THE COMPLETE ENCYCLOPEDIA OF DIY AND HOME MAINTENANCE

Edited by
Julian Worthington

Book Club Associates, London

Acknowledgments

Photographers: Jon Bouchier, Simon Butcher, Paul Forrester, Jem Grischotti, Keith Morris, Karen Norquay, Ian O'Leary and Roger Tuff.
Artists: Roger Courthold Associates, Drury Lane Studios, Bernard Fallon, Nick Farmer, Tony Hannaford, Trevor Lawrence, Linden Artists, David Pope, Peter Robinson, Mike Saunders, Ian Stephen, Will Stephen, Craig Warwick, Brian Watson, Gary Watson and David Worth.

This edition published 1984 by
Book Club Associates by arrangement with
Orbis Publishing Limited, London

under licence from
Whinfrey Strachan Limited
315 Oxford Street
London W1R 1AJ

Printed in Italy by SAGDOS, Milan

CONTENTS

INTRODUCTION

To appreciate your home fully and get the most out of it, you will need to look after it. This not only involves maintaining the overall appearance, both inside and out, but also making sure that all the systems are working properly.

It is an often painful fact of life that problems occur at the most inconvenient times – and this is as true in the home as anywhere. So a basic knowledge of DIY around the house will come in very handy when your are faced with an emergency.

Even when the job that needs doing is not that urgent, the fact that you are in a position to handle it yourself will certainly save you money – and maybe time as well.

The Complete Encyclopedia of DIY and Home Maintenance is invaluable in either situation, for the information it provides will ensure that, whatever the job, you will get it right. And, of course, this is just as important as being able to do it yourself, since there is little point in carrying out work or making a repair if it is not done correctly. In this case, the problem is almost certain to occur again – and this time it may cost you a lot more to put it right.

You must pay particular attention to planning and preparation. The golden rule in any situation is to stop and think about what needs to be done. Are you clear in your mind exactly how to tackle the work? Have you considered all the possible problems you are likely to encounter. Have you got the right tools to hand? Have you bought all the materials you need?

All these may seem obvious, but it is surprising how often people rush into the work without giving it proper consideration and either hit a snag halfway through or end up with a sub-standard result.

Never rush into a job, particularly if it is one you are tackling for the first time. By taking a little longer to plan and prepare thoroughly, you will save time and effort in the end. Bear in mind what it would cost to do the job again.

Never neglect safety. Although a job may appear simple, there could be unseen hazards in using worn or damaged tools. For this reason you should always look after your tools, store them carefully and treat them with respect. This way they will not only do the job you want them to do – and correctly – but they will also last a lot longer.

If you are working at a height, make sure you are standing on a secure base. This applies just as much when reaching for the ceiling as when working outside from the top of a ladder.

There are certain basic precautions that must be taken when working on the domestic systems. With electricity it is essential that you switch off the power or isolate the relevant circuit when handling electrical fittings and connections. On the plumbing system, make sure you have turned off the supply and drained the relevant part of the system before starting any repair, maintenance or installation work.

If there are young children in the house, keep them well away from the work area and never leave tools lying around for them to play with. Pets, too, should be kept away while you are working.

The guideline should always be – think before you act. It is far easier and safer to get the job right from the start than to have to iron out problems later.

The Complete Encyclopedia of DIY and Home Maintenance gives you the information you need to plan and prepare for each job, and its step-by-step guide to techniques will help ensure you get it right. In achieving the best results each time, you will have the satisfaction of knowing that each job you do is a job well done.

CHAPTER 1

Painting

PAINTING WOOD

Painting is the most popular way of decorating and protecting much of the wood in our homes. As with so many do-it-yourself jobs, getting a good finish depends on your skill. Here's how to paint wood perfectly.

Wood is used extensively in every part of our homes — from roof trusses to skirting boards. Structural timber is usually left rough and unfinished, while joinery — windows, doors, staircases, architraves and so on — is usually decorated in some way. Wood has just one drawback; as a natural material it's prone to deterioration and even decay unless it's protected. Painting wood is one way of combining decoration and

protection, and the popularity of paint is a testimony to its effectiveness. Properly applied and well looked after, it gives wood a highly attractive appearance and also provides excellent protection against dampness, dirt, mould, insect attack, and general wear and tear.

Of course, paint isn't the only finish you can choose for wood. If its colour and grain pattern are worth displaying, you can use

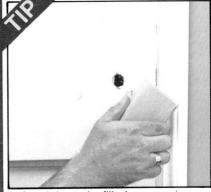

PREPARING WOOD FOR PAINT

1 Before you can apply the paint you must fill any cracks or holes with wood filler (applied with a filling knife) and leave to dry.

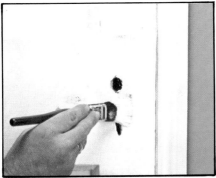

2 Sand down the filled areas using medium-grade glasspaper. Wrap the abrasive around a sanding block or wood offcut so it's easier to use.

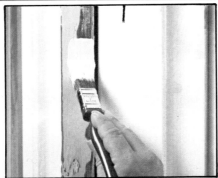

3 Where paint has been chipped off, sand down the area and apply an ordinary wood primer to the bare wood using a small paintbrush.

4 When the surface of the wood is smooth, apply undercoat (as the maker recommends) and leave to dry before you put on the top coat.

PREPARING PAINT

1 Remove the lid from the paint can using the edge of a knife as a lever – don't use a screwdriver or you'll damage the lip of the lid.

2 Stir the paint (if recommended by the maker) using an offcut of wood, with a turning, lifting motion, or use an electric drill attachment.

3 Decant some paint into a paint kettle, which you'll find easier to carry than a heavy can. Top up the kettle from the can as you work.

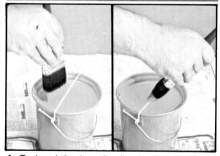

4 To load the brush, dip the bristles into the paint to one-third of their length and wipe off excess on a string tied across the kettle rim.

---

oils, stains or varnishes to enhance the overall effect and protect the surface. But as most of the wood used in our houses is chosen more for performance and price rather than looks, bland and uninteresting softwoods are generally the order of the day for everything from windows and door frames to staircases, skirting boards and door architraves. And painting them offers a number of distinct advantages.

Firstly, paint covers a multitude of sins — knots and other blemishes in the wood surface, poorly-made joints patched up with filler, dents and scratches caused by the rough and tumble of everyday life — and does it in almost every colour of the spectrum. Secondly, paint provides a surface that's hard-wearing and easy to keep clean — an important point for many interior surfaces in the home. And thirdly, paint is easy to apply ... and to keep on applying. In fact, redecorating existing paintwork accounts for the greater part of all paint bought.

What woods can be painted?

In theory you can paint any wood under the sun. In practice, paint (solvent-based or emulsion, see *Ready Reference*), is usually applied only to softwoods — spruce (whitewood), European redwood (deal), pine and the like — and to man-made boards such as plywood, blockboard, hardboard and chipboard. Hardwoods and boards finished with hardwood veneers can be painted, but are usually given a clear or tinted finish to enhance their attractive colour and grain pattern.

Paint systems

If you're decorating new wood, there's more to it than putting on a coat of your chosen paint. It would just soak in where the wood was porous and give a very uneven colour — certainly without the smooth gloss finish expected. It wouldn't stick to the wood very well, nor would it form the continuous surface film needed for full protection. All in all, not very satisfactory. So what is needed is a paint system which consists of built-up layers, each one designed to serve a particular purpose.

The first in the system is a primer (sometimes called a primer/sealer) which stops the paint soaking into porous areas and provides a good key between the bare wood and the paint film. Next, you want another 'layer' — the undercoat — to help build up the paint film and at the same time to obliterate the colour of the primer, so that the top coat which you apply last of all is perfectly smooth and uniform in colour. With some paints — emulsions and non-drip glosses — an undercoat is not always used and instead several coats of primer or two

---

HOW TO APPLY PAINT

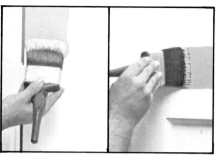

1 Apply the paint along the grain; with non-drip paint (left) you can apply a thicker coat in one go without further spreading (brushing out).

4 Now you must 'lay off' the paint with very light brush strokes along the grain to give a smooth finish that's free from brush marks.

---

top coats are applied with the same result.

The general rule to obey when choosing primer, undercoat and top coat is to stick with the same base types in one paint system, particularly out of doors and on surfaces subjected to heavy wear and tear (staircases and skirting boards, for example). On other indoor woodwork you can combine primers and top coats of different types.

If the wood you are painting has been treated with a preservative to prevent decay (likely only on exterior woodwork) an ordinary primer won't take well. Instead use an aluminium wood primer — not to be confused with aluminium paint — which is recommended for use on all hardwoods too. Oily woods such as teak must be degreased with white spirit and allowed to dry before the primer is applied.

As far as man-made boards are concerned, chipboard is best primed with a solvent-based wood primer to seal its comparatively porous surface. Hardboard is even more porous, and here a stabilising primer (a product more usually used on absorbent or powdery masonry surfaces) is the best product to use. Plywood and blockboard should be primed as for softwood. There's one other

2 Still working with the grain and without reloading the brush, paint another strip alongside the first one and blend the two together.

3 Reload the brush and apply strokes back and forth across the grain over the area you've just painted to ensure full, even coverage.

5 Paint an area adjoining the first in the same way, blending the two sections together by about 50mm (2in) and laying off as before.

TIP

6 Brush towards edges, not parallel with them or onto them, as the paint will be scraped onto the adjacent face, forming a ridge.

WHAT CAN GO WRONG WITH PAINT

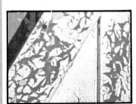

Left: Lifting and flaking occurs if paint is applied over a surface that is damp or powdery.

Right: Crazing is caused when paint is applied over a previous coat that was not completely dry.

Left: Blistering occurs when damp or resin is trapped beneath the paint film and is drawn out by heat.

Right: Cratering results from rain or condensation droplets falling onto the wet paint surface.

Left: Running, sagging or 'curtaining' happens when paint is applied too thickly on vertical surfaces.

Right: Wrinkling or shrivelling can occur on horizontal surfaces if paint is applied too thickly.

Ready Reference

HOW MUCH PAINT?

Large areas – in all cases coverage per litre depends on the wood's porosity and the painter's technique:
Wood primer 9-15 sq metres (95-160 sq ft)
Aluminium primer 16 sq metres (170 sq ft)
Primer/undercoat 11 sq metres (120 sq ft)
Undercoat 11 sq metres (120 sq ft)
Runny gloss or satin 17 sq metres (180 sq ft)
Non-drip gloss or satin 13 sq metres (140 sq ft)
Runny emulsions 15 sq metres (160 sq ft)
Non-drip emulsions 12 sq metres (130 sq ft)

Small areas – add up all the lengths of wood to be painted. One sq metre is equivalent to:
● 16m (52 ft) of glazing bars
● 10-13m (33-43 ft) of window frame
● 6m (20 ft) of sill
● 10m (33 ft) of narrow skirting
● 3-6m (10-20 ft) of deep skirting

CHOOSING BRUSHES

The best brushes have a generous filling of long bristles and are an even, tapered shape. Cheaper brushes have short, thin bristles and big wooden filler strips to pack them out. The ideal sizes for wood are:
● 25mm (1in) or 50mm (2in) for panel doors, skirtings
● 50mm (2in) or 75mm (3in) for flush doors, skirting, large areas
● 25mm (1in) cutting-in brush for window glazing bars
● 12mm (½in), 25mm (1in) or cheap paintbox brush for spot priming, applying knotting

Alternative to brushes
Paint pads are more widely used on walls than on woodwork, but the crevice or sash paint pad will do the same job as a cutting-in brush. It should be cleaned with white spirit or hot water and washing-up liquid (paint solvents might dissolve the adhesive between the mohair pile and foam).

TIP: PREPARING A BRUSH

Before using a new (or stored) brush work the bristles against the palm of your hand to remove dust and loose hairs.

thing you need to know. If the wood you want to paint has knots in it you should brush a special sealer called knotting over them to stop the resin oozing up through the paint film and spoiling its looks. If the knots are 'live' — exuding sticky yellowish resin — use a blow-torch to draw out the resin and scrape it off before applying knotting.

Paint on paint

You'll often want to paint wood that has already been painted. How you tackle this depends on the state of the existing paint-work. If it's flaking off and is in generally poor condition, you will have to remove the entire paint system — primer, undercoat and top coat — by burning off with a blow-torch, applying a chemical paint stripper or rubbing with an abrasive. You then treat the stripped wood as already described for new wood.

Where the paintwork is in good condition, you simply have to clean it and sand it down lightly to provide a key for the new paint and to remove any small bits that got stuck in the surface when it was last painted. Then you can apply fresh top coat over the surface; the paint system is already there. You may, of course, need two top coats if you add a light colour to a dark one to stop the colour beneath from showing through.

If the paintwork is basically sound but needs localised attention, you can scrape or sand these damaged areas back to bare wood and 'spot-treat' them with primer and undercoat to bring the patch up to the level of the surrounding paintwork, ready for a final top coat over the entire surface.

Painting large areas

Though the same principle applies to wood as it does to any other large surface area — ie, you divide it into manageable sections and complete one before moving on to another — if you're using an oil-based gloss paint you have to make sure that the completed area hasn't dried to such an extent that you cannot blend in the new. On the rare occasion that you might want to paint a whole wall of wood you should make the section no wider than a couple of brush widths and work from ceiling to floor.

With emulsions there isn't the same problem for although they are quick drying the nature of the paint is such that brush marks don't show.

You might think that a wide brush is the best for a large area but the constant flexing action of the wrist in moving the brush up and down will tire you out fast. Holding a brush is an art in itself and aches are the first indication that you're doing it wrongly. A thin brush should be held by the handle like a pencil, while a wider brush should be held with the fingers and thumb gripping the brush just above the bristles.

You'll find a variety of paint brushes on sale — some are designed to be 'throwaway' (good if you only have one or two jobs to do), others will stand you in good stead for years. But remember before using a new brush to brush the bristles back and forth against the palm of your hand — this is called 'flirting' and will dislodge any dust or loose hairs that could spoil your paintwork.

It is wise to decant the paint to save you moving a heavy can from place to place — a paint kettle which resembles a small bucket is made for the purpose. Plastic ones are easier to keep clean than metal ones.

Never be tempted to dip the bristles too far into the paint and always scrape off excess from both sides. Paint has the habit of building up inside the brush and if this happens on overhead work, you risk it running down the handle and onto your arm.

Painting small areas

These tend to be the fiddly woodwork on windows, around doors and lengths of stairs or skirting boards — and the hardest bit about all of them is working out how much paint you'll need (see *Ready Reference*).

Special shaped or narrow brushes can make painting these areas easier — for example, they prevent you 'straddling' angles in wood (like you find on mouldings) which damages the bristles in the middle of the brush. With windows and panelled doors you should also follow an order of working to

---

ORDER OF PAINTING

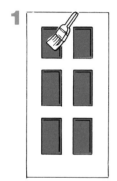 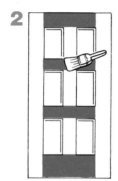 

Panel doors: *tackle any mouldings first, then the recessed panels, horizontal members, vertical members and lastly the edges.*

Casement windows: *start with any glazing bars, then paint the opening casement itself (the hinge edge is the only one which should match the inside); lastly paint the frame.*

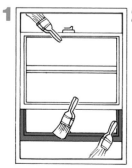 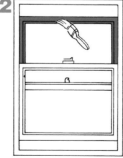 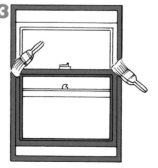

Sash windows: *paint the inside top and bottom and a little way up and down the sides of the frame first. Then paint the bottom of the outer sash. Move the sashes and do the rest of the outer sash, the inner sash and finally the frame.*

avoid causing overlap marks on the parts you've already painted.

Fiddly or not, they are the jobs you have to do first if you are putting up wallcoverings (if you're painting a room, the walls should be done before the woodwork) so that the drops can be placed against finished edges. If you want to touch up the paint without changing the wallpaper, it's best to use a paint shield.

Getting ready to paint

Ideally, before painting doors and windows you should remove all the 'furniture' — handles, fingerplates, keyholes, hooks etc — so you can move the brush freely without interruption. You should also take time to read the manufacturer's instructions on the can. If, for example, they tell you to stir the paint, then stir it for this is the only way of distributing the particles which have settled.

If you open a can of non-drip paint and find a layer of solvent on the top, you should stir it in, then leave it to become jelly-like again before painting.

All your brushes should be dry — this is something to remember if you are painting over several days and have put them to soak overnight in white spirit or a proprietary brush cleaner. If you don't get rid of all the traces of the liquid it will mess up your paint-work. They should be rinsed, then brushed on newspaper till the strokes leave no sign.

Cleaning up

When you've finished painting clean your brushes thoroughly, concentrating on the roots where paint accumulates and will harden. They should be hung up, bristles down, till dry, then wrapped in aluminium foil for storage. Don't ever store them damp for they can be ruined by mildew.

If there's only a small amount of paint left, you can either decant it for storage into a dark glass screw-topped jar so you can use it to touch up damaged spots — it's important to choose a suitable sized jar so there's very little air space. Air and dust are both potential paint spoilers and there are two ways to keep them out if you're storing the can. Either put a circle of aluminium foil over the paint surface before putting the lid on securely, or — and this is the best way if the lid is distorted — put on the lid and then invert the can to spread the paint round the inner rim to form an airtight seal. Set it back the right way for storage.

If despite these safeguards a skin forms on the paint (usually over months of storage) you have to cut round the edge of it with a sharp knife and carefully lift it off.

PAINTING WINDOWS

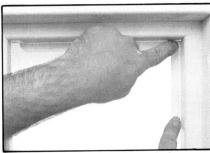

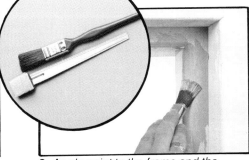

1 Apply masking tape to a window pane to prevent paint getting onto the glass – leave 3mm (1/8in) of glass exposed so the paint forms a seal.

2 Apply paint to the frame and the glazing bars using a small brush, or (inset) a cutting-in brush or a sash paint pad.

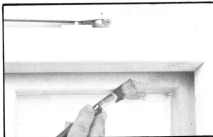

3 Apply the paint along the grain; remove the tape when the paint is almost dry – if it dries completely you might peel it off with the tape.

4 An alternative way of keeping paint off the glass is to use a paint shield or offcut of plywood but, again, leave a paint margin on the glass.

PAINTING WALLS AND CEILINGS

The quickest and cheapest way to transform a room is to paint the walls and ceiling. But, for a successful result, you have to prepare the surfaces properly and use the correct painting techniques.

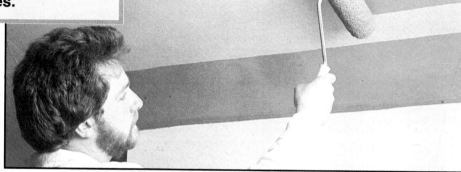

Dulux Russet over Dulux Cameo

Paint is the most popular material used to protect and decorate walls and ceilings in the home. Whereas many people hesitate before hanging wallpaper or sticking more permanent wall and ceiling coverings in place, few would worry about wielding a paint brush for the first time.

One of the chief advantages of painting a room is that it doesn't take much time; large areas can be given two or even three coats of emulsion paint in a day. The paints now available are hardwearing and totally unlike earlier distemper and water paints. They are easy to apply by brush, roller or pad and can be safely washed at frequent intervals to keep them looking fresh.

Any drawbacks are usually caused by faults in the wall or ceiling surface, rather than by the paints. A standard paint alone cannot cover up defects in the same way that some other wallcoverings can, so a surface which is to be painted usually needs more careful preparation than one which is to be papered.

The majority of walls and ceilings are plastered and this type of surface, when in sound condition, is ideal as a base for emulsion and other paints. But it is not the only surface finish you are likely to come across.

Previous occupiers of the house may well have covered the walls with a decorative paper and even painted on top of that. At the very worst there may be several layers of paper and paint, making it very difficult to achieve a smooth paint surface. In this situation it is invariably better to strip the surface completely down to the plaster and to start again from scratch.

This does not mean that no paper should be overpainted. Certain types such as plain white relief wallcoverings and woodchips are intended to be so treated, and actually look 'softer' after one or two redecorations. In short, most wall or ceiling surfaces you are likely to encounter will be paintable. All you have to do is select the right paint for the job and get the surface into as good a condition as possible.

Choosing paints

Vinyl emulsion paints are the most commonly used types of paint for painting walls and ceilings. They are easy to apply and come in a wide range of colours. You will usually have a choice of three finishes: matt, silk, or gloss.

There are also textured paints which are increasing in popularity, particularly for ceiling use. These are vinyl emulsion paints with added 'body' so they can be applied more thickly and then given a decorative textured finish.

Oil-based eggshell paints can be used where a more durable surface is needed or where you want to use the same colour on both walls and woodwork. Resin-based gloss paint is used occasionally also on walls and ceilings, particularly in humid rooms like kitchens and bathrooms.

You should choose paint carefully. The fact that one make is half the price of another may indicate that it has only half the covering power and you would therefore need to apply two coats of the cheaper paint. Also, if you're using white paint, you may find that one brand is noticeably 'whiter' than another.

Tools and equipment

Few specialised tools are needed for wall and ceiling paintwork. If you are content to work with only a brush you will require two sizes: one larger one for the bulk of the work, and a smaller brush for working into corners. It is worth decanting quantities of paint into a paint kettle which is easier to carry around than large heavy cans.

Rollers make the job of painting large areas of wall or ceiling much quicker and also help to achieve a better finish. But you will still need a small brush for working into corners and for dealing with coving, cornices etc.

To prepare a new fibre roller for painting, soak it in soapy water for 2 to 3 hours to get rid of any loose bits of fibre, then roll it out on the wall to dry it off. One point to remember: if you intend using silk vinyl emulsion paint, it's best not to use a roller as this tends to show up as a stippled effect on the silk surface.

Large paint pads will also enable you to cover big expanses of wall or ceiling very quickly. You can use a brush or a small paint pad for work in corners.

Apart from these paint application tools you'll need a variety of other items for preparing the surfaces so they're ready for the paint. The walls must be cleaned, so you'll need washing-down equipment: sponges, cloths, detergent, and a bucket or two of water.

You'll need filler for cracks and a filling knife about 75mm (3in) wide. When any filler is dry it will need to be sanded down, so have some glasspaper ready for wrapping round a cork sanding block. A scraper will also be needed if old wallpaper has to be stripped from the walls.

Finally, because of the height of the walls and ceiling, you'll need access equipment, such as a stepladder, to enable you to reach them safely and comfortably.

Preparing the surface

No painting will be successful until the

PAINTING THE CEILING WITH A ROLLER

1 *Use a brush to paint a strip about 50mm wide round the outside edge of the ceiling; a roller cannot reach right into angles or corners.*

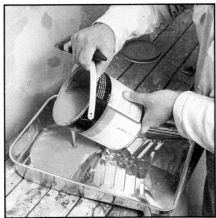

2 *Pour paint into the roller tray; don't put in too much at a time or you risk overloading the roller and splashing paint out of the tray.*

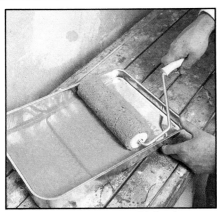

3 *Dip the roller in and pull it back so there is paint at the shallow end of the tray. Push the roller back and forth in the paint at the shallow end.*

4 *Run the roller over the ceiling so there is a band of paint next to the strip of paint you have brushed along the edge of the ceiling.*

5 *Reverse the roller's direction so you join up the two strips of paint into one band. Then finish off by running the roller over the band.*

6 *Now start the next section by running the roller alongside the completed band. Work your way round the ceiling in bands.*

Ready Reference

LINING WALL SURFACES

You can use lining paper to do the same job for paint as it does for wallpapers, covering minor cracks and defects on the wall or ceiling and providing a smooth surface for painting.

TIP: SEAL STRONG COLOURS

Wallcoverings with strong colourings, and particularly those tinted with metallic inks, will almost certainly show through the new paint. To prevent this they should be stripped off, or sealed with special aluminium spirit-based sealer.

FILLING HAIRLINE CRACKS

You may not be able to push enough filler into hairline cracks to ensure a good bond:
● it is often better to open the crack up further with the edge of an old chisel or screwdriver so the filler can penetrate more deeply and key better to both sides of the crack
● when using a textured vinyl paint there is no need to fill hairline cracks, but cracks wider than 1mm (^{1}/$_{32}$in) should be filled.

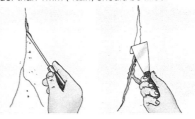

DEALING WITH FITTINGS

Protect electrical fittings so paint or water can't enter them during cleaning and decorating:
● ideally, power to these fittings should be cut off and the fittings removed
● if items cannot be removed, use masking tape to protect them.

SELECTING PAINTS

When choosing paints, remember that:
● emulsion paints are quicker to apply, dry more quickly and lack the smell of resin- or oil-based paints. They are also cheaper and can be easily cleaned off painting equipment with water
● non-drip paints are best for ceilings and cover more thickly than runny ones, cutting down on the number of coats
● a silk or gloss finish will tend to highlight surface irregularities more than a matt finish
● textured paints are suitable for use on surfaces which are in poor condition since they will cover defects which a standard emulsion paint cannot.

PAINTING THE WALL WITH A BRUSH

1 Use a small brush to cut in at the wall and ceiling join and in corners. With a larger brush paint the wall in bands. First, brush across the wall.

2 Move the brush across the wall in the opposite direction. The bands of paint should be about 1m wide and you should be working downwards.

3 When you are working at the top of the wall your next strokes should be downwards to complete the area you have covered with crossways strokes.

4 At the bottom two-thirds of the wall continue working in crossways strokes, but this time finish off each section by brushing upwards.

USING PAINT PADS

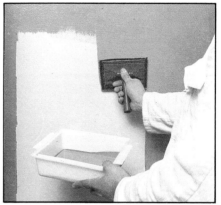

1 Thin the paint a little (with water for emulsions, turps for oil-based ones). Cut in with a small brush or pad and use a larger pad to paint in bands.

2 For precise work you can use a small pad like this. Ensure that you cover areas you don't want painted with masking tape.

surface beneath has been properly prepared. Unless wallpaper is of a type intended for painting it is usually better to strip it off, and walls which have been stripped of their previous wallcoverings need a thorough washing to remove all traces of old paste. Make sure the floor is protected against debris by covering it with a dust sheet or sheets of old newspaper. Emulsion-painted walls also need washing to remove surface dirt. In both cases, use warm water with a little household detergent added. Then rinse with clean water.

If you decide to leave the wallpaper on the walls you will have to wash it down before you paint. Take care to avoid overwetting the paper, particularly at joins. When the surface is dry, check the seams; if any have lifted, stick them down with a ready-mixed paste.

Ceilings should be washed in small areas at a time and rinsed thoroughly before you move onto another section systematically.

If the surfaces are left in perfect condition, they can be painted as soon as they are dry.

It's possible that walls or ceilings may have been painted with distemper, which may only become apparent after you have removed the existing wallcovering. Unless it is the washable type, you will have to remove it completely since emulsion paint will not adhere well to it. Use hot water, detergent and a scrubbing brush to soften and get rid of the coating; this is hard work, but you could use a steam stripper to speed up the process.

With all the surface cleaned, the next job is to fill any cracks and repair defects such a as indentations caused perhaps by knocks or the blade of a carelessly handled wallpaper scraper (see Ready Reference).

Whenever a filler has been used it should be sanded down flush with the wall surface, once dry, and the resulting dust should be brushed away.

If the plaster is in bad condition and obviously covered in cracks you should consider covering it completely with liningpaper, woodchip or other relief wallcovering before painting it. The paper will provide a good base for redecoration, and will save a great deal of preparation time. However, this can only be done if the plaster itself is still bonded securely to the wall. If it is coming away in chunks or sounds hollow behind the cracks, then the wall should be replastered.

Cracks which have developed round door and window frames are best filled with a flexible sealant, which will be unaffected by movement of the frames. Acrylic-based sealants are available for this purpose and they can be easily overpainted.

After all the preparation work has been

PAINTING PROCEDURE

Paint the ceiling first in 1m-wide bands (1 & 2). Paint round a ceiling rose (3), then complete the rest of that band (4). On walls work downwards (1). At a window, paint along the top band (2) and repeat the process at the bottom (3). Work from right to left unless you are left-handed.

completed, have a good clear-up in the room so that when you begin painting you do not stir up dust and have to work around numerous bits and pieces scattered over the floor space.

Re-lay dust sheets and set up your access equipment before even opening the first can of paint. Make sure your brushes or rollers are clean and ready for use.

Painting sequences

If possible, do all your painting in daylight hours. Artificial light is less easy to work by and can lead to small areas being missed.

Painting is always done from the highest point downwards, so ceilings are the first areas to be tackled. The whole ceiling will be painted in bands across the room no wider than you can easily reach without stretching on your stepladder or platform. This generally means that at any one time you will probably be painting a band no wider than 1m and less than 2m long unless you are using scaffolding boards to support you.

You start at the edges first and then work into the main body of the room.

Linking one section to another is seldom

difficult with emulsion paint and is simply a matter of blending the paint from the new section back into the previous one.

Walls are treated similarly, starting at the top and working downwards in sections about 1m wide, cutting in at the ceiling and at return walls.

Painting tips

The number of coats required will depend on the previous colour and condition of the surface and the type of paint. If another coat has to be applied, be sure that the previous one is fully dry first. With modern vinyl emulsion paint it may be that because the paint is water-based it will cause the paper underneath to swell and bubble; however, you shouldn't worry about this because as the water in the paint dries out the paper and paste behind the paint surface will begin to flatten again.

If the paper is badly hung with a lack of adhesive at the edge, seams may lift as the paint dries. They will have to be stuck down in the same way as if they had lifted during washing. Careful preparation would prevent this problem anyway.

APPLYING TEXTURED FINISHES

Textured finishes which you can paint on walls or ceilings are an inexpensive way of covering up poor surfaces. They also give you the chance to exercise your ingenuity in creating relief patterns on them.

Textured wall and ceiling finishes can provide a relatively quick form of decoration. You don't, for example, need to apply more than one coat. And, unlike relief wallcoverings (another type of product commonly used to obtain a textured wall or ceiling surface), you don't have to go through the process of pasting, soaking, cutting, hanging and trimming; you simply spread the finishes on the surface with a paint brush or roller.

One of the advantages of using a 'texture' on walls is that it will tend to mask the effect of any general unevenness in the surface. Similarly, ready-mixed textures are often marketed specifically as a solution to the problem of improving the appearance of old ceilings. They are very suitable for this and can save a lot of tedious repair work.

However, there is no need to think of textures just as a cover-up. You may simply prefer a textured surface to a flat, smooth one. If you use patterning tools, the range of textured effects you can achieve is practically endless, depending only on your skill and imagination.

Choosing textured finishes

One of the factors which will influence your choice of finish is, obviously, how much you are prepared to pay. The traditional compound which you buy in powder form to mix with water is the cheapest type, but, like ordinary plaster, is rather porous and needs to be painted over. Even so, the cost of coverage, including over-painting, is very reasonable. Ready-mixed types are rather more expensive but you don't normally need to paint over them, and some brands offer a reasonable range of colours.

The traditional powder type, thickly painted on a wall or ceiling, has a slow setting time, which makes it ideal for creating a decorative impression with a patterning tool. Ready-mixed products can also be given a textured finish in the same way as the powdery type, but doing so will tend to vary the thickness of the finish so that overpainting might be necessary. (If you just paint them on without carrying out any follow-up patterning treatment, you will be left with a random textured

effect.) Some of the textured products suitable for exterior use can also be patterned with tools; check the manufacturer's instructions for guidance here.

Tools and equipment

Apart from the texture finish itself, and paint if you're going to overpaint, you will need a brush or roller to apply the finish. The most suitable type of brush is a 200mm (8in) distemper brush. The type of roller you use will affect the pattern created and special rollers are available to create certain effects (see step-by-step photographs). Sometimes you paint the material on first with an ordinary roller (or a brush) and then work it over with a patterning roller; follow the manufacturer's instructions for the type of roller you will need.

If you are dealing with a ceiling you will need some form of access equipment; two stepladders with a plank resting between them will usually suffice. Textured finishes, especially when applied with a roller tend to spray and spatter about, so it's best to have goggles and a mask to protect your eyes and mouth when you are looking up; also, don't forget to protect your hair. In addition, whether you're painting walls or ceiling, you'll need a dust sheet or some other form of protective covering for the floor.

You may also require a plumb bob and line (see *Ready Reference*) and any equipment required for filling cracks or joints such as a caulking tool, jointing tape knife, filling knife, filler and so on.

Where you intend to texture the surface after painting on the finish you will also need your patterning tool(s). These can be proprietary or home-made; you can even use equipment which was chiefly designed for other purposes which you may decide will create the pattern you want. Apart from patterning rollers, the proprietary tools available include combs (some of which can give special effects within the combed patterns such as 'rose' and 'flower'), stipple brushes and pads and special 'swirl' brushes. You can also buy a tool called a 'lacer' to dull any sharp ridges; however a plastic straight edge or the blade of a filling knife is a suitable alternative.

Preparing the surface

Textured finishes can be applied to bare or painted surfaces but the surface must be sound and, in some cases, treated. You should not, for example, think of textured finishes as a means of covering up walls which really need replastering or a ceiling which should be replaced.

All porous surfaces should first be treated

SEALING JOINTS

1 *To seal a joint between boards, first use a caulking tool to apply cellulose filler (or a thicker mix of texture compound) along it.*

2 *Use a special taping knife to press a length of jointing tape into the filler so it's securely embedded and free of air bubbles.*

3 *Spread on another layer of filling material, again using the caulking tool, but this time so the filler covers the jointing tape.*

4 *Use a damp sponge to wipe away surplus filler and to feather the edges so the joint surface becomes flush with the plasterboard.*

Ready Reference

PROPRIETARY TOOLS TO USE

You can buy various tools designed for patterning textured finishes. They include combs, patterned rollers, various types of brushes and a 'lacing' tool for smoothing high points.

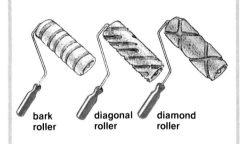

bark roller   diagonal roller   diamond roller

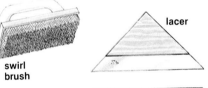

swirl brush   lacer

comb

MAKE YOUR OWN COMB

You can make a comb with a wooden handle and a rigid plastic blade (cut, for example, from an old ice-cream carton). Cut your own designs out of the plastic.

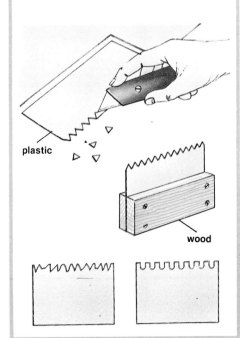

plastic   wood

---

with a stabilising primer recommended by the manufacturer of the finish so that the setting of the texture material is not spoilt by suction. Surfaces requiring such treatment include brick, render, concrete, plaster and some types of wallboards.

Texture finishes can be used to hide very fine hairline cracks and are usually marketed for their flexible ability to cope with normal movement so cracks don't reopen. However, none of them can cover cracks or joints of more than 1.5mm (1/16in) with any guarantee that these will remain covered up. You will have to caulk the cracks or joints with texture compound (perhaps thickened with a little ordinary filler). Ideally, joints between boards of any kind should also have a layer of jointing tape over them between layers of whatever types of filler you are using (see step-by-step photographs). Make sure you feather the edges of the filling material so there is no

noticeable ridge when the texture covers it.

Painted surfaces should be clean, sound and sanded lightly to provide a key for the finish. Distemper and low-quality emulsion paint may not hold the texture; test by pressing adhesive tape on a small area first and remove any painted surface that has a tendency to delaminate when the tape is peeled off. If the surface has been painted in a dark colour it's best to paint over it in a light colour first before you apply the texture.

You will have to remove wallpaper or light tiles such as polystyrene tiles. You can, however, safely apply a textured finish over ceramic tiles provided they are clean, the gaps are filled and they are primed with a coat of PVA adhesive, diluted according to the manufacturer's instructions.

Do check that lath-and-plaster ceilings are strong enough to support the extra weight of the textured coating. If they are

MAKING TEXTURED PATTERNS

Textured materials can be applied by brush or roller. If you are applying this type of finish to walls it's best, if possible, to work in an upwards direction to minimise the amount of material which gets sprayed over you and the floor. Apply the finish to the wall in bands and apply it thickly so the texture will stand out. You can roll it on with an ordinary foam roller (see left) which will give a stipple effect and then leave the surface to dry as it is. Alternatively, you may prefer to go ahead and use other tools to create other kinds of textured effects.

showing any signs of sagging, lift a floorboard in the room or loft above and check that the laths are still nailed firmly to the joists, and the plaster is well keyed to the laths.

Where there are fixing nails or screws which will be embedded in the texture material, you should paint them over with gloss paint to prevent them from rusting.

You will have to prime wood-faced wallboards if they are absorbent and it's best to treat wood-effect plastic boards with PVA adhesive in the same way as ceramic tiles. In the case of thin wallboards there is a risk that movement will cause the texture material to crack, so test them for flexibility and remove them if necessary.

Applying textured finishes

It's best to apply a textured finish thickly; remember you will only be applying one coat and the thicker the coat the more protection it will provide for the wall or ceiling surface. Also, if you intend using a patterning tool, working on a deep, even coat of texture will give the best results. Apply the finish in bands across the room until the entire wall or ceiling is covered.

Exterior textures are normally applied with a natural bristle brush, though on smooth surfaces where you want a coarser texture you can use a foam roller. Whenever possible, you should work in the shade. If you are painting near drainpipes, you should tape newspaper round the pipes to protect the area you wish to avoid painting. Similarly, use masking tape to protect window frames (outdoors and inside) and also window reveals, light fittings, ventilator grilles and so on. If it does get on any of the areas, wipe it off with a damp rag immediately.

Using patterning tools

The drying time for textured finishes varies from 12 to 24 hours, though the working time for patterning can be much lower, depending on atmospheric conditions. You will normally have at least 4 hours to complete your patterning, but it would make sense to complete one wall or ceiling at a time as far as possible. If in doubt, study the manufacturer's instructions for the particular product you are using.

A random pattern will usually be quicker to achieve than a regular one where you will have to take care in matching up the pattern. In the latter case, it may be better to spread the texture on in strips and pattern each strip as you go rather than covering the whole wall or ceiling and then patterning it.

Finishing off

After patterning, it is normal practice to 'lace' the pattern (to dull any sharp ridges) just as the material begins to dry. Even after it has dried you may still need to remove sharp points; use the blade of a filling knife to knock them back, or, if you want to go to the trouble, wrap fine glasspaper round a sanding block and sand them down. If you don't remove sharp ridges and points, the surface may cut someone who leans against it or brittle parts may break off.

Textured finishes can usually be covered with either an emulsion or oil-based paint but check the manufacturer's recommendations.

Cleaning and maintenance

Most texture finishes are designed to last, which is just as well as it's a messy, time-consuming and difficult job to remove them. Maintenance will normally consist of redecorating them with a coat of paint when they show signs of wear or hard-to-remove dirt or stains. Surfaces should be kept clean: to do so, apply warm soapy water with a paint brush to loosen dirt and dust.

3 A specially designed, grooved 'bark' effect roller is being run over the textured material to produce a bark pattern on a wall surface.

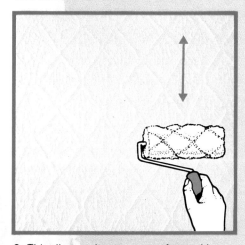

6 This diamond pattern was formed by a purpose-designed roller. With a regular pattern like this you should check that the pattern rows match.

1 A straightforward and at the same time striking effect can be produced by running a purpose-designed diagonal roller up and down across the surface.

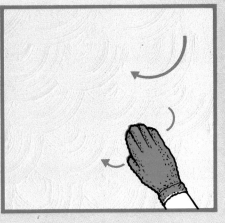

2 A wide variety of tools, proprietary or otherwise, can be used to form patterns on texture materials; here a coarse nylon mitt produced a swirled effect.

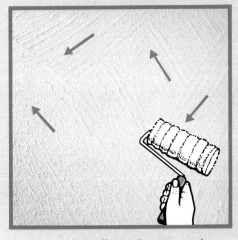

4 Here a 'bark' effect roller was again used but this time in a random sweeping motion to create a curved criss-cross variation of the basic pattern.

5 The fine stipple effect (left) was made using an ordinary foam roller; the coarser stipple (right) by dabbing with a sponge wrapped in plastic.

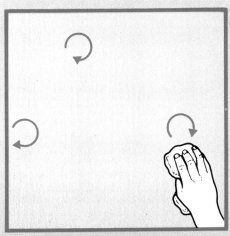

7 Another design: the background pattern was produced by running a 'bark' roller over the surface; a sponge was then used to make circles on this.

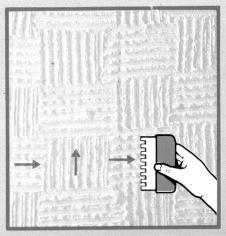

8 This criss-cross pattern of alternate facing 'squares' could be created using a comb but here a serrated scraper was used instead.

Ready Reference

TYPES OF FINISH

There are various types of textured finishes available. They include:
● the traditional type, which is a powder compound, generally available only in white, which you mix with water; it needs to be painted afterwards
● textured 'paints', which are ready-mixed products containing similar light aggregates and binders to the traditional type but also plasticised like modern paints; they come in a range of colours and usually don't have to be painted over (though you can if you wish)
● textured paints and coverings suitable for exterior use.

HOW FAR WILL THEY GO?

Powder compounds will cover about 2.5sq m per kg (12sq ft per lb) of unmixed powder and are available in 5, 10, 12½ and 25kg bags. Ready-mix materials will cover 2 to 2.5sq m (22 to 27sq ft) per litre and are supplied in 5, 10 and 12½ litre tubs.

BEWARE ASBESTOS

Traditional compound powder textures sometimes contain asbestos (check the manufacturer's instructions); such types should be mixed in well-ventilated conditions to protect you against a potential health risk.

THE RIGHT TEMPERATURE

Texture finishes can be affected by extremes in temperature so:
● don't apply ready-mix products to a ceiling which incorporates a heating system
● don't carry out application when the temperature is below 5°C or above 40°C or when the temperature is likely to exceed these limits before the material is dry.

You can apply a traditional compound type of texture over 'hot' surfaces such as heated ceilings and chimney breasts, but you should first seal the surface with a good quality alkali-resisting primer.

Don't apply either type in freezing conditions.

CREATING REGULAR PATTERNS

If you are creating a regular pattern which requires matching, use a plumb bob and line to mark guidelines on the walls (or to snap chalked lines on the ceiling); paint and pattern in bands between the straight lines.

TIP: REMOVE MASKING QUICKLY

If you have used tape or newspaper to protect window frames, pipes or fittings, remove it before the texture dries; it may be difficult to remove later when the texture has set.

EXTERIOR PAINTING preparation

Whether you like it or not, preparing the outside of your house before painting it is a job that has to be done. If you provide a sound surface the paint will last much longer.

If your house is in good order and has been decorated regularly, then the paintwork may need no more than a quick wash down and a light sanding before it's ready for re-painting. But if your house is in a rather worse state than this, take some time now to make a really good job of the preparation and you'll have a much easier time in the future. The preparation may seem rather time-consuming, but don't be tempted to miss out any of the steps. Properly applied, paint will protect your house for several years, but it won't stick to an unsound surface.

The most convenient order of working is to start at the top of the house and work down, and to do all the preparation before you start to paint so that dust and grit won't fall on wet paint. When working at a height, make sure the ladder or platform is firm and secure.

Gutters and downpipes

Gutters manage to trap a surprising quantity of dirt and old leaves, so clear this out first. It's a good idea to check that the gutter is at a regular slope towards the nearest downpipe. You can easily check this by pouring a bucket of water into one end and seeing if it all drains away. If puddles form, you'll need to unscrew some of the gutter brackets and adjust the level of the gutter until the water flows away freely. Check all the joints for leaks and if you do find any, seal them with a mastic compound applied with a gun.

Plastic gutters need little maintenance, and they don't need painting. But if you want to change their colour, simply clean them thoroughly and wipe them over with a rag dipped in white spirit or turps to remove any grease spots before starting to paint. There's no need for a primer or undercoat, but you may need two top coats for even coverge.

Metal gutters and pipes need more attention as all rust has to be removed. Scrape off flaking paint first, then use a wire brush and emery paper to remove the rust. A wire brush attachment on an electric drill would make the cleaning easier (but wear a mask and goggles while using one). You can buy an anti-rust chemical from paint shops which is useful for badly rusted metalwork. It works by turning iron oxide (rust) into phosphate of iron which is inert and can be painted over. In any case, prime all bare metal immediately with either a red lead primer or a zinc chromate metal primer. Metal primers contain a rust-inhibitor which protects the metal against further corrosion, so don't miss them out. If the gutters and pipes are in good condition with no sign of rust, simply wash them down and sand the surface lightly to key it ready for repainting.

Fascias and barge boards

Fascias and barge boards run along the top of a wall just below the roof. Fascias support the guttering below pitched roofs and edge flat ones, while barge boards are fitted beneath the roof tiles on gable ends. Because they are so high up, don't worry too much about their appearance; the main consideration is protection as they are in such an exposed position. Clean out well behind the gutters as damp leaves or even bird's nests can be lodged there. Then, using a wide scraper, remove all loose flaking paint, sand down the whole board surface and prime the bare patches. Fill holes and cracks with an exterior-grade filler or waterproof stopping and smooth it level while still damp using a filler knife. You can prime the filler when it's dry.

Walls

The main surface materials and finishes used on the outside of your house are brick, stone, wood and render.

Walls of brick and stone, especially when weathered, have a beauty all of their own and don't really need painting. But the surface can become cracked and dirty and a coat of paint will cover up repairs that don't match the original surface, and protect the wall from further damage. Examine the pointing and, if it has deteriorated, rake out the damaged parts and re-point with fresh mortar. Use a mixture of about 1 part cement to 4 parts of fine sand, or buy a bag of ready-mixed mortar. Use a small trowel and try to match the original pointing in the surrounding brickwork. Don't worry about hairline cracks as these will easily be covered by the paint. The white crystalline deposit which sometimes appears on brickwork is known as efflorescence. It is caused by water-soluble salts in the brick being brought to the surface, and should be brushed off with a dry brush. Don't try to wash it off as this will only make it worse.

The main types of render are plain, roughcast and pebbledash. Plain render can be applied to give a smooth finish or a textured 'Tyrolean' finish, for example. Roughcast consists of pebbles mixed with mortar before application, and with pebbledash the pebbles are thrown on while the mortar is still wet. Pebbledash deteriorates more quickly than the other types of render as, over the years, differences in rates of expansion between each pebble and the surrounding mortar may result in small surface cracks causing the pebbles to become loose and fall out. Paint will bind in the pebbles and protect small cracks.

PREPARING THE WALLS

1 *Before painting an exterior wall, brush it down well to remove any loose material. Start at the top and use a fairly stiff brush.*

2 *Kill mould and algae with a solution of 1 part bleach to 4 parts water. Leave for two days, then wash down and brush off.*

3 *Rusty metal and leaky gutters can easily cause stains, so cure the leaks and clean and prime all metal first. Sterilise the stain and brush down.*

4 *Holes in the wall are often created when old downpipe brackets are removed. Brush them out well and damp the surface with a little water.*

5 *Fill the hole with a sand and cement mixture using a small trowel. Small bags of ready-mixed mortar are ideal for jobs of this size.*

6 *If the wall is powdery or highly porous, or if a cement-based paint has been used previously, seal the surface with a stabilising primer.*

Ready Reference

CHOOSE THE RIGHT PRIMER

Different materials require different primers; be sure to choose the right type.

Wood

softwood & hardwood	wood primer or acrylic primer
resinous wood	aluminium wood primer

Metal

iron and steel	calcium plumbate primer, zinc chromate primer or red lead primer
galvanised iron (new)	calcium plumbate primer
(old)	calcium plumbate or zinc chromate primer
aluminium	zinc chromate primer
brass, copper and lead	none necessary: allow new lead to weather

Masonry etc

brick, stone, concrete & render	stabilising primer alkali-resisting primer, acrylic primer

Other materials

asbestos	stabilising primer, alkali-resisting primer or acrylic primer
bitumen-coated wood	aluminium wood primer
bitumen-coated metal	aluminium spirit-based sealer

PROPERTIES AND COVERAGE

Where there is a choice of suitable primers, it's often helpful to know something more about each type. For instance, many primers are toxic and you should choose a non-toxic one if you're painting anything in a child's room.

● Acrylic primer – white or pastel shades, water-based, quick drying, non-toxic, 13-18m^2 (140-190sq ft) per litre.

● Alkali-resisting primer – needs two coats on very porous surfaces, non-toxic, 3-10m^2 (30-110sq ft) per litre.

● Aluminium wood primer – dull metallic grey, self-knotting, non-toxic, 16m^2 (170sq ft) per litre.

● Calcium plumbate primer – off-white, rust inhibiting, toxic, 8-12m^2 (90-130sq ft) per litre.

● Lead-free wood primer – white or pink, non-toxic, 10-12m^2 (110-130sq ft) per litre.

● Red lead primer – bright red, rust inhibiting, only for exterior use, toxic, 12-17m^2 (130-180sq ft) per litre.

● Lead-based wood primer – white or pink, only for exterior use, toxic, 12-14m^2 (130-150sq ft) per litre.

● Zinc chromate primer – yellow, rust inhibiting, non-toxic, 11m^2 (120sq ft) per litre.

PREPARING THE WOODWORK

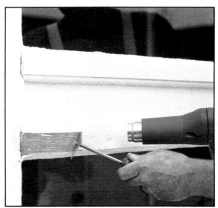

1 Start preparing the woodwork by scraping off all the loose flaking paint. Large areas of unsound paint are better if stripped completely.

2 Sand and prime all the bare wood, taking care to work the primer well into cracks and any exposed end grain, then leave the surface to dry.

3 Where joints have opened up, scrape off the paint and rake out the gap with a knife or shavehook. Clean out all the loose debris.

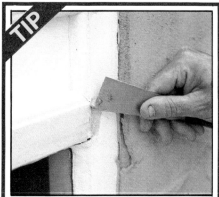

TIP

4 Small cracks can be filled with putty, but use exterior-grade filler or waterproof stopping for larger cracks and holes.

5 Gaps often appear between the window frame and the wall. Fill these with a mastic compound to provide a continuous water-tight seal.

6 Make sure the drip groove underneath the window sill is clear of paint, then thoroughly sand down the whole of the window frame.

REPLACING OLD PUTTY

1 Old, damaged putty must be raked out. Scrape old paint from the glass, and clean the glass with methylated spirit to remove any grease spots.

2 Work the putty in your hands until it has an even consistency. If it's too oily, roll it on newspaper first. Press it firmly into the gap.

3 Smooth the new putty level with the old using a putty knife, then run a soft brush over it to make a water-tight seal with the glass.

TREATING KNOTS

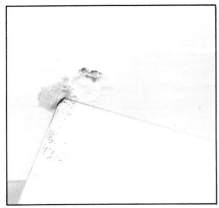

1 *Active knots like this ooze out a sticky resin which quickly breaks through the paint surface, leaving a sticky and unsightly mess.*

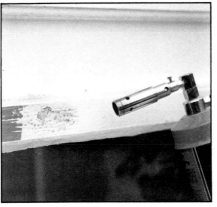

2 *The paint must first be stripped off to expose the knot. Use any method of stripping, and scrape the paint off with a shavehook or scraper.*

3 *Use a blow-torch to heat the knot until the resin bubbles out. Scrape off the resin and repeat until no more of it appears.*

4 *Sand the knot with fine glasspaper, then wipe over the area with knotting applied with a soft cloth. Prime the wood when it has dried.*

When repairing any of these surfaces, try and achieve the same finish as the original, or as near as you can, so that when it's repainted the repair won't be too noticeable. Stop up cracks with mortar, using a mix of 1 part cement to 5 parts sand. Chip away very wide cracks until you reach a firm edge, then undercut this to provide a good key for the new mortar. Dampen the surface, then stop up with a trowel. Use a float if the surface is plain, or texture the surface to match the surrounding area. Where the rendering is pebble-dash, throw on pebbles with a small trowel while the mortar is still wet, then press them into the mortar lightly with a flat piece of wood.

Mould and stains

If there's any sign of mould or algae on the wall, treat this next. Mix up a solution of 1 part household bleach to 4 parts water and paint this on the affected area. Be generous with the solution and cover the area well. Leave for 48 hours for the bleach to kill off all the growth, then wash off thoroughly and brush down with a stiff brush.

Rusty gutters, pipes and metal fittings can all cause stains if rusty water drips down the wall. So cure any leaks first and clean and prime all metal to ensure there's no trace of rust. Mould and algae thrive on damp walls; even if you can't actually see any growth on a damp patch, there may be some spores lurking there, so you should make absolutely sure that you sterilise all stains with the bleach solution just to make sure.

Dusty or chalky walls

All walls, whether dusty or not, should be brushed down thoroughly to remove any loose material. But if, after brushing, the wall is still dusty or chalky, if a cement-based paint was used previously to decorate it, or if the wall is porous, you'll have to brush on a stabilising solution. This will bind together loose particles to allow the paint to stick, and it will seal a porous surface and stop paint from being sucked in too much. The stabiliser also helps to waterproof the wall and you can paint it on as an extra layer of protection whether it's really necessary or not. Most stabilisers are colourless, but off-white stabiliser/primers are available and this would be a good choice if you were planning to paint your house in a light colour, as it could save one coat of the finishing colour. These off-white stabilisers, however, are not recommended for use on surfaces painted with a cement-based paint.

Stabilisers must be painted on a dry wall and should be left to dry for 24 hours before painting on the top coat. Don't paint if rain is expected. Clean your brush in white spirit or turps as soon as you stop work.

Timber cladding

If the cladding or weatherboarding is bare and you want to leave the natural wood surface showing, it should be treated with a water-repellent wood preservative to give protection against damp penetration and decay. The preservative is available clear or pigmented with various colours.

If the wood has been varnished, scrape off the old varnish and sand down well, following the grain of the wood. Fill cracks and holes with plastic wood or a tinted stopper to match the colour of the wood.

If you wish to paint the surface you'll have to wait a year or so for the water-repellent agents in the preservative to disperse before priming with an aluminium wood primer.

Woodwork

If the paintwork on the windows is in good condition all you need do is give them a wash and a light sanding. If the paint is cracked and flaking, a little more preparation is needed. To check if the paint surface needs stripping, lay on a piece of sticky tape and see if it lifts off any paint. Occasional chipped or blistered portions can be scraped off and cut back to a firm edge. As long as the edge is feathered smooth with glasspaper, it shouldn't show too much. If previous coatings are too thick for this treatment, build up the surface with outdoor grade hard stopping until it is just proud of the surrounding paint, then sand level when it's dry. Don't allow the stopping to extend too far over the edge of the damage or it'll be difficult to sand it smooth.

There comes a time, however, when the condition of the old coating has become so bad that complete stripping is advisable.

A blow-torch or an electric hot air stripper are the quickest tools to use. Start at the bottom softening the paint, and follow up immediately with a scraper. Hold the scraper at an angle so the hot paint doesn't fall on your hand, and don't hold it above the flame or it may become too hot to hold. Try not to concentrate the flame too long on one part or you're likely to scorch the wood

PREPARING METAL

1 Metal pipes and gutters are often in a very bad state of repair and need a lot of preparation. Scrape off all the old flaking paint first.

2 Brush well with a wire brush to remove all traces of rust. Badly rusted pipes should be treated with an anti-rust chemical.

3 Hold a board or a piece of card behind the pipe to keep paint off the wall, and paint on a metal primer, covering every bit of bare metal.

4 A small paint pad on a long handle is a useful tool for painting behind pipes, especially when they are very close to the wall.

New doors and windows

New wooden windows and doors may already have a coat of pink primer applied at the factory, but it's best not to rely on this for complete protection. Knots, for instance, will rarely have been properly treated, and the primer film will have been damaged here and there in transit. So sand down the whole surface, treat any knots with knotting compound and apply another coat of wood primer overall. It may be advisable to paint doors while they're lying flat; certainly it's vital to paint the top and bottom edges before you hang them in place. It's very important to paint the bottom as rain and snow can easily penetrate unpainted wood causing it to swell and rot. Paint also protects the wood against attack from woodworm.

Metal and plastic windows

Metal doors and windows should be treated in the same way as metal pipes and gutters. So sand them down and make sure all rust is removed before priming. Aluminium frames can be left unpainted, but if you do want to paint them you must first remove any surface oxidation which shows as a fine white deposit. Use a scraper or wire brush, but go very gently and try not to scratch the surface. Prime with a zinc chromate primer. Plastic window frames should not be painted.

Galvanised iron and asbestos

You're likely to find galvanised iron used as corrugated iron roofing, gutters and down-pipes. The zinc coating on galvanised iron is to some extent 'sacrificial', so that if a small patch becomes damaged, the surrounding zinc will, in time, spread over to cover the damage. But this weakens the coating and an application of paint will prolong its life. If the galvanising is new and bright, simply clean it with a rag dipped in white spirit or turps to remove any grease, and apply a calcium plumbate primer. If it's old and grey-looking, first remove any existing paint by rubbing lightly with a wire brush, trying not to scratch the surface. Then clean with white spirit or turps and apply zinc chromate primer.

Asbestos is often used for guttering, fascia boards, as walls on out-houses and as corrugated sheeting for roofs. Asbestos is a very dangerous material and for this reason great care should be taken when dealing with it. It'll probably need cleaning before painting and the only safe way is to wet it thoroughly first and scrub it down with a scrubbing brush. Be sure to wear rubber gloves and a face mask. Leave it to dry, then prime it with a stabilizing primer, an alkali-resisting primer, or simply a coat of thinned-down emulsion paint. Asbestos is very porous, so always paint both sides of any asbestos sheet to prevent damp penetrating from the back.

though this rarely matters on exterior wood-work which will be over-painted again. Always be extremely careful when using a blow-torch, and keep a bucket of water or sand nearby in case something does catch fire. A chemical paint stripper is the best method to use near glass in case the glass cracks under the heat of a blow-torch.

Knots, putty and holes

Check the woodwork for any live knots which are oozing out resin. If you find any, strip off the paint over them and then play a blow-torch or electric hot air stripper over them to burn out the resin. Sand lightly and treat with knotting, then prime when dry.

You should also check the putty fillet round each pane of glass, and if any has disintegrated, rake it out with an old knife. Then sand and prime the wood and bed in new putty using a putty knife. Use linseed oil putty on wood and metal glazing or all purpose putty on metal-framed windows. Smooth the putty with a damp cloth and leave it for about a week before painting.

Rake out any cracks in the wood and cut back wood which is starting to rot. If a large amount of wood is rotten – usually along the bottom edge of a sash window – a larger repair is needed. This could involve replacing a section or all of the window. Prime the bare wood, working the primer well into cracks and end grain as this is where the weather gets in. Small cracks can be filled with putty, but larger ones should be filled with exterior grade hard stopping or filler. Sand level when dry and spot-prime. Gaps between the window frame and wall should be filled with a flexible, waterproof, mastic compound applied with a special gun.

Finally, sand down the whole of the wood-work to make it ready for repainting.

EXTERIOR PAINTING

completing the job

The first two parts of this article described how to prepare the outside of your house to make it ready for repainting. This last part shows you the best way to paint the walls, pipes, windows and doors to give a professional look to your home.

If you have completed all the cleaning, repairs and preparation on the outside of your house, and if the weather has been dry for the past couple of days and looks settled for a while, you are now ready to start painting. Tackle the painting in more or less the same order as the preparation, starting at the top and working downwards.

Gutters, fascias and barge boards

If you have plastic gutters and want to paint them, simply apply a thin coat of gloss paint to the outside surface. This is the only case outside where paint is used purely for decoration rather than protection. Iron gutters can be painted on the inside with a bituminous paint as this will provide a waterproof coating and protect the iron. Paint the outside of gutters and downpipes with the usual gloss paint system. You'll need a small paint pad or crevice brush to get into the narrow gaps at the back of gutters and pipes. Protect the fascia with a piece of board held behind the guttering. Don't miss out these awkward bits as this is where the rust will start up again. You can use bitumen paint on the inside of asbestos gutters too, but it's best to use

TEXTURED WALLS

1 Use a 'banister' brush or 'dust pan' brush for painting rough-textured finishes such as pebbledash or a randomly-textured finish.

2 Paint brickwork with a well-loaded old brush. Small cracks are bridged by the paint, but larger cracks have to be filled first with exterior filler.

3 Alternatively, use a roller on brick to give a thicker coat of paint and a slightly textured finish. Special rollers give even deeper textures.

emulsion paint rather than solvent-based gloss ones on the outside. Asbestos is porous and needs to be able to 'breathe'. Gloss paint would trap moisture within the asbestos, and this would eventually cause the paint to blister.

Fascias and barge boards are so exposed that it's best to give them an extra coat of gloss. You'll need your crevice brush or paint pad again to paint behind the gutters.

Walls
There is a wide range of paints available for exterior walls, and full information is usually available from suppliers. As for tools, a 100mm (4in) brush is the easiest size to handle; anything larger would put too much strain on the wrist. An alternative is a long-pile roller which has the advantage of being much quicker to use – about three times quicker than a brush. An extra long-pile roller is needed for roughcast or pebbledash; choose one with a pile 32mm (1¼in) deep, or use a banister brush instead. Use a cheap disposable brush or roller for cement paints as they are almost impossible to clean afterwards.

A large plastic bucket or paint kettle is essential when working up a ladder. Stir the paint thoroughly first, then pour some into the bucket until it's about one third full. If you're using a roller, use a special roller tray with a large paint reservoir, or else stand a short plank in the bucket (see step-by-step photographs, page 27) to allow you to load the roller evenly.

Hook the bucket or tray onto a rung of the ladder with an S-hook to leave both hands free. Lay a dust sheet below to catch any drips and you're ready to start.

Application
Start at the top of the wall and paint a strip across the house. Work from right to left if you're right-handed, and left to right if you're left-handed. Be sure to secure the ladder to prevent it slipping and allow a three-rung overlap at the top.

Use a brush to cut in under the eaves or fascia boards and to paint round obstacles, then fill in the larger areas with a brush or roller. Paint an area only as large as you can comfortably manage and don't lean out too far, your hips should remain between the ladder's stiles at all times.

If you have an awkward area which is too far away to reach, push a broom handle into the hollow handle of the roller, or buy a special extension handle. Protect pipes by wrapping them in newspaper, and mask any other items you don't want to paint. Leave an uneven edge at the bottom of each patch so the join won't be too noticeable, then move the ladder to the left (or right) and paint another strip alongside the first. The principle is always to keep working to the longest wet

edge so the joins won't show. When you've done the top series of strips, lower the ladder and paint another series across the middle. Lower the ladder again or work from the ground to do another series along the bottom. Working across the house like this means you have to alter the ladder height the least number of times.

Woodwork
You can choose either a non-drip gloss or a runny gloss for the exterior woodwork. The non-drip jelly paints combine the properties of undercoat and finishing coat so a separate undercoat is not required. But this single coat won't be as long-lasting as the undercoat-plus-runny-gloss system and you'll have to apply two or three coats to build up a thick enough paint film to give adequate outside protection. Inside, however, one coat of non-drip paint would be quite sufficient.

The sequence of painting all jointed woodwork – windows, doors and frames – is determined by the method of construction. In nearly all cases the rails (horizontal bars) are tenoned into mortises cut into the stiles (uprights). Therefore, you should paint the rails and cross bars first, then deal with the stiles. By painting in this way, any overlaps of paint from the rails and bars are covered up and leave a neater finish. An even edge on the glass is best achieved freehand, but if you doubt the steadiness of your touch, use a paint guard or masking tape. Bring the paint onto the glass for up to 3mm (⅛in) to protect the edge of the putty. If you are using masking tape, remove it shortly after painting round each pane; the paint may be peeled off if it is left to harden completely before the tape is removed.

When a visitor calls at your house, he'll stand face to face with your front door and have nothing to do but examine it while he awaits your answer. So it's here you should put in your best work. Remove all the door furniture such as knobs, knockers, locks, keyhole covers and letterbox. Prepare the woodwork carefully and wipe it down with a tackrag (a soft cloth impregnated with a sticky varnish) to collect any remaining dust. Tackrags are obtainable from any good paint shop. Use a perfectly clean brush, preferably one that has been used before so that no loose bristles will come adrift. Wedge the door ajar and cover the floor with a dust cloth or old newspapers. Use paint which doesn't need straining, and pour about 50mm (2in) into a small container or paint kettle.

All coats of paint should follow the grain of the wood. Don't attempt to cross-hatch – that is, apply a primer in one direction, undercoat at right angles and finishing coat in the direction of the primer. If you do, you'll get a crisscross effect when the paint dries which produces a poor finish.

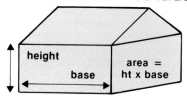
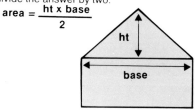

PAINTING WALLS

1 A roller is much quicker to use than a brush, but make sure you have a large enough bucket to dip the roller in. Fill this about ⅓ full.

2 Cut a short plank of wood to the same width as the roller and put it in the bucket so you can load the roller evenly by pressing against it.

3 When painting the house wall, start at the top right hand corner (if you are right-handed) and use a brush to cut in round the edges.

4 Using the roller, cover a strip on your right-hand side. Don't lean over too far and only make the strip as long as you can easily manage.

5 Move the ladder to the left and paint another strip by the first, without overlapping too much. Touch in round obstacles with a brush.

6 Using the brush again, carefully paint round the window. Try to leave a neat edge with the woodwork and wipe off any splashes with a damp cloth.

7 Continue painting a strip at a time from right to left, then lower the ladder and paint a further series of strips until the wall is covered.

8 Protect pipes by wrapping old newspaper round them and securing it with adhesive tape. Use a brush to paint the wall behind the pipes.

9 Be very careful when painting the bottom edge of the wall, and don't load the brush too thickly or paint will run onto the path.

Ready Reference

HOW MUCH GLOSS PAINT?

The coverage of a litre of gloss paint depends on several factors, including the smoothness of the surface and whether it is interrupted by edges and mouldings. Also, a lot depends on the painter's technique. However, as a general guide, for one litre of paint:
● runny gloss covers 17m² (180sq ft)
● non-drip gloss covers 13m² (140sq ft).

CALCULATING AREAS

It would be very difficult to calculate the area of every bit of wood and metal you wanted to paint. But you need to make a rough estimate so you'll know how much paint to buy. The following examples are intended as a rough guide and they should give you an idea of how much paint you'll need, assuming you're using **runny gloss** and you give everything **two coats of paint.** If you're using non-drip gloss you'll have to buy about 25% more paint:
● a panelled front door will take ⅓ litre (½ pint)
● a flush door will take about ⅕ litre (⅓ pint)

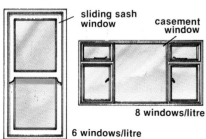

panelled door — **3 doors/litre**

flush door — **5 doors/litre**

● a sash window, about 2x1m (6ft 6in x 3ft 3in) with an ornate frame will take about ⅙ litre (¼ pint)
● a modern picture window of the same size with a plain frame will take only ⅛ litre (⅕ pint)

sliding sash window **casement window**

8 windows/litre

6 windows/litre

● to find the area of a downpipe, simply measure round the pipe and multiply by the height, then add a little for clips and brackets. For two coats of paint, one litre will cover 18m (60ft) of 150mm (6in) diameter pipe and 27m (90ft) of 100mm (4in) pipe.

PAINTING WINDOWS

1 Start to apply undercoat at the top of the window. Prop the window open, tape up the stay and paint the frame rebates first.

2 Paint the rebates on open casements next. If you get paint on the inside surface, wipe it off immediately with a cloth dipped in white spirit or turps.

3 Close the window slightly and paint the area along the hinged edge. You may need to use a narrow brush (called a fitch) to reach this part.

4 A neat paint line on the glass is best achieved free-hand, but if you find this too difficult, use a paint shield or apply masking tape.

5 The general order of painting is to do the cross bars (rails) first, followed by the uprights (stiles) and then the window sill.

6 When the undercoat is dry, sand it down with a fine grade glasspaper, then apply the top coat in the same order as the undercoat.

PAINTING SEQUENCES

Windows and panelled doors are tricky areas to paint properly but you shouldn't have any trouble if you follow the correct sequence of painting shown here.

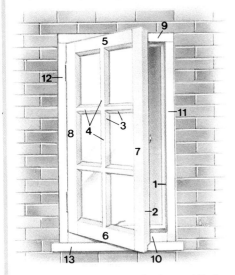

Start with the rebate on the frame (1), then paint the outside edge of the window (2). Do the putty (3) next, followed by the glazing bars (4) and the rails and stiles (5 to 8). Paint the frame (9 to 13) last.

Wedge the door ajar and paint the frame (1 to 3), the hinged edge of the frame and door. Do mouldings and panels next (4 to 13) followed by the muntins (14,15), the rails (16 to 19) and finally the stiles (20, 21).

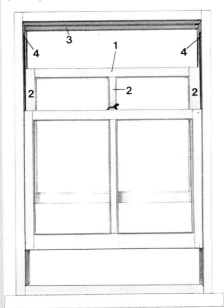

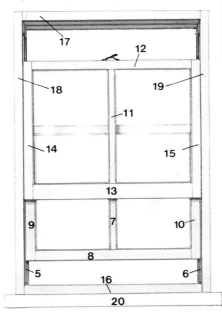

Sliding sash windows need to be painted in two stages. Pull down the top sash and paint the top rail of the inside sash (1) and the sides as far as you can go (2). Do the runners at the top of the frame (3) and a short way down the outer runner(4). Almost close the windows, then paint the bottom runners (5,6), and the remainder

of the bottom sash to meet the other paint (7 to 10). Paint the whole of the top sash including the bottom edge (11 to 15) and finally the window frame (16 to 20). This view shows the interior of the window: for the exterior the sequence is identical except of course, that you start with the top sash.

Deal with the door frame first (the top, then the sides) so that any splashes can be wiped off an unpainted surface immediately. Then do the door itself, following the sequence of painting shown on this page. Don't put too thick a coat on the inner edge of the door frame because although gloss paint dries fairly quickly, it won't oxidise (ie, thoroughly harden) for about a week. So in that period, when you close the door, paint may 'set-off' from the frame onto the door, producing a vertical streak an inch or so from the door's edge. A good idea to prevent this is to insert a thin strip of polythene sheeting round the door's edge after the paint has become touch dry, and leave it until the paint has thoroughly hardened.

If you want to apply two finishing coats, wait at least 12 hours but not more than a week between coats. There's no need to sand down between coats because the solvent used in modern gloss paints is strong enough to dissolve the surface of the previous coat and so to ensure a firm bond between the two layers.

Weatherboards

Weatherboards and timber cladding can be left in their natural state as long as you treat them with a wood preservative, and you can use wood stains to enhance or change their colour. If you prefer a glossy finish, use a suitable external varnish such as an oil-resin varnish (marine varnish), rather than a one-pack polyurethane varnish which can prove brittle and difficult to over-coat in future. If you wish to paint the wood you'll have to apply one coat of wood primer, followed by an undercoat and two finishing coats of gloss.

Galvanised iron and asbestos

Because it is waterproof, bituminous paint is best for galvanised or asbestos roofs. In addition to the customary black it can be obtained in shades of red, green or brown to simulate or match tiles. These colours are more expensive than black and may have to be ordered specially from a builders' merchant. Bitumen soon loses its gloss and its surface tends to craze under a hot sun. But that doesn't matter as roofs are not usually visible.

Paint the walls of asbestos outhouses with outdoor-grade emulsion in a colour to match the rest of the house. Thin the first coat to allow for the porosity of the asbestos and follow this with a normal second coat. Apply emulsion on the interior surface as well to minimise moisture absorption. Galvanised iron on vertical surfaces should be painted with gloss paint.

When painting corrugated surfaces, give the high parts a preliminary touch-up with paint, leave it to dry and then paint the whole lot. If you apply paint all over in one go it will tend to flow from high to low parts, giving an uneven coating.

STRIPPING WOOD

Wood has a natural beauty, but it's often a beauty concealed by layers and layers of paint. Doors, window frames, even skirting boards and architraves can all become attractive features in themselves when stripped back to reveal the wood. Even if you prefer to repaint, using the right techniques to strip off the old will give the best possible surface on which to work.

Stripping wood of old paint or layers of ancient varnish isn't the easiest of jobs. It's usually only done because you're after a natural finish, or because the painted surface has degenerated to such an extent that further coats of paint simply can't produce a smooth finish. Either way, once wood has been stripped back to its natural state, it then has to be sealed again — to protect it from moisture which can cause cracking, warping and ultimately decay. Both varnishes and paints act as sealants, giving a durable finish. But which one you choose might depend on the wood itself — and you won't know what that's like until you've stripped it. If you're unsure of its quality, it's advisable to strip a test area first.

Some of the timber used in houses is of a grade that was never intended for a clear finish – large ugly knots, cracks, splits or even an unattractive grain are some of the signs. In cases like this it is probably better to treat the problems (eg. applying 'knotting' – a special liquid sealer – to make the knots tight and prevent them 'bleeding', filling cracks and splits to give a flush surface) and then paint to seal.

If you are set on having the wood on show and don't want to paint it – because it wouldn't fit in with a colour scheme or make the feature you want – you can give it a better appearance and extra protection with stain or coloured varnish.

Stripping with abrasives

For dry stripping there are several different kinds of powered sanders available, all of which use abrasive papers of some kind to strip the surface off wood. On large areas such as floors it is best to use a purpose-made power sander which you can hire. A drill with a sanding attachment, however, is useful for getting small areas smooth after paint has been removed by other methods.

One such attachment is a 'disc sander' and is quite tricky to use effectively without scoring the wood surface. Hold it at a slight angle to the wood and present only half the disc to the surface. Work in short bursts and keep the disc moving over the surface – if it stays too long in one place it can damage the wood.

A 'drum sander' attachment has a belt of abrasive paper stuck round the edge of a cylinder of foam, and if used along the grain only is rather easier to handle than a disc

USING SCRAPERS

1 *A triangular shavehook needs two hands when paint is thick. Hold the blade at an angle to the wood so it doesn't cause gouges.*

2 *A combination shavehook has round, straight and pointed edges to help remove paint and varnish from mouldings round windows and doors.*

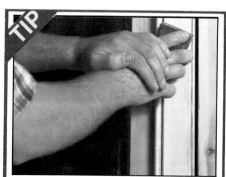

3 *A special hook scraper has a sharp replaceable blade suitable both for scraping paint off flat surfaces and for getting into awkward crevices.*

sander. Whichever type is chosen, a fine grade abrasive should be used for finishing stripped wood.

Orbital sanders (which are also known as finishing sanders) usually come as self-powered tools – although attachments are available for some drills. These have a much milder action and as long as the spread of wood isn't interrupted by mouldings they smooth well and are useful for rubbing down between coats. These sanders are rectangular and should be moved over the surface in line with the grain. Make sure you choose the right type of sander, depending on the work in hand.

For sanding by hand – hard work, but much better for finishing – there are many grades of glasspaper from the coarse to the very fine. On flat surfaces it's best to wrap the paper round a small block of wood. As an alternative to glasspaper, there's also steel wool, which is most useful when you're trying to smooth down an intricate moulding. Always sand backwards and forwards *with the grain of the wood*, not across it. Scratches across the grain will always be highlighted by a clear finish. To remove remaining bits of paint use medium grade glasspaper; for finishing, a fine grade is better. Renew the glasspaper frequently as the paint will clog the surface.

although a useful tip is to try cleaning clogged paper with a wire brush. It'll work once or twice, but after that the abrasive surface is usually lost. Alternatively pull the sheet backwards and forwards, abrasive side uppermost, over a table edge to dislodge paint particles.

A useful tool for cleaning paint from corners and mouldings is a hand scraper with replaceable blades. These 'hook' scrapers are also used for 'smoothing' and often need two-hands – they slightly raise the surface of a clear run of wood, giving an attractive finish under a clear seal. Use with the grain.

Heat stripping

Heat stripping is the quickest way to remove paint or varnish, but it needs a lot of expertise if you are to avoid charring the wood. So it is best reserved for stripping out of doors where a less-than-perfect surface will be less noticeable. A gas blow-torch is used along with metal scrapers to lift the finish off the wood while it's still warm. Blow-torches with gas canister attachments are light to use and a flame spreader nozzle makes the job easier (it can be bought separately).

Where there's no glass, it's a two-handed operation. Light the blow-torch and hold it a

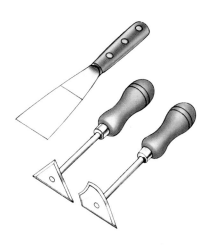
HEAT STRIPPING

1 Play the blow-torch onto the paint and when it begins to bubble, start to scrape. Protect floor and sills with a sheet of non-flammable material.

2 When stripping paint near windows one hand must hold protection for glass. When paint hardens again, return the flame to the area.

3 Working overhead can be tricky if using a blow-torch. Protect your hands with gloves, your eyes with safety goggles and cover surfaces below.

4 To strip paint overhead, remove torch (be careful where it points), blow out flames and scrape quickly. As the paint loses heat it hardens.

little way from the surface. Move it back and forth, going nearer and withdrawing, till the paint starts to wrinkle and blister. Now begin to scrape – be careful where you point the flame at this stage or you may damage other surfaces. As soon as the paint is hard to move return the flame to the area. Wear gloves to save your hands from being burnt by the falling paint, and cover areas below where you are working with a sheet of non-flammable material to catch the scrapings. In awkward areas, especially overhead, you should wear protective goggles for safety's sake.

Chemical stripping
Chemical strippers are probably the easiest way to strip wood. Available in liquid, gel and paste forms, their methods of application and removal vary, so always remember to read the manufacturer's instructions before you begin. Though all of them will remove paint and varnish, if you are dealing with a large area of wood they can work out to be very expensive – they're also very messy.

Liquid and gel strippers, decanted if necessary into a more convenient-sized container (read the instructions as to whether it can be heavy gauge plastic or should be glass or metal), are stippled onto the surface with a brush and left till the paint bubbles before scraping. Usually these strippers will work through only 1 layer of paint at a time so several applications can be necessary. If stripping a chair or table, stand the legs in old paint cans or jam jars so that any stripper which runs down the legs can be recycled. Artists brushes rather than paint brushes are useful when applying these strippers to mouldings or beading in windows and No 2 steel wool is useful for removing it.

After liquids or gels have been used, the surface must be cleaned down with white spirit or water (it depends on the stripper used) to remove any trace of chemical and must be left till completely dry before any stain or seal is applied.

Pastes are mostly water soluble and manufacturers stress important conditions for using them safely (eg, not in direct sun, in well ventilated rooms, the wearing of protective gloves, etc). Bought in tubs ready-mixed or in powder form to be made up, they are spread in thick (3-6mm) layers over the wood which must then be covered with strips of polythene (good way of using up plastic carrier bags) or a special 'blanket' (supplied with the tub) which adheres – when you press it – to the paste. They have to be left for between 2 and 8 hours after which the paste can be scrubbed off (with a firm brush) or washed down. Frequent changes of water are needed; follow manufacturer's advice about additives (eg, vinegar). Pastes are particularly effective with extraordinarily stubborn paint or varnish in very awkward places (eg, windows, bannisters etc); or where using a scraper might damage old wood. Some pastes are unsuitable for certain types of wood and can stain it – so read instructions carefully. Washing down should not be done, for example, with valuable furniture for this can raise the grain of the wood.

Bleaching
If the wood is discoloured once stripped (either from the stripper used or from some other source) you can try and achieve an overall colour with bleach – the household type, used diluted 1:3 with water to begin with and more concentrated if necessary, or better still a proprietary wood bleach.

Clean the surface of the stripped wood with paint thinner and steel wool and leave for 15 minutes to dry. Cover areas you don't want bleached with polythene, then brush bleach on generously. Work it into the wood *with the grain* using medium steel wool.

Leave for 2-4 minutes, then wipe off with rags. Leave to dry (up to 5 hours) before sanding after which you can finish the surface as desired.

CHEMICAL STRIPPING

1 *Liquid strippers are stippled onto wood with a brush. First pour the liquid into a smaller container — but remember it will dissolve light plastic.*

2 *When paint is bubbling use a scraper to remove it. Work upwards and be careful not to gouge the wood with the blade.*

3 *Several applications of liquid may be needed as chemicals often only eat through one layer at a time. Use gloves to protect your hands.*

4 *After all paint has been stripped off, wipe the wood down with white spirit or water so that the chemicals are neutralised.*

5 *A good way to deal with mouldings is to apply a thick layer of stripping paste. This needs to be covered while it works, but is very effective.*

6 *After leaving for the specified time (can be several hours) wash the paste off with sponge or a scrubbing brush, changing the water often.*

CHAPTER 2

Papering

PAPERING WALLS
the basics

No other wall covering can quite so dramatically alter the look and feeling of a room as wallpaper. Correctly hung paper makes the walls sharp and fresh, and to achieve this finish there are important things to know. What do you do if the walls are out of true? Where's the best place to start? How do you prevent bubbles and creases? The answers are here.

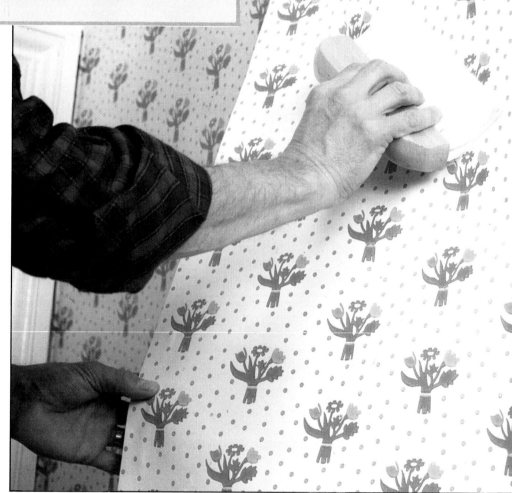

Wallpapering isn't so much an art, it's more a matter of attention to detail. And perhaps the first mistake that's made by many people is expecting too much of their walls. Rarely are walls perfectly flat, perfectly vertical and at right angles to each other. So the first and most crucial part of hanging wallpaper is to prepare the walls properly. Obviously you can't change their basic character – if they're not entirely flat or vertical, you're stuck with them – but you can make sure that the surface is suitably prepared so that the new paper will stick.

This means that any old wallpaper really should come off before you do anything else. Papering on top of old wall coverings won't *always* lead to disaster, but it will quite often simply because the new adhesive will tend to loosen the old. The result will be bubbles at best and peeling at worst.

Adhesives

Always use the correct adhesive for the wallcovering and follow the manufacturers instructions for mixing. Using the wrong paste can result in the paper not sticking, mould growth or discoloration of the paper.

A cellulose-based adhesive is used for all standard wallcoverings. There are two types, ordinary and heavy-duty which relates to the weight of the paper being hung. Heavy-duty pastes are for heavyweight wallcoverings. Certain brands of paste are suitable for all types of wallcoverings – less water being used for mixing when hanging heavy papers.

Since vinyls and washable wallcoverings are impervious, mould could attack the paste unless it contains a fungicide. Fungicidal paste is also needed if the wall has previously been treated against mould or if there is any sign of damp.

Some wallcoverings (like polyethylene foam, some hessians and foils) require a specially thick adhesive which is pasted onto the wall. Follow manufacturers' instructions.

Ready-pasted papers are exactly that and require no extra adhesive – although it's useful to have a tube of latex glue handy for finishing off corners and joints which mightn't

have stuck. (The same applies to all washable wallpapers).

Glue *size* (a watered down adhesive) is brushed over the walls before papering to seal them and prevent the paste from soaking in to the wall. It also ensures all-over adhesion and makes sliding the paper into place easier.

Although size can be bought, most wallpaper pastes will make size when mixed with the amount of water stated in the instructions.

If you buy a proprietary size and the wallcovering you are using needs an adhesive containing fungicide, make sure that the size you buy also contains a

fungicide. Use an old brush to apply and a damp cloth to clean off any that runs on to paintwork. It can be difficult to remove after it has dried. Sizing can be done several days or an hour before.

Where to begin

The traditional rule is to start next to the window and work away from it, but that is really a hangover from the days when paper was overlapped and shadows showed up joins. Today, papers butt up, so light isn't the problem. But as inaccuracies can occur with slight loss of pattern, you have to be able to make this as inconspicuous as possible. In an average room, the corner nearest the door is the best starting point. Any loss of pattern will then end up behind you as you enter the room. In a room with a chimney breast, hang the first drop in the centre and work outwards from both sides of the drop.

Problem areas in a house (recesses, arches, stairwells) are dealt with later in this chapter.

Measuring and cutting

Measure the height of the wall you want to paper using a steel tape measure and cut a piece of paper from the roll to this length, allowing an extra 50mm (2in) top and bottom for trimming. This allowance is needed for pattern matching, and to ensure a neat finish at skirting board and ceiling.

Lay the first drop — that's the name given to each length of paper — pattern side up on the table and unroll the paper from which the

second drop is to be cut next to it. Move this along until the patterns match, then cut the second drop using the other end of the first as a guide. Subsequent lengths of paper are cut in exactly the same way, with each matching the drop that preceded it.

Remember some wallpapers have patterns that are a straight match across the width, while others have what is called a drop pattern that rises as it extends across the width. With drop match papers the second length will begin half a pattern repeat further along the roll. Length 3 will match length 1, length 4 will match length 2 and so on.

For things to run smoothly, you should establish a work routine when paper hanging. Cut all the wall drops first (so you only have to measure once) and cut bits for papering above windows and doors as you come to them. If you paste say 3 drops, the first will have had its required soaking time

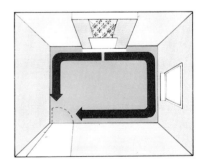
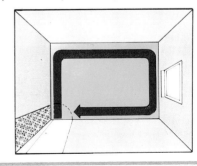
HOW TO CUT AND PASTE

1 Mark the pasting table with lines at 150mm (6in) and 300mm (1ft) intervals. Measure wall drop and use guidelines to cut your first length.

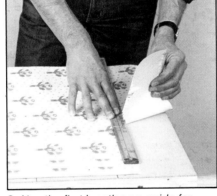

2 Use the first length as a guide for the other drops, matching the pattern carefully. Tear off the waste against a wooden rule.

3 Lay all the drops pattern down, overhanging the far edge of the table. Pull the first drop to the near edge and paste it from centre to edges.

4 Fold pasted end, paste the rest and fold in. Now fold up the whole drop and leave it to soak. The top of the longer fold always goes to the top of the wall.

PAPER HANGING TECHNIQUES

1 Place chosen pattern on ceiling line with waste above. Align side edge with vertical and turn waste onto adjacent wall. Brush up to ceiling first, then corners and edges, and then down. Open out short fold last.

2 Mark cutting line for waste at ceiling and skirting board with a pencil — ends of scissors won't fit creases neatly and can give a thick line which causes you to cut the paper inaccurately and will give an uneven look at ceiling and skirting.

3 To cut waste, pull short length of paper away from wall so pencil line catches the light. Cut using full length of blades — hurried, short cuts can make the edges jagged. Brush paper back on wall so that it is perfectly flat.

4 Reduce waste on adjacent wall to 6mm (¼in) to lessen bulk when paper overlaps from other direction.

5 Continue along wall matching the pattern horizontally. Press drop onto wall so long edges butt.

6 As each drop is hung, brush up first, then to edges and finally down to remove any trapped air.

7 To turn a corner, measure between hung paper and corner at the top, middle and bottom of wall. Add 6mm (¼in) to widest width, then use this measurement to cut the pasted and folded drop into two. Set aside offcut for new wall.

8 Hang drop to complete wall, brushing the waste round the corner. Find the new vertical and mark the line the width of offcut from the corner. Check this measurement at the top, middle and bottom of wall. If the same, hang offcut.

9 If corner is out of true, offcut and wall measurements will differ. To disguise pattern loss, hang the offcut so waste laps onto completed wall. Brush into corner, run pencil down crease line and cut waste.

(with medium weight paper) by the time the third is pasted and folded and is ready to be hung. With heavy papers paste, fold and soak 6 drops at a time as extra soaking time is needed.

Avoiding bubbles

The purpose behind soaking time (apart from making paper supple enough to handle) is to give it time to expand to its natural limit. On the width this can be 6mm-12mm (¼in-½in) and the average wall-size drop will gain 24mm (1in) on the length – this explains why you have more to cut as waste than you started with.

If you haven't given paper the time it needs, it will expand on the walls – but its spread will be contained by adjoining drops and so you get bubbles in the central part.

Soak medium weight papers for 3-4 minutes, heavy weights for about 10. Ready-pasted papers don't need too long a soaking, but to ensure they get wet all over, roll drops loosely and press into water till they are completely covered.

Pasting and soaking

Position the paper with its top edge at the right-hand end of the table (or at the other end if you're left handed). Paste it carefully to ensure that all parts, the edges especially, are well covered. Work from the centre outwards in herring-bone style using the width of the brush to cover the drop in sweeps, first to the nearest edge, then the other – excess paste here will go onto second drop, not the table. Cover two-thirds of the drop, then fold the top edge in so paste is to paste. Move the drop along the table and paste the remainder, folding bottom edge in paste to paste. Because the first folded part is longer than the other, this will remind you which is the

top. Fold the drop up and put aside to soak while you paste the others.

This technique will give you a manageable parcel of paper to hang no matter what length the drop – but always remember to make the first fold longer – this is the one offered to the ceiling line. If in doubt mark the top edge lightly with a pencil cross.

Hanging pasted paper

Wallpaper must be hung absolutely vertical if it is to look right, so always work to a vertical line (see Ready Reference).

Position your step ladder as close as possible to where you want to work, and climb it with the first length of paper under or over your arm. Open out the long fold and offer the top edge up, placing the pattern as you want it at the ceiling with waste above. Align the side edge of the drop with your vertical guide line, allowing the other side edge to turn onto the adjacent wall if starting at a corner. Smooth the paper onto the wall with the paperhanging brush, using the bristle ends to form a crease between wall and ceiling, and at corners. When brushing paper into place, always work up first then to the join, then to the side edge, then down. This will remove trapped air.

As soon as the paper is holding in place, work down the wall, brushing the rest of the drop in position, opening out the bottom fold when you reach it. Again use the bristle ends to form a good crease where paper meets the skirting board.

The next step is to trim off the waste paper at the top and bottom. Run a lead pencil along the crease between the ceiling or skirting and the wall — the blades or points of scissors wil make a line that's too thick for accurate cutting. Gently peel paper away from the wall and cut carefully along the line with your scissors. Finally brush the paper back in place.

Hanging the second drop is done as the

Estimator

Most wallpaper is sold in rolls 10.05m (11yds) long and 530mm (21in) wide. Calculate rolls needed by measuring perimeter of the room and height from skirting board to ceiling.

WALLS	Distance around the room (doors and windows included)										
Height from skirting	10m 33'	11m 36'	12m 39'	13m 43'	14m 46'	15m 49'	16m 52'	17m 56'	18m 59'	19m 62'	20m 66'
2.15–2.30m (7'–7'6")	5	5	5	6	6	7	7	8	8	9	9
2.30–2.45m (7'6"–8')	5	5	6	6	7	7	8	8	9	9	10
2.45–2.60m (8'–8'6")	5	6	6	7	7	8	9	9	10	10	11

The number of rolls needed can be greatly affected by the frequency of pattern repeat. With a large pattern repeat, buy an extra roll.

first except that you have to butt it up against the edge of the first length, matching the pattern across the two. The secret here is not to try and do it all in one go. Get the paper onto the wall at the right place at the ceiling join but just a little way away from the first length. Now press against the paper with the palms of your hands and slide it into place. Using well-soaked paper on a wall that's been sized makes this easy, but if you're using a thin wallpaper press gently as it could tear. Butt the paper up after pattern matching and brush into place.

When trimming waste from drops other than the first, cut from where the lengths butt to ensure even ceiling and skirting lines.

Hanging ready-pasted wallpaper

With these you won't need pasting table, bucket and pasting brush but you will need a special light plastic trough made for the purpose. Put it below where the first drop is to be hung and fill with water – covering the floor with layers of newspaper will soak up accidental spillages. Don't try to lift the trough; slide it along the floor as the work progresses.

Cut each drop so patterns are matching, then roll the first one loosely from the bottom up with the pattern inside. Place it in the trough and press it down so water can reach all the parts covered with paste. Leave for the required soaking time (check manufacturers' instructions but, it's usually between 30 seconds and 2 minutes), then pick the drop up by the two top corners and take it to the ceiling line. Press onto the wall using an absorbent sponge to mop up and push out air bubbles. Press firmly on the edges with the sponge or a seam roller, then trim waste.

COPING WITH WALL FITTINGS ... AND CREASES

Few walls present a perfectly clear surface for paperhanging. Almost all will contain such small obstacles as light switches and power points, while some may carry wall-mounted fittings such as curtain tracks and adjustable shelving. Small obstacles can be papered round with some careful trimming, but larger obstacles are best taken down from the wall and replaced when you have finished decorating. That way you will get a really professional finish.

Creases can also spoil the look of your work. If they occur, take steps to remove them before the paste dries. Here's how.

1 Use matchsticks, pushed head out into wall plugs, to show where wall fittings have been taken down.

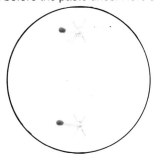

2 Brush paper firmly over match heads so they pierce it. With hanging complete remove matches and replace fittings.

1 To cut round light switches, mark centre of plate, insert scissor tips and cut out towards plate corners.

2 Crease tongues of paper against edges of plate, lift away from wall, trim along line and brush back into place.

3 With washable and vinyl papers push a strip of rigid plastic against plate edges and trim with a sharp knife.

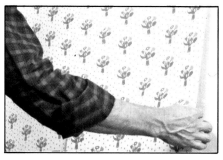

1 Creases are a common fault where the wall is out of true or if you haven't brushed the paper out properly.

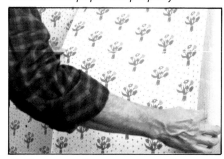

2 To remove the crease, peel the paper from the wall to a point above the crease – to the ceiling if necessary.

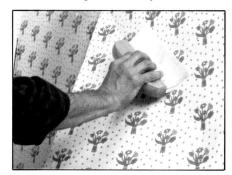

3 Brush the paper back into position – across towards the butt join, then to the other edge and down to the bottom.

PAPERING A STAIRWELL

Even if the walls are flat, papering a stairwell presents problems. The awkward angles, height of the walls and long lengths of wallcovering make for special difficulties of access and handling, but you'll find that these can be overcome.

Hanging wallpaper in an ordinary room is not too difficult. But with stairwells there are awkward corners and long lengths to cope with.

Gaining access

The chief problem in wallpapering a stairwell is that of gaining access to the walls you are papering. This is because of the height of the walls and the awkward angles involved.

It is essential to have a safe working platform and to set this up in the right way to suit the layout of the stairwell and the way the stairs rise. You can hire special platforms for decorating the stair/hall area, or use the components of a tower platform. Alternatively, you can use ladders and steps linked with scaffold boards (see page 41).

A particularly useful item of equipment is a hop-up, a small platform which you can make yourself (see *Ready Reference*).

Preparation

Before you start decorating, remove the handrail and any other wall-mounted obstacles so you can get at the wall. Then prepare the walls properly so the new wallcovering will stick. Always remove any old wallcovering; some will peel off, although with most types you will have to soak and scrape them off.

Once the walls are stripped, you can work out where to begin hanging. You should position the longest drop of wallcovering first, and to establish where this will be, measure the height of each wall in the stairwell. (You will need a long tape and someone to help you when you are measuring the wall in a stairwell.) Then, starting as close as possible to this point but about 50mm away from any obstacles – such as a door or window opening – take a roll of the wallcovering you are going to use and move it along the wall to estimate where succeeding widths will fall. If, according to your calculations, there will be a join between lengths within 50mm of an external corner (at another window opening, for example), change your starting point slightly and measure again so you avoid this. Then mark off where this first drop will be hung.

When you have established where you will hang the first drop, use a plumbline to work out a true vertical at this point. Coat the line with chalk, pin it to the top of the wall and allow it to hang. Then, at the skirting, hold the plumb bob with one hand, pluck the string with the other and let it snap back against the wall to leave a vertical chalk line on the wall. Alternatively, instead of coating the plumb line with chalk, fix it in place, allowing it to hang down, and then place a long straight timber batten so the edge is exactly against the line, and use the batten as your guide to draw a true vertical line down the wall. Remember to plumb a new line every time you turn a corner.

Hanging the wallcovering

The decorating sequence is the same as for any other area – see the techniques already covered. If the wall is bare plaster, start by applying size to the wall to prevent the paste soaking in. Then measure and cut the wallcovering to length, remembering to allow for the angle of the skirting board if applicable, paste it and allow it to soak. If you are using a ready-pasted wallcovering, place your water trough in the hall or on the landing, not on the stairs where you are likely to knock it over. Wallcoverings hung by the

Ready Reference

SAFETY FIRST IN STAIRWELLS

Falls from ladders and steps cause many deaths and injuries in the home. To prevent the risk of an accident
● make sure ladders and steps can't slip by resting their feet against a batten screwed or nailed to the floor or tread on which they are standing
● always secure boards to whatever they are resting on – with rope, or bolts dropped through pre-drilled holes
● never trust a handrail to support your weight or that of a board.

MAKE A HOP-UP

As part of your access equipment, make a hop-up from 150mm x 25mm (6in x 1in) timber nailed or screwed together. It should be about 460mm (18in) high and 760mm (30in) wide.

PREPARATION

1 To prepare the wall surface you will have to remove the existing wallcovering. In this case it is vinyl which is easy to remove; it is simply peeled off.

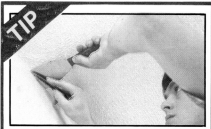

2 Before you remove lining paper it's worth cutting along the paper at ceiling level or you may find you tear off the ceiling paper with the lining paper.

3 When working at a high level make sure that the ladders and scaffold boards you are working from are firmly secured and well supported to ensure safety.

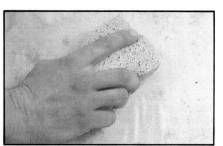

4 To remove paper from the wall when preparing to hang a new wallcovering, soak it thoroughly with a damp sponge. Leave for a while, then soak again.

5 Use a scraper to take the paper off the wall and scrape off old flaking paint at the same time. Wash the wall down to remove any remaining bits.

6 When you have established where you will hang the first length, use a plumbline to make sure you get a true vertical and mark a pencil line on the wall.

HANGING THE WALLCOVERING

1 Place the first drop up against the wall, using the line you have drawn as a guideline to get it straight. Get someone to help you hold the long drop.

2 Use a soft-bristled wallpaper-hanging brush to smooth the covering into place. Leave an overlap at the top and bottom for trimming when the drop is fixed.

3 Hang subsequent lengths of wallcovering so they butt join and so the pattern matches. Trim each piece; a scraper will help as a guide.

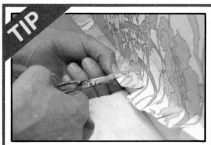

4 Where there is a curve cut into the overlap so the paper will fit round the curve easily without puckering.

5 You can then trim off the overlap in the same way as at a door surround, using a scraper to help guide the knife as you trim along the bottom edge.

6 For convenient paper hanging you will have to remove a wall handrail. This can be replaced when the wallcovering is fixed and the adhesive completely dry.

SAFE WORKING PLATFORMS

1 stairs with quarter landing

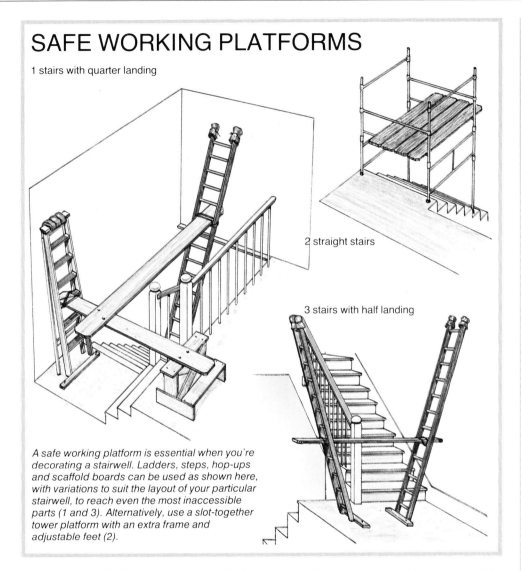

2 straight stairs

3 stairs with half landing

A safe working platform is essential when you're decorating a stairwell. Ladders, steps, hop-ups and scaffold boards can be used as shown here, with variations to suit the layout of your particular stairwell, to reach even the most inaccessible parts (1 and 3). Alternatively, use a slot-together tower platform with an extra frame and adjustable feet (2).

Ready Reference

CARRYING LONG LENGTHS

To make it easier to carry a long length of wallcovering, fold it in concertinas and then drape it over your arm.

BEWARE ANGLED SKIRTING

When measuring up remember that lengths meeting the stairs skirting must be measured along their longer edge, not their shorter one.

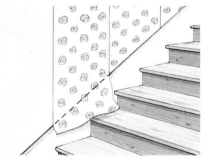

EQUAL SOAKING TIME

To minimise the risk of stretching
● allow the same amount of soaking time between pasting and hanging on each length
● if you do find the paper has stretched, match the pattern as best you can at eye level, where bad matching would be most noticeable.

YOU'LL NEED HELP

It's best not to try hanging long lengths of paper by yourself; the weight of the paper may cause it to stretch or tear. Get someone to take the weight and unfold the paper as you work down the wall.

TIP: TRIM NARROW PIECES DRY

Where long narrow strips are needed, measure up and trim the drop approximately to size before pasting. This is easier to handle than having large waste pieces covered in paste flapping around.

OVERLAPS WITH VINYL

Vinyl will not stick to vinyl where you are using ordinary paste. If an overlap is unavoidable use a special vinyl overlap adhesive.

paste-the-wall technique are particularly easy to hang in stairwells, because you are handling lengths of dry wallcovering.

Because the lengths of paper for the wall at the side of the stairs will all be of a different size – caused by the rise of the stairs – it is better to cut and paste one length at a time, unlike straightforward rooms where you can cut and paste several lengths at a time.

Hang the first and longest length of wallpaper, using the vertical line you have marked on the wall as a guideline to get it straight. Then work round the stairwell from this length, making sure the pattern matches as you go along.

If your staircase is curved at the bottom the wallcovering is likely to pucker as it fits around the curve. To prevent this, you can snip into the overlap at the foot of the wall at intervals so the paper is more flexible in its fit.

Coping with long drops

A problem unique to stairwells is the length of paper you are handling – often as much as 4.5m (15ft) long. Apply paste liberally so it is less likely to dry out before you have fixed the bottom of the length. (It's worth keeping a small amount of adhesive ready to apply where the adhesive has dried out before the wallcovering is fixed.) Fold the pasted paper in concertinas (see *Ready Reference*) and then gather up the folds and drape the folded-up length over your arm to carry it.

Because the weight of the paper may cause it to stretch or tear as you are hanging it, try to get someone to help you take the weight. Where there is no one available to help, you will have to sit on your scaffold board, or other form of support, and allow the bottom of the drop to unfold gently to skirting board level. Then you can take the top up to the ceiling and start brushing it into the correct place.

Remember too, that when you are trimming along the bottom of a length of wallcovering that meets the staircase skirting, you will be trimming at an angle rather than horizontally as at the foot of a wall in a room.

PAPERING AWKWARD AREAS

The techniques for papering round tricky areas like corners and reveals are quite basic. But care and patience is required if you are going to get really professional results from your paperhanging.

Although the major part of wallpapering, hanging straight lengths is fairly quick and straightforward. The tricky areas – corners, doorways and so on – which call for careful measuring, cutting and pattern matching are the bits that slow the job down. There's no worse eye-sore than a lop-sided pattern at a corner; but if you use the right techniques you can avoid this problem.

You have to accept in advance that the continuity of a pattern will be lost in corners and similar places; even a professional decorator can't avoid this. However, he has the ability to match the pattern as closely as possible so that the discontinuity is not noticeable, and this is what you have to emulate.

Things would, of course, be a lot simpler if all corners were perfectly square, but this is rarely the case. When you wallpaper a room for the first time you are likely to discover that all those angles that appeared to be true are anything but.

You can, however, help to overcome the problem of careful pattern matching at corners by choosing a paper with the right design (see *Ready Reference*). The most difficult of the lot to hang are those with a regular small and simple repeat motif. The loss of pattern continuity will be easy to spot if even slight errors are made. The same is often true of large, repeat designs. With either of these types, a lot more time will be involved and it could well take a couple of hours to hang a few strips around a single window reveal.

Sloping ceiling lines are another problem area and certain patterns will show it up clearly. You can understand the nuisance of a sloping ceiling by imagining a pattern with, say, regular rows of horizontal roses. Although the first length on the wall may be hung correctly to leave a neat row of roses along the ceiling line the trouble is that as subsequent lengths are hung and the pattern is matched, you will see less and less of that top row of roses as the ceiling slopes down. And, conversely, if the ceiling line slopes upwards, you will start to see a new row of roses appearing above. So, despite the fact that each length has been hung

vertically, the sloping ceiling will make the job look thoroughly unsightly.

Internal and external corners
Before you begin papering round a corner, you must hang the last full length before the corner. Your corner measurement will be done from one edge of this length. You can use a steel tape or boxwood rule to measure the gap to the corner (see *Ready Reference*) and then cut the piece required to fill it, plus a margin which is carried round onto the new wall. Since it's likely that the walls will be out of square and that the margin taken round the corner will not be exactly equal all the way down, it's obvious you would have a terrible job hanging the matching offcut strip to give a neat butt join.

For this reason you must hang the matching offcut which goes on the 'new' wall to a true vertical and then brush it over the margin you've turned onto this wall. You should aim to match the pattern at the corner as closely as possible. Since the paper overlaps, the match will not be perfect, but this is unavoidable and will not, in any case be noticeable as the overlap is tucked into or round the corner out of sight (see *Ready Reference*).

Papering round window reveals
Unless you intend to paper just one or two walls in a room you will eventually have to cope with papering round a window. Pattern matching is the problem here, but you should find cutting the paper to fit above and

below a window is not too difficult provided you work in a logical order (see box opposite). But you may have to be prepared for lots of scissor work when you cut out strips of paper for the two sides and top of the reveal to ensure the pattern matches the paper on the facing wall. (It's worth getting into the habit of marking some sort of code on the back of each piece of paper before it's cut up so you will be able to find matching pieces quickly.)

Make sure that you don't end up with a seam on the edge of the reveal, where it will be exposed to knocks and liable to lift. Before you begin work on the window wall, take a roll of wallcovering and estimate how many widths will fit between the window and the nearest corner. If it looks as though you will be left with a join within about 25mm (1in) of the window opening you should alter your starting point slightly so that, when you come to the window, the seam will have moved away from the edge of the reveal.

Where the lengths of paper are positioned on the window wall obviously depends on the position of the window, its size and the width of the wallpaper. But the ideal situation occurs when the last full length before you reach the window leaves a width of wall, plus window reveal, that measures just less than the width of the wallpaper. You can then hang the next length so its upper part goes on the wall above the window, the lower part on the wall below it and (after making two scissor cuts) turn the middle part to cover the side of the window reveal. The edge of

PAPERING ROUND A WINDOW

Top: Fill the narrow gap left on the underside of the reveal with a small offcut.
Above: The papering sequence; piece 7 fills the gap left on the reveal by piece 6.

the middle part can then be creased and trimmed so it fits neatly up against the window frame.

Go on to hang short lengths of wallpaper above the window, cutting them so their lower parts can be taken on to the underside of the top window reveal, and again trim them so they fit neatly up against the window frame. When you reach a point where the reveal on the opposite side of the window is less than the width of the wallpaper away from the last edge hung, you should stop and repeat the papering process below the window between the sill and skirting board, trimming as you go.

You can then hang the next full length in the same way as the one you hung on the first side of the window. You should, first, however, hang a plumbline over the pieces in place above the top and bottom of the window then hang the full length to the plumbline, trimming any slight overlap on the new length if necessary. (By doing this, you will ensure that the lengths to be hung on the rest of the wall will be truly vertical.)

Often, however, the position of the last full length at the window will fall so that the paper does not cover the reveal at the side of the window, and in this case you will have to cut matching strips to fill the gap. Similarly, you

will have to cut strips to fill the gaps on the underside of the reveal at the top of the window.

Dormer windows

In attics and loft rooms there will be sloping ceilings and dormer windows with which you will have to contend. If you decide to paper rather than paint the sloping ceiling, then you treat it in the same way as you would a vertical wall; there are no unusual problems involved, other than the peculiar working angle. Remember, too, that if you choose the wrong type of paper the irregular pattern-matching could give unfortunate results.

Paper the wall alongside the window and then round the window itself, moving on to the wall below the other side of the sloping ceiling (see step-by-step photographs). Finally, you can paper the dormer cheeks.

Chimney breasts and fireplace surrounds

Special rules apply to chimney breasts. For a start, since they are a focal point in the room, any pattern must be centralised. The design of the paper will affect where you begin to hang the wallpaper. Where one length of paper contains a complete motif, you can simply measure and mark off the central point of the chimney breast and use a

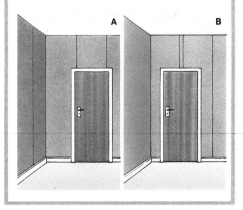

PAPERING AN INTERNAL CORNER

1 *Hang the last full length before the corner. Then measure the gap (see Ready Reference) to determine the width to be cut from the next length.*

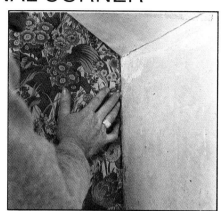

2 *Cut from the next length a piece which will overlap 12mm (¹/₂in) round the corner. Then paste and fix it in position so it fills the corner gap.*

3 *Measure the width of the matching offcut strip of paper and use a plumbline to mark a guideline on the wall this distance from the corner.*

4 *Hang the offcut so its cut edge overlaps the matching edge of the first corner piece and its 'good' edge aligns with the vertical guideline.*

FLUSH WINDOWS

1 *Fix the last full length of paper before the window and pull the excess across. Cut round the sill and fix the paper beneath it.*

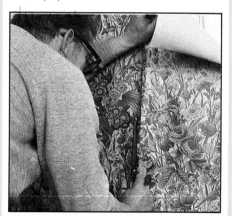

2 *You can then trim off the excess paper which runs alongside the window. Now press and brush the pasted paper into position.*

3 *Work along the wall underneath the window, fixing, creasing and trimming as you go. Afterwards you can fix the paper on the other side of the window.*

plumbline at this point to help you draw a vertical line down the centre. You can then begin hanging the wallpaper by aligning the first length with this line.

On the other hand, if it is the type of paper where two lengths, when aligned, form a motif, you will first have to estimate the number of widths which will fit across the chimney breast and then draw a line as a guide for hanging the first length of paper so the combined motif will, in fact, be centralised.

Your order of work should be from the centre (or near centre) outwards and you will then have to turn the paper round the corners at the sides so you form an overlap join with the paper which will be applied to the sides of the chimney breast. Follow the usual techniques for measuring and papering round external corners, remembering in particular not too take too much paper round the corner.

When it comes to fireplace surrounds, there are so many varying kinds of mantelshelfs and surrounds that only general guidance can be given. Usually the technique is to brush the paper down on to the top part of the wall and then cut it to fit along the back edge of the mantelshelf. You can then cut the lower half to fit the contours of the surround. If it's a complicated outline then you'll have to gradually work downwards, using a small pair of sharp scissors, pressing the paper into each shape, withdrawing it to snip along the crease line, then brushing it back into place.

If there is only a small distance between the edge of the mantelshelf and the corner, it's a lot easier if you hang the paper down to the shelf and then make a neat, horizontal cut line in the paper. You can then hang the lower half separately and join the two halves to disguise the cut line.

PAPERING ROUND A DORMER

1 Where the dormer cheek meets the junction of the wall and ceiling, draw a line at right angles to the wall on the ceiling by the dormer cheek.

2 Draw a vertical line at right angles to the first line on the dormer cheek. You can then fix the first length of paper in place on the dormer cheek.

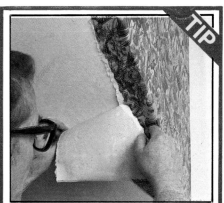

3 Work along towards the window, trimming as you go. Gently tear along the overlap to feather its edge so you won't get a bulky join later.

4 At the window, crease along the side of the frame by running the edge of the scissors along it. You can then carefully trim along the creased line.

5 Return to the small gap which needs to be filled at the narrow end of the dormer cheek; fix this piece in position, crease and trim.

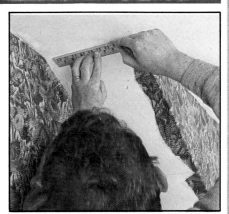

6 Mark a straight line on the sloping ceiling to serve as a guideline for fixing the first length of paper on the underside of the dormer cheek.

7 Cut a piece of paper so it reaches from the point you have marked up to the window and brush it into position ensuring that it covers the feathered edges of the overlap.

8 At the junction of the wall and ceiling you will have to cut round awkward angles. You can then go ahead and brush the paper into its final position.

9 Finally, you can brush the strip of paper which fills the gap between the wall and the underside of the dormer cheek into position to finish off the dormer area neatly.

PAPERING CEILINGS

One way to cover up a ceiling with cracks or other imperfections is to use lining paper or a textured wallcovering and then paint over it. But a good alternative is to make a special feature of the ceiling by using decorative paper.

Papering ceilings can be a rather daunting prospect, even to the experienced home decorator. In fact, once you have mastered the basic technique of paperhanging, ceilings are quite straightforward and you are likely to be presented with far fewer problems than on walls. There will be no windows, few (if any) corners and not so many obstacles with which you have to deal.

If you intend to paint the ceiling it's usually best to hang a lining paper or a textured paper like woodchip first to hide the inevitable blemishes of a plaster ceiling. Or you might decide to choose a fine decorative paper and make a feature of the ceiling with it. Most of the papers that are suitable for walls can also be used for ceilings.

But before you opt for papering, it makes sense to consider the alternative: if the sole objective is to get a textured surface which will cover up cracks and bumps, you can do it just as well with a textured paint. Using a woodchip paper would only make sense if you were skilled at papering and wanted to save money; in any case, you'll still have to paint it. However, if you want a smooth ceiling or a decorative surface of distinction then papering is for you.

The equipment you'll need
You will need the same equipment as for papering walls, with the addition of a safe working platform that spans the width of the room (see *Ready Reference*). You should check with your supplier that the paper of your choice is suitable for ceilings (some heavier types may not be) and ask him to provide a suitably strong adhesive, including fungicide if it is a washable vinyl paper. Such papers are extremely suitable for high humidity environments like bathrooms and kitchens.

Preparing the surface
The surface to which you fix the paper must be clean and sound. This means washing down existing paintwork with detergent or sugar soap and then sanding it with a fine abrasive paper or pad to provide a key for the adhesive. Distempered ceilings, often found in old houses, must be scrubbed to remove the distemper, or the paper will not stick.

If the ceiling has been papered before, you should remove the old paper completely. If you try to hang another paper over it there will be blobs and bubbles where the dampness of the new paper separates the old paper from the plaster. Any surface which is at all porous, such as bare plaster, will tend to absorb moisture from the pasted paper at too fast a rate for a successful adhesion. Such surfaces should be sized by brushing them over with a proprietary size, or a diluted version of the actual paste you're going to use. Let the size dry before proceeding.

New plasterboard, often used in modern construction, needs painting with a primer/ sealer before decoration. It is also wise to fix a layer of lining paper before your main decorative paper if you are hanging heavyweight or fabric wallcoverings.

Decorating perfectionists always recommend using lining paper anyway, whatever the surface. There is no doubt it does improve the final appearance, particularly on older surfaces or with thinner papers. Lining paper comes in different thicknesses or 'weights' and you should consult your supplier about a suitable grade.

One last preparation tip: don't leave cracks and dents in ceilings for the paper to cover. Fill them and sand them smooth, particularly at joins between plasterboards, and at the wall/ceiling angle. Think of your paper as a surface that needs a good smooth base, and not as a cover-up for a hideous old mess.

Planning the job
Consult the estimator panel (see *Ready Reference*) to gauge the approximate number of rolls you will need; also think about the pattern of your intended paper. Can you cope with a complex drop pattern on a ceiling, or would you be better off with a straight match? A bold paper that looks fine on walls might be a bit overpowering above your head. Is your ceiling good enough for a plainish paper, or do you need texture to draw the eye away from the ravages of time that appear in all old lath-and-plaster ceilings?

Modern papers are designed for the strips to be butted against each other, not overlapped. This means the traditional pattern of working away from, but parallel to, the main source of natural light is not essential. You will generally find it easier working across the narrowest dimension of the room. Wellapplied paper will tend not to show the joins too much anyway, particularly if the pattern draws the eye.

All ceiling papering starts from a line which is strung or marked across the ceiling 10mm (⅜in) less than the width of the paper away from the wall. The 10mm (⅜in) on the length of paper which runs next to the wall allows for the walls being out of square and its overlap is trimmed off at the wall and ceiling junction. You can chalk a line and snap it against the ceiling between two tacks to make a mark, or just pin it temporarily in place and butt the first strip of paper against it.

MARKING UP AND PASTING

1 *Measure in from the width of the paper minus 10mm (³/₈in), to allow for an overlap at the wall, and mark this distance on the ceiling.*

2 *Make another mark at the opposite end, the same distance from the wall. Use a chalked line to link the marks, then snap the line onto the ceiling.*

3 *Cut or tear the lengths of paper. You should allow 100mm (4in) excess on each piece to give an overlap of 50mm (2in) for trimming at each end.*

4 *Apply paste to the back of the paper and fold it into concertina folds as you go. Paste enough lengths to allow adequate soaking time.*

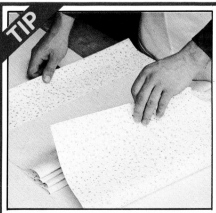

5 *Take the last fold in the length to meet the first, short, fold so the edges meet without paste getting on the front of the paper.*

6 *Slip a spare roll of paper under the folded-up length; this will serve as a support for the paper so you can carry and hold it easily.*

Ready Reference

ESTIMATOR

Distance around room	Number of rolls 10.05m x 530mm (33ft x 21in)
10-12m (33-39ft)	2
12-14m (39-46ft)	3
14-18m (46-59ft)	4
18-20m (59-66ft)	5
20-22m (66-72ft)	6

TIP: WHISK YOUR PASTE

To speed up the process of mixing paste, use a kitchen whisk to beat up the mix.

A SAFE WORKING PLATFORM

Set up two stepladders and a solid plank, at a height where you can comfortably touch the ceiling with the palm of your hand.

TIP: HAVE TOOLS TO HAND

Have the necessary tools with you (in the pocket of an apron or overall) when you're on the working platform to save you scrambling up and down more than you need.

PREVENT WASTAGE

If you are pattern matching, paper in the direction which will save long bits of waste paper left over after cutting the lengths.

LINING PAPER

If you are hanging lining paper, remember that it should be hung at right angles to the paper which goes over it.

PAPERING TECHNIQUE

With the concertina-folded paper supported by the spare roll held in your left hand (if you are right-handed; vice versa if you are left-handed) pull one fold out taut and then brush it into place, working outwards from the centre to avoid trapped air bubbles. Repeat with the other folds.

TIP: TRIM ROSES NEATLY

Don't be tempted to remove the cover of a ceiling rose to trim the paper round it; inaccurate cutting may mean there are gaps when the cover is replaced.
Instead:
● trim round the fitting with the cover in place leaving a slight overlap (see step-by-step photographs)
● remove the cover and press the overlap into place.

FINAL TRIMMING

When the last piece of paper has been hung you may need to spend some time on final trimming if the walls and ceiling do not meet squarely and evenly.

HANGING STRAIGHT LENGTHS

1 *Hang the first length on the 'room' side of the chalk line, not next to the wall. Brush the paper into place gently but firmly.*

2 *Brush the ends carefully into the angles where walls and ceiling meet, and trim. Then hang the next length alongside the wall.*

3 *The lengths should be butt-jointed. Use a seam roller to ensure well-stuck edges by running it gently over the length of the seam.*

4 *Trim off the overlap at the ends and side (if necessary) of each length of paper. Use a scraper as a guide for the knife for accurate cutting.*

5 *Wipe off any excess adhesive where the overlap has been before it dries, or it will leave ugly marks on the wall surface.*

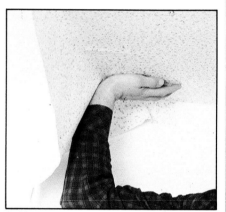

6 *You can now go ahead and hang the next length on the other side of the first piece hung. Continue until you have covered the entire ceiling.*

It makes sense to get all the lengths measured and cut out in advance, and pasted up in batches of twos or threes (depending on your speed of working) to give adequate soaking time for the type of paper you are hanging; check the manufacturer's instructions on this point. Cut all the strips, including those which will be trimmed for chimney breasts, to full room dimensions plus 100mm (4in) excess for trimming.

The concertina fold
The secret of successful ceiling papering is the correct folding technique, as you paste, so that the paper can be transferred to and laid out against the ceiling surface in a smooth manner. Each fold of the concertina should be 300mm (1ft) wide approximately, apart from the first, which can be shorter (see step-by-step photographs). It's worth practising folding with dry paper first.

Hanging the paper
Assemble the working platform securely at the correct height across the whole length of the room, beneath the area where the first strip is to be pasted. Before you get up there with a fold of wet, pasted paper, make sure you have the tools you will need to hand.

The last-to-be-pasted section of each length is first to go on the ceiling; tease off this first section and brush it into place. Continue to unfold the concertina in sections, brushing it down as you go and checking it is straight against the guideline.

Trimming and seam rolling
When you trim, you should make sure the paper butts exactly up to covings, but allow a 5-10mm (¼-⅜in) overlap down to the surface of the walls you intend to paper later. Except with embossed papers, you should roll the butt joints between strips with a seam roller.

Light fittings or shades should always be removed, leaving just the flex hanging down. Turn the power off, to ensure safety.

If a chimney breast falls parallel to the run of the paper, you will need your scissors handy to take out an approximate piece as you work along the platform. It's worth anticipating this before you get up there; mark a rough line on the paper at the approximate position of the chimney breast. Cut out the chimney breast piece, leaving an excess of about 15mm (⅝in) for detailed trimming when the whole strip is in place.

If the strip ends at a chimney breast there are less problems. Remove any vast unwanted sections as you work and trim to fit later. External corners are dealt with by making a V-cut so that one flap of the paper can be folded down the inside alcove edge of the chimney breast (or trimmed there if you are working to a coving).

PAPERING ROUND OBSTACLES

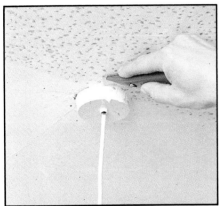

1 If there is a ceiling rose, use a knife or scissors to make a little slit in the paper so it fits round the rose; don't cut too deep.

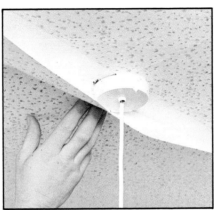

2 Hang the next length so it butts up against the previous one; at the rose take the paper over the top of the obstacle.

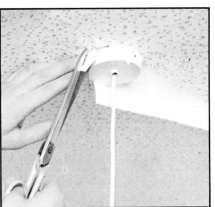

3 Again, make slits in the paper so it fits round the rose; this will allow you to brush the rest of the length of paper in place.

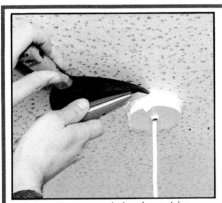

4 When the paper is in place, trim round the rose. Place the edge of a scraper between the knife and ceiling so there's a slight overlap.

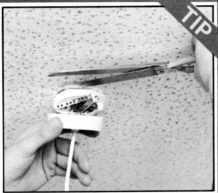

TIP

5 Turn off the power, remove the rose cover and press the overlap into place. When the cover is replaced it will conceal the cut edges completely.

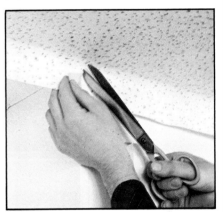

6 Where the paper meets an alcove, make a slit in the paper in line with one corner of the alcove and then in line with the other.

7 You can then brush the paper into place in the normal fashion so it fits neatly into the gap between the two corners. Trim the overlap along the wall leading to the alcove.

8 Fix the next length so it butts up against the previous one. Adhesive may ooze out when seams are rolled; so long as the paper is colourfast you can remove it with a damp sponge.

9 Measure up and cut the last narrow piece, allowing for an overlap of about 25mm (1in) at the wall and ceiling junction. Paste and brush it into place; trim to complete the job.

HANGING RELIEF WALLPAPER

If you want a change from the flat surface which ordinary wallpaper gives, you can hang a relief wallcovering with a raised, embossed pattern for a different look on walls or ceilings.

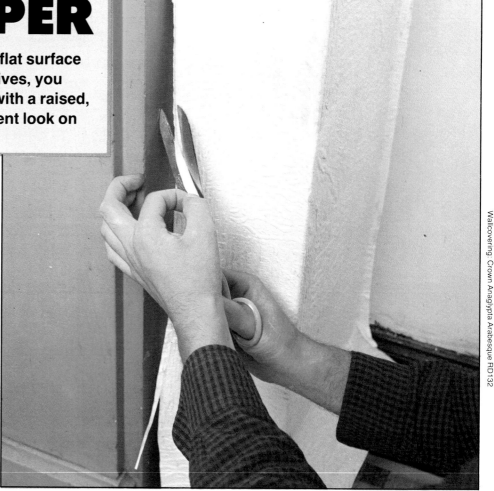

Wallcovering: Crown Anaglypta Arabesque RD132

One way of covering up a poor wall or ceiling surface is to use a relief or embossed wallcovering. It must be stressed at the outset that the wall or ceiling should be in sound structural condition, but these types of wallcoverings will provide an ideal disguise for minor defects such as hairline cracks, a rough finish or slight unevenness in the surface. Even where the surface is perfect, you may simply decide that you like the look which a raised pattern can give.

Frequently, embossed or relief wallcoverings are referred to as 'whites' because they come only with a white finish. Most of them require overpainting (you can, of course, paint them white, if you wish) so the paper is protected against dirt, moisture and reasonable wear and tear. Painting over a wallcovering normally means that it won't be an easy job to remove it later, so it's usually best to hang a relief wallcovering only if you intend leaving it in place for some time. (Although a steam stripper will make removal easier.)

There is a wide range of relief wallcoverings available which vary in design, thickness, depth of embossing, quality, strength, method of manufacture and price.

Woodchip wallpapers

One of the most commonly used of the 'whites' apart from lining paper is woodchip wallpaper. This relatively thick paper is made from soft wood-pulp with small, medium or large chips of wood added during the manufacturing process. These chips create the textured surface.

Woodchips are hung in normal fashion; you paste the back with a paste suitable for medium weight papers and butt-join lengths of paper before trimming off the overlaps. The cut lengths must be allowed to soak and become supple before hanging, but be careful that you don't oversoak them (follow the manufacturer's instructions as to the length of soaking time) or it is more likely you will tear the paper when trimming.

Low-relief embossed papers

This range of wallpapers, which includes Anaglypta, is also made from pulped wood fibre. During manufacture two sheets of paper are bonded together with a water-resistant adhesive. Before the adhesive dries, the paper is run through shaped steel rollers, one with a raised pattern and the other with corresponding indentations, to stretch the soft paper and create the embossed effect.

The back surface of the paper has hollows and you need to take extra care when hanging these types of wallcoverings to ensure that the hollows are not squashed flat against the wall. You should use a heavy-duty adhesive and allow the paper to soak (usually for 10 minutes) and become supple before hanging. Take care that the edges are well pasted.

High-relief embossed papers

The majority of good quality high-relief 'whites' are made in a similar manner but often using cotton linters (short cotton fibres), china clay and resins rather than pulped wood fibre to produce the 'paper'. These ingredients give a more durable wallcovering and enable it to be given a greater depth of embossing. Supaglypta is the best known example of this type of paper.

Depending on the design, high-relief embossed papers can often require some depth of drop matching to maintain pattern repeats. Soaking times (use a heavy-duty adhesive) should therefore be kept as constant as possible so that each length stretches, before and during hanging, to the same degree.

Blown vinyls

Classed as 'whites' and intended to be overpainted, blown vinyls are made from a type of vinyl bonded to a paper backing. During manufacture the vinyl is heated to make it expand, then before it cools it is passed through a machine which embosses a pattern into the surface. The result is a wallcovering with a slightly soft, spongy feel. But despite this softness, blown vinyls are strong, easy to handle and create few hanging problems.

You should hang a blown vinyl wallcovering with a heavy-duty or ready-mixed paste containing a fungicide; these types of wallcovering do not require soaking. You can

PREPARING ANAGLYPTA

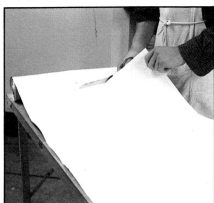

1 *Measure and cut the paper so there will be a 50mm (2in) overlap at the top and bottom. Mark the top so you'll hang the lengths the same way.*

2 *To ensure accurate pattern matching place the length to be cut alongside a cut length and make a slight tear to indicate where to cut.*

3 *Brush on the adhesive, filling all the hollows. If it is the correct consistency the brush will lift the paper from the table for a few seconds.*

4 *Fold the paper, taking care not to crease the folds, and leave the length to soak for 10 to 15 minutes (follow the instructions on the roll.)*

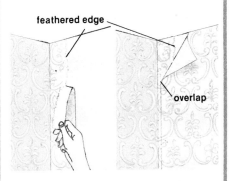
then paint them like any other relief wallcovering, and they can be scrubbed clean. When you want to remove the wallcovering you peel off the vinyl layer leaving the paper lining on the wall. This can be left in place to serve as a lining paper for the next covering, or else it can be soaked and stripped off completely.

Pre-finished vinyl reliefs
Another type of relief wallcovering comes with a textured or plain vinyl surface. It is pre-finished so it does not require over-painting (though you can paint it if you wish), and it is bonded to a paper backing. These can be regularly wiped clean and are easily removed by peeling them off.

There are also vinyl relief wallcoverings with a printed decorative embossed surface designed to give the appearance of wall tiles, wood panelling or other effects.

Lincrusta types
Lincrusta is a heavy, solid, embossed wallcovering made from a combination of oxidised linseed oil and fillers bonded to a paper backing. During manufacture the putty-like surface is embossed while still soft, and is then left for 14 days to mature and dry out. It is available in two versions – one intended to be overpainted and the other already finished.

As this type of wallcovering is heavy and will easily pull away old, poorly-adhering emulsion or other paints, you should take special care in preparing the wall surfaces. They must be thoroughly clean, made good and should also be given a coat of size.

To hang Lincrusta, first cut it into drop-matched lengths, allowing an extra 50mm (2in) for later trimming at the base. The top edges of each length should be cut to fit precisely. Then trim the edges of the lengths

HANGING ANAGLYPTA

1 Mark where the first length will fall (here the edge just reaches the central point of the chimney breast) and then gently brush it in place.

2 To give you a clear guideline for trimming the relief paper, mark off the cutting line by running a pencil along the wallcovering.

3 Use scissors to trim the paper. Don't use a knife as you are more likely to tear the paper because of its softness (from soaking).

4 Fix the next length of wallcovering, butting it up against the previous length. Don't overlap; any slight gap will be filled by overpainting.

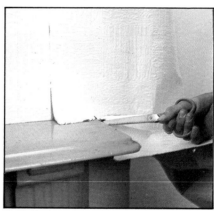

5 To fit the paper round a mantelpiece cut into the overlap at several places. Make sure that you don't cut too deep.

6 Similarly, where the paper will have to fit round an external corner, make a cut into the overlap at the top and bottom.

7 At a fire surround mark off the cutting line with a pencil, use scissors to trim the overlap, then brush the trimmed edge into place.

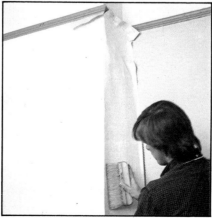

8 There should be at least 25mm (1in) of paper lapping round an external corner (here there's much more) which you brush into place.

9 At an internal corner brush one length into the corner. Ideally, tear the overlap (see Ready Reference), and cover it with the next length.

using a straight edge and a sharp knife. (Lincrusta is one of the few wallcoverings which require edge trimming). Offer each length up to its intended position and make any cutouts required for light switches or other obstacles.

You should then dampen the paper backing with warm water applied with a sponge to allow the material to expand fully and make hanging easier. Leave it to soak for up to 30 minutes on a flat surface with two lengths laid back to back, then wipe off any excess water.

Brush special Lincrusta glue onto the damp backing paper; work fairly quickly and aim for even coverage. Position each length immediately after it is pasted, and use a soft cloth to press the wallcovering gently but firmly into position, working from the top downwards. Trim the bottom length with a sharp knife and you can then go ahead and hang the other lengths, butting each tightly up against the next. Because of its thickness and the nature of its surface, Lincrusta does not easily bend round corners so you will have to cut and butt join it at corners as neatly as possible. As with other types of wallcoverings, you're unlikely to get perfect pattern matching at corners because the walls will probably be slightly out of true.

It is very difficult to remove Lincrusta and you are quite likely to damage the wall behind in the process if you try to remove it, so it's worth thinking carefully before you decide to hang this type of wallcovering. It is, however, extremely durable, so can be used where ordinary relief wallcoverings might be prone to damage – in stairwells, for example.

Novamura

Although not really a relief wallcovering and certainly not a 'white', there is another slightly textured wallcovering worth describing which is made from an unusual material and hung in an unusual manner.

This is Novamura, which is a foamed polyethylene wallcovering. It is extremely lightweight and supplied in standard-size rolls in a wide variety of designs. It is soft and warm to touch and possibly the easiest wallcovering to hang.

Instead of pasting lengths cut from the roll, the paste is applied directly to the wall; the roll is unfurled down the wall onto the pasted area and then trimmed. This method eliminates the need for paste tables, mixing buckets and other paperhanging paraphernalia and takes comparatively little time.

Novamura must nevertheless be treated with some care and should not be overstretched. Although it can be wiped clean it should not be scrubbed.

To remove it you simply peel it away from the wall, with no soaking or pre-treatment required.

PAINTING ANAGLYPTA

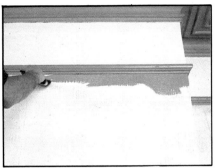

1 Use a brush to cut in at the edges; applying a silk-finish emulsion paint will emphasise the embossed effect more than a matt one.

2 The job will go more quickly if you use a roller to paint the rest of the wallcovering; paint it in bands, working down the wall.

HANGING NOVAMURA

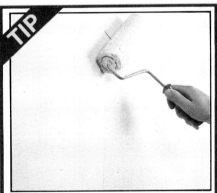

1 Apply adhesive containing a fungicide to the wall, covering an area slightly wider than the width of the wallcovering.

2 Apply the wallcovering directly from the dry roll without cutting individual lengths. Smooth it into place with a damp sponge.

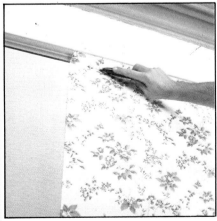

3 Crease the wallcoverings at the joins between wall and ceiling (or picture rail) and skirting, then trim with scissors or a sharp knife.

4 Hang the next piece in the same way, butting it up against the preceding piece and making sure the pattern matches as you hang it.

CHAPTER 3

Tiling and Flooring

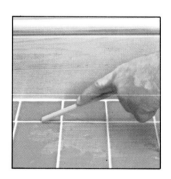 

CERAMIC TILES for small areas

Ceramic tiles are easy-clean, hygienic and hard wearing. By starting with a small area in your home where these qualities are needed – like splashbacks or worktops – you'll not only grasp the basics but also gain confidence to tackle bigger things.

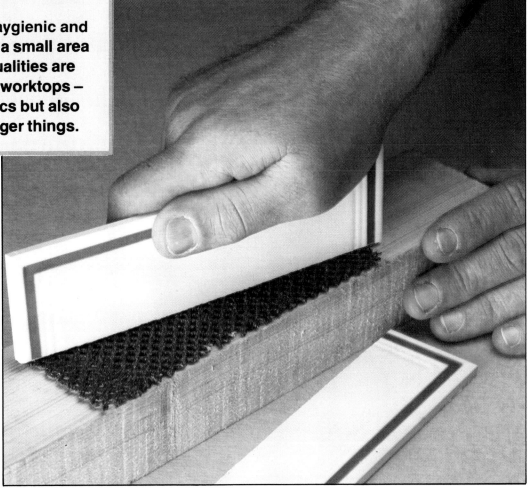

Modern ceramic tiles are thin slabs of clay, decorated on one side with coloured glazes. These are baked on to give the tile a hard, glassy surface resistant to water, heat and almost all household chemicals. The clay from which tiles are made, which is known as the biscuit, varies and you need to know the differences before you choose the tile to use. The thinnest ones with a pale coloured biscuit are good on all vertical surfaces (including doors where extra weight puts stress on the hinges).

If the biscuit is reddish/brown it has been high baked (vitrified). The thicker and darker coloured it is the more strength the tile has — floor tiles, for example, are usually big in size as well as thick in biscuit.

Work surfaces need tiles that are strong to withstand weights of heavy pots, while splashbacks and bathroom surfaces can take lighter, thinner ones.

Types of tiles

Within each range of tiles there are usually three types. *Spacer* tiles have small projections on each edge called lugs which butt up to the neighbouring tile and provide the correct space for grouting (with these it is very hard to vary the width of the grouting). *Border* tiles are squared off on all sides but are glazed on two adjacent edges — these give a neat finish to outer corners and top or side edges. *Universal or continental* tiles have no lugs and are square on all edges. All three can be used successfully in small areas, but do remember that if tiles do not have lugs you have to include grouting space in your calculations — the thinnest tiles need to be spaced by nothing more than torn-up pieces of cardboard, 6mm (¼in) tiles are best with a matchstick width in between.

Tiles are sold by the sq metre, sq yd, boxed in 25s or 50s, or can be bought individually. Boxed tiles usually advise on adhesive and grout needed for specific areas. When buying, if there's no written information available always check that the tile is suitable.

How to plan the layout

When tiling small areas you don't have much space to manoeuvre. The idea in all tiling is to create a symmetrical effect, using whole tiles or, if any have to be cut, making them equal.

Knowing about the different sizes of tiles helps in the planning. For example, if you know the width and height or depth of the surface you intend to tile, you can divide this by the known size of tiles until you find the one that gives the right number of whole tiles. Remember that the width of grouting has to be added to the measurement with non-lugged tiles – and except with the very thinnest tiles this can be slightly widened if it saves cutting a tile.

If you're prepared to incorporate cut tiles into the planning remember:

● on the width of the tiled area, place equal cut tiles at each end

● on the height, place cut tiles at the top edge

● on the depth (eg, window-recesses) put cut tiles at back edge

● frame a fitting by placing cut tiles at each side and the top

A mix of patterned or textured with plain tiles is best done first on metricated graph paper. This will help you see where you want the pattern to fall.

Fixings should be made in the grouting lines where possible. Some tile ranges have soap dishes, towel rails etc attached to tiles so they can be incorporated in a scheme, but if these don't suit your purposes, you can drill the tiles to screw in your own fitting (see page 58).

A working plan

All tiles should be fixed level and square so it's important to establish the horizontal and vertical with a spirit level. Draw in the lines with pencil. If you plan to tile where there is no support (eg, on either side of a basin or sink) lightly pin a length of 50 x 25mm (2 x 1in) timber below the tiling line – the batten will prevent the tiles slipping.

On doors you may have to consider adding a timber surround to keep the tiles secure as they will be subjected to movement (also see section on *Adhesives* below).

Adhesives and grouting

The choice of both of these depends on where the tiles are to be fixed. In a watery situation (eg, a shower cubicle or a steamy kitchen) it is important to use a waterproof variety of both, even though you might have

Ready Reference

TILE SHAPES AND SIZES

Ceramic tiles for walls are usually square or oblong in shape. The commonest sizes are shown below. The smaller sizes are usually 4mm (5/32in) thick, while larger tiles may be 6mm (1/4in) or more in thickness.

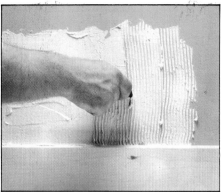

▼200x200mm   6x6in▼

100x100mm▲
▲4¼ x 4¼in   50x50mm▲

HOW MANY TILES?

Square or oblong areas
● measure lengths and width of the area
● divide each measurement by the size of tile you're using, rounding up to the next whole number if you get a fraction
● multiply the two figures to give the number of tiles needed

Awkwardly-shaped areas
● divide area into convenient squares or oblongs
● work out each one as above adding up the area totals to give the final figures

Patterns using two or more different tiles
● sketch out design on graph paper, one square for each tile (two for oblong tiles); use colours to mark where different tiles fall
● count up totals needed of each pattern, counting part tiles as whole ones

Add 10% to your final tile counts to allow for breakages

ADHESIVE/GROUT

For each square metre of tiling allow:
● 1.5kg (about 1 litre) of adhesive
● 150g of grout

TIP: AVOID NARROW STRIPS

Less than about 25mm/1in wide is very difficult to cut. When planning, if you see narrow strips are going to occur you can:
● replan the rows to use one less whole tile with two wider cut pieces at either end
● or increase the grouting space slightly between every tile in the row

HOW TO HANG TILES

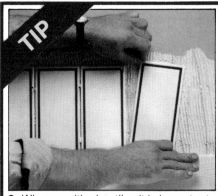

1 Spread ceramic tile adhesive to cover 1 sq metre, then 'comb' with notched spreader. To support tiles where no other support exists, pin a horizontal timber batten to the wall.

2 When positioning tiles it is important to twist them slightly to bed them. Don't slide them as this forces adhesive between joints.

3 Form even grouting spaces between tiles without lugs with pieces of matchstick. Or you can use torn-up cardboard from the tile packaging or similar if you want only a narrow grouting space.

4 Remove matchsticks or card after all tiles are hung, and grout 12-24 hours later. Press grout into the spaces using a small sponge or squeegee, making sure no voids are left in either vertical or horizontal spaces.

5 After 10 minutes, wipe off excess grouting with soft cloth. Use fine dowelling (sand the end to round it) to even up and smooth the lines. Fill any voids that appear with fresh grout to prevent water penetration.

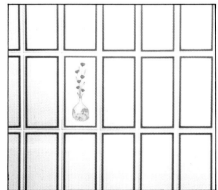

6 When grouting is dry, polish the tiles with a soft cloth so the area is smooth. All the surface needs now is an occasional wipe-down although non-waterproof grout may tend to discolour as time goes by.

to wait for 4-5 days before exposing the tile surface to use.

All ceramic tile adhesives are like thin putty and can be bought ready mixed in tubs or in powder form to be made up with water. They are what is known as thin-bed adhesives in that they are designed to be applied in a thin layer on a flat even surface. The spread is controlled by a notched comb (usually provided by the manufacturer but cheap to buy where you bought the tiles) to make furrows of a specified depth. When the tiles are pressed on with a slight twist, the adhesive evenly grips the back of the biscuit.

Special latex-based adhesives (usually, two-part products which have to be mixed before using) have much more flexibility and are good for tiles where there is any movement (eg, on doors).

Spread the adhesive on an area no more than 1 sq metre (1 sq yd) at a time, or it will lose its gripping power before you have time to place the tiles. If you remove a tile, before refixing comb the adhesive again.

Grout gives the final finish to the tiled area, filling the spaces between the tiles and preventing moisture getting behind them and affecting the adhesive. Grouting can be done 12-24 hours after the last tile has been pressed into place. Grout can be standard or waterproof (with added acrylic), and both are like a cellulose filler when made up.

If you only make up one lot of grouting, you can colour it with special grouting tints – but remember that it's hard to make other batches match the colour. Waterproof grouting cannot always take these tints.

Press grout between the tiles with a sponge or squeegee and wipe off excess with a damp sponge. Even up the grouting by drawing a pencil-like piece of wood (eg dowelling) along each row first vertically, then horizontally. Do this within 10 minutes of grouting so it is not completely dry.

Leave the tiles for 24 hours before polishing with a clean dry cloth. Wash clean only if a slight bloom remains.

Tiles should never be fixed with tight joints for any movement of the wall or fittings will cause the tiles to crack. Similarly where tiles meet baths, basins, sinks etc, flexibility is needed – and grout that dries rigid cannot provide it. These gaps must be filled with a silicone rubber sealant

Techniques with tiles

To cut tiles, lightly score the glaze with a tile cutter to break the surface. Place the tile glazed side up with the scored line over matchsticks and firmly but gently press the tile down on each side. If using a pencil press on one side, hold the other. Smooth the cut edge with a file. Very small adjustments are best done by filing the edge of the whole tile.

CUTTING TILES

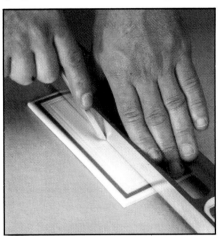

1 *Before a tile will break, the glaze must be scored — on the edges as well as surface. Use a carbide-tipped cutter against a straight-edge.*

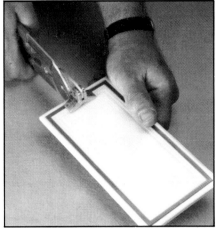

2 *Another type of cutter has 'jaws' which clasp the tile during breaking. (It also has a small 'wheel' for scoring through the glaze on the tile).*

3 *No special tools are needed with other tile-breaking methods. For medium thick tiles use a pencil, for thin tiles use matchsticks.*

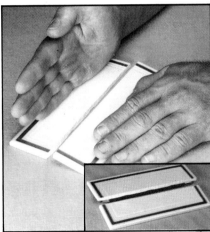

4 *Place pencil centrally under tile and score line, hold one side and press firmly on other. With thin tiles, press lightly both sides.*

To remove a narrow strip of tile, score the line heavily by drawing the tile cutter across the tile more firmly several times in the same place. Then use pincers to 'nibble' the waste away in small pieces and smooth the edge. Glaze on broken tiles is as sharp as glass, so be careful not to cut yourself.

Templates for awkwardly shaped tiles are not difficult to make. Cut the shape in card, place on a tile and score a line freehand with the tile cutter. Any straight score marks can be deepened afterwards, using a straight edge for support. Then nibble away the waste with pincers. If there's a large amount to be cut away, score the waste part to divide it into sections, then nibble away. A good tip is to do this on a soft or padded surface so the tile doesn't break in the wrong place.

Suitable surfaces

The ideal surface for tiling is one that's perfectly flat, dry and firm. Small irregularities will be covered up, but any major hollows, bumps or flaking, need to be made good.

Plastered walls and asbestos cement sheets: perfect for tiling, but wait a month after any new plastering to allow the wall to dry out completely. Unless surface has been previously painted, apply a coat of plaster primer to prevent the liquid in the tile adhesive from being absorbed too quickly.

Plasterboard: again, ideal for tiling as long as it's firmly fixed and adjacent boards cannot shift. (If they did the joins would probably crack). To prepare the surface, remove all dust, wipe down with white spirit

Ready Reference

TOOLS FOR TILING

Tile cutter: essential for scoring glaze of tiles before breaking them. Score only once (the second time you may waver from the line and cause an uneven break).
Pincers: these are used for nibbling away small portions of tile, after scoring a line with the cutter. Ordinary pincers are fine for most jobs, but special tile nibblers are available.
Special cutter: combines a cutting edge (usually a small cutting wheel) with jaws which snap the tile along the scored line.
Tile file: an abrasive mesh, used as a file to 'shave' off small amounts.

TIP: TO DRILL A TILE

● make a cross of masking tape and mark the point where you want the hole
● drill after adhesive and grouting have set using lowest speed or a hand drill with masonry bit — too much speed at the start will craze the tile
● once through the glaze, drill in the normal way

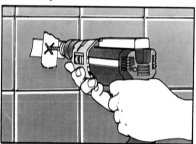

● cut tile into two along line corresponding with centre point of pipe; offer up each half to the pipe
● mark freehand semi-circles on tile to match edge of pipe; score line with tile cutter and nibble away waste with pincers

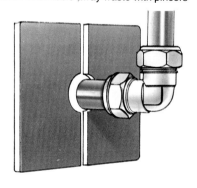

SHAPING TILES

5 Edges of broken tiles need to be smoothed off — use a special tile file mounted on wood, a wood file or rub against rough concrete.

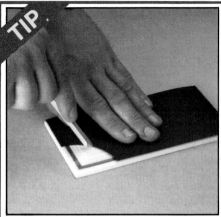

6 To cut an awkward shape, make a card template. Place it on the tile and score glaze on the surface and edges with the tile cutter.

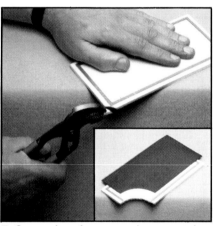

7 On a soft surface, use pincers to take tiny nibbles out of the tile. If you're over enthusiastic you'll break off more than you intended.

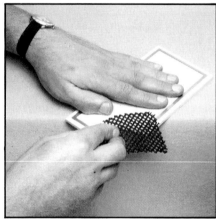

8 Once the waste has been slowly but surely nibbled away, smooth up the edge. Files are also useful when a whole tile needs a slight trimming.

to remove grease, then treat with primer.
Paint: old emulsion-paint needs to be cleaned thoroughly with sugar soap or detergent to remove all traces of dust and grease. Gloss paint needs to be cleaned thoroughly; remove any flaking paint then roughen up whole surface with a coarse abrasive to provide a good key for the adhesive.
Wallpaper: DO NOT tile directly onto wallpaper, as this can be pulled away from the wall by the adhesive. Strip it off completely.
Wood and Chipboard: perfect for tiling as long as it is flat and adjacent boards cannot shift. Treat with an ordinary wood primer.
Laminates: joins and small, minor blemishes in the surface can be covered up so long as the entire sheet is soundly fixed and absolutely flat. Its smooth face must be roughened with course abrasive to provide a key for the tile adhesive.
Old ceramic tiles: the thin biscuit ceramic tiles are excellent for tiling over as they add little to the wall's thickness and won't protrude beyond existing fittings. Loose and cracked tiles will have to be removed. Scrape out the grouting surrounding the tile using an old, thin screwdriver or something similar, then, beginning in the centre and working outwards, remove the tile using a club hammer and cold chisel.

Small sections or mis-shapen pieces (as around a new fixture) can be built up level with neighbouring tiles with cellulose filler.

The area should then be sealed with plaster primer or emulsion paint to finish the surface.

CERAMIC TILING WALL TO WALL

Ceramic tiles are an ideal decorating material for they make a room look good for years and require virtually no maintenance. But covering several walls with tiles is a large-scale job which needs a methodical and careful approach if you are to achieve the best results.

The all-in-one look that wall-to-wall tiling can give has to be planned carefully to avoid expensive and time consuming mistakes. How to do this may depend on whether you want to include special patterns in the design, but following certain rules will give a desirable symmetry to the look.

One of the hardest tasks will probably be choosing the tiles for there's a vast array of shapes, sizes and colours available. Having picked out the ones you want though, don't buy until you've done the planning – for the plans of each wall should tell you whether the pattern will work in the room or would be lost in the cutting or amid the fittings.

Plans on paper also give you an instant method of working out how many tiles to buy (counting each cut one as a whole, and adding 2-5% for unintended breakage) including the number which will need to be border (two glazed edges) or mitred (on square or rectangular universal tiles) for the top row of half-tiled walls or external corners. Buy all the tiles at once, but do check each carton to make sure there's no variation in the colour (this can occur during the firing of different batches).

Planning on paper

The best possible way to start planning for a large expanse of tiling is not on the wall, but on paper. Graph paper is ideal, particularly if you intend including a mix of plain and patterned tiles, or a large motif that needs building up. Of course, advance planning is also essential if you're tiling round major features like windows, doors, mirrors, shower cubicles and so on.

You need separate pieces of graph paper for each wall you intend tiling. Allow the large (1cm) squares on the paper to represent your tiles — one for a square tile of any size, two for a rectangular tile; this will give you a scale to work to. Now mark up sheets of greaseproof paper with your actual wall sizes using the scale dictated by the tile size on the graph paper. Measure and outline on the see-through paper the exact position and in-scale dimensions of all fixtures and fittings (see the planning pictures on page 60).

At this stage, the objective is to decide how to achieve the best symmetrical layout for your tiles — the 'ideal' is to have either whole or equal-size cut tiles on each side of a fixture.

First you have to mark in the central guide lines. For instance, on *walls with a window* draw a line from the sill centre to the floor, and from the centre of the top of the window to the ceiling. If there are *two windows* also draw in the central line from floor to ceiling between them. Mark the centre point above a *door* to the ceiling and also indicate the horizontal line at the top of the door. In the same way draw in a central line from the top of a *basin or vanity unit* to the ceiling.

For all these lines use a coloured pen for you have to be aware of them when deciding where whole tiles should be positioned. But they're only the starting point — other potential problems have to be looked at too.

Place the see-through paper over the tile sizes on the graph paper so you can see how the tiles will fall in relation to the guide lines. Now take into account the following important points:

● The first row above the lowest level — either the floor, the skirting board or a wall-to-wall fitting — should be whole tiles. If necessary, change this to prevent a thin strip being cut at the ceiling.

● Check where tiles come in relation to fittings. If very thin strips (less than 38mm/1½in) or narrow 'L' shapes would need to be cut, move the top sheet slightly up, down, left or right till the tiles are of a cuttable size — areas to watch are around windows, doors and where one wall meets another.

Placing patterns

When you are satisfied that you have a symmetrical and workable arrangement you can tape the top sheet in the right position on the graph paper, then start to plan where you're going to position your patterned tiles. Use pencil this time in case you change your mind and want to make adjustments. These are the points to watch:

● Don't place single motif patterns at internal corners where they would have to be cut — you won't find it easy to match up the remaining piece on the adjacent wall.

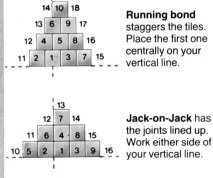

● If the pattern builds up vertically and horizontally over four or more tiles, 'centre' the pattern on the wall so that cuts are equal at both ends. If pattern loss can't be avoided with designs of this type at least it can be kept to internal corners.

● Whole tiles should be used on both faces of external corners.

Now butt each of the wall plans up to the other to make sure that the patterns relate both vertically and horizontally.

Planning on the wall

When there are no complicated tiling patterns involved and walls are free of interruptions such as windows, it's often easier to do the planning directly on the wall itself. Here, the simple objective is to place the tiles symmetrically between the corners. And to do this, all you need is a tiling gauge which you can make.

A tiling gauge is like a long ruler, except that it's marked off in tile widths. Use a long, straight piece of timber ideally about 25mm square (1in square) and remember to include the grouting gap between tiles as you rule off the gauge. If you're using rectangular tiles, mark the widths on one side, the lengths on the other.

Holding the gauge against the walls —

first vertically, then horizontally — tells you instantly where the whole tiles will fit in and where cut tiles will be needed. But first you must find the centre of each wall. Measure the width — doing this at three places will also tell you if the corners are vertical (hang a plumb line or use a spirit level to make absolutely sure) — and halve it to find the centre point. Use the tiling gauge to mark this vertical centre line with a pencil, then hold the gauge against it. Move it up or down until you have at least a whole tile's width above the floor or skirting board — this can be adjusted slightly if it avoids a thin piece of tile at ceiling height — then mark off the tile widths on the vertical line itself.

Now hold the tiling gauge horizontally, and move it to left or right of the vertical line if thin pieces of tile would have to be cut near windows or fittings, or to make cut tiles at both ends of the wall equal. Following this adjustment, mark the wall and draw in a new vertical line if necessary. The wall can now be marked horizontally with tile widths. Keeping to the same horizontal, mark up adjacent walls in the same way.

At corners, whether internal or external, don't assume they're either square, vertical or even. An internal corner is the worst place to start your tiling for this very reason, but it

doesn't matter if you position cut tiles there. On external corners use the tiling gauge to work inwards in whole tile widths.

You can also use the tiling gauge to check that your graph plan is accurate, and make any necessary adjustments.

Putting up battens

Once you have determined that your plan is correct, fix a length of perfectly straight 50mm x 25mm (2in x 1in) battening across the full width of the wall — use a spirit level to ensure that the batten is horizontal. Use masonry nails to fix it in place but do not drive them fully home as they will have to be removed later. If using screws the wall should be plugged. The batten provides the base for your tiling and it's important that its position is correct.

If more than one wall is being tiled, continue to fix battens around the room at the same height, using the spirit level to check the horizontal. The last one you fix should tie up perfectly with the first. If there are gaps, at the door for example, check that the level either side is the same, by using a straight-edge and spirit level to bridge the gap.

Once the horizontal battens are fixed, fix a vertical batten to give yourself the starting point for the first tile. Use a spirit level or plumb line to make sure it's positioned accurately.

Fixing tiles

Begin tiling from the horizontal base upwards, checking as you work that the tiles are going up accurately both vertically and horizontally. Work on an area of approximately 1 sq metre (1 sq yd) at a time, spreading the adhesive and fixing all the whole tiles using card or matchsticks as spacers as necessary. Make sure no excess adhesive is left on the surface of the tiles.

Next, deal with any tiles that need to be cut. You may find the gap into which they fit is too narrow to operate the adhesive spreader properly. In this case spread the adhesive onto the back of the tiles.

When all the tiling above the base batten has been completed wait for 8-12 hours, before removing the battens, and completing the tiling. Take care when removing the base batten that the tiles above are not disturbed — the adhesive is unlikely to be fully set.

Dealing with corners

Your original planning should have indicated how many border or mitred tiles you will need for tiling external corners or for the top line of tiles on a half-tiled wall. You will find external corners, those which project into the room, in virtually all tiling situations — around boxed-in pipework, or around a window or door reveal, or in an L-shaped room.

Where you are using universal tiles at an

PLANNING TILE LAYOUT ON PAPER

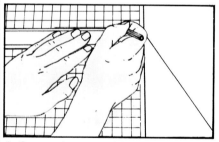

1 On graph paper with large (eg, 1cm) squares, let each square represent one whole square tile. Strengthen the grid lines with coloured pen if necessary.

2 On tracing paper, draw the outline of each wall to be tiled, and mark in doors and windows. Use the scale 1cm = the actual tile size (eg, 150mm).

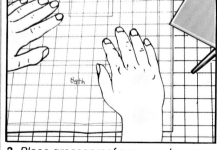

3 Place greaseproof over graph paper and move it around till you get the most manageable size cut tiles, especially near fixtures, ceiling and floor.

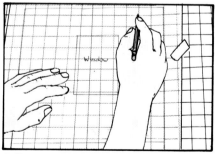

4 Tape the top sheet in place, then mark the pattern in with pencil. Do each wall the same so that the alignment of the horizontal is correct.

Jem Grischotti

external corner, start at the corner with a whole tile — it should project by the depth of the mitre so that the mitre on the other face neatly butts up against it with a fine space for grouting in between.

With window reveals the correct method is to tile up the wall to sill level, cutting tiles if necessary. Fit whole tiles either side of the reveal, then again cut tiles to fill the space between those whole ones and the window frame. Attach whole border or mitred tiles to the sill so they butt up against the wall tiles. If using square-edged tiles the ones on the sill should cover the edges of those on the wall so the grouting line is not on the sill surface. If the sill is narrower than a whole tile, cut the excess from the back — not the front. If the sill is deeper than a whole tile, put cut tiles near the window with the cut edge against the frame. Continually check the accurate lining up of tiles with a spirit level.

Some vertical external corners are not as precisely straight and vertical as they should be and this can lead to problems of tile alignment. The use of a thick-bed adhesive will help to straighten out some irregularities where a corner goes inwards (a thin-bed helps where the wall leans outwards). Buying a 'flexible' adhesive will give you both qualities. As a general rule it is

PLANNING ON THE WALL

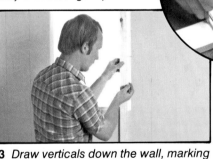

1 (inset) Mark the tiling gauge in tile widths (and lengths if they are rectangular).

2 Use a plumb line to check that the wall is vertical.

3 Draw verticals down the wall, marking off the exact tile widths to give an accurate guide.

4 Check each horizontal with a spirit level, then mark tile positions from floor to ceiling.

Jem Grischotti

5 Place horizontal batten at least a tile's width above floor or a fitting using masonry nails or screws.

6 Fix vertical batten and begin to tile where the battens meet. Spread adhesive to cover 1 sq metre (1 sq yd).

Ready Reference

TACKLING TILING PROBLEMS
Whenever a fitting, a door or window interrupts the clean run of a wall, it becomes the focal point of the wall. So you have to plan for symmetry *round* the features. Here are some guidelines:

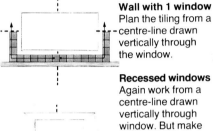

Wall with 1 window
Plan the tiling from a centre-line drawn vertically through the window.

Recessed windows
Again work from a centre-line drawn vertically through window. But make sure that whole tiles are placed at the front of the sill and the sides of the reveals. Place cut tiles closest to the window frame.

Wall with two windows
Unless the space between the two windows is exactly equal to a number of whole tiles, plan your tiling to start from a centre-line drawn between the two.

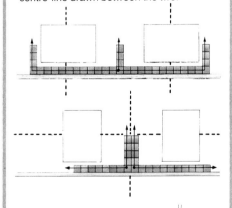

Wall with door
If the door is placed fairly centrally in the wall, plan your tiling from a centre-line drawn vertically through the door. If, however, the door is very close to a side wall, the large expanse of wall is a more prominent focal point. So plan the tiling to start one tile's width from the frame. If the frame is not exactly vertical, you'll be able to cut tiles to fit in the remaining space.

MAKE YOUR OWN TILE BREAKER

1 Use a timber offcut wider than the tile as the base. Use 3mm (1/8in) ply for the top and sides.

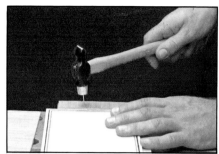

2 Stack ply strips on both sides till the same height as the tile, then pin. Nail on the top piece.

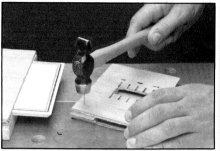

3 The breaking part needs to be as wide and deep as the tile, with the opening on the top a half tile long.

4 Score the glaze on the top and edges with a carbide-tipped cutter. Put the tile into the main part.

5 Slip on the breaking part so the score line is between the two. Hold one side while you press the other.

6 The tile breaks cleanly. This aid costs nothing and will save you time when tiling a large expanse.

TILING CORNERS

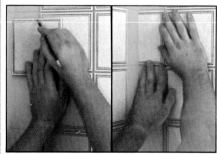

1 At an internal corner, mark amount to be cut at top and bottom. Break the tile, then fit in position.

2 File the remainder until it fits the adjacent area with enough space left for a fine line of grout.

3 On a window sill, use a whole tile at the front and make sure that it overlaps the one on the wall-face underneath.

4 Mitred edges of universal tiles and glazed edges of border tiles give a better finish to external corners.

better to concentrate on lining up your border or mitred tiles perfectly vertically with only minute 'steps' between tiles, then bedding spacer or ordinary tiles behind to correspond with the line. Don't forget that if you do have to create a very slight stepped effect, you can reduce the uneven effect between the corner tiles and others by pressing in extra grouting later.

Internal corners seldom cause serious problems as cut tiles can be shaped to suit fluctuations from the truly vertical. Don't assume when cutting tiles for a corner that all will be the same size — the chances are that they will vary considerably and should be measured and cut individually. Another point: don't butt tiles up against each other so they touch — leave space for the grouting which will give the necessary flexibility should there be any wall movement.

Tiling around electrical fittings

When tiling around electrical fittings it is better to disconnect the electricity and remove the wall plate completely so that you can tile right up to the edge of the wall box. This is much neater and easier than trying to cut tiles to fit around the perimeter of the plate. Cut tiles as described in the illustrations on pages 57 and 58 and fit them in the normal way with the plate being replaced on top, completely covering the cut edges of the tiles. This same principle applies to anything easily removable. The fewer objects you have to tile around the better, so before starting any tiling get to work with a screwdriver.

You have the greatest control over the end result if at the planning stage you work out where you want to place fittings such as towel rails and soap dishes, shelves and the like. Some tile ranges offer them attached so it's only a matter of fitting them in as you put the tiles up.

Tiling non-rigid surfaces

On surfaces which are not totally rigid or which are subject to movement, vibration or the odd shock, tiles should not be attached using adhesive which dries hard as most standard and waterproof types do. Instead use adhesives which retain some flexibility. These may be cement-based types with a latex rubber content, or acrylic adhesives. You may have to surround a non-rigid surface with wooden lipping to protect the tiles.

TILING AROUND FIXTURES

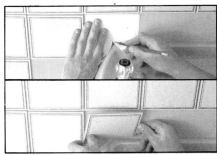

1 *At awkward corners use card to make a tile-size template. Place it on the tile and score the shape, then gently nibble out the waste with pincers — the smaller the bits the better.*

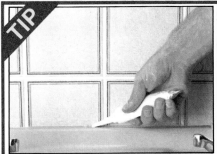

2 *Where basins, baths, kitchen sinks or laundry tubs meet tiles, seal the join with silicone caulking to keep out water. Caulking comes in various colours to match fixtures.*

3 *After the adhesive has had time to set, the tiles are grouted both to protect them and to enhance their shape and colour.*
Accessories can be bought already attached to tiles, can be screw mounted after drilling the tile, or if lightweight can be stuck on to tiles with adhesive pads.

DECORATING WALLS WITH CORK

Cork in tile, panel or sheet form provides an easy-to-fix wallcovering which is highly decorative and warm to the touch. It will also add to your peace and quiet by insulating against noise.

You may decide to decorate one or more walls of a room in your house with cork simply because you like the look of it. But there are practical advantages in doing this as well. You will also be providing extra insulation as, apart from its decorative qualities, cork deadens sound, is warm to the touch and keeps heat in and cold out. Also, it doesn't cause condensation and will absorb a certain amount of moisture. It can be quite hardwearing, taking its share of knocks and bumps without bruising, and many of the ranges of cork tiles, panels, sheets and rolls available are treated to be fully washable and steam-proof.

Where to use cork

Because of its highly decorative quality and natural texture, cork usually looks best as a feature wall, or forming a focal point on a chimney breast, or in an alcove, or behind some display shelves. But because of its insulating quality it is ideal on the inside of walls which face away from the sun, particularly if a bedhead or seating is placed next to them. Cork tiles on a ceiling can help reduce noise and also add warmth; in children's rooms, teenage bedsitting rooms, family living rooms, hobby areas, even the kitchen, a panel of cork can also provide a place to pin pictures, posters and memos. Pre-sealed cork is practical for kitchens and bathrooms so long as it does not come in direct contact with the bath, sink or basin edge (you can isolate it with a row of ceramic tiles). It can also be used to face doors, cover window seats and ottomans, or cover screens and bath panels – so long as you select the right product.

Types of cork

Cork for walls comes in several different types. Some is made by pressing the cork into layers, or mixing cork chippings with a binder, and then cutting it into sheets, tiles or panels of various sizes, thicknesses and textures. Sometimes, to get a rougher home-spun look, the actual bark of the cork tree is peeled, mounted on a backing and sold for decorative purposes. The backing may be coloured, and if the cork is slivered thinly

enough, this backing will show through, giving a hint of colour to the cork. This type may be sold as panels or sheets.

Another attractive cork wallcovering is made by shaving the cork so thinly that it is almost transparent and because of the natural uneven texture, the effect is like hand-crocheted lace. This is then mounted onto a foil backing which glints through the layer of cork. This type is usually sold in sheets or by the roll, as wallpaper.

A new development is a wallcork which is laminated to crêpe paper so it is extremely flexible and can be bent round curved surfaces. This type comes in a natural finish, which can be painted, and also in several colours. It is sold by the linear metre, off the roll.

Most wallcorks are presealed, either waxed or treated with a sealant, which makes them washable; some come unsealed including some of the heavily textured types and the very open granular tiles.

Buying and planning

Cork tiles, panels and sheet come in various sizes. When you have decided on the type you want to use you will have to work out how much you will need to order from your supplier. Remember the cardinal rule that you should always order more than will be exactly required to cover the wall, to allow for any mistakes, accidents or errors when you are putting the cork up.

You may decide to fix tiles or panels in a particular pattern, for example, so they create a diamond or herringbone design. If so, it's best to work out the design on paper

first; then, after you've prepared the surface, you can square up the wall and mark the position of each tile or panel on it. (Remember you can also create interesting effects by using light and dark tiles to form a chequerboard pattern or to form a border or 'framed' effect; but you shouldn't need to mark up the wall for this.)

Preparing the surface

As with any other form of decoration, cork must be hung on a properly prepared surface. If you are going to cover a wall with cork which has already been decorated you should strip off old wallpaper, scrape off any flaking paint and fill any deep holes; cut and re-plaster any crumbling 'live' areas. If the plaster is porous, prime with PVA primer diluted 1:5 with water.

Gloss or emulsion-painted walls can be keyed by rubbing over them with glasspaper to roughen the surface, but as the paint can sometimes cause the adhesive to break down, most cork suppliers recommend lining a painted wall with heavy lining paper before fixing the cork in position. Follow the instructions supplied with the particular product you intend using. If you are going to use lining paper, remember to cross-line the walls, that is, hang the paper horizontally just as you would before hanging a good quality wallpaper or fabric wallcovering to avoid the risk of joins coinciding.

If you are hanging sheet cork wallcovering and using a heavy-duty wallpaper paste to fix it, it may be necessary to prime the wall surface first with a coat of size or diluted wallpaper paste.

FIXING THE FIRST TILE

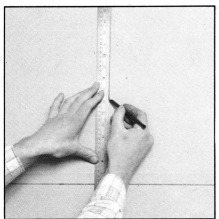

1 *Work out how the tile pattern will fall on the wall by drawing central horizontal and vertical lines. Adjust these to avoid awkward cuts.*

2 *Starting at the centre, spread adhesive in one of the angles formed by the lines. (With contact adhesive apply it to the back of the tile as well.)*

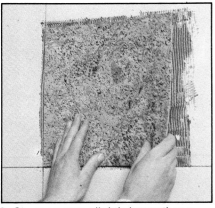

3 *Cover an area slightly larger than a tile, then align the first tile using the horizontal and vertical lines as a guide to the exact position.*

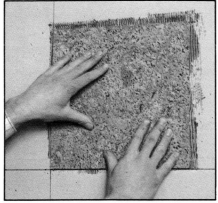

4 *Press the tile into place flat against the wall, taking care not to let it slip out of line as you do this. It's crucial you get the tile correctly positioned.*

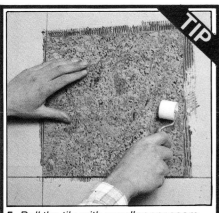

5 *Roll the tile with a wallpaper seam roller to get a better bond particularly at the edges. Be careful not to get adhesive on the roller.*

6 *If any adhesive gets onto the face of the tile wipe it off with a damp cloth before it sets. With some adhesives you may need to use white spirit (turps).*

Ready Reference

CHOOSING THE RIGHT CORK

Cork swells when it gets wet and could become distorted and start peeling off the wall. It therefore makes sense to
● use a pre-sealed type for kitchens, bathrooms and areas where you are going to have to wipe off sticky finger marks, or
● use a type of cork which can be sealed after hanging in these areas.

TIP: CONCEAL CUT TILES

When you are planning the layout of the tiles you are going to use on a wall, aim to place cut tiles where they won't draw attention. For example:
● it's best to have cut tiles at the skirting rather than at the ceiling
● on a chimney breast, butt cut tiles up to the junction between the chimney breast and wall rather than to the outer corner of the chimney breast.

TIP: MAKE DEMOUNTABLE PANELS

Because of the adhesive used to fix them, cork tiles can be difficult to remove once they are up; if you try to scrape them off you may either have large lumps of cork left stuck to the wall or large holes left in the plaster. To help you make it easier to have a change of decor later:
● fix the cork to panels of plasterboard, hardboard, partition board, chipboard, plywood or other dry lining
● fix the panels to battens which are screwed to the wall; these can be unscrewed and removed when you choose.

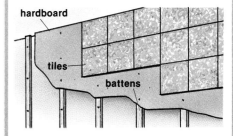

TILES IN HOT SPOTS

If you are fixing cork tiles to a chimney breast where a fire will be used, behind a radiator or other 'hot spot', it is best to put adhesive down the edges of the tiles as well as on the back to make extra sure of a secure bond.

PREVENT FIRE RISK

Many adhesives suitable for use with cork are highly inflammable. Therefore, when using them, make sure all pilot lights are switched off and turn off any electric or gas fires. Don't smoke or work near a naked light, and provide adequate ventilation.

FIXING OTHER TILES

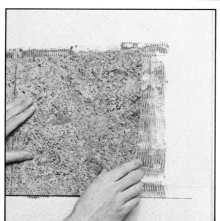

1 *Apply more adhesive then butt the second tile into place using hand pressure and a roller. Then continue to fix all the whole tiles.*

2 *Where the tile has to be cut, for example, to fit at the edge of a chimney breast, you should first place it over the last whole tile in the row.*

3 *Butt another tile up against the corner so that it overlaps the tile to be cut; use this as a guide to mark off a cutting line with chalk or pencil.*

4 *To cut the tile, place it on a firm surface then use a sharp kife to cut along the marked line. Use a straightedge as a guide.*

5 *Coat the exposed wall with adhesive and fix the cut tile in the same way you've fixed the whole tiles. Continue marking up, cutting and fixing the tiles.*

6 *When you've completed the front of a chimney breast you can tile the sides. Work so the cut edges go into the junction with the wall.*

Tools and equipment

You are already likely to have most of the tools and equipment required for covering walls with cork, particularly if you have hung some other type of wallcovering before. You will need a sharp knife to trim the cork, a straightedge, a notched adhesive spreader (sometimes supplied with the adhesive) or a pasting brush, a plumbline and chalk or pencil, a T-square or set square, a wallpaper seam roller and (for sheet cork) a wallpaper hanger's roller (which is wider than a seam roller). You will also require a tape measure and, to cut bark-type cork, a fine-toothed tenon saw. A pasting table (or some other suitable surface) may be needed; put this in a good light so you can see that the back surface of the tile or sheet (where these are pasted on the back rather than pasting the wall for fixing) is completely covered. As you'll be working at a height for part of the fixing process you'll need a stepladder. Make sure this is in sound condition so it will provide you with safe, secure access.

Fixing the cork

When you are fixing cork tiles or panels, as with all tiling, the setting-out is vitally important. The tiles should always be centred on a focal point or wall, so you end up with cut tiles or panels of equal width in the corners or at the edge of a chimney breast. Once you have established your central point and squared up the wall for the first line of tiles, tiling should be quite straightforward; the tiles are fixed with contact adhesive applied to the back of the tile and the wall or with an adhesive which is applied to the wall only.

Sheet cork is hung in different ways (see *Ready Reference*). The crucial thing here is to hang the lengths of cork to a true vertical and to plan the layout so cork which has to be cut to fit in width will come at the corners where any unevenness (due to the walls being out of square) will be least likely to be noticed.

Finishing touches and maintenance

If you put up cork tiles, panels, or sheet cork which are not sealed you can seal them with a transparent polyurethane varnish (a matt finish looks best). Dust the surface thoroughly and apply two or three coats of varnish; you may find a spray-on type is easier to apply than one which you brush on but this is only economical if you don't have too large an area to cover.

Most wall corks (whether sealed or unsealed) can be cleaned by dusting them down (use a cloth or the soft brush attachment on your vacuum cleaner). Most of the sealed corks and the crêpe-backed cork can be wiped with a damp cloth. The paper and foil-backed corks may not be wipable, so check before you buy, and don't hang them in a place where they will get dirty quickly.

HANGING SHEET CORK

1 Use a plumb line to mark off a guide line for fixing the first length. It should be less than the width of the cork sheet away from the corner.

2 Mark off more lines the width of the cork sheet apart along the wall. You can then apply the adhesive; in this case with a notched spreader.

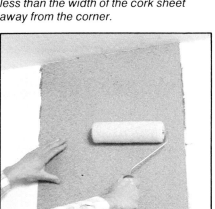

3 Trim the first length to size at the ends and then fix it in place; work down the wall and use a wide roller to help you smooth the cork in place.

4 Fix the next length by applying adhesive and then butting the cork up against the first length. Continue to fix cork lengths along the wall.

5 At a corner, measure the width at several places down the wall. Transfer these measurements to the cork and cut it to fit exactly.

6 Fix the corner length in place. It should have been cut to fit an out of square wall. The other adjacent (cut) corner length butts up to it.

Ready Reference

FINISHING RAW EDGES

If you will get a 'raw' edge down the side where you are fixing tiles to the face of a chimney breast only or where thick, soft types of tiles will meet at an exposed corner, protect the tile edges with a wooden lipping or moulding. For this you:
● attach the lipping (of the same thickness as the tiles) with pins or adhesive down each vertical angle before you start tiling
● tile up to the lipping as if it were an internal angle
● stain the lipping the same colour as the tiles so it will be barely noticeable or coat it with clear varnish to make it more of a feature in the decorative scheme.

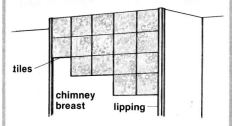

tiles

chimney breast   lipping

TIP: REMOVE EXCESS ADHESIVE

If you inadvertently get adhesive on the front of the cork you may be able to remove it by rubbing with your finger when the adhesive is partly set. If it dries before you notice it, rub it gently with a cloth moistened with white spirit (turps). You may need to reseal or touch up the surface with wax polish when the cork is dry in order to hide the marks.

FIXING CORK SHEET

Cork in sheet form can be fixed in various ways. When you are fixing it, remember that
● with some types you use a special cork adhesive, applied to the wall
● with others you apply a heavy-duty wallpaper adhesive to the back of the cork or to the wall (check with the manufacturer's instructions)
● unlike wallpaper, which you trim after fixing, each length of cork should be cut exactly to fit before you hang it
● the joins between the lengths of cork shouldn't be rolled with a seam roller, as this will simply make the joins more obvious and spoil the overall look.

BARK-TEXTURED CORK

It's a pity to seal a really heavily textured bark cork, as part of its appeal lies in the matt, almost crumbly surface. Another point is that this type of cork should not be hung where it gets constantly knocked or touched, nor used as a noticeboard or pinboard or it will show signs of wear.

LAYING CERAMIC FLOOR TILES

You can lay ceramic tiles to provide a floor surface which is particularly resistant to wear and tear. If you follow a few basic rules you shouldn't find it too difficult a task and you could at the same time turn the floor into a decorative feature.

Ceramic floor tiles provide a floor-covering which is attractive, extremely hard-wearing and easy to maintain and keep clean. The wide variety of tiles available means you should easily find a pattern which suits your colour scheme.

Floor tiles are usually thicker than ceramic wall tiles (they are generally at least 9mm/³⁄₈in thick), very much stronger and have a tough hardwearing surface to withstand knocks as well as wear from the passage of feet.

The backs of the tiles have a brownish appearance caused by the extra firing – done at a higher temperature than for wall tiles, which are often almost white on the back.

Types of tiles
Square tiles are commonest, in sizes from 150 x 150mm (6 x 6in) to 250 x 250mm (10 x 10in). Besides square tiles you can choose oblong ones in several sizes, hexagons or other interlocking shapes. Surfaces are usually glazed but are seldom as shiny as those of wall tiles or scratch marks would inevitably become apparent as grit was trampled in. So most floor tiles are semi-glazed; others have a matt, or unglazed finish.

Patterned ceramic tiles are quite frequently designed in such a way that several tiles can be laid next to one another to complete a larger design. The commonest is built up by laying four identical tiles in a square, each tile being turned at 90° to its neighbours. The full impact will only be achieved if a sufficiently large area of floor is being tiled.

Patterned and plain tiles can also successfully be intermixed to create unusual designs, but it is essential that the tiles are all supplied by the same manufacturer, and ideally come from compatible ranges, to ensure uniformity of thickness and size.

Some manufacturers supply floor tiles designed to co-ordinate with wall tiles, and in addition make matching panels to act as skirtings between wall and floor tiles.

Types of adhesives
There are several types of adhesives for laying floor tiles. Some come ready-mixed, others in powder form to be mixed with water. A number are waterproof and where the floor will be subjected to frequent soakings (as, for example, in a shower cubicle) or heavy condensation you will need to use one which is water-resistant. Usually the adhesive does not become waterproof until it has set completely, which means that you can clean tools with water and do not require a special cleaner.

On a solid floor with underfloor heating you should use an adhesive which is also heat-resistant or the adhesive will fail and the tiles will lift necessitating continual re-fixing.

A cement-based floor tile adhesive is suitable for use on good, level concrete whereas a suspended wooden sub-floor will need an adhesive with some degree of flexibility built in. Combined cement/rubber adhesives are available for this purpose but even these should not be used on suspended wooden floors which are subject to a lot of movement – you will have to add a covering of man-made boards to provide a more stable surface before fixing the tiles.

Manufacturers' instructions give guidance as to the type of adhesive suited to a particular situation and you should study these carefully before making your choice. You should also follow their recommendations as to the thickness of adhesive bed required; most resin-based ready-mixed adhesives are used as thin beds (3 to 6mm/⅛ to ¼in), while cement-based powder adhesives may be laid up to 12mm (½in) thick. Usually a spreader is supplied with the adhesive to make applying it a straightforward job.

Planning
As when tiling a wall, it is well worth planning your layout on paper first, particularly if you intend using a complicated design. For rectangular or square tiles make a scale drawing on graph paper; for hexagons or other specially-shaped tiles, draw the shapes to scale on tracing paper, to act as an overlay to a scale floor plan of the room. From your scale drawings you can see if the layout you have in mind is going to work. It will help you set out an attractive design and it will also enable you to work out the number of tiles you will require.

Mark on your plan the position of fixtures such as a WC, wash or sink stand, cupboards or pipes to indicate where cutting will be required – where necessary adjust your plan so you will not have to cut pieces which are too narrow for convenient cutting.

Similarly, your layout should be designed so you avoid having to cut narrow pieces of tile to

MARKING UP

1 *Choose the corner at which you wish to start tiling, and use a tiling gauge to find out how many whole tiles will fit alongside one wall.*

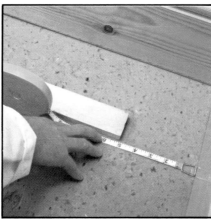

2 *Measure the gap left and halve it to give the width of the cut pieces for each end. Allow one less whole tile in the row to avoid very narrow cut pieces.*

3 *Measure in the width of one cut piece, plus grouting gaps, from the adjacent wall. Mark a line to show where one edge of the first whole tile will be placed.*

4 *Repeat the measuring process along the adjacent wall to establish the position of the other edge of the first whole tile. Mark this line on the floor too.*

5 *Lay a batten on the line drawn in **4** and nail it to the floor alongside the first wall to act as a guide for laying the first complete row of tiles.*

6 *Pin a second batten alongside the other wall, its edge on the line drawn in **3**, and check that the two battens are at right angles to each other.*

Ready Reference

THE RIGHT TILES
Always check that the tiles you buy are suitable for use on floors.
● floor tiles are usually 6mm (¼in) or more thick and have brown backs
● some are flat-backed, others have projecting studs.

TILE SHAPES
Most floor tiles are square or oblong. Common sizes, and the number of each needed to cover 1 sq metre (11 sq ft), are:
● 150 x 150mm (6 x 6in)   : 44
● 200 x 200mm (8 x 8in)   : 25
● 250 x 250mm (10 x 10in) : 16
● 300 x 200mm (12 x 8in)   : 17
Hexagons usually measure 150mm (6in) between opposite edges. You need 50 per sq m (11 sq ft).

ADHESIVES AND GROUT
● use a *thin-bed* (3mm/⅛in) adhesive for *flat-backed tiles* – you'll need about 3.5kg (8lb) per sq metre (11 sq ft)
● use a *thick-bed* (6-12mm/¼-½in) adhesive for *tiles with studs* or if the floor is uneven – you'll need double the above quantities
● allow 1.2kg (2½lb) of *grout* per sq metre (11 sq ft) for joints 6mm (¼in) wide.

TILING SPACING
● space tiles that build up to form a larger pattern about 2mm apart. With plain tiles a wider gap looks better. Use a tile on edge as a spacer

● dry-lay a row of tiles along each wall to see how wide an edge piece you will need at each end of the row.

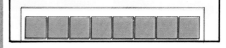

● avoid having to cut thin edge pieces by laying one whole tile less in each row.

TILE GAUGE TO MAKE
Use a straight 1830mm (6ft) long timber batten and mark its length with tile width and grouting space.

TIP: BUYING TILES
Add on a few extra tiles to allow for breakages during laying and replacements in the future.

LAYING TILES

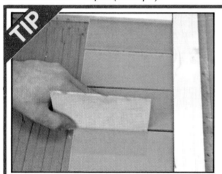

1 In the corner framed by the two battens, spread enough tiling adhesive with a notched spreader to cover an area of about 1 sq m (10 sq ft).

2 Lay the first tile in position in the angle between the two battens, pushing it tightly up against them, and bed it into place with firm hand pressure.

3 Continue laying tiles along the first row, butting them against the batten to keep the edge straight. Use a cardboard spacer to create even gaps.

4 Lay tiles until you have reached the edge of the adhesive, using the spacer as before. Carry on area by area until all whole tiles are laid.

fit around the perimeter of the room. Floor tiles, being so much tougher, are less easy to cut than wall tiles and attempting to obtain narrow strips is likely to cost you several broken tiles.

Where you are not using a complicated design you can plan your layout directly on the floor. For this you will need a tiling gauge (see *Ready Reference*).

Preparing the floor surface

Surfaces to be tiled should be dry, flat, stable, clean and free from grease, dirt and unsound material. A flat, dry, level concrete floor can be tiled without special preparation. If, however, there are small depressions in the concrete these should be filled with a mortar mix of 3 parts sharp sand and 1 part cement. A more uneven floor should be screeded with a proprietary brand of self-levelling flooring compound.

The screed should be left for two weeks to allow it to dry thoroughly before fixing tiles. If the floor is a new concrete one, it should be left for a minimum of four weeks to allow all moisture to disperse before you begin covering it with tiles.

Existing ceramic floor tiles, quarry tiles or terrazzo surfaces can be tiled over. They should be checked to ensure that there are no loose or hollow-sounding areas. Any defective sections must be made good before you lay new tiles on top.

You can tile on suspended wooden floors, but it is important that the floor should be made as rigid and firm as possible. To achieve this, cover the floorboards with a layer of water-resistant resin-bonded plywood at least 12mm (½in) thick. Alternatively, you can use chipboard of the same thickness.

Before laying tiles over timber floors cover the surface thoroughly with a priming coat – either a special priming agent from the adhesive manufacturer, or else diluted PVA building adhesive.

Finding the starting point

The first whole tile you lay will determine where all the other tiles are laid, so it is important that you get this positioning correct. Choose the corner in which you wish to start tiling and, laying your tile gauge parallel to one of the walls, measure how

many whole tiles will fit along that side of the room. There will almost certainly be a gap left over. Measure this gap, and divide the answer by two to find the width of the cut tiles that will fill the gap at each end of the row. (These should be of equal size.)

If these cut tiles turn out to be less than one quarter of a tile-width across (and therefore tricky to cut), reduce the number of whole tiles in the row by one. The effect of this is to increase the width of each cut tile by half a tile – much easier to cut.

Return to the corner and with your tile gauge parallel to the wall along which you have been measuring, move it so the end of the gauge is the width of one cut tile away from the adjacent wall. Mark this position off on the floor – it indicates where one edge of the first whole tile in that row will fall.

Repeat this same measuring process along the adjacent wall to establish the positioning of the row at right angles to the one you've just set out; you will then be able to mark off where the other edge of this same first tile will fall, and so fix its position precisely. Once that is done, every other tile's position is fixed right across the floor.

You can then place this first tile in position. Mark off and cut the boundary tiles between it and the corner. Remember to allow for the width of the grouting gap when measuring each cut tile.

Each cut tile should be measured individually because the wall may not be perfectly straight. You may then go ahead with laying whole tiles, starting from your original corner.

Laying tiles

In the corner area spread adhesive evenly on the floor over an area of about 1 sq m (11 sq ft) – it is important to work on only a small area at a time, otherwise the adhesive may have begun to dry out by the time you reach it. With a gentle, twisting motion, place the first tile in the corner, and use light hand pressure to bed it firmly in the adhesive. Place the second tile alongside the first, using the same gentle pressure, and placing spacers of cardboard or hardboard between the tiles if they don't have spacer lugs. Continue laying tiles, building up a rectangular area, until you have reached the edge of the adhesive bed.

Use a spirit level to check that the tiles are level; if any are too low, lever them off the bed as quickly as possible with a wide-bladed trowel, add adhesive and re-set them, pressing them down gently.

With the first square metre of tiles laid, you can spread another layer of adhesive over a further area, and lay the next area of tiles.

As you lay the tiles, it is worth checking every now and again that adequate contact with the adhesive is being made and that there are no voids beneath the tiles – any gaps or

FITTING BORDER TILES

1 *Mark the width of each border tile in turn, using the spacer to allow for the necessary grouting gap. Kneel on a board so you don't disturb the whole tiles.*

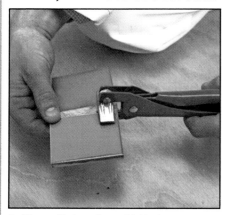

3 *Use a tile breaker with V-shaped jaws to break the tile along the scored line. Floor tiles are usually too thick to break over a straight-edge.*

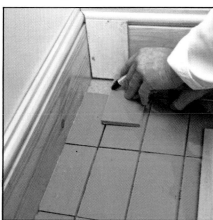

5 *Finally mark and cut the piece of tile to fit in the corner of the room, lay it and leave the newly-tiled floor for 24 hours to allow the adhesive to set.*

2 *Score across the tile surface at the mark with a tile cutter. Press firmly so its tip cuts the glaze cleanly; scoring again may cause a ragged edge.*

4 *Butter adhesive onto the back of the cut piece, and press it into position. Use the spacer to form an even grouting gap at either side of the cut piece.*

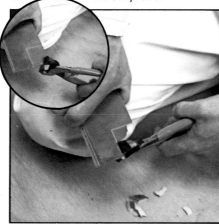

6 *To cut an L-shaped piece of tile, score the surface carefully and nibble away the waste with tile pincers. Work from the corner (inset) in to the score lines.*

Ready Reference

TIP: CUTTING FLOOR TILES

Because of the high-baked clay back, floor tiles can be hard to snap by hand. Save time and breakages by buying a tile cutter with angled jaws, or hire a special floor tile cutter from a tool hire shop.

TIP: ALLOW 48 HOURS SETTING

● don't walk on the floor for at least 48 hours after tiling
● where access is essential, lay plywood or chipboard sheets over the tiles to spread the load
● avoid washing the floor until the grout and adhesive have set completely (1 to 2 weeks).

DON'T FORGET DOORS

Tiling will raise the floor level. Remove inward-opening doors from their hinges before starting tiling or they will not open when tiling reaches the doorway.

● measure the depth of tile plus adhesive laid
● plane the door bottom down by this amount
● fit a sloping hardwood strip across the door threshold

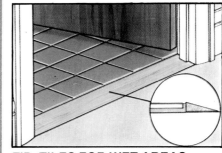

TIP: TILES FOR WET AREAS

Unglazed tiles are less slippery than glazed but ones with a textured surface reduce the chance of accidents in bath and shower rooms.

GROUTING TILES

1 When the adhesive has set, you can grout the joints. Use a sponge or a rubber squeegee to force the grout into all the gaps.

2 Wipe off the excess grout as you work with a damp sponge; if you allow it to set hard it will be very difficult to remove later.

3 Use a piece of thin dowel with a rounded end to smooth off the joints. Don't be tempted to use a finger as grout could irritate your skin.

4 Leave the grout to set for the recommended time, and then polish the surface all over with a clean, dry cloth to remove the last traces of grout.

PREPARING FLOOR

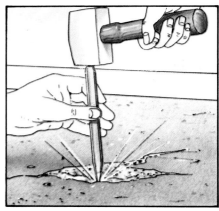

Clean out the small depressions and cracks to be filled with a club hammer and chisel. Beware of flying chippings.

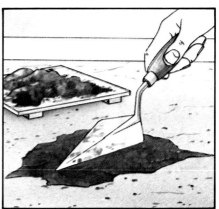

Use a trowel to fill in the depressions with mortar and to level off to provide a suitable surface for the tiles.

---

hollows under the tiles will become weak points later on.

You can proceed with the tiling in 1 sq m sections until all the tiles are in place, then leave them for at least 24 hours. The tiles must not be walked on during this time so that any risk of them being knocked out of place or bedded too deeply is avoided. If you have to walk on the tiles, lay a sheet of plywood or chipboard over them first to spread the load. When 24 hours – or longer; check the manufacturer's instructions – are up, you can remove the spacers. Check with the adhesive manufacturer's instructions to see whether you need to allow extra time after this before you begin grouting.

Cutting tiles

You will have to cut each tile individually since you will almost certainly find variations around the room. Place the tile which is going to be cut against the wall and on top of the adjacent whole tile. Mark it off for cutting.

Using a straight edge as a guide, score the tile surface and edges with a scribing tool. You *can* use a hand tile cutter to cut and break the

tile along the scoreline; but its probably worthwhile hiring a special floor tile cutter to make the job easier.

To cut a tile to give an L-shape you will need to use tile nips to nibble away at the waste area. You can use a tile file, carborundum stone or coarse glasspaper to smooth off the rough edge. For curved shapes (eg, to fit round a WC pedestal), you will need to make a template and again use tile nips to nibble away at the tile.

Grouting the tiles

Mix the grout according to the manufacturer's instructions; make up only a small amount at a time and, as with adhesive, work in areas of 1 sq metre (11 sq ft). Apply it with the straight edge of a rubber float, or a sponge or squeegee, making sure the joints are properly filled. Pack the grout firmly into the joints and smooth off using a small rounded stick – don't try using a finger as the grout is likely to irritate your skin.

It's best to remove excess grout (and adhesive) as soon as possible. If it sets it will be difficult to remove.

Filling cracks and hollows

If you have a concrete floor which is flat, dry and level you can go ahead and lay tiles without further preparation. Often, however, the floor is not level or there are cracks and small hollows on the surface. Indentations should be filled with mortar (a 3:1 sand:cement mix is suitable) mixed to a creamy but not too runny consistency. For mortar with a good bond add some PVA bonding solution to the mix. Cut back the holes to a clean shape and brush out any loose material so it doesn't mix in with the mortar making it difficult to get a smooth surface. You can also coat the holes with a PVA bonding solution to help the mortar adhere.

SURFACES FOR TILING

1

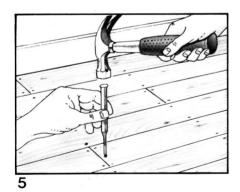

3

2

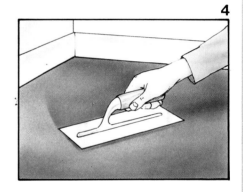

4

5

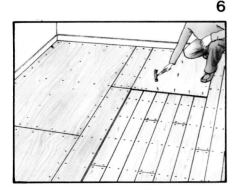

6

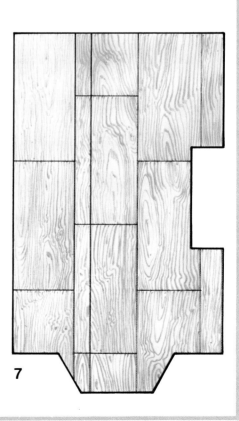

7

Levelling a concrete floor

A concrete floor which is out of true can be levelled using a self-levelling flooring compound so it is suitable for tiling. For the compound to form a smooth, even surface it should only be applied to a floor which is clean and free from dust, oil, grit or grease so you should first sweep the floor and then scrub it thoroughly (1). You may find you have to use a proprietary cleaner to remove stubborn greasy patches. The compound comes in powder form and you will have to mix it up according to the manufacturer's instructions so it forms a runny paste (2).

If you try covering the entire floor in one operation, it's likely the compound will set into large pools which are difficult to join up. It's better to work in small areas; you can delineate your working area by forming a bay using timber battens. Pour the compound onto the floor (3) and then spread it out as evenly as possible using a steel float (4), any marks from the float will disappear quickly. The compound will set within a couple of hours. If you want extra thickness you can apply a second coat once the first is hard.

Laying plywood over a timber floor

A floor which is subject to movement will disrupt tiles laid over it so if you intend tiling over a suspended wooden floor you will first have to make the surface as firm as possible by covering it with a layer of man-made boards. Water-resistant resin-bonded plywood is a suitable material as it will resist penetration by the damp adhesive you will be spreading over it and you will avoid the problem of rotting boards. The boards should be at least 12mm (½in) thick. To prepare the floor to take the plywood you should punch any protruding nails below the surface (5) at the same time checking that the floorboards are firmly secured. You can then go ahead and fix the sheets of plywood to the floor (6) using nails spaced at 225mm (9in) intervals across the middle of the sheets and at 150mm (6in) intervals round their perimeter. You will have to cut the boards to shape round any recess or alcove (7), and where there is a pipe run, fix narrow strips of plywood over the pipes to make access to them easier. Make sure you stagger the joints; this will prevent any floor movement causing the tiles to break up in a run across the floor.

LAYING CORK TILES

Cork tiles will provide you with a floor surface which is warm, wears well and is quiet to walk on. In addition, they are the easiest of tiles to lay.

You can use cork floor tiles in bathrooms, kitchens, dining rooms and children's rooms; anywhere, in fact, where any other resilient floorcovering (eg, vinyl sheet or tiles, or thermoplastic tiles) could be used. They are warmer and quieter than most other floorcoverings and tend not to 'draw the feet', unlike, for example, ceramic tiles, which are very tiring if you have to stand round on them for long periods. They will look particularly elegant if they are softened with rugs or rush matting and blend equally well with modern or traditional style furniture and décor.

Ordinary cork tiles are made from granulated cork, compressed and baked into blocks; the natural resins in the grain bond the particles together, though sometimes synthetic resins are added to improve wearing and other qualities. The tiles are cut from these blocks so they are 5mm (1/4in) or more thick. 'Patterned' cork tiles (see below) are made by alternating wafer-thin cork veneers with thicker layers of insulating cork and sealing with a protective PVC surface.

Types of tiles

Cork tiles have an attractive natural look; usually they are a rich honey-gold, although there are some darker browns and smoky tones. Dyed cork tiles are available in many different colours ranging from subtle shades to strident primary colours. There are also 'patterned' tiles which have an interesting textured, rather than a heavily patterned look; these come in natural colours as well as red, soft green and rich dark smoky brown: the colour tends to 'glow' through the top surface of cork. One design gives a subtle miniature checkerboard effect. Other tiles come with designs (such as geometric patterns) imprinted on them.

For floors that are likely to get the occasional flood or where spills and 'accidents' are inevitable, such as in kitchens, bathrooms and children's rooms, it is wiser to use pre-sealed types of tiles (see *Ready Reference*). The cheaper seal-it-yourself types are, however, perfectly adequate for living rooms, bedsitting rooms and halls.

Preparing the surface

As with other types of tiles and resilient floor-coverings the subfloor surface on which you lay cork tiles must be smooth, clean and free from lumps, bumps, protruding nails, tacks or screws. Where floorboards are uneven, it's best to cover them up with flooring-grade chipboard, plywood or flooring quality hardboard, either nailed or screwed down securely. Remember to stagger the sheets of chipboard or other material to avoid continuous joins. Then, if there is any floor movement it will not disturb the tiles fixed on top and cause them to lift or be moved out of alignment.

There must also be adequate ventilation underneath a wooden subfloor. Poor ventilation can cause condensation which could lead to the rotting of the floorboards and the floorcovering above them. If the floor is laid at ground level, or directly to joists or battens on ground level concrete, you should protect the cork from moisture penetration by covering the timber with bituminous felt paper before laying hardboard or plywood. The paper should be fixed with bituminous adhesive; and you should allow a 50mm (2in) overlap at joins and edges.

Solid subfloors, such as concrete or cement and sand screeds, should be thoroughly dry. Make sure the floor incorporates an effective damp-proof membrane before laying the tiles: this can

ESTABLISHING THE STARTING POINT

1 *Find the centre points of two opposite walls. Stretch a string line between them, chalk it and snap a line across the floor.*

2 *Repeat the procedure, but this time between the other two walls. Where the two lines intersect is the exact centre of the floor.*

3 *Dry-lay a row of tiles along the longest line from the centre point to one wall. Adjust the other line if necessary (see Ready Reference).*

4 *Lay a row of tiles along the other line from the centre point and again adjust to avoid wastage or very narrow strips at the edges.*

be in polythene sheet form, a cold-poured bitumen solution, or a hot pitch or bitumen solution. If the subfloor is porous or flaky and tends to be very dusty, you can use a latex floor-levelling compound to cover it. This is also practical for very uneven floors. The solution is poured on, left to find its own level and then allowed to dry out before the final floorcovering is laid.

Other floors, such as quarry or ceramic tiles, can have cork laid on top, but they have to be degreased, dewaxed and keyed by rubbing them with wire wool; once again, a floor-levelling compound may be necessary. With flagstones laid directly on the ground there could be damp or condensation problems; it may be best to take up the existing floor and re-lay it, probably a job for a professional to do. Alternatively, the floor could be covered with a layer of rock asphalt at least 16mm (⅝in) thick but you will need to call in

professional help for this. (Always seek expert advice if you are worried about the state of the subfloor; the expense incurred will be worth it to get successful results when you are laying the final floorcovering.)

If there is already a linoleum, vinyl sheet, tile or other resilient floorcovering on the floor, you are advised to take this up, then resurface or rescreed it if necessary; alternatively, use a floor-levelling damp-resistant latex powder mix, or an epoxy surface membrane. If it is not possible to remove the old floorcovering, you should use a proprietary floor cleaner to degrease and dewax it and then key the surface by rubbing over it with wire wool.

Planning
Measure the room, at floor level, using a steel tape or wooden measure; don't use a cloth tape as these stretch in use. If the room

is irregularly shaped, divide it into rectangles and measure each one separately. If you take these measurements to your supplier, he should be able to help you calculate the quantity of tiles you will require. Or, as many tiles are sold ready-boxed with a guide to quantities printed on the box, you can study the guide to work out the number of tiles you'll need.

If you plan to buy tiles of contrasting colours, and to form a border pattern, or to lay them so you get a checkerboard effect, you should plan out the design on squared paper first. Divide up the floor area so each square represents a tile, and colour the squares in different colours to represent the different colours of the tiles so you can judge the effect. You can then calculate the quantity needed by reference to your plan.

Laying tiles
Whichever type of tile you are laying, it is best to work at room temperature, so don't switch off the central heating. Leave the tiles in the room overnight to condition them.

Make sure you have enough tiles and adhesive on the spot; you don't want to have to stop work halfway through the job and go out and buy extra. Collect together the necessary tools: measure, chalk and string, pencils and ruler or straight edge, notched trowel or spreader, sharp knife, cloth and white spirit. If you are using the seal-later type of tile you will need a sander and brush or roller plus sealer.

As with other types of tiles, cork tiles look best if they are centred on the middle of the room and any narrow or awkwardly shaped tiles come at the edges. So you'll have to establish your starting point (see *Ready Reference*) at the centre of the room. You can then begin laying whole tiles, working from the centre outwards. It's best to work on a quarter of the floor at a time; when all four quarters of whole tiles are laid, you can cut and fix the border tiles. If you are using adhesive, you may have to spread only about one square metre (1 square yard) at a time before it is ready to take the tiles. In other cases it will be best to cover a larger area with adhesive, so you don't have to wait too long to bed the tiles, increasing the length of time it will take to complete the job. Since the length of time needed before the adhesive is ready to take the tiles does vary depending on the type of adhesive, you should follow the manufacturer's instructions.

If tiles have to be cut to fit round obstacles such as door architraves, WC bases, or wash stands you can use a scribing block to mark the outline you require. Make up a paper template or use a special tracing tool (which has little needles which retract to fit the shape) if the shape is particularly complicated.

Ready Reference

MARKING OUT

For a balanced look, aim to cut your edge tiles to equal size on both sides of the room. To do this, establish the centre point of the floor, using chalked string lines (see step-by-step photographs, page 582):
● if, when you've dry-laid a row of tiles from the centre point out to the wall, a gap remains of more than half a tile-width at the wall end (A), adjust your chalked line half a tile-width off-centre (B); this will save undue wastage later when you are cutting the perimeter tiles.

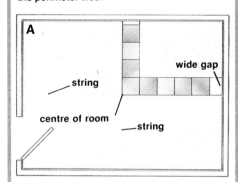

A

string

centre of room

string

wide gap

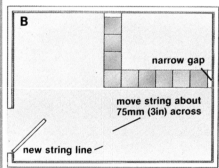

B

narrow gap

move string about 75mm (3in) across

new string line

● if, however, by moving the chalked line you are left with very narrow perimeter strips (less than 75mm/3in wide) leave the centre of the floor as your starting point; there will be wastage but narrow cut perimeter tiles won't look very good and should be avoided if possible
● when marking out, avoid narrow strips at door thresholds where they will be subjected to a lot of wear
● adjust your starting point so you don't end up with narrow strips round a feature of the room, such as a chimney breast.

CHECK UNSEALED TILES

Be sure to lay unsealed tiles the right way up. They have a smooth top surface and a bottom surface which is rougher to provide a key for the adhesive. You can judge which surface is which by running your fingers over the tile.

LAYING WHOLE TILES

1 *Use a notched spreader to apply adhesive to a quarter of the floor area, using the marked lines as a guide to the area to be covered.*

2 *Place the first whole tile in the centre right angle which has been coated with adhesive. Check that it aligns with the guidelines.*

3 *Lay a row of tiles following the guidelines, treading each tile down gently but firmly to make sure it is securely bedded.*

4 *Work across the floor until that quarter is covered with whole tiles. Then lay tiles on the other quarters of the floor area.*

For some awkard shapes (eg, fitting tiles round an L-shape or in an alcove) you can mark out the pieces to be cut by placing a whole tile or tile offcut up against the skirting and the tiles which are already in place and draw the required shape on it. Cork tiles are very simple to cut: all you need is a sharp knife and a straight edge to guide it; there is no risk of breakages as there may be with other tiles which are more difficult to cut, such as ceramic types.

Sealing tiles

If your tiles are the seal-after-laying type, you will have to sand the floor carefully, using a powered sander, to ensure the surface and joins are smooth. Dust carefully; you can wipe the tiles with a slightly damp cloth to remove excess dust but take care not to saturate the tiles. Leave them to dry and then seal them, using a brush or roller to apply the sealer.

If you attach your applicator to a long handle, you can avoid bending or crawling on all fours; work from the furthermost corner, backwards to the door. Leave each coat to dry thoroughly, before applying the next one. There will always be more than one coat of sealer but the exact number will depend on the type of wear to which the floor will be subjected (see *Ready Reference*).

Ideally, you should leave the sealer to dry for a few days before you walk on the floor, but if you have to use the room, seal half the room at a time. Cover the unsealed part with brown paper so it can be walked on without damaging or marking the cork. When the sealed part is completely dry, you can seal the other half.

Don't wash a new cork floor for at least 48 hours after laying and sealing; ideally it should be left for at least five days. It's worth

LAYING BORDER TILES

1 *To cut border tiles accurately to size, place the whole tile to be cut exactly on top of the last whole tile in a particular row.*

2 *Place a second tile over it, this time butting it up against the skirting. Use its edge as a guide to scribe a line on the first tile.*

3 *Remove the tile to be cut and make a deeper mark. The tile should then break through cleanly when gentle pressure is applied.*

4 *Place the cut border tile in position against the skirting. You may need to apply extra adhesive to its back to ensure secure fixing.*

TILING AN L-SHAPE

1 *As when cutting other border tiles, use a tile as a guide to scribe the outline of one side of the L onto the tile to be cut.*

2 *Move the tile to be cut and the guide tile to the other side of the L and use the same method to scribe its outline for cutting.*

3 *Remove the loose tiles, cut through the back of the tile along the scribed lines and then fix the tile in position so it aligns with the whole tiles.*

putting up with grubby marks for a few days rather than running the risk of moisture penetrating the flooring and reducing its useful life.

Care and maintenance

Once pre-sealed tiles are laid, or the unsealed type has been properly sealed, it will probably be unnecessary to do more than wipe over the floor with a damp mop or cloth to keep it clean. To remove grease or dirt, add a few drops of liquid detergent to the washing water; wipe over again with a cloth rinsed in clean water to remove any traces of detergent. If there are some particularly stubborn marks, made, for instance, by rubber-soled shoes, or paint or varnish spots, you should be able to remove them by rubbing gently with a little white spirit on a damp cloth.

An important point to remember when you are cleaning your cork floor is that you must take care not to overdampen the floor or the tiles may lift. Also, never use strong abrasive cleaners as these can damage the PVC wear layer.

If you like a fairly glossy surface or are worried about scratches on the floor, you can use an emulsion wax polish on top of the sealed tiles. However, never use a wax floor polish as the surface could become too slippery.

Sometimes a tile can become damaged. If the area which needs repair is small (a cigarette burn hole, for instance) you can fill it with shavings from a cork out of a bottle and reseal the tile. For more extensive damage, you should remove the tile carefully and replace it with a spare one; reseal if this tile is an unsealed type with the number of coats of sealer required to give it adequate protection.

Ready Reference

TIP: STORE TILES FLAT

If you take tiles out of their box, weight them down to keep them flat when you are storing them.

FIXING TILES

Fixing methods and adhesives vary. Some adhesives should be applied to both the back of the tiles and floor, others to the floor only; follow the manufacturer's instructions. Remember:
● pre-sealed tiles are always fixed with adhesive
● unsealed tiles are often fixed by driving in 5 headless pins, one at each corner and one in the centre, a technique which may be combined with adhesive (the pin holes can be filled, if necessary, and will then be covered up by the sealer).

REMOVE EXCESS ADHESIVE

As you lay the tiles, wipe off any adhesive from the front of the tiles with a soft cloth which has been dipped in white spirit.

CUTTING ROUND PIPES

To cut a tile so it fits round a pipe, make a cardboard template of the shape required and trace the shape onto the tile. Then cut a slit from the hole made for the pipe to the skirting board; this line will be almost invisible when the tile is fixed in place.

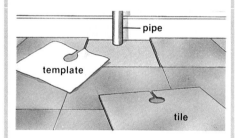

SEAL TILES PROPERLY

Cork is porous and fairly absorbent, so proper sealing is essential; if the tiles get wet, they swell and lift and have to be trimmed and re-stuck. For unsealed tiles, several coats of sealer will be necessary for real protection:
● in areas of ordinary wear, apply two or three coats of sealer
● in heavy wear areas you will need to apply 4 or 5 coats.

TRIM DOORS

To allow doors to open freely after the cork floor has been laid you may have to trim along the bottom of the door to give adequate clearance.

LAYING TILES IN AN ALCOVE

1 Place a tile over the fixed tiles with its corner butting up against the skirting and make a mark on the 'wrong' side at the correct distance.

2 Repeat this procedure, this time to make a mark on the adjacent edge. Transfer the marks to the front of the tile and draw a line between them.

3 Cut along the drawn line to give the required shape and then place the cut tile in position so it aligns properly with the whole tiles.

4 Use the same techniques to cut the next tile. If there is a pipe against the wall, butt the tile up to it and mark where it's to be cut.

5 Cut the triangular-shaped piece required to fill the gap between the two larger shaped pieces and fix this in position so that it butts right up against the skirting.

6 To complete the job, cut the corner piece to shape and fix it in place. For economy, you can cut these smaller shaped pieces from any tiled offcuts which you may have available.

LAYING SHEET VINYL

Vinyl provides a tough, easy-to-clean floor surface which is ideal in kitchens, bathrooms and other areas of the house where floors are likely to be subjected to heavy wear or spillages. It's also straightforward to lay.

Vinyl flooring was developed in the 1960s and revolutionised the smooth (and resilient) flooring market. At first it was a thin and rather unyielding material. But it was something which could be laid fairly easily by the DIY enthusiast; and this was a breakthrough because its predecessor, linoleum, had had to be professionally laid. Since then, vinyl flooring has been greatly improved and there are now several different types available.

Types of vinyl

The cheapest type of vinyl is known as a 'flexible print' and has a clear wear layer on top, with the printed pattern sandwiched between this and the backing. Then there are the cushioned vinyls, which are more bouncy underfoot and have a soft inner bubbly layer between the wear layer and the backing. They are often embossed to give them a texture, which is particularly successful when the embossing enhances the design, as with simulated cork or ceramic tile patterns. Finally, the most expensive type is solid flexible vinyl, made by suspending coloured vinyl chips in transparent vinyl to create colour and design which goes right through the material and consequently wears longer.

All three types come in a wide variety of colours and designs ranging from geometric and floral patterns to simulated cork, wood block, parquet, ceramic tiles, slate and brick. Some ranges include special glossy no-polish surfaces. Also, there is a special 'lay-flat' type which does not have to be stuck down, except on very heavy wear areas or at doorways. Some vinyls can be folded without cracking, but as with carpets, a good guide to durability is price: the more expensive the flooring, the longer-lasting it is likely to be.

Buying vinyl

To work out the amount of vinyl you'll need, measure up the floor using a metal tape; note down the measurements and then double-check them. Draw a scale plan of the room on squared paper, marking in all the obstacles, door openings and so on.

Take the measurements and plan to your supplier, who will help you to work out quantities. Remember to allow for walls which are not quite true and for trimming the overlap (see *Ready Reference*).

Whatever the type, vinyl is available in standard sheet widths (see *Ready Reference* again). Choose one in a wide width for use on a floor where you do not want to have a seam. (A wide sheet can be difficult to lay so make sure you have someone to help you – If you are going to lay sheets of a narrower width which will have to be joined, remember to allow for pattern matching when buying.

Check the manufacturer's instructions for fixing and order the correct adhesive and other sundries. Make sure you get the right amount; there is nothing worse than running out of adhesive halfway through the job.

A roll of vinyl is usually 30 to 40m (100 to 130ft) long and the retailer will cut off the length you want, re-rolling it for you. Take the roll of vinyl home and leave it, loosely rolled, in the room where it is to be laid for about 48 hours. This will allow it to become acclimatised and it should then be easier to lay. Do not stand it on edge as this can crack the material and take care not to damage the ends when you are transporting or storing the roll.

Preparing the sub-floor

Vinyl must be laid on a sound, reasonably smooth and even sub-floor if the best results

Ready Reference

SHEET SIZES
Sheet vinyl usually comes in three different widths: 2m (6ft 6in), 3m (9ft 9in) and 4m (13ft).

SUITABLE SURFACES
Vinyl can be laid over concrete, wood or tiles. Don't attempt to lay it over old vinyl, linoleum or cork; these should be removed or covered with hardboard.

PREPARING A WOOD FLOOR
To prepare a bumpy wood floor for laying vinyl, cover it with large sheets of flooring-grade chipboard or hardboard. Stagger the joints between sheets.

If you are using hardboard, place the shiny side down as the rough side provides a better grip for the vinyl.

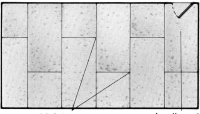

staggered joints   hardboard

LAYING HARDBOARD SHEETS

1 Fix sheets of hardboard, rough side up, by nailing them to the old floor surface. The nails should be spaced about 100-150mm apart.

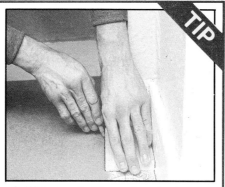

2 Where part of the wall protrudes, use a scribing block to provide a guide when marking off the contour of the wall on the hardboard.

3 Cut along the line you have marked on the hardboard, using a sharp knife and a straight edge to guide the knife.

FITTING AND FIXING VINYL

1 Lay the flooring out fully across the room; with a large width such as this you will probably need help to get it roughly into position.

2 Make diagonal cuts at each corner, taking care not to cut too deep, to make accurate positioning much easier.

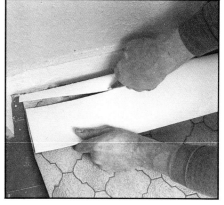

3 With the vinyl in position, use a sharp knife to trim off the excess, starting at the longest straight wall. Remember to allow an overlap.

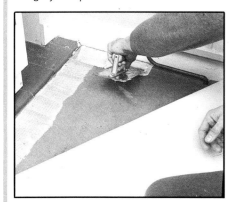

5 With the excess trimmed away from the longest straight wall and the adjacent wall, pull back the vinyl and spread adhesive on the floor.

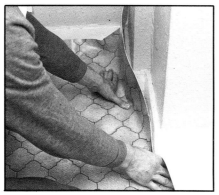

6 Push the vinyl down onto the adhesive making sure it is firmly stuck down. Smooth out the surface as you go so there are no air bubbles.

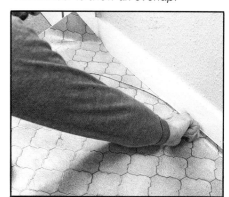

7 Trim off the overlap on the edges where the vinyl has been stuck down. Continue fitting, fixing and trimming round the rest of the room.

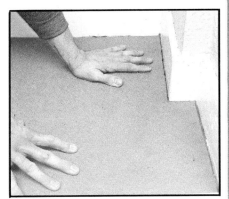

4 *After you have cut out the required shape, push the hardboard into place, making sure it butts up against the bottom edge of the skirting.*

4 *At a doorway, cut into the corners (see* Ready Reference) *and again trim off the excess, allowing for an overlap for later, final trimming.*

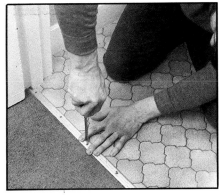

8 *At the entrance to a room, fasten down the fixed vinyl with a threshold strip to cover the join between the vinyl and the carpet.*

are to be achieved and the flooring is to give adequate wear. The floor must also be free from dirt, polish, nibs of plaster or splashes of paint, but above all it must be damp proof, so deal with this first.

In an old property with no damp-proof course (dpc), it may be necessary to install one or to have some other form of damp-proofing carried out. The floor may have to be rescreeded or old floorboards taken up and replaced. But whatever is needed must be done before laying the new flooring. A cover-up job will never be satisfactory and the new material will start to perish from the back.

Remember that screeding a floor will raise its level and so doors will almost certainly have to be taken off their hinges and trimmed at the bottom to accommodate the new floor level.

Where the existing floor covering does not provide a suitable surface for laying vinyl you will have to remove it. You can remove old vinyl by stripping it off from the backing, then soaking any remaining material in cold water, washing-up liquid and household ammonia before scraping it off with a paint scraper.

With a wooden sub-floor you should remove any protruding tacks, nails or screws, or punch them down level with the floor. Any rough or protruding boards should be planed smooth and wide gaps between boards filled with fillets of wood; small holes or gaps can be filled with plastic wood. If the floor is very bumpy it can be covered with man-made boards.

Fitting seamed lengths

Measure for the first length of vinyl along the longest unobstructed wall unless this brings a seam into the wrong position (see *Ready Reference*). After measuring you can cut the first length from the roll. Butt the edge of the vinyl right up to the skirting at one end of the room, tucking the overlap underneath the skirting if possible so you don't have to trim this edge. Then cut the material off across the width, allowing for an overlap at the other end, at doorways and obstacles.

To fit the first doorway you will have to cut slits at the door jambs and then ease the vinyl round the door recess and supports, cutting off a little at a time, until you get a perfect fit. Next, either tuck the overlap of the vinyl under the skirting which runs along the length of the room if you can, or trim along the wall or skirting, allowing for a good (but not too tight) fit. Smooth down the flooring as you work along its length and then cut the vinyl to fit at the other end.

If the wall is uneven you will have to 'scribe' its contour onto the vinyl. You pull the vinyl slightly away from the wall and then run a wooden block, in conjunction with a pencil,

PROVIDING A FOIL LINING

It may be necessary to cover a preserved timber or bitumen-protected floor with a non-porous foil lining paper before laying vinyl on top.

WARNING: ASBESTOS DUST

Don't attempt to remove old vinyl or thermoplastic by sanding or grinding. Asbestos fibres contained in the material may be released into the air.

STORING VINYL

Don't stand the roll of vinyl on end when you're storing it or you run the risk of spoiling its appearance as it will be liable to distort or crack.

WHERE TO SEAM

If you are going to join vinyl, avoid having seams in doorways or heavy traffic areas:
● seams on wood floors should run across the boards
● seams over chipboard or hardboard should be no closer than 150mm (6in) to the joints in the board sheets.

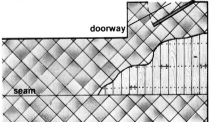

OVERLAP ALLOWANCE

When fitting vinyl allow for a 50-75mm (2-3in) overlap all round for trimming.

ADJUSTMENT PERIOD

Leave flooring laid out for 1 hour before fitting and trimming to allow it to adjust to room temperatures.

DEALING WITH UNEVEN WALLS

Where the wall is not perfectly straight you will have to use a technique known as 'scribing' to transfer the contour of the wall or skirting to the vinyl. For this you will need a small block of wood (about 75-100mm/3-4in) wide, called a 'scribing block' and a pencil.

LAYING VINYL IN A RECESS

1 *With the vinyl fixed in place at the straightest edges of the room, deal with awkward areas like a recess. First trim at the corners.*

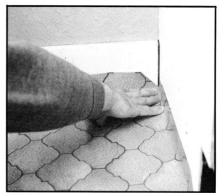

2 *Turn back the vinyl and spread a band of adhesive round the edges of the recess. You can then push the floorcovering firmly into position.*

3 *To complete the job, use a sharp knife to trim off the overlap. Again, make sure there are no bubbles by smoothing the vinyl down.*

along the wall so its profile is marked on the vinyl. To cut along this line you can use a knife and straight edge (with the straight edge on the vinyl which will be used), or if the line is very wobbly, use scissors.

With the first length fitted, you can then place the next length of vinyl parallel to the first, matching the pattern exactly, and cut off the required length, again allowing for extra overlap at the ends and sides. Some people cut all the required lengths first before fitting, but if the room is not perfectly square and several widths are being used, there could be a mismatch.

If the two sheets overlap, the excess will have to be trimmed away. Place one on top of the other, aligning the design carefully, and cut through the two sheets together at the overlap, using a knife and straight edge. Remove the trimmings and then adjust the second sheet to fit doors, skirtings and so on, trimming where necessary.

Where there are more than two sheets, repeat the fitting procedure, making sure the pattern matches.

If you are renewing the skirting, to get a perfect fit you can fit the material first and put the skirting on after the vinyl is laid. Remember, though, that this may make it difficult to take up the floorcovering when you need (or want) to change it.

Fitting extra-wide flooring
The technique is largely the same as for fitting strips of vinyl except there will not be any seams to stick, or pattern matching to do. You should start by laying the flooring out fully – you will probably need help for this – and try to find a long straight wall against which the first edge can be laid. Then make diagonal cuts at each corner to allow the flooring to be positioned roughly, with the

excess material 'climbing up' the skirting board or wall. Trim away the excess, leaving a 50 to 75mm (2 to 3in) overlap all round. Scribe the first wall, if necessary, then trim and ease the flooring back into its exact position. Deal with corners, projections, and obstacles as you work your way round the room, leaving the same overlap; finally trim to a perfect fit.

Fixing vinyl
How you fix vinyl will depend on the type; always follow the manufacturer's instructions. As vinyl can shrink it's wise to stick it down immediately before or after trimming it. To stick the edges you should first turn them back and apply a 75mm (3in) wide band of adhesive to the sub-floor, using a serrated scraper in a criss-cross motion, and then press the vinyl into position immediately. This will usually be at doorways, round the edges of the room, or round obstacles. Where heavy equipment will be pulled across the floor regularly (a washing machine for example) it is worth sticking down the entire area.

At the seams, you should make the width of the spread adhesive generous – 150 to 200mm (6 to 8in). Again, turn back the edges, apply the band of adhesive to the sub-floor and press the vinyl back into position immediately. Wipe away any adhesive which seeps through the seam or round the edges of the vinyl immediately, as this can discolour the flooring if it hardens.

At the entrance to rooms, particularly in heavy traffic areas, or if you have used the 'lay-flat' type of vinyl, you can fasten down the vinyl with a ready-made threshold strip. These come in metal, wood or plastic and are also used to cover joins between two different materials, such as vinyl and carpet.

Cleaning and maintenance
Once you have laid your floor you will need to look after it. Always wipe up any spills immediately, particularly hot fat and grease. It is also wise to protect the surface from indentation by putting heavy pieces of furniture on a piece of hardboard, or standing legs and castors in castor cups.

Some of the more expensive vinyls have a built-in gloss, so they do not need polishing. This type can be mopped with a damp cloth.

Never use a harsh abrasive cleaner on any type of vinyl floor as this could damage the surface layer. The glossy surface should not wear away, but if it does become dull in heavy traffic areas, it can be recoated with a special paint-on liquid provided by the manufacturer.

The less glossy vinyls will need regular sweeping or vacuuming and mopping. It also makes sense to use a clear acrylic polish, applied very sparingly according to the manufacturer's instructions and then buffed gently. Wash occasionally with warm water and a mild liquid detergent, and don't apply lots of coats of polish, or you will get a thick discoloured build-up, which spoils the look of the floor; 2-4 coats over a 12-month period is plenty. Always let the floor dry thoroughly before walking on it, after it has been washed or polished.

Once several coats of polish have built up, you will have to strip off the polish and start again. To do this, add a cupful of household ammonia to a bucket of cold water, to which a little washing-up liquid has been added. Scrub the floor with this, taking care not to saturate it too much. When the old surface begins to break down, wipe it with an old soft cloth, rinse thoroughly with warm, clean water and dry before applying a new protective coating.

CUTTING ROUND OBSTACLES

The best way to get a neat floor when fitting vinyl round obstacles such as bathroom fittings is to make a template of paper or cardboard which is slightly larger (by about 25mm/1in) than the obstacle. Place one sheet of paper up against the basin pedestal, WC base or whatever, and tear it round so you have half the obstacle's shape on it. Then repeat the procedure with another sheet of paper for the other half.

Fit the template round the obstacle and use a scribing block and pencil to give the exact profile. Then lay the pattern over the flooring and use the block and pencil to reverse the procedure and transfer the exact outline onto the vinyl by running it round the inside of the line. You can then cut and fit; you will have to make a slit in the edge of the vinyl in some cases to get a snug fit at the skirting. Carefully trim away any excess material round the obstacle once the flooring is placed in position. Fix the vinyl according to the manufacturers' instructions.

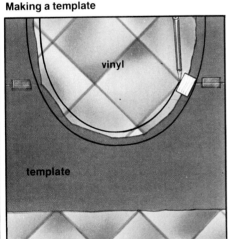

Making a template

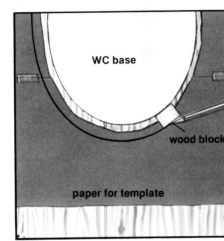

Scribing the contour onto the template

Scribing the contour onto the vinyl

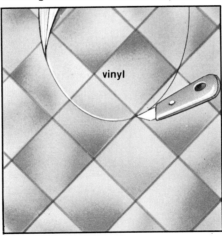

Cutting the vinyl

Ready Reference

FITTING CORNERS

To fit vinyl:
● at internal corners, gently push the vinyl into the corner and cut away the excess, diagonally across the corner, until it fits. Cut a little at a time and pare the edge carefully
● at external corners, press the vinyl into the corner, pull up the excess and cut to allow the vinyl to fall into place round the corner; then trim the excess.

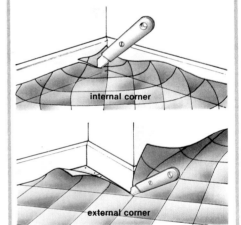

FIXING METHODS

Sheet vinyl can be fixed either by sticking it down all over or only at the edges and seams. Check the manufacturer's instructions.

'Lay-flat' vinyls do not have to be stuck down but they must be firmly fixed at doorways by glueing, or another method. Double-sided tape may be used to secure seams.

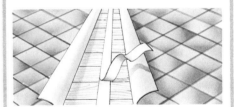

TIP: SMOOTH OUT BUMPS

If there are any bumps in the vinyl after you have laid it fill a pillowcase with sand and drag this round the floor to iron them out.

TIP: HIDING GAPS

If you have an unsightly gap between the skirting and the floor, because the walls are very uneven or your vinyl has shrunk, you can pin painted quadrant beading to the skirting round the room to hide the gap.

If you wipe up spills at once you should not get any stains on vinyl flooring, but sometimes they become marked from tar or grit trodden into the house; some types of shoe can leave black scuff marks, and cigarette burns are not unknown.

If normal cleaning doesn't remove marks rub them very gently with a very fine grade wire wool, used dry. Take care not to rub too much of the surface layer away. Wipe with a damp cloth, and reseal/polish the area if necessary. Some grease marks can be removed with white vinegar, others with petrol or lighter fuel. Always, however, wipe the area immediately with clean water.

Any badly discoloured or damaged area may have to be patched, so save any offcuts of sufficient size for this purpose.

LAYING VINYL FLOOR TILES

Vinyl tiles are supple, easy to handle and don't take much time to lay. They come in many colours and designs so you should have no trouble finding tiles of the type you want.

Vinyl tiles are ideal for use on kitchen and bathroom floors because they are water-proof and resistant to oil, grease and most domestic chemicals. They have the advantage over vinyl sheet flooring in that they are easier to handle, and also, if you make any mistakes when cutting, they will be confined to individual tiles. So if you have a room where you will have to carry out quite a lot of intricate cutting to make the floorcovering fit round obstacles or awkwardly shaped areas, it would be well worth considering laying tiles rather than sheet material.

The tiles come in a wide variety of patterns and colours, with a smooth gloss finish or a range of sculptured and embossed designs. They can be bought with or without a cushioned backing. Cushioned tiles are softer and warmer underfoot, but more expensive than uncushioned tiles. However, even among tiles without a cushioned backing there is a wide variation in price. The cost of a tile is usually a fair indication of its quality, so, in general, the dearer the tile the longer it will last. However you don't need to be greatly concerned about this: even the cheapest tiles can have a life of twenty years in average domestic use, and long before then you will probably wish to remove or cover up the tiles. (On average floorcoverings are changed every seven years.) So your choice of tiles will probably be based simply on the fact that you like the colour or pattern and feel it will fit in well with the rest of the decorative scheme in the room.

Preparing the surface

The floor surface on which you intend to lay vinyl tiles should be free of dust and dirt, so you should go over it first of all with a vacuum cleaner. Then check that the subfloor is in sound condition.

If it is a timber floor you will have to repair any damaged boards, and if the floor has been treated in whole or in part with stains and polishes these will stop the tile adhesive from adhering properly, and will have to be removed with a proprietary floor cleaner. There may be gaps between the boards and they could possibly be warped and curling at the edges. You can cure these faults by

lining the floor with hardboard without adding much to the cost of the job or the time it takes to do it. First inspect the floor; punch home any protruding nails and countersink any screws. Replace missing nails. Where a board squeaks because it is loose, screws will hold it in place more securely than nails.

Hardboard sheets 1220mm (4ft) square will be a manageable size for this type of work. To condition them, brush water at the rate of 1/2 litre (2/3 pint) per 1220mm (4ft) square sheet onto the reverse side of the sheets. Then leave them for 48 hours stacked flat back to back in the room where they will be laid so they will become accustomed to its conditions. When fixed they will dry out further and tighten up to present a perfectly flat subfloor.

You can begin fixing the hardboard in one corner of the room. It's not necessary to scribe it to fit irregularities at the walls; small gaps here and there at the edges of the boards will not affect the final look of the floor.

Fix the sheets in place with hardboard pins at 150mm (6in) intervals round the edges and 225mm (9in) apart across the middle of the sheets. Begin nailing in the centre of a convenient edge and work sideways and forwards so the sheet is smoothed down in place. On a floor where there are water pipes below, use pins of a length which will not come out on the underside of the floorboards.

The sheets should normally be fixed with their smooth side down so the adhesive will grip more securely; also the pin heads will be concealed in the mesh.

Nail down the first sheet and work along the wall. When you come to the end of a row of sheets, you will have to cut a sheet to fit. Don't throw the waste away; use it to start the next row so the joins between sheets will not coincide. When you come to the far side of the room you will have to cut the sheets to width. Again, don't worry about scribing them to fit the exact contours of the wall.

On a solid floor, check to see if there are any holes or cracks and whether it is truly level and smooth. Fill in holes and small cracks with a sand/cement mortar. Large cracks could indicate a structural fault and, if in doubt, you should call in an expert. To level an uneven floor, use a self-levelling compound, applying it according to the manufacturer's instructions.

When dealing with a direct-to-earth floor you will have to establish whether it is dry or not. There's no point in attempting to lay the tiles on a damp floor: you will get problems with adhesion and in time the tiles themselves will curl and lift.

One difficulty is that dampness in a floor is not always immediately apparent, especially if there is no floorcovering. (If the floor has a sheet covering you should lift up a corner of the covering and inspect beneath for any signs of damp.) A slight amount of damp can rise up through floors of quarry tiles or concrete and evaporate in a room without being noticed.

To test for damp you can heat up a plate of metal over a gas ring or blowlamp, or heat a brick in the oven for about an hour, then

LAYING SELF-ADHESIVE TILES

1 *Sponge primer over the floor and leave it to dry for 24 hours. It will help the tiles to form a secure bond when they are fixed in place.*

2 *Snap two chalk lines which bisect at the floor's centre. Dry-lay a row of tiles along one line to find out the width of the cut border tiles.*

3 *Adjust the first (centre) tile if the cut tiles will be too narrow. Fix the tiles in place by peeling off the backing and pressing them down.*

4 *With the first row in place, continue fixing the tiles, working in sections, until all the whole tiles are laid. You can then lay the cut border tiles.*

5 *Place a tile over the last whole tile in a row and another one over it butted against the wall to use as a guide to mark the cutting line.*

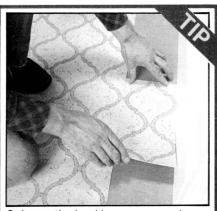

6 *Leave the backing paper on when cutting the tile with a sharp knife. Remove the paper and press the cut border tile in place.*

Ready Reference

TILE SIZES
Vinyl tiles are sold in packs sufficient to cover 1 square metre (1 square yard). The most common size tile is 300mm (12in) square.

FIXING TILES
Some tiles are self-adhesive; you simply pull off a backing paper, then press the tile down in place. Others require adhesive; this should be special vinyl flooring adhesive.

TIP: MAKE A TRAMMEL
A simple device called a trammel can help you find the centre of a room. Take a batten about 900mm (3ft) long and drive a pin through the batten near each end.

FINDING THE CENTRE OF THE ROOM
In an irregularly-shaped room you can find the room's centre in this way:
● strike a chalk line to form a base line, parallel to and 75mm (3in) away from the wall with the door
● place the centre of your trammel on the centre of the base line (A) and use the trammel to mark points B and C on the chalk line
● with one pin of the trammel placed in turn on points B and C, scribe two arcs, meeting at D
● strike a chalk line through points A and D to the wall opposite (this line will be truly at right angles to the base)
● find the centre of the line through A and D to give the centre point of the room (E), then draw a line across and at right angles to it using the same technique.

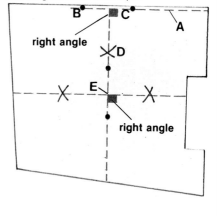

TILING AN L-SHAPE

1 At an external corner, place the tile to be cut over the last whole tile in one of the rows of tiles which adjoin at the corner.

2 Place another tile over the tile to be cut, but butted up against the skirting and use it as a guide to mark the cutting line.

3 Place the tile to be cut over the last whole tile in the other row leading to the corner. Use another tile as a guide for marking off.

4 Cut the tile along the marked lines with the backing paper on. Test if the cut tile fits, then peel off the paper and fix it in place.

TILING ROUND AN ARCHITRAVE

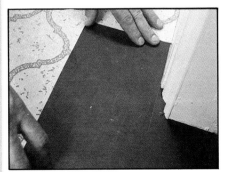

1 Make a template of the area round the architrave. Always test a template out: put it in place before using it on the tile to be cut.

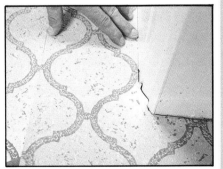

2 When the template fits, use it to mark out the required shape on the tile. Cut the tile, remove the backing paper and press it in place.

place it on the floor. If a damp patch appears on the floor or moisture gathers underneath the metal or brick this indicates that damp is present. Another test is to place a sheet of glass on the floor, seal its edges with putty, then leave it for a couple of days. If moisture appears underneath it is again a sign of damp. These methods are, however, rather hit-and-miss and you may feel it's worth calling in an expert to give a true diagnosis.

Curing a damp floor is a major undertaking which may involve digging up the existing floor and laying a new one with proper precautions taken against damp. You should seek professional advice here.

Existing sheet floorcoverings should be removed before you start laying vinyl tiles. You can, however, lay them over existing vinyl tiles provided these are in sound condition and are securely fixed. If they are not, you will have to remove them before you fix the new tiles. To lever them up, use a paint scraper, or even a garden spade (the long handle will give you plenty of leverage).

Marking up

You should start laying tiles from the middle of the floor. To find the centre of a room which is a reasonably regular shape you should take one wall and, ignoring any bays, alcoves or projections, measure and mark its centre. Go to the wall opposite and do the same. Between these two centre points you should snap a chalked line. Snap a second chalk line from the middle of the other two walls: the point where the lines meet is the centre of the floor.

If you are going to tile an irregularly-shaped room you should strike a chalk line, to form a base line, parallel to and 75mm (3in) away from a wall which has a doorway in it. You can then strike a line at right angles to the base line and stretching to the wall on the other side. The centre of this line will be the centre point of the room; draw a line through this centre point parallel to the base line. (Instead of using a large square to help you draw the lines at true right angles, you can use what's known as a trammel; see *Ready Reference*.)

Laying the tiles

When you come to lay the tiles, the first one is all-important. There are four possible positions for it. It can go centrally on the centre point; neatly inside one of the angles where the centre lines cross; centrally on one line and butting up to the second, or centrally on the second line and butting up to the first.

You should choose the position that gives you the widest border of cut tiles round the room. Very narrow cut strips at the edges will tend to give an unbalanced look, especially if you are laying the tiles in a dual colour or chequerboard pattern. So set out the tiles dry

TILING ROUND A WC

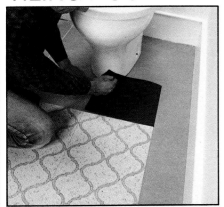

1 *Butt a paper template, which is the same size as a tile, against the base of the WC and mark off the shape of the WC on the template.*

2 *Cut the template to shape, then test to see if it fits exactly round the WC base and between the base and the whole laid tiles.*

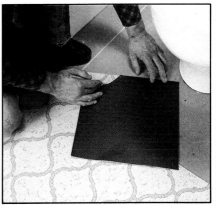

3 *Place the template over a whole loose tile (check the tile is the right way round for pattern matching) and mark off the cutting line.*

4 *Use a sharp knife to cut the tile to shape following the marked line. You can then remove the backing paper and fix the tile.*

5 *Aim to get the tile position right first time. Tiles can be taken up and restuck, but will lose some of their adhesive in the process.*

6 *Continue to make templates and fix shaped tiles round the curved WC base. You can then fix the cut border tiles next to the walls.*

(that is, not stuck down) to find out which position for the first tile gives you borders with the largest cut tiles. In a regularly-shaped room this will be quite straightforward; a couple of dry runs should make things clear. In an awkwardly shaped room, especially if it has a lot of alcoves or projections, you will have to make several of these practice runs. When you've decided on your final starting position, draw round the outline of the first tile to be placed.

When you've stuck down your first tile you can begin laying the rest. If you are laying tiles which require adhesive, you should apply this to as large an area as you can cope with in one go; possibly a square metre (square yard). Butt all the tiles accurately up against each other, and check that they are precisely aligned. Then apply firm hand (or foot) pressure to bed them firmly in place.

It's normal practice to stick down all the full tiles, known as the 'field', leaving a border of cut tiles to be fitted round the edges.

If you are laying self-adhesive tiles, you simply peel off the backing paper and press each tile into place. Where you have to cut tiles, don't peel off the backing until the cutting-to-size is completed. Should a tile be misplaced, lift it quickly and relay it correctly; the adhesive 'grabs' quickly and later attempts to lift the tile will probably tear it.

Cutting tiles

Vinyl tiles can be quite easily cut using a sharp knife and a straightedge. For an intricate shape make a template first.

Border tiles can be marked up for cutting in the usual way; that is, you take the tile to be cut, place it on the last complete tile in the row, place another tile over the first one but jammed hard against the wall and use this tile as a guide for marking off the cutting line

on the first tile (see step-by-step photographs). The main thing wrong with this method is that it can leave a narrow border in which it is difficult to apply adhesive, with the consequent risk that the border tiles will not adhere properly.

Another method, which avoids this problem, is to lay the field except for the last full tile in each row. Then take a tile and place it against the last full tile in the field. Place another tile on top of the first one and jammed against the wall. Use this second tile as a guide to cut through the first (and it will itself become the last full tile fixed in the relevant row).

The two tiles can temporarily be placed on top of the field, adjacent to the position they will occupy, while you cut the rest of the border. When you come to stick the border tiles down you will have plenty of room in which to wield your adhesive spreader and ensure adequate coverage.

CHAPTER 4
Repairing

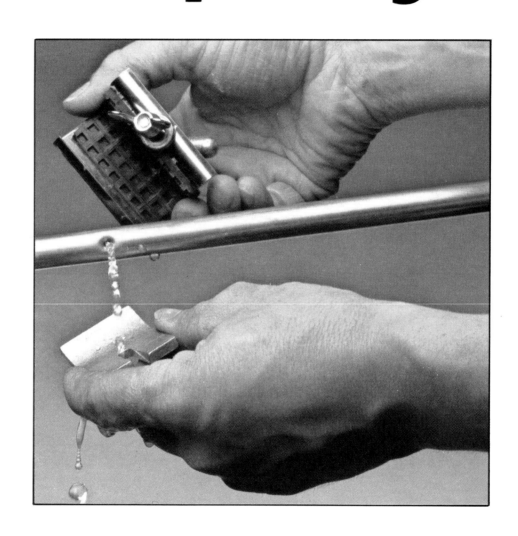

MAKING GOOD
walls and ceilings

If you're making a lot of alterations to your house, you'll probably pull out cupboards, partitions, remove fixings and strip off old wallcoverings. Don't worry if you cause some damage, since you can quite easily put it right.

No matter what sort of decorating you intend to do, the surface you're covering must be sound. If you paint, paper or tile over cracks or loose plaster you're wasting your time. The professionals call this preparation 'making good' — and the reason is obvious. Without time spent here the end result will be less attractive, won't last very long, and you won't be getting value for the money you've spent on decorating materials. Making good takes time, but it is never wasted. Here is a guide for the sort of problems you'll face in making good walls and ceilings ready for decorating.

Cracks

There are two types of cracks in walls to watch for. A structural one will be large, deep, and often wider at one end than the other — this has been caused by subsidence and you should seek the advice of a professional before any attempt is made to repair it. The second type is usually just a crack in the surface covering of the wall — the plaster, for instance — and because it's only superficial it can be easily repaired.

For such superficial cracks in plaster, first detach all loose material with the edge of a stripping knife and brush out thoroughly. If more plaster than you bargained for comes away, the plaster must have been weak — in which case, treat as large holes. Fill hairline and small cracks with cellulose filler, bought as powder and mixed with water to a thick creamy paste (mix only small quantities to avoid waste). Smooth it on with a filling knife and sand it down when dry.

In wood, cracks and opened grain can again be filled with cellulose filler — but it will show up rather than blend. If the wood is going to be painted, this probably won't matter. But if you're going to finish the wood with a clear varnish, plastic wood or stopping should be used to ensure the best possible finish.

Gouges

These are superficial marks caused by a badly-used shavehook or stripping knife (held at the wrong angle or because it slipped) or an electric abrasive tool which during the smoothing created ridges in the surrounding plaster. Fill as in cracks with cellulose filler, making it slightly proud of the surface. Leave it to dry hard and then sand flush with medium glasspaper. Gouges in wood should be treated in exactly the same way as cracks.

Holes

Small holes are often left when old screws and nails are removed or if wires have been chased in — for these the remedy is simple. Large holes, however caused, can require a lot more attention especially if they're deep as well as wide (eg, if a partition has been removed leaving gaps in walls or ceilings).

It can boil down to a question of cost — cellulose filler bought in the quantity required for a large hole will be more expensive than a small bag of plaster. Plaster, however, has its own problems — it's difficult to mix properly, sets very fast and takes some skill to get it to stick to the wall in the first place. In small areas there are ways around this (see page 92 for *Ready*

STRIPPING WALL COVERINGS

● Brush wallpaper with a solution of warm water and washing-up liquid or a proprietary stripper. Leave for about 5 minutes to allow the water to soak through to the old paste. Ease the stripping knife under the paper at a join and lift the paper off and away. This will prevent gouges in the plaster.

● If the paper clings stubbornly, soak it again but add a handful of wallpaper paste to the water. This will help the water soak in.

● Vinyl wallcoverings are removed simply by lifting the plastic coating at the bottom edge of the drop, then pulling it upwards and off in a complete sheet. Strip off the thin paper backing if it is damaged by soaking as above.

● Washable or gloss painted heavy wallcoverings will resist water. If you can get a scraper behind the paper at a join or at the top, spray water containing some wallpaper paste in with a pot-plant spray. Leave for a few minutes, then move the scraper backwards and forwards between the wall and the paper. Or you can break down the surface. Use either a wire brush or a serrated scraper.

Ready Reference

WHICH FILLER TO USE

Cellulose filler or ready-mixed filler for
● superficial cracks in plaster and plasterboard
● small holes (up to 50mm/2in) across
● gouge marks in plaster
● joint cracks in plasterboard or coving
● filling dents and cracks in wood to be painted.

Finishing plaster or brush-on skim plaster for
● large holes (over 50mm/2in) across
● deep cracks in plaster
● patches where unsound plaster has been stripped off
● skim coats on plasterboard.

Wood stopper in matching shade for
● wood to be given a natural finish.

Flexible mastic or ready-mixed filler for
● gaps between woodwork and walls (round windows and door frames).

TOOLS FOR MAKING GOOD

● a *filling knife* with a 25-50mm (1-2in) wide blade. This has a more flexible blade than a wallpaper stripping knife, and is useful for small repairs

● a *hawk* for holding plaster close to the work (something you can make yourself from a square of plywood 450 x 450mm with a piece of thick dowelling for the handle)

● a *plasterer's trowel* (also called a steel float) used for applying plaster and polishing the surface

● an *angle trowel* is also useful for making neat right-angled internal corners

---

Reference on plaster and fillers).

Very large holes need to be treated in the same way as plastering a wall — you start with an 'undercoat' plaster (it's much coarser than a 'finishing' plaster) to fill to about 6mm (¼in) from the surface, and this provides a key for two coats of finishing plaster which is applied with a float. As it dries it has to be 'polished' by applying water and smoothing with the float. Because of the speed at which plaster dries, this can be a difficult skill to master and telltale ridges may remain where the plaster has dried before the polishing began. Experience will overcome this problem.

Large or small holes in a plastered wall first have to be thoroughly cleaned out. Chip out all loose material and undercut the edges with a knife, then brush out thoroughly to remove all the dust.

If the wall is block or brick underneath, and the hole is no more than 100mm (4in) in diameter, then use a small trowel and build up the surface with thin layers of filler.

With a wall constructed of laths (thin strips of wood) and plaster, you first have to expose the laths, removing all loose plaster in the same way as above. But you won't be able to undercut the edges so easily, so you have to make sure that the filling goes between the slats. If the slats are damaged then treat as plasterboard. Otherwise, build up the filler in layers.

Always overfill a large hole, and to get it flush use a batten (long enough to bridge it) in a sawing action to reduce excess or redistribute it till the required level is reached. Finally smooth the finished surface with a filling knife or trowel, and sand down when dry with glasspaper or an orbital sander.

If holes aren't too large but are deep, an alternative method is to press in balls of wet newspaper, then skim a layer of plaster or cellulose filler over the top.

If there's a hole or holes where walls meet to make an external corner, nail a batten vertically along the edge of one wall and fill the hole on the other as described above. When this patch is dry remove the batten and repeat on the other wall. If the damage to an exposed corner is extensive, or if it is particularly vulnerable, greater reinforce-

SURFACE CRACKS

1 *These tiny cracks usually occur in plaster and are superficial. Use the edge of a stripping knife to remove any loose material along its length.*

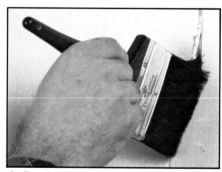

2 *Brush out the crack thoroughly so there's no dust left. In a small carton mix some cellulose filler to a creamy paste with water.*

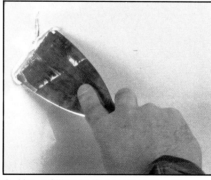

3 *Use a filling knife to press the filler onto the wall surface over the tiny cracks. Leave the filler slightly proud as it will shrink a little.*

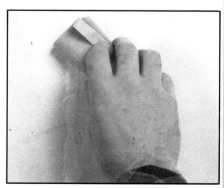

4 *When the filler has dried (it will lose the grey look and turn white) use glasspaper wrapped round a wood block to make the surface flush.*

HOLES IN PLASTERBOARD

1 *With large holes in ceilings or walls use a handyman's knife and straight edge to cut back the plasterboard to the nearest joists or studs on each side.*

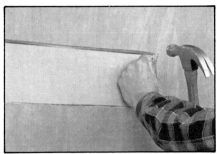

2 *The new piece of plasterboard should fit the hole fairly neatly. Press it in and fix to joists or studs on either side using galvanised plasterboard nails.*

3 *Use a steel trowel to press finishing plaster well into gaps. Then smooth the whole area keeping the top of the trowel angled away from the wall.*

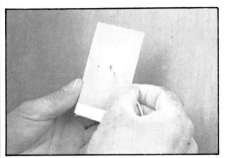

4 *For small holes, cut a piece of plasterboard a little larger than the hole (but small enough for you to get it through) and drill a hole in the middle.*

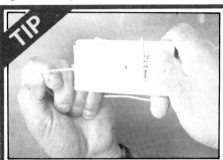

TIP

5 *Feed a short length of string through the hole, then tie a nail to one end — this will keep the string secure and prevent it being pulled out later.*

6 *Dab freshly mixed plaster onto both ends of the piece of plasterboard, then guide it into the hole. Pull on the string to position it in the hole.*

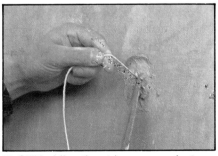

7 *Still holding the string, press plaster into the hole then use a trowel to remove the excess so that it's not quite flush with the surface.*

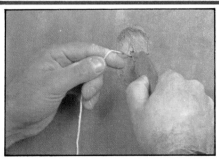

8 *When the plaster is hard cut off the length of string with a handymans' knife. After the cut is made there should be no sign of the string.*

9 *Apply a thin finishing coat of plaster to the surface. Lightly flick water onto the surface as you use the trowel to polish the surface smooth.*

ment may be desirable. Cut back the plaster as described under weak plaster (see page 92) to beyond the limit of the damage and square off to neaten edges. Then fix an expanded metal corner-piece to the underlying wall with dabs of plaster and plaster over it using the batten technique. Internal corners are a bit trickier. There are two methods. Either fill one side, smooth with batten, then leave to dry before doing the other. Or fill both and when semi dry, smooth down with an angle trowel.

For small holes in plasterboard use cellulose filler. Edges of larger holes should be cleaned up with a handyman's knife and can be covered with a patch of scrim cloth (available from most builders' merchants and hardware shops) stuck in place with dabs of plaster. Or you can use an offcut of plasterboard (see the photographs above). When secure, gently plaster over using a creamy mixture of filler or finishing plaster and allow to dry. Finally sand smooth.

Large holes in plasterboard must be patched with plasterboard offcuts. To nail in position it will be necessary to cut a hole big enough to expose the nearest wooden supports (in a wall these are called 'studs', in a ceiling 'joists'). On a ceiling, if you can get at it from above, the hole can be cut square and battened along each side, the battens being nailed to the joists. Use 30mm or 40mm galvanised nails to fix the plasterboard in place, then fill in gaps as above.

Holes in wood are best filled with wood, and if the hole is circular, use a piece of

SEALING GAPS

1 *Gaps between woodwork and walls can be filled with a flexible sealer. The nozzle is directed into the space with the help of a special gun.*

2 *For a smooth finish, lightly sprinkle the sealer with water then run down the corner with a flexible bladed knife. It can be painted 24 hours later.*

dowelling glued in place with PVA adhesive. With some holes, you can achieve the same result with a wedge — hammered into place, and then planed off for a flush finish. Alternatively, use plastic wood or stopping and sand the finish down when dry. If knots are loose and very dry, they should be cut out and the hole filled with a small piece of dowelling, glued in place.

Gaps

Where gaps occur between woodwork and walls (eg, near windows, architraves and skirting boards), a flexible sealant will fill them. Bought as 'cartridges', they have a nozzle which can be directed straight into the gap. A 'gun' attachment gives even more control and is especially useful in awkward places. The sealant can be painted 24 hours later. Cellulose filler can also be used for gaps but take care to get it smooth. If the gaps are particularly deep partly fill them with strips of folded newspaper and apply flexible sealer over the top. If they're wide, use thin wood to fill and wood filler to finish, then sand down when dry.

Gaps in plaster cornices (the shaped moulding where walls meet ceilings) occur when a framework (eg, an old cupboard) has been pulled away. Clean up the gap and apply liberal quantities of cellulose filler. When the filler is 'stiff' but not hard take a profile comb (you can make this yourself from a piece of card cut to the same 'profile' or shape as the coving) and run it along from the existing coving onto the filler. When the match is perfect allow the filler to dry and then gently smooth with the folded edge of a sheet of glasspaper.

Weak plaster

Old plaster may be loose against its backing and will move when you press it. If this is the case in any more than small areas, then complete replacement may be necessary. Unsound plaster will sound hollow when you tap it gently with your knuckles.

The extent of the weak area should be found by tapping, then lines drawn around it with a pencil. Using a club hammer and a bolster, gently chip out the weak area starting at the outside edges of the patch and working inwards (cover the floor below to catch the mess). If you don't start at the edges of the weak areas and work inwards, you may end up removing half the wall. When the patch has been removed you should fill as in holes. With larger areas you may need a professional plasterer. If the weakness was caused by damp the underlying wall should also be treated with a suitable damp sealant before repairing.

Mould

This may be found in steamy conditions which encourage its growth or where condensation is a problem (eg, in kitchens and bathrooms). Mould appears as grey, green or black spots or patches, and first should be treated with a fungicidal solution. Alternatively you can use a three parts water to one part household bleach solution. The wall should be dry before redecoration. If the problem persists, then you'll have to tackle the underlying cause — which may be damp penetrating the wall from outside or from below, or lack of insulation and ventilation which causes persistent condensation.

Old adhesives

Where ceramic tiles have been removed tile cement may remain fixed to the wall. In some situations — if you're retiling, for instance — this won't matter because as long as the surface is fairly flat any new adhesive will stick perfectly well. In the case of polystyrene tiles on a ceiling there may be dabs of adhesive left when you remove them and

REPAIRING HOLES

1 Mark straight guide lines slightly beyond the weak area. Use a bolster and club hammer to cut back to the brick, block or laths underneath.

2 Brushing out any dust and then dampening the surface with a little water helps the plaster stick and stops it drying too quickly.

3 Apply a plaster backing coat to the hole — use either a coarse type which sets slowly, one-coat gypsum with an added retarder, or 'brush-on' plaster.

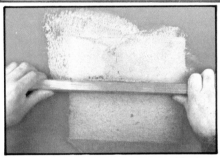

4 To level, use a batten with a side-to-side sawing action. As the plaster hardens, cut it back with a trowel so it's not quite flush with the wall surface.

5 When putting on the finishing coat, scoop plaster from the hawk onto the trowel, then angle the bottom edge of the trowel in to the wall.

6 Keep the trowel moving at all times. Smooth upwards, then from side to side. To 'polish' flick on drops of water, and move the trowel in a circular motion.

CORNERS

1 Repairing corners is a two-stage job. Brush out the damaged area, then fix a batten on one side. To ease removal, don't drive the nails fully home.

2 Use the edge of the trowel to fill in the hole with traditional quick setting gypsum plaster. When it's dry move the batten to the other side.

3 Fill in the rest of the hole, damping down with water. Leave to dry, then remove the batten. Gently smooth the new edge to match the old.

---

the surface has to be cleaned off. The only answer to this is an arduous, bit by bit, removal of each dab. (In places, plaster may come away with the tile or adhesive in which case treat as holes in plaster.) Gently ease the adhesive or cement away from the surface using a stripping knife and a mallet. Then sand the area smooth before decorating. If cork tiles have been taken down, any adhesive remaining will have to be sanded off with an orbital sander — another time-consuming but essential job — if you're decorating with paint or wallpaper.

Paint problems

If the paint on plaster, plasterboard or wood has flaked, blistered or bubbled scrape off the damaged area with a scraper or a coarse abrasive until a sound paint edge is reached. Wash down the exposed surface, allow to dry and prime before repainting.

If paint on wood repeatedly blisters or discolours, this could mean that there's a knot there that's giving out resin. Use a blow-torch to burn off the discoloured part then play the flame gently on it to draw the resin out. Scrape this off, sand the surface and

wipe off all traces of dust, then apply two coats of 'knotting' sealer (available from most hardware shops) to the patch. It must be dry before painting.

Crazing is another common problem, visible as very fine hair-like cracks in a painted surface. On a plastered wall it's often caused by applying the paint before the plaster is completely dry. On wood it may be because the paint underneath the top coat had not completely dried. The remedy is to scrape off the surface and repaint (see also pages 30-32).

REGLAZING A WINDOW

Windows may be a vital barrier against the elements but they're also quite fragile and can be broken easily. When this happens the glass has to be replaced. It's not a complicated job and few specialist tools are required – it does, however, need a degree of care.

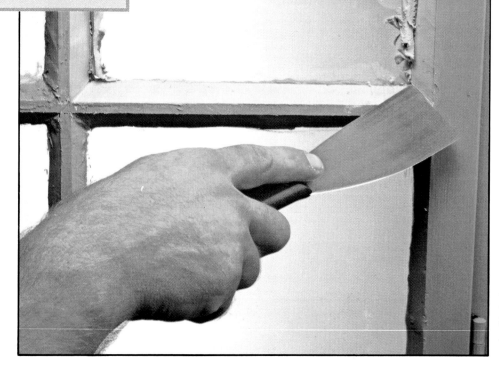

Jem Grischotti

Windows may be all shapes and sizes but basically all have a main frame containing one or more fixed or opening frames. The glass is held in a rebate – a narrow 'shelf' – on the outer face of the window, and is kept in place with either angular metal nails called sprigs (on wooden frames) or wire clips (on metal frames). These are then covered with putty, a pliable material which hardens when exposed to the air and provides a water-proof bedding for the glass (see *Ready Reference*).

The technique for reglazing a window depends mainly on what the window frame is made from – and wooden ones are by far the most common.

Removing the glass
Obviously, this has to be done carefully. If necessary, tap the old pane with a hammer until it is sufficiently broken to let you pull out most of the pieces by hand – you should wear thick gloves for protection. Any tiny fragments embedded in the putty can be tugged out with pincers, but don't worry if they refuse to budge. They can wait until the putty is removed.

Preparing the frame
The professional glazier uses a tool called a hacking knife to chop out the old putty. It's an

inexpensive tool to buy. If you have an old chisel, you could use this in conjunction with a mallet. If the putty is very old it can be quite stubborn, so take care not to damage the window frame. On multi-paned windows, you should also avoid using so much force

that surrounding panes crack.

As soon as the rebate is clear, brush it out. Rub it down with medium grade glasspaper until it is clean and smooth, then give it a coat of ordinary wood primer – not paint because this will prevent the putty drying.

PREPARING A WOODEN FRAME

Jem Grischotti

1 Tap out most of the broken glass with a hammer, then remove the remaining splinters by hand – but wear thick gloves for protection.

2 Chop out the old putty from the rebate using a hacking knife. Tap it with a hammer if necessary. Be careful not to damage the window frame.

3 Pull out the old glazing sprigs with a pair of pincers. If the sprigs aren't damaged you can re-use when fitting the new pane of glass.

Buying new glass

It's important to choose the right type of glass, but don't try to cut it to size yourself. Your local glazier will do a much better job, and is less likely to break the pane in the process. There's also no financial advantage to doing the job yourself for you'll be left with unusable off-cuts. And don't think you can use up that odd piece of glass you may have lying about. Old glass does not cut well at all, and tends to break in the wrong place even when you've scored it with a carbide-tipped glasscutter.

So measure the width and height of the rebate into which the glass must fit; double check the measurements to be sure, and order the glass to be cut 3mm (⅛in) smaller on each dimension. This allows for any slight inaccuracy in your measurements, and avoids the risk of the glass cracking due to expansion or contraction of the frame. If you need patterned glass, make a note of which way the pattern runs.

The fixing process

First you must line the rebate with putty. You can either take a ball of putty in the palm of your hand and squeeze it out between thumb and forefinger using your thumb to press it in; or you can roll the putty into finger-thick sausages and press these into place. Wet your hands before handling putty to prevent it sticking to your fingers, and knead it until it is pliable and any surface oils are thoroughly mixed in.

Next, press the pane into the puttied rebate with the palms of your hands, so that putty oozes out, around and behind the glass. Apply pressure around the edges rather than in the centre of the pane and check that, when you've finished, the glass is separated from the frame on the inside by a bed of putty which is 2mm to 3mm (up to ⅛in) thick.

Now for the unnerving part – nailing the glass in place. It's best to use glazing sprigs,

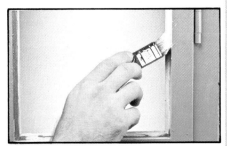

4 Clean the rebate using medium-grade glasspaper, then remove any dust and prime the rebate with a narrow paintbrush.

but you could make do with 19mm (¾in) panel pins that have had their heads nipped off with pliers. You'll need at least two per side, spaced no more than 230mm (9in) apart, and you must be sure to drive them squarely into the wood so they don't pinch and crack the glass. When you've finished, just over 6mm (¼in) of pin should be showing.

The final stage is to fill the rest of the rebate with a triangular fillet of putty that neatly covers the pins. Apply the putty in the same way as when lining the rebate, and use a putty knife or an ordinary filling knife to do the shaping, mitring the corners of the fillet as neatly as possible. Wet the knife blade to prevent the putty sticking to it as you draw it over the fillet.

Clean off the excess putty – including any that oozed out inside the pane earlier – and allow to dry hard before painting.

When you need to reglaze a window that isn't at ground level, you'll have to work from a ladder. Obviously you'll have to be organised when working at a height. Tap out most of the glass first from inside – and make sure there's no one standing below as you do so. Put all the tools and equipment in a bucket which you can hang on a hook attached to the ladder at the top. Don't try to carry the glass – it's best to get someone to pass it through the window.

Modern windows

Conventional steel-framed windows are reglazed in almost the same way as wooden ones, except that the glass is fixed with wire clips fitting into holes in the frame, rather than with glazing sprigs. Remove these and re-use them to fix the new pane – along with the right type of putty – after priming with a metal primer.

Because putty needs paint to protect it, and because modern aluminium and plastic windows aren't meant to be painted, a different method is used to hold the glass. Normally, it's a variation on the rubber gasket system used to keep the windows fixed in a car.

Just how easy these windows are to reglaze depends on the design; different manufacturers have their own systems and unless it is obvious how the glass fits in, all you can do is ask the window manufacturer for his advice. In some cases, he will prefer to do the repair himself.

Replacing double glazing

There are few problems where secondary double glazing is involved. This system uses a completely separate window frame to hold the extra pane of glass. All you do is treat each element of the system as a single glazed window. One complication you may come up against is where a do-it-yourself

PUTTING IN NEW GLASS

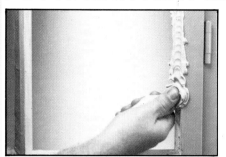

1 When the primer is dry line the rebate with putty. Hold the putty in the palm of your hand and squeeze it out between your forefinger and thumb.

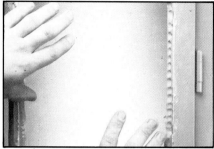

2 Position a new pane of glass in the rebate. Press it in place gently from the sides to avoid pressure on the centre, which could shatter the glass.

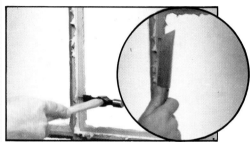

3 Knock in glazing sprigs using a cross-pein hammer or (inset) the back of a hacking knife. Slide the tool across the surface of the glass.

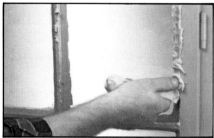

4 When all the glazing sprigs have been inserted, apply putty to the rebate to cover the edges of the glass. Press it into the angle with your thumb.

5 Shape the putty fillet into a slope using the straight edge of a putty knife. The slope shouldn't extend beyond the rebate line on the inside of the frame.

6 When you've shaped the putty into a slope, mitre each corner with the square edge of a filling knife, laying the blade on lightly to smooth out any ridges.

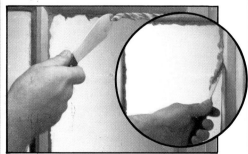

7 Trim off any surplus putty – from the surface of the glass and (inset) from the inside face of the pane – by running the putty knife along the rebate.

8 Leave the putty to dry for about a fortnight, then prime, undercoat and top coat. Allow the paint to extend 2 or 3mm (1/8in) onto the glass surface.

Cross-pein hammer Stanley Tools

Jem Grischotti

double glazing kit has been used. In this case the extra 'frame' may be no more than plastic channelling clipped over the edge of the glass, so it's more a case of remaking this frame than reglazing it.

Replacing double glazing where both panes are mounted in the same frame is more involved, and how you approach it depends on whether factory-made sealed units or two ordinary panes of glass have been used.

In the latter case, you merely fix two new panes in the same way as if reglazing an ordinary window. Just be sure you don't get marks on the panes facing into the double glazing's air gap – you can't clean them off once the second pane is in place.

Factory-made sealed units are also sometimes fitted like a single pane of glass but, more often, you'll have a modern gasket system to contend with. In any case, the most important thing is to order the new sealed units to exactly the right size. They cannot be trimmed if you make a mistake.

Dealing with leaded lights

Strictly speaking, to reglaze a leaded light, you must remove the putty and glazing sprigs from the main window frame and lift out the entire glass and lead latticework, so it can be worked on flat. You may, however, get away with working in situ if you get a helper to hold a sheet of hardboard or something similar against the other side of the pane, to keep it flat while you carry out the repair.

Whichever approach you adopt, you must lever away the lip of lead (called the 'came') holding the glass in place by using an old chisel. Cut the lead near the corners of the pane with a knife to make this easier. Remove the broken glass, clean out the putty from the channel in the lead, apply new putty and then fit the new pane – this should be cut to fit the dimensions of the rebate exactly. Finally, smooth back the lead with the handle of the chisel to hold it in place. To finish, make good the knife cuts with solder, or with a proprietary plastic repair compound.

There's more about this type of repair in another section.

Why glass?

You may be wondering why nobody has come up with a glass or glass substitute that never breaks. Well, they have. Leaving aside bullet-proof glass and the like, there are a host of plastic glazing materials on the market ranging from the familiar Perspex to compounds with complicated chemical names. But they all have two major drawbacks – they are comparatively expensive to buy, and they scratch so easily that they lose their transparency.

REPAIRING AND REPLACING GUTTERING

The chances are you won't realise there is anything wrong with your home's guttering until it leaks. Note where the water is coming from and, once the rain has stopped, get up a ladder and see what's wrong

The gutters on your home are supposed to capture all the rain falling on the roof and channel it to one or more downpipes. In turn these downpipes take the water into the main drain, a storm drain, or to a soakaway in your garden. This efficient removal of rainwater is important to keep your outside walls sound. Any missing, damaged, or blocked guttering will result in water cascading down the face of your wall, leading to dampness, and eventually mortar and brick decay. You may be able to repair it; or you may be faced with having to replace whole sections or the complete system.

Until the mid-1940s most guttering was made of cast iron, although asbestos enjoyed a brief popularity. Cast iron had the disadvantage of being very heavy to work with – as you'll find if you take some of it down. It is also prone to rusting if not properly maintained. Asbestos was heavy, looked rather bulky in appearance and was easily damaged. When plastic piping and guttering was introduced, it became an obvious choice. It is light to work with, doesn't need painting and its smooth surface allows water to flow through it more effectively. In any case, cast iron is very expensive these days, and not particularly easy to obtain.

Blockages

You should check why a blockage has occurred in the first place. This may be due to sagging, or poor installation preventing a free run for the water. Or the blockage may be combined with a faulty joint which may be possible to repair. But if cast iron guttering is at all cracked it needs replacing.

If your gutter overflows during heavy rain, the chances are that it's blocked with leaves.

PREPARING FOR WORK

1 Access is always a problem when working on guttering – a convenient garage roof made this job a lot easier. Scaffold towers are useful on high roofs.

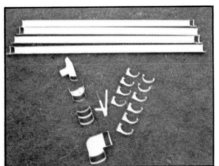

2 Before you start work assemble all the components you will need. You can check them off against the existing guttering.

REMOVING OLD GUTTERING

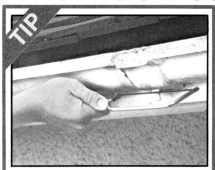

1 *Gutter sections are usually bolted together and these bolts won't come out easily. Saw through the nut.*

2 *When the nut has been detached try to hammer the bolt out but don't use too much force as the gutter itself may crack and collapse dangerously.*

3 *You may need to use a hammer and chisel to get the joints moving. Loosen the joints before unscrewing the gutter sections.*

4 *Cast iron guttering is supported by brackets or screws depending on its profile. You can lift it off brackets, or in this case unscrew it.*

5 *Start to take down the guttering at the point closest to the down pipe – it should come free quite easily even if it's attached directly to the pipe.*

6 *Detach and lift off each succeeding section in turn – remember that cast iron is heavier than it looks. Be careful not to overbalance.*

7 *Always carry pieces of guttering down to the ground, never throw them down – you may cause the cast iron to splinter dangerously.*

8 *Thoroughly brush down the fascia board to remove dirt and cobwebs, then fill any holes using a filler suitable for outside work.*

9 *If the fascia board has not been painted, use this opportunity to do the work. Sand down first and then apply primer and topcoats.*

You can use an old dustpan brush to clean it out, scraping the debris into piles and scooping them out with gloved hands. But prevent any bits from getting into the downpipe or this may get blocked as well.

Coping with sags

If a section of guttering has sagged, making it lower than the top of the downpipe, the water will not drain away properly. And you will be able to see this from puddles of water collecting in the guttering itself. You must decide whether to raise the sagging section, or lower the mouth of the downpipe to bring everything back into line. If you flex cast iron guttering more than about 25mm (1in) you'll break the seal on the joints, causing a leak. So choose the option that involves moving the guttering least.

In order to reset the guttering to the correct gradient you'll need to fix a piece of string taut between two nails hammered into the fascia board. You can then use this as a guide as you reposition each gutter support in turn.

Leaking joints

Joints in cast iron gutters are made by overlapping the two lengths of gutter, and bolting them together with a layer of sealant in between to form a watertight seal. As this sealant begins to deteriorate with age, the joint starts to leak.

To make the repair, first remove the bolt holding the joint together. Often this is too rusty to undo, so hacksaw off the bolt between the nut and the guttering, or drill out the rest of the bolt. Lever the joint apart with an old chisel, and scrape away all the old sealant. Clean up the joint with a wire brush, then apply a finger-thick sausage of new sealant and bolt the sections back together using a new nut and bolt and a couple of washers. Scrape off any sealant that has oozed out before giving the repair a coat of bitumen-based paint on the inside of the gutter.

Dealing with rust
If one bit of guttering has rusted right through, it won't be long before the rest follows suit, so you may as well save yourself a lot of trouble and replace it all. If meanwhile you want a temporary repair, there are several suitable repair kits on the market. They consist of a sort of wide metal sticky tape which you apply inside the guttering and over the holes with bitumen adhesive.

Choosing a replacement
Assuming you won't be using cast iron again – you'll have a job getting hold of it and even more of a job putting it up, apart from the fact that it's expensive – your choice is between aluminium and plastic. Plastic guttering is made of UPVC (unplasticised polyvinyl chloride). It's probably the better choice for a do-it-yourself installation: it is far more widely available than aluminium, and has the edge in terms of cost and durability.

Two different cross-sections are commonly available – half-round and 'square'. The latter is often given a decoratively moulded face similar to the more ornate ogee cast iron guttering. In addition, a semi-elliptical guttering is available – it looks a bit like half-round but is deeper and more efficient. This, together with some brands of conventional profile, can be camouflaged by being boxed in with a clip-on fascia panel. Which type you choose is largely a matter of personal taste, but try to choose something that blends into the style of your home.
· More important than looks is the size of the gutter. Too small, and it will be forever over-flowing; too large, and you will have paid more for the installation than is necessary. It's all to do with relating the amount of water the guttering can carry to the amount of water likely to come off the roof during a heavy rainstorm. These calculations are complicated, but you can assume that they were done when the guttering was originally installed. Just measure the existing

guttering at its widest point to find its size, and buy the same again. The most commonly available sizes are 75mm (3in), 100mm (4in), 112mm (4½in), 125mm (5in), and 150mm (6in). If in doubt, consult the manufacturer's literature.

The actual cross-section of the gutter may vary from brand to brand; this can make it difficult to join with existing guttering: for example, the guttering belonging to a neighbour on a semi-detached or terraced house. Most firms offer adaptors to link their product with cast iron guttering, or with a different size from within their range. However, they tend not to offer adaptors to tie in with the equivalent size from another brand, so if possible stick to one brand throughout the installation. If you have to link up with a neighbour's gutter, find out which brand was used, and try to use the same.

There are many different fittings as well as lengths of guttering available on the market. Before you start buying your new guttering get hold of a manufacturer's brochure from the stockist you use and carefully check to ensure you have all the fittings you will need. Make sure you understand how the particular system works before you buy anything.

Taking down old guttering
Cast iron guttering is heavy, and may also be rusted into place, so removing it can be tricky. But there is no need to be gentle with it: it doesn't matter if it breaks. The important thing is to work in safe conditions. If you are wrenching things apart, do it in a controlled way so you don't fall off the ladder, and so that great chunks of gutter don't fall down. Try not to drop cast iron guttering to the ground: it shatters easily, and, if it lands on a hard surface, dangerous fragments can fly off. If you toss the guttering clear of the house you might overbalance and fall off the ladder, so aim to lower larger sections gently to the ground with a rope.

Begin with the section linking gutter and downpipe. Cut through the old bolts holding the sections together. Then, if you lift the gutter slightly, you should be able to pull it free from the downpipe. Once it's out of the way, unmake the joints between the sections of gutter (as if you were repairing them), and lift the guttering off its supporting brackets. It may, of course, be screwed directly to the fascia board.

You can now turn your attention to the brackets themselves. These are usually screwed to the fascia board just beneath the eaves of the roof, and can either be unscrewed or levered off with a claw hammer. In older houses the brackets may be screwed to the tops or sides of the roof rafters, to support the weight of the iron guttering. If there is a fascia board to which

PUTTING UP PLASTIC GUTTERING

1 If you are joining onto your neighbour's gutter you'll need a special adaptor. Line it with a lump of mastic and bolt it into place.

2 Fix a string at the level of the bottom of the adaptor or end furthest from the downpipe. Hammer a nail into position to hold it in place.

3 Pull the string taut and fix it with a nail at the other end of the gutter run. Make sure it is horizontal by using a spirit level.

4 Fix the brackets at intervals of about 1 metre. Drop the first by 6mm (about ¼in) firom the string line, the second by 10mm (about ⅜in) and so on.

5 You can now put in the first section of guttering so that it is resting on the brackets, and connect it to the end piece or adaptor.

6 Each manufacturer has a different system for making joints. Here the next section rests in the previous one and is then firmly held with a clip.

7 You will very likely have to cut a section of guttering. Measure it exactly at roof level, then cut it squarely.

8 In this system, once a section is cut, new notches must be made in the end for the clip. To do this you can use a proprietary notch cutter or a wood file.

9 The final corner piece and downpipe fitting is made up on the ground which is the easiest procedure when dealing with small sections.

you can fit the new gutter, the ends of the brackets can be hacksawed off. Otherwise, you will have to lift off some of the roofing to remove them.

When all the old guttering has been removed, inspect the fascia board to make sure it is sound and securely fixed. If it is, fill the old screw holes and paint it before fixing the new guttering. If it isn't, it will have to be replaced. You'll find more information about this in another section.

Fixing new guttering

The obvious first step is to assemble the various bits and pieces you need, and you can use the old guttering system as a model to decide what's required. It's best to measure up the length of the guttering itself, allowing a little extra to be safe.

At the end of the run furthest from the downpipe, fix a gutter support bracket as high up the fascia as possible, and about 150mm (6in) from the end. The fixings here, and elsewhere, are made with 25mm (1in) screws. Choose ones that are galvanised to stop them rusting. Insert a nail into the fascia board level with the bottom bracket.

At the other end of the run, 150mm from the downpipe, fix another nail, tie a length of string tightly between the two, and use a spirit level to check that this string is level. When it is, lower the second nail by the amount needed to ensure that the guttering runs downhill towards the outlet. This 'fall', as it's called, varies according to the type of guttering, so check the manufacturer's recommendations. Usually, it is in the region of 5mm for every metre of gutter run. Once you've found the right line for the gutter, fix another bracket level with the lowest nail.

The next job is to fix the next bracket 1m (39in) from the one at the downpipe

end of the run, using the string as a guide to set it at the correct level. Use these two brackets to support a length of gutter with the downpipe outlet attached.

Exactly how you join the gutter to the outlet – or indeed make any other joins in the guttering – will vary from brand to brand. With some, you slip the ends of the components into a special jointing piece called a union, and clip the whole lot together. With others, one of the components will have a union built into its end.

Now work your way along, building up the gutter run as you go and adding additional support brackets as required, again using the string as a guide. In most cases, you will need a bracket every metre, plus one on each side of every join – though some ranges contain combined unions and support brackets. Check the manufacturer's recommendations.

The only problem you may run into is when you have to cut the guttering to length, either to go round a corner, or to finish the run with a stop end. Do the cutting on the ground using a hacksaw, making sure that you cut the end square. Any roughness left by the saw should be cleaned up with a file. If you want to turn a corner, fix the corner piece before cutting the straight piece of gutter to length. You can then use it to work out exactly how long the straight gutter length needs to be. When cutting to finish at a stop end, it is usual to leave about 50mm (2in) of gutter projecting beyond the ends of the fascia.

When you've finished the job and checked to see that all the joints are properly connected, take a bucket of water to the highest point of the gutter and pour it down. If the gutter doesn't drain all the water then go back and check your work.

10 *The made-up section is fixed in place taking care to locate the downpipe end into the hopper head. Any pipe connection needs a sealant joint.*

11 *When the whole system is up, you should check that it will work by pouring water in at the point furthest from the downpipe.*

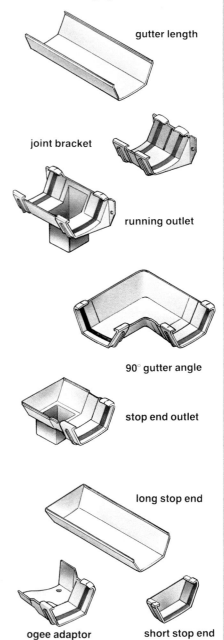

STOPPING TAPS LEAKING

Although taps are in frequent use, they rarely need maintenance. But if one starts to leak don't ignore it. Leaking taps are not only annoying and wasteful, but also, if they are hot taps, expensive — you've paid to heat the water going down the drain.

A tap is a device for controlling the flow of water at an outlet point, and is opened and closed by turning a handle. This may be a 'tee' or 'capstan' type (so called because of the shape) fitted onto a spindle rising from the body of the tap. Or it may be a 'shrouded head', covering all of the upper part of the tap.

Turning the handle clockwise forces a jumper unit down onto a valve seating in the waterway of the tap and stops the flow of water. Because metal against metal doesn't make a very tight seal, a synthetic rubber disc — a washer — is attached to the base of the jumper so that it beds firmly onto the seating.

Turning the handle anti-clockwise raises the jumper from the seating and allows water to flow. An exception to this is the Supatap where the nozzle is rotated to control the flow. When you open a tap water pressure will also force water round the jumper unit and, unless there is some way of preventing it, this would escape from round the spindle. To get round this problem some taps have 'O' ring seals fitted to the spindle while older taps have greased wool packed tightly in a gland around the spindle. More modern taps have rubber tube for packing.

Mixers work in exactly the same way as ordinary taps except that they have only one

spout that combines the flow of water from the hot and cold supplies. On kitchen mixers particularly this spout can be swivelled so that it can be pushed to one side to give better access to the sink or can supply a double sink.

When a tap starts to leak, there's a strong temptation either to ignore it or to try to stop it by closing it as tightly as you can. Such action is invariably ineffective and could lead to the valve seating being permanently damaged.

Where leaks occur
Basically there are three places a tap can leak: at the spout, in which case the washer and perhaps the seating will need looking at; at the spindle when the tap is turned on, which means either the packing in the gland or the 'O' ring has failed; or at the swivel point at the spout of a mixer tap, which means that the 'O' ring is at fault. All these repairs are easy to deal with. But first you must know the type of tap and the terminology related to it.

How washers are replaced
Conventional pillar tap This is the basic type of tap design and provides a good example of the procedure to follow when replacing a washer. These taps are commonly used for the hot and cold water supply over the kitchen sink and in this position they are probably the most frequently used taps in the house. It's quite likely that sooner or later the washers will need replacing.

To do this you'll first have to turn off the

water supply either at the mains or, if you're lucky, at isolating stop-valves under the sink which when shut cut off the supply either to the hot or cold tap without affecting the rest of the system (see section on emergency repairs on pages 107-109). Turn on the tap fully so it is drained before you start work.

Usually with a pillar tap the spindle rises out of a dome-like easy-clean cover, which you should be able to unscrew by hand. If this proves too difficult, you can use a wrench, but pad the jaws thoroughly with rag to avoid damaging the finish on plated taps.

With the tap turned on fully you can then raise the cover sufficiently to slip the jaws of a wrench under it to grip the 'flats' of the headgear — the main body of the tap which has a nut-shaped section to it. If you can't do this you'll need to take off the tap handle and easy-clean cover. First you'll have to remove the tiny grub-screw in the side of the handle which can then be lifted off. If this proves difficult a good tip is to open the tap fully, unscrew, then raise the easy-clean cover and place pieces of wood (a spring-loaded clothes peg will do) between the bottom of the easy-clean cover and the body of the tap. By turning the tap handle as if you were trying to close it the upward pressure on the easy-clean cover will force it off the spindle. However, you then have to replace it over the spindle just sufficiently to enable you to turn the tap on. When this is done take it off again and remove the easy-clean cover. While you are doing all this make sure you hold the tap steady. If the headgear is stiff and the entire tap turns you could damage the part of the sink into which the tap fits.

You can now put the headgear to one side. You should be able to see the jumper, with the washer attached, resting on the valve seating within the body of the tap (though sometimes it gets stuck and lifts out with the headgear). Often the washer is held in position on the jumper by a tiny nut which has to be undone with pliers before the washer can be replaced. This may be easier said than done, and rather than waste time attempting the all-but-impossible, it's probably better to fit a new washer and jumper complete rather than just renewing the washer. Once this has been done the tap can be reassembled, and as you do this smear the screw threads with petroleum jelly.

Jem Grischotti

Supatap: Deltaflow   Blue enamelled taps: Zazzeri   Others: Folkard Bolding

Bib with capstan handle

Pillar with capstan handle

Supatap

Pillar with shrouded head

PILLAR TAP

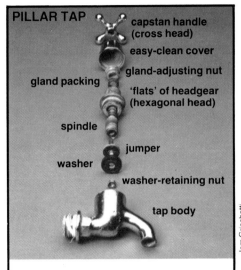

- capstan handle (cross head)
- easy-clean cover
- gland-adjusting nut
- gland packing
- 'flats' of headgear (hexagonal head)
- spindle
- jumper
- washer
- washer-retaining nut
- tap body

New taps rarely need repairs – and the actuality is more likely to be taps like these which won't be bright and clean inside. In hard-water areas lime scale will have accumulated which can cause the tap to jam so remove it with wire wool when the tap's dismantled. This will also help you identify the parts.

SHROUDED HEAD TAP

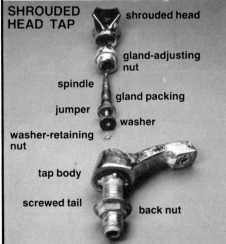

- shrouded head
- gland-adjusting nut
- spindle
- gland packing
- jumper
- washer
- washer-retaining nut
- tap body
- screwed tail
- back nut

Tap with shrouded head This is basically a pillar tap where the spindle is totally enclosed by an easy-clean cover that also acts as a handle to turn the tap on and off. Some shrouded heads are made of plastic and care is therefore needed when using wrenches. But the mystery of this tap is how to get to the inside — and methods vary with the make of tap.

Some shrouded heads can simply be pulled off, perhaps after opening the tap fully and then giving another half turn. Some are secured by a tiny grub-screw in the side. But the commonest method of attaching the head is by a screw beneath the plastic 'hot' or 'cold' indicator. Prise the plastic bit off with a small screwdriver to reveal the retaining screw (normally a cross-headed screw). When the shrouded head has been removed you'll find that you can unscrew the headgear to reach the interior of the tap in the same way as with an ordinary pillar tap. Rewashering can then be done in the same way.

If the jumper is not resting on the valve seating in the body of the tap, but is 'pegged' into the headgear so that it can be turned round and round but can't be withdrawn, it's slightly more of a problem to remove the washer-retaining nut. The easiest way is to fasten the jumper plate in a vice (although pliers will do) and turn the nut with a spanner. Some penetrating oil will help to free the thread. If after this you still can't loosen the nut, a good tip is to slip the blade of a screwdriver between the plate of the jumper and the tap headgear and lever it to break the pegging. A new jumper and washer can then be fitted complete, although the stem should be 'burred' or roughened with a file to give an 'interference fit' when it is slipped into the headgear.

Bib taps These taps are treated in exactly the same way as a conventional pillar tap. You might find with a garden tap that there's no easy-clean cover, so the headgear is already exposed.

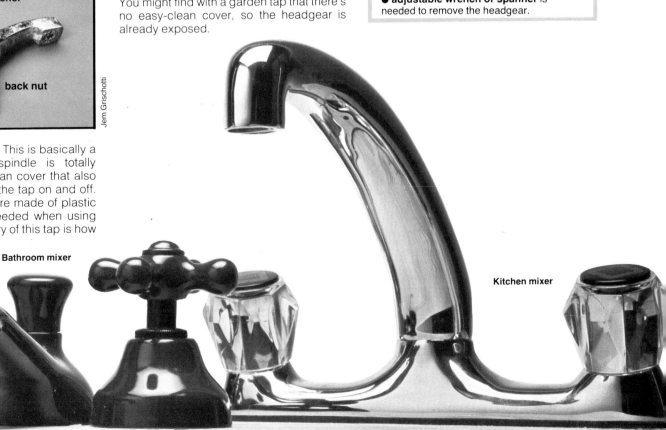

Bathroom mixer

Kitchen mixer

REPLACING A PILLAR TAP WASHER

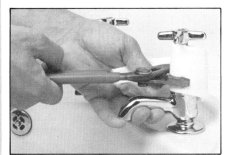

1 Pillar taps should be opened fully after turning off the water supply. Now unscrew the easy-clean cover.

2 Lift up the easy-clean cover so you can slip an adjustable spanner or wrench in to undo the headgear.

TIP

If there isn't enough space for the spanner or wrench, undo the grub-screw and then remove the handle.

If the handle won't come out, put a wedge under the cover and try to close the tap and force the cover up.

3 With the handle fully opened, the headgear can be removed and the jumper unit pulled away.

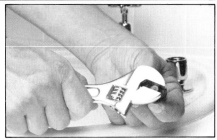

4 Some taps have the washer fixed to the jumper unit by a nut; in others it has to be prised off.

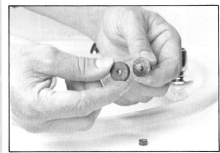

5 Push a washer of the correct size over the end of the jumper unit. If held by a nut clean it with steel wool before replacing it.

6 Push the jumper unit back onto the headgear and replace in the tap. Turn the handle to half close the tap, then restore the mains supply.

SHROUDED TAP

1 With a shrouded head tap, you can either pull it off or prise off the indicator cap with a screwdriver after turning the water supply off and the tap on.

2 Undo the retaining screw (probably a cross-headed type so you'll need the right screwdriver) and then you will be able to pull off the head.

3 Hold the spout to prevent damaging the basin while you unscrew the headgear either using a spanner or an adjustable wrench.

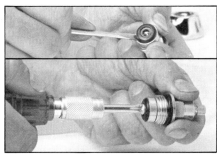

4 Unscrew the retaining nut, remove the old washer and replace with one of the correct size. Reassemble the tap, then restore the water supply.

Jem Grischotti

RE-WASHERING A SUPATAP

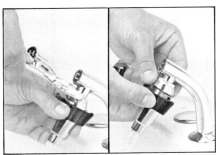

1 Turn on the tap slightly and hold it while you do the top nut. Open the tap fully, then turn the nozzle to unscrew it from the headgear.

2 As the nozzle comes away in your hand, a valve in the tap will automatically cut off the water so that you can make the repair.

3 Tap the nozzle on a hard surface so you can shake out the antisplash device to which will be attached the jumper unit and the washer.

4 Prise the old washer and jumper unit from the antisplash device and press in a new complete unit. Now you can reassemble the tap.

Jem Grischotti

Supataps Changing the washer on this type of tap can be carried out in minutes, without the need to cut off the water supply first. Before you begin, check that you have a replacement Supatap washer and jumper unit. Once you've undone the retaining nut at the top of the nozzle you have to open up the tap fully — and then keep on turning. At first the flow will increase, but then, just before the nozzle comes off in your hand, a check-valve inside the tap will fall into position and stop the flow. You can separate the anti-splash device, (containing the washer and jumper unit) from the nozzle by turning it upside down and tapping the nozzle on a hard surface — not a ceramic sink or basin. The washer and jumper unit then need to be prised from the anti-splash device — you can use a knife blade or the edge of a coin to do this. A new washer and jumper unit can then be snapped in. When reassembling the tap it's necessary to remember that the nozzle has a left-hand thread and so has to be turned anti-clockwise to tighten it.

Repairing a poor seating
Sometimes a tap will continue to drip although you've changed the washer. This is usually because the valve seating has become scored and damaged by grit from

the mains, so the washer can't make a water-tight connection.

You can use a reseating tool to put the problem right. This entails removing the headgear after the water has been turned off, inserting the tool into the body of the tap and turning it to cut a new seating. It won't be worthwhile buying one of these tools for what is a once-in-a-lifetime job, but you may be able to hire one from a tool hire company.

An alternative method, and certainly one that's a lot easier, is to use a nylon 'washer and seating set'. Again with the water supply off, the headgear and the washer and jumper are removed from the tap end and the nylon liner is placed in position over the seating. The jumper and washer are then inserted into the headgear, which is screwed back onto the tap. The tap handle is then turned to the off position. This action will force the liner into and over the old seating to give a watertight joint.

You can't, of course, use one of these sets to reseat a Supatap. However, the makers (Deltaflow Ltd) will supply a reseating tool on request, but these taps very rarely need reseating.

You can also use a domed washer to cure a poor seating. It increases the surface area in contact with the waterway and so

Ready Reference

WHAT'S GONE WRONG?
Check out the problem first.
Washers may be worn or disintegrating. Replace with 12mm (½in) or 18mm (¾in) synthetic rubber washers, available from hardware stores. A good tip for a temporary repair is to reverse the old washer.

'O' rings that look worn may also cause leaks. Choose the same size so they fit snugly.

Valve seating is damaged if rough and uneven. You can:
● use a domed, not a flat, washer

● fit a washer and seating set which covers up the damage

● buy or hire a reseating tool to grind the damaged seat smooth

TIPS TO SAVE TIME AND TROUBLE
● If you can't undo the nut holding the washer to the jumper, buy an all-in-one jumper and washer set.

● If a metal easy-clean cover is stuck pour very hot water over it. It should then unscrew.
● After repairing a tap, leave the water to run gently for 15 minutes to remove any air trapped in the pipes.

LEAKAGE UP THE SPINDLE

1 *If the tap has a stuffing box round the spindle, first try to tighten the gland-adjusting nut.*

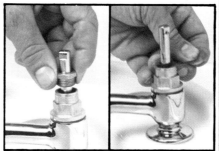

2 *If this fails to stop the leak, remove the nut and then pick out the old greased wool stuffing.*

3 *Smear petroleum jelly on a length of knitting wool, then wind it around the spindle, packing it down tightly.*

4 *Alternatively you may be able to use a rubber packing washer which just has to be slipped on.*

REPLACING 'O' RING SEALS

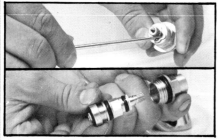

1 *To get to the seals on a tap, remove the headgear and prise off the circlip which holds the spindle in place.*

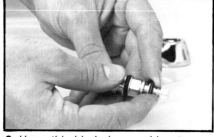

2 *Use a thin-bladed screwdriver to work off the worn 'O' rings and then replace them with new ones.*

3 *At the swivel point of a spout, first undo any grub-screw. Now twist the spout to one side and gently ease it from the mounting.*

4 *Prise off the worn seals with a screwdriver and then slip new ones into position. Replace the spout back in the mounting, restore water.*

effectively cuts off the flow when the tap is turned off even though the top of the valve seating may not be smooth.

Repacking a gland
This is necessary when you turn the tap on and water bubbles up the spindle towards the handle. At the same time the tap can be turned on and off far too easily — you might even be able to spin the handle with a flick of the fingers. This fault is a common cause of water hammer — heavy thudding following the closure of a tap or float-valve — that can result in damage to the plumbing system.

Leakage up the spindle is most likely to occur in rather old fashioned — but still very common — taps in which the spindle passes through a gland or 'stuffing box' filled with greased wool. It's inevitable that water containing detergent will be splashed onto the tap and this may result in the grease being washed out of the gland. The leakage can also be created if you run a garden or washing machine hose from the tap.

Fortunately, to make a repair you don't have to cut off the water supply to the tap, but you must be able to get at the gland-adjusting nut. This is the first nut through which the spindle passes.

Giving the gland-adjusting nut about half a turn may be enough to stop the leakage up the spindle, but eventually all the adjustment available will be taken up and you'll then have to repack the gland. When the gland-adjusting nut has been unscrewed and removed, the old gland packing material can be taken out and replaced with knitting wool saturated with petroleum jelly. The wool is wound round the spindle and packed down tightly before the gland-adjusting nut is put back and tightened until the tap handle can be turned fairly easily but without any leaks occurring.

Replacing an 'O' ring
Many modern taps have 'O' ring seals instead of a packed gland or stuffing box. If an 'O' ring fails the remedy is simply to undo the gland-adjusting nut, pick out the old 'O' ring and replace it with a new one. Leaks from taps with this fitting are rare. 'O' rings are also found at the swivel point of many mixer taps and if a leak occurs here you have to remove the spout to make the change – but this is usually only held with a grub-screw.

Older Supataps aren't fitted with an 'O' ring seal but if water leaks from the top of the nozzle you can fit a ring round the valve casing. Modern Supataps have an 'O' ring already fitted and if it needs replacing, it's a simple matter of slipping it off and pushing on another — but choose one that fits snugly and doesn't move about. If this doesn't cure the leak you'll have to replace the anti-splash device which could have become worn.

EMERGENCY PIPE REPAIRS

A leaking pipe is no joke. First you have to stop the water – so you need to know where to turn if off – and then to make some kind of emergency repair, even if it's just a holding operation.

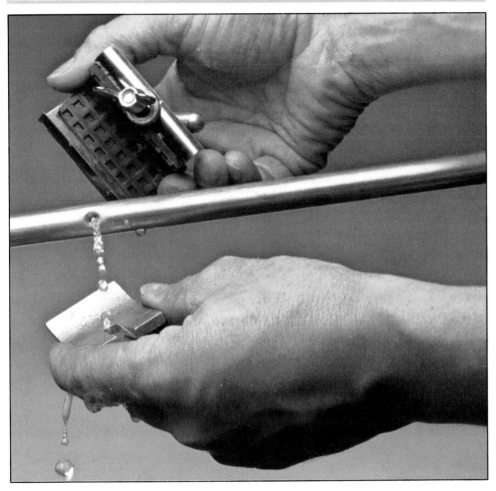

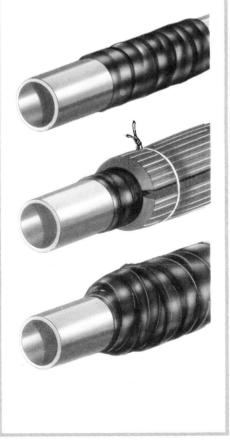

Ready Reference

TURNING OFF THE STOP TAP

Make sure the family knows where the mains stop tap is.

● do not force the handle if it has seized up — it could break it off.
● use hammer or wrench to tap the fitting while pouring penetrating oil down spindle.
● if you can't free it call the water authority emergency service — they can turn the water off where your supply pipe leaves the mains.
● don't reopen stop valve fully when turning on the supply until a permanent pipe repair is made. This reduces water pressure on a temporary seal.

TIP: MAKESHIFT REPAIRS

If you don't have the right materials to hand (see next page) try this:
● bandage insulating tape round the pipe and hole
● cover with a 150mm (6in) piece of garden hosepipe slit along its length and tie with wire at each end, twisting ends of wire together with pliers
● wrap more tape tightly over this

Leaks in domestic plumbing systems have a nasty habit of happening at the most inconvenient of times, often when it isn't possible to carry out a proper permanent repair. What you need is a plumbing emergency first aid kit, and there are now several proprietary products available that will at least enable you to make a temporary repair and get the water flowing again.

With any leak, the vital first step is to stop the flow of water. Even a small leak can create a surprisingly large pool of water in no time. Stopping the flow in any pipe is relatively easy provided that you know the locations of the various stop-taps or valves that isolate parts of your water system, or cut it off completely from the mains supply.

Water comes into the house through a pipe known as the rising main, and because water in this pipe (and others leading from it) is under mains pressure, leaks from it will be particularly serious. It enters the house underground, and from there leads either to all the cold taps and a water heating system, or to just the cold tap in the kitchen and to a cold water storage tank.

Leaks can result from a number of causes. Pipework may have been forced or strained at some point, resulting in a leak at one of the fittings connecting the lengths of pipe together, or in a fracture at a bend.

Corrosion within pipes may lead to pin-holes in pipe lengths, while frost damage can lead to bursts and splits in pipes and to leaks at fittings caused by ice forcing the fitting open. Whatever the cause, cutting off the water supply to the affected pipe is the first vital step.

Where to turn off the water

1 Cold water supply pipes connected directly to the mains: in the UK these pipes usually only supply the kitchen cold tap, the cold water storage tank and sometimes instantaneous water heaters. In Australia and other countries, the pipes may supply *all* cold water taps and the hot water storage cylinder. The simple way of deciding whether any pipe or tap is supplied directly by the mains is by the pressure – taps supplied from a tank are what's known as gravity-fed and the pressure of water is relatively low compared to mains pressure.

To turn off the water, look for the mains stop-valves. There may, in fact, be two: one inside the house where the mains pipe enters (under the kitchen sink, in the utility room, or even under the stairs); the other outside – either just inside the boundary of the property (near to a water meter, if you have one), or under the footpath outside the garden fence. Outdoor stop-valves may be set as much as a metre (3 ft) down beneath a hinged cover or metal plate, and you may need a special 'key' which is really just a long rod with a square socket on the end which fits over the tap to

turn it. In most cases, however, it's simply a matter of reaching down to turn it off by hand or with a wrench. Some outdoor stop-valves also control a neighbour's water supply, so do warn them if you're turning it off.

The stop-valve inside will either be a wheel type or an ordinary T-shaped type. The only possible complication is if it hasn't been touched for years and is stuck fast. A little penetrating oil and tapping it with a hammer will usually loosen it sufficiently. (It's worth closing the stop-valve now and again to see that it doesn't get stuck.)

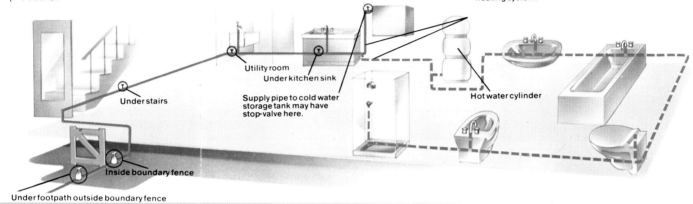

Supply feeds cold water storage tank *or* runs directly to all other cold water outlets and water heating system.

Under stairs

Utility room
Under kitchen sink

Supply pipe to cold water storage tank may have stop-valve here.

Hot water cylinder

Inside boundary fence

Under footpath outside boundary fence

2 Cold water supply pipes from a cold water storage tank: in the UK these pipes usually supply the bathroom cold taps, the WC cistern and the hot water cylinder.

To close off the water supply in these pipes there's often a stop-valve immediately alongside the cold water tank where the pipe exits. Turn this off first and then open all cold water taps. They'll run dry almost immediately. If there isn't a stop-valve, you have to drain the whole tank. So first you stop water entering the tank by either turning off the mains (as above) or by tying up the ball-valve in the tank so that it remains closed. Then you open all the taps in the house.

3 Hot water pipes: these are all supplied from a hot water cylinder, which in turn gets its cold water either from the cold tank or from the mains.

Since hot water leaves the hot water storage cylinder from the top, it's only the pressure of water going in at the bottom of the cylinder that forces the water out. Turn off the supply of cold water (either at the cold water tank, or at the mains) and you stop the flow. In this sort of situation the hot water cylinder remains full. If for any reason you need to drain this as well, use the drain cock near the bottom. It's essential in this case to turn off either the immersion heater or boiler.

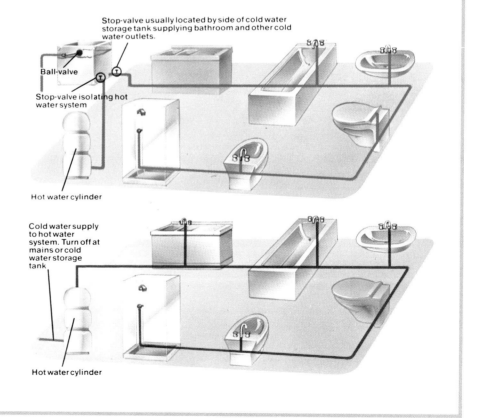

Stop-valve usually located by side of cold water storage tank supplying bathroom and other cold water outlets.

Ball-valve

Stop-valve isolating hot water system

Hot water cylinder

Cold water supply to hot water system. Turn off at mains or cold water storage tank

Hot water cylinder

EMERGENCY REPAIRS

● One type of repair kit is based on a two-part **epoxy resin plastic putty** supplied as two strips of differently-coloured putty in an airtight pack. When the strips are thoroughly kneaded together the putty is packed firmly round the pipe, where it will harden to form a seal. However, this hardening process takes up to 24 hours and the water supply will have to remain off for this period. (If you don't need to use all the pack in one go, reseal it immediately).

Equal amounts of putty should always be used and mixed together thoroughly until a uniform colour results, otherwise it won't harden properly. It's also essential that the pipe or joint is scrupulously rubbed down and cleaned with methylated spirit or nail polish remover. This will ensure a good bond between the putty and the metal.

● One of the most valuable aids is a multi-size **pipe repair clamp** which has the added advantage of being reusable. It consists of a rubber pad which fits over the hole (for this repair it's not necessary to turn off the water) and a metal clamp which draws the rubber tightly against the pipe when it is screwed in place.

Position the pad and one side of the clamp over the hole, and link the two parts of the clamp together, making sure that the pad is still in place. Tighten the wing nut fully. If the position of the hole makes this difficult, use blocks of wood to hold the pipe away from the wall. This method of repair cannot, of course, be used to mend leaks occurring at fittings.

● Another proprietary product uses a two-part **sticky tape** system which builds up waterproof layers over the leak — in the true sense this does form an instant repair. The area round the leak should be dried and cleaned and then the first of the tapes is wrapped tightly round the pipe, covering the leak and 25mm (1in) either side of it. Then 150mm strips of the second tape, with the backing film removed, are stuck to the pipe and stretched as they are wound round, each turn overlapping the previous one by about half the width of the tape. This covering should extend 25mm beyond either end of the first layer of tape. The job is completed by wrapping the first tape over all the repair.

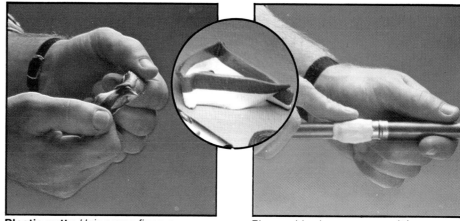

Plastic putty *Using your fingers, mix together equal amounts of the two putty strips. It's ready for use when the colour is even all through.*

Thoroughly clean area round the leaking pipe, then pack putty round fitting. It can be sanded smooth when it's completely hard.

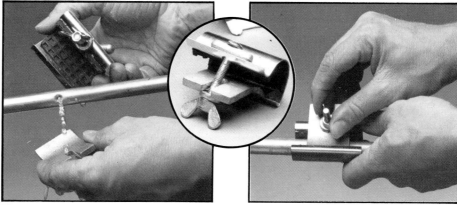

Pipe clamp *Place rubber pad and one side of metal clamp directly over leak in pipe. There's no need to turn off the water with this type of repair.*

Link the two parts of clamp togther, being careful to keep it in position. Screw down wing nut to secure rubber pad against pipe.

Sticky tape *Start winding first tape round pipe about 25mm (1in) from the leaking fitting. Continue over the joint and for 25mm on other side.*

Stretch and overlap 150mm strips of second tape round pipe. Continue 25mm (1in) either side of first tape. Finish off with layer of first tape.

STOP-VALVES AND BALL-VALVES

The valves that control your household water system aren't difficult to understand – or to fit or repair. So the next time one of yours goes wrong, be prepared to put it right yourself.

Stop-valves, gate-valves and ball-valves are all plumbing fittings that in different ways do precisely the same thing, which is to regulate the flow of water through pipes. Each of the three types of valve performs an important function in your water system, and it is therefore in your interest to know not only what they do and how they do it, but also how to put right any of the faults to which they are prone.

Stop-valves
Your main stop-valve is perhaps the single most important plumbing fitting in your house. In the event of almost any plumbing emergency the very first thing that you should do is turn it off. This will stop the flow of water into your house and reduce the extent of any damage. Looking like a very basic brass tap, your main stop-valve will be found set into the rising main not far from the point where this pipe enters your house. Often it will be located under the kitchen sink.

If your house is fairly old then it could be that it won't be provided with a main stop-valve. If this is the case, then you will have to use the local water authority's stop-valve instead. You will find it under a hinged metal flap set into your garden path or the pavement outside your property. This sort of stop-valve usually has a specially-shaped handle that can only be turned with one of the water authority's turnkeys. So that you can deal promptly with any emergency you should make sure that you either have one of these turnkeys, or at least that you have ready access to one. However, both for the sake of convenience and because specialist gadgets like turnkeys have a habit of disappearing when they're most needed, you may decide to install a main stop-valve yourself – not a difficult task if the rising main is made of copper pipe (see step-by-step photographs).

The internal construction of a stop-valve is identical to that of an ordinary tap, and so it is prone to the same types of faults (see *Ready Reference*). But one further trouble that may afflict your stop-valve – which doesn't crop up with ordinary taps – is that of jamming in the open position as a result of disuse. It's a problem cured simply by applying penetrat-

ing oil to the spindle. However, you can prevent this happening by closing and opening the stop-valve regularly, and by leaving it fractionally less than fully open – a quarter turn towards closure will do.

Gate-valves
Whereas stop-valves are always fitted to pipes that are under mains pressure, gate-valves are used on pipes that are only subject to low pressure. They are therefore found on hot and cold water distribution pipes and on those of the central heating system. Gate-valves differ from stop-valves in as much as they control the flow of water through them, not with a washered valve, but by means of a metal plate or 'gate'. You can distinguish them from stop-valves by the fact that their valve bodies are bigger, and by their wheel – as opposed to crutch – handles. Due to the simplicity of their internal construction gate-valves require little attention (see *Ready Reference*). Unlike stop-valves, which have to be fitted so that the water flowing through them follows the direction of an arrow stamped on the valve body, you can install a gate-valve either way round.

Mini stop-valves
Mini stop-valves are useful little fittings that you can insert into any pipe run. Their presence enables you to re-washer or renew a tap or ball-valve (see below) or repair a water-using appliance such as a washing machine without disrupting the rest of your

water system. They can also be used to quieten an excessively noisy lavatory flushing cistern that is fed directly from the rising main, since by slowing down the flow of water to the ball-valve you can reduce the noise without materially affecting the cistern's rate of filling after flushing. You usually fit a mini stop-valve immediately before the appliance that it is to control; and they can be turned off and on either with a screwdriver, or by turning a small handle through 180°.

Ball-valves
Ball-valves are really just self-regulating taps designed to maintain a given volume of water in a cistern. While there are a number of different patterns they all have a float – not necessarily a ball these days – at one end of a rigid arm which opens or closes a valve as the water level in the cistern falls or rises. There are basically two types of ball-valves: the traditional type, generally made of brass, in which the water flow is controlled by a washered plug or piston; and the type that has been developed more recently in which the flow is controlled by a large rubber diaphragm housed within a plastic body.

Croydon and Portsmouth ball-valves
The oldest of the traditional types of ball-valves is the Croydon pattern. You can easily recognise one of these by the position of its piston, which operates vertically, and by the fact that it delivers water to the cistern in two insufferably noisy streams. Due to their noisi-

FITTING A STOP-VALVE

1 When installing a main stop-valve use the type that has compression fittings. If it isn't combined with a drain-cock then fit one separately.

2 Make sure that you fit the stop-valve the right way round. The direction of the water flow is clearly indicated by an arrow stamped on the valve body.

3 Take care when marking off the rising main. The extent to which the pipe will penetrate the fitting is indicated by a shoulder; use this as your guide.

4 Turn off the water authority's stop-valve and cut it at the mark with a hacksaw. Some water will flow out as you do this; be prepared for it.

5 Spring the stop-valve into the cut pipe so that the two ends meet the pipe stops within the fitting. The valve handle should be angled away from the wall.

6 Tighten up the nuts, restore the water supply at the water authority's stop-valve, then turn on the stop-valve and check the fitting for leaks.

HOW A STOP-VALVE WORKS

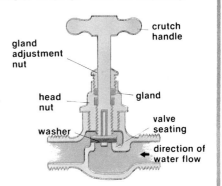

Because a stop-valve works in the same way as an ordinary tap its washer and gland are also subject to wear. You can:
● remove headgear to replace a worn washer (see pages 102-106), and
● deal with a worn gland by tightening the adjustment nut, or by re-packing the gland.

HOW A GATE-VALVE WORKS

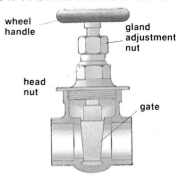

A gate-valve requires little attention. The only thing that may give trouble is the gland, which sometimes needs adjusting or renewing.

DEZINCIFICATION

In areas where the water supply is unusually acidic the zinc content of pipe fittings made of brass (an alloy of copper and zinc) can be dissolved by the water. This phenomenom is known as dezincification, and it results in the fittings losing their structural strength. When it presents a problem, fittings made of gunmetal (an alloy of copper and tin) are usually used though cheaper corrosion-resistant brass fittings are also available. These usually have CR stamped on the valve body.

VALVE TYPES

Apart from the float arm the only moving part on a diaphragm-type valve is a small plunger. When prompted by the float arm this plunger presses a large rubber diaphragm against the valve nozzle to close it.

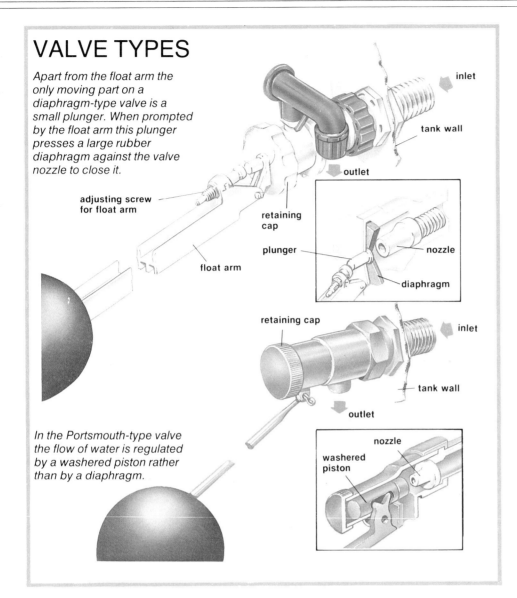

adjusting screw for float arm

float arm

retaining cap

plunger

outlet

inlet

tank wall

nozzle

diaphragm

retaining cap

inlet

tank wall

outlet

nozzle

washered piston

In the Portsmouth-type valve the flow of water is regulated by a washered piston rather than by a diaphragm.

REPAIRING A BALL-

1 *The first thing you do when faced with a faulty Portsmouth valve is examine the piston. In order to get at it you will first have to remove the float arm.*

5 *A piston usually consists of two parts. If it's hard to unscrew, slip a screwdriver into the slot and turn the washer-retaining cap with a wrench.*

---

ness, Croydon valves are now by and large obsolete, and if you do come across one you will almost certainly want to replace it. The traditional type of valve that superseded the Croydon pattern was the Portsmouth valve (see illustration). You can distinguish it from the former type by the fact that its piston operates horizontally; and as it is still popular with plumbers despite the development of more sophisticated diaphragm type valves, it is a pattern that you may well find in your home.

When one of your ball-valves goes wrong the first thing you will notice is water dripping from an outside overflow pipe. If the valve is a Portsmouth pattern then it is likely to have developed one of three faults. First, it could have jammed partially open as a result of the build-up of scale or the presence of grit; or, secondly, it could need re-washering. In either of these cases this will necessitate you turning off the water supply so that you can either clean the ball-valve or fit a new washer

to it (see step-by-step photographs). Lastly, the valve could have been incorrectly adjusted to maintain the proper water level in the cistern – which should be about 25mm (1in) below the overflow pipe. Even modern Portsmouth valves are rarely provided with any specific means of adjusting the water level, so if you need to do so you will have to resort to bending the float arm.

Noise can be a problem with Portsmouth valves. It is caused either by the inrush of water through the valve nozzle, or by vibration created by the float bouncing on ripples on the surface of the water ('water hammer'). As silencer tubes are now banned by water authorities, you will have to try other methods to deal with this problem. Reducing the mains pressure by closing the rising main stop-valve slightly may help, and as vibration can be magnified by a loose rising main it is worth making sure that this pipe is properly secured with pipe clips. Another measure

you could take would be to improvise a stabiliser for the float using a submerged plastic flowerpot tied to the float arm with nylon cord. However, if all the above measures fail you will have to consider replacing the Portsmouth valve with one of the modern diaphragm types.

Diaphragm ball-valves

Diaphragm ball-valves, which are also referred to as BRS or Garston ball-valves, were specially developed to overcome the noisiness and inherent faults of the Croydon and Portsmouth valves. Since the moving parts of a diaphragm valve are protected from incoming water by the diaphragm (see illustration) there is no risk of them seizing up as a result of scale deposits; and the problem of noisy water delivery is often overcome nowadays by an overhead sprinkler outlet which sprays rather than squirts the water into the cistern. Should you need to adjust the water

VALVE

2 *Then unscrew the retaining cap and push out the piston. Do this by inserting a screwdriver into the slot on the underside of the valve body.*

3 *If you can't get the piston out or if you suspect that your ball-valve needs a clean rather than a new washer, then you will have to remove the whole valve body.*

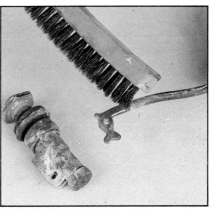

4 *If a build-up of scale does turn out to be the cause of your problem, clean the valve and the end of the floam arm with a wire brush.*

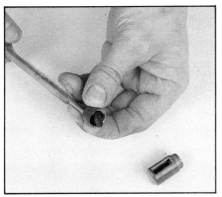

6 *You'll find the old washer seated in the cap. Poke it out and substitute a new one. Smear the piston with petroleum jelly before replacing it in the valve.*

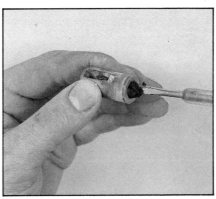

7 *Rather than risk damaging a piston that refuses to unscrew, pick out the old washer with a point and force a new one back in its place.*

8 *Debris caught in the valve nozzle can interrupt the water flow. Cure this problem by dismantling the valve and removing the debris with a nail.*

level in a cistern fitted with a diaphragm valve, then invariably you can by means other than bending the float arm. The only problems you are likely to encounter with diaphragm valves are jamming of the diaphragm against the valve nozzle, and obstruction of the space between the nozzle and diaphragm with debris from the main. You remedy these problems by unscrewing the knurled retaining cap and either freeing the diaphragm with a pointed tool or removing the debris.

High and low pressure water supply

The water pressure under which a ball-valve operates is an important factor, as the size of the hole in the nozzle of the valve will be either smaller or larger according to whether it is under high pressure (ie, mains pressure) or low pressure (ie, supplied by water from a storage tank). Older Portsmouth valves have either HP (high pressure) or LP (low pressure) stamped on their bodies, and will only operate

satisfactorily under the pressure for which they are designed. Modern valves, on the other hand, have interchangeable nozzles which allow you to convert them from low to high pressure or vice versa. If you fit a high-pressure valve (or nozzle) in a situation where a low-pressure one is required this will result in an agonisingly slow re-fill. A constantly dripping overflow may be the sign of a low-pressure valve that has been fitted to a cistern that is fed by the mains.

In some areas, mains pressure varies considerably throughout a 24-hour period. During the day, when demand is high, pressure will be low, whereas in the evening as demand falls off the pressure increases. These fluctuations in pressure don't affect low pressure valves but they do affect high pressure ones, which can perform erratically as a result. You can overcome this problem if it affects you by replacing your high pressure ball-valves with equilibrium valves.

Equilibrium ball-valves

You can buy Portsmouth and diaphragm equilibrium valves. These are both designed to allow a small quantity of water to pass through or round the washered piston (or diaphragm) into a watertight chamber beyond. Acting as it does on the rear of the piston, and being at the same pressure as the mains, the water in the chamber ensures that the piston is held in equilibrium. What this means in practice is that the valve is operated solely by the movement of the float arm, rather than by a combination of the movement of the float arm *and* the pressure of the incoming water as is the case in an ordinary high-pressure valve. In addition to re-filling your cistern promptly regardless of any fluctuations in mains pressure, equilibrium valves also eliminate the 'bounce' as the valve closes – a common cause of water hammer. A diaphragm equilibrium valve will give you a particularly rapid and silent refill.

CLEARING BLOCKAGES

There are few plumbing emergencies quite as unpleasant as a blocked drain or waste pipe. However, it's usually possible to cure the problem if you know what to do when you've tracked down the blockage and you have the right equipment.

Professional plumbers rarely relish being called out to deal with a blockage. There *are* specialist drain clearance firms, but they can't always be contacted quickly in an emergency – and their charges reflect what can sometimes be the unpleasantness of the job. Drain or waste-pipe clearance is usually well within the capacity of the householder, and there are certainly few more cost-effective do-it-yourself jobs about the house.

Coping with blocked sinks

The outlet of the sink, usually the trap immediately beneath the sink itself, is the commonest site of waste-pipe blockage. Usually the obstruction can be cleared quickly and easily by means of a sink-waste plunger or force cup. This is a very simple plumbing tool obtainable from any do-it-yourself shop, ironmongers or household store. It consists of a rubber or plastic hemisphere, usually mounted on a wooden or plastic handle. Every household should have one.

To use it to clear a sink waste blockage, first press a damp cloth firmly into the overflow outlet, holding it securely with one hand. Then pull out the plug and lower the plunger into the flooded sink so that the cup is positioned over the waste outlet. Plunge it up and down sharply half a dozen or more times. Since water cannot be compressed, the water in the waste between the cup and the obstruction is converted into a ram to clear the blockage. The overflow outlet is sealed to prevent the force being dissipated up the overflow.

If your first efforts at plunging are unsuccessful, persevere. Each thrust may be moving the obstruction a little further along the waste pipe until it is discharged into the drain gully or the main soil and waste stack.

Should plunging prove unsuccessful you'll have to gain access to the trap. Brass and lead U-shaped traps have a screwed-in plug at the base. With plastic U-shaped and bottle traps the lower part can be unscrewed and removed – see *Ready Reference*. Before attempting this, put the plug in the sink and place a bucket under the trap; it will probably be full of water unless the blockage is immediately below the sink

WHERE BLOCKAGES OCCUR

Blockages can occur in several different places around your home's waste and drain systems. The commonest sites are:

1 *traps under basins, baths and sinks;*

2 *WC traps;*

3 *waste pipes running to soil stacks, hoppers or gullies;*

4 *rainwater or yard gullies;*

5 *underground drain runs between house and manhole;*

6 *intercepting chambers (see* Ready Reference*);*

7 *underground drain runs between manhole and sewer.*

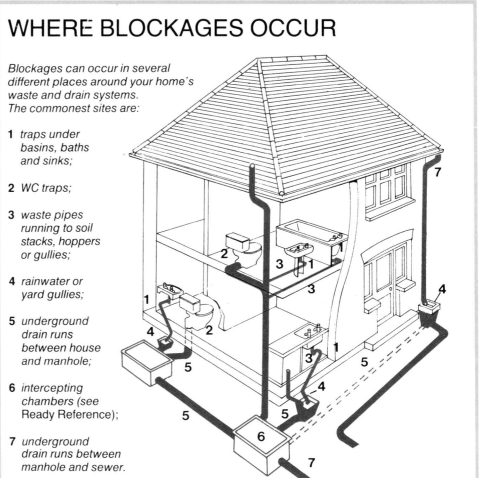

CLEARING BLOCKED TRAPS

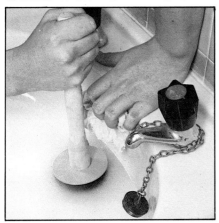

1 *Try using a plunger to clear blocked sinks, basins, baths or WCs. Cover the overflow with a damp cloth, then push the plunger down sharply several times.*

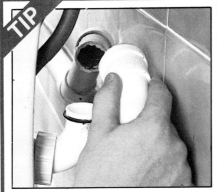

3 *In a confined space like this, you may find it easier to remove the next push-fit elbow before tackling the connection to the waste outlet itself.*

5 *Before reassembling the trap fully, check that the next section of the waste pipe is clear by poking a length of wire down it as far as you can reach.*

2 *If the blockage persists, you will have to open up the trap. Put the plug in the basin and have a bucket handy to catch the trap contents.*

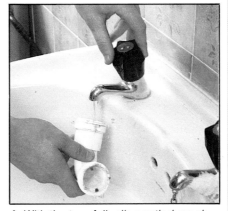

4 *With the trap fully dismantled, wash each component thoroughly to remove the blockage and any scum clinging to the pipe sides. Leave the plug in.*

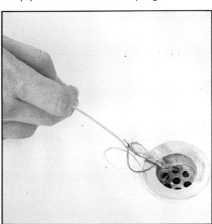

6 *A build-up of hair and scum can often block basin wastes just below the outlet. Fish out as much as possible with a slim wire hook passed through the grating.*

Ready Reference

TYPES OF TRAP

On old plumbing systems you may still come across lead traps, which have a removable rodding eye in the base. On more modern systems plastic traps will have been installed, and it is easy to unscrew part of the trap to clear a blockage.

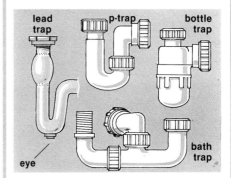

TIP: SUPPORT LEAD TRAPS

Lead traps are very soft, and may bend or split if you use force to open the rodding eye. To avoid this:
● insert a piece of scrap wood into the U-bend of the trap
● undo the rodding eye with a spanner, turning it in the direction shown while bracing the trap with the scrap wood
● reverse the procedure to replace it.

RODDING INTERCEPTING TRAPS

The manhole nearest the main sewer may be an intercepting trap, designed to keep sewer gases out of the house drains. To clear a blockage between it and the sewer,

feed your rods into the rodding arm. To prevent the stonware plug from being dislodged and causing a blockage you can have a glass disc fitted.

outlet, and the chances are that opening the trap will release it. Having done so, probe into the trap, and into the waste pipe itself. You can buy purpose-made sink waste augers for this purpose, but you'll find that a piece of expanding curtain wire, with a hook on the end, can be equally effective.

Blocked baths and basins

Basin and bath wastes are less likely to be totally blocked than sink wastes but, when blockages do occur, they can usually be cleared in the same way. They are, however, very subject to partial blockage. The waste water is often found to run from the bath or basin ever more slowly. This may be due to a build-up of scum, scale and hair on the inside of the waste pipe, and the use of a proprietary drain-clearing chemical will usually clear it. These frequently have a caustic soda base, so they should be kept away from children and handled with care, strictly in accordance with the manufacturer's instructions. Before spooning them into the bath or basin waste outlet it is wise to smear petroleum jelly over the rim of the outlet to protect the chromium finish, especially with plastic baths or fittings.

Partial blockage of a wash basin waste may often be caused by hair suspended from the grid of the outlet. This may be all but invisible from above, but probing with a piece of wire (the old standby of a straightened-out wire cotahanger is useful) can often produce festoons. If you can't clear the hair by this means, unscrew the nut that connects the threaded waste outlet to the trap and pull the trap to one side. Now use a pair of pliers to pull the hair away from beneath the grid.

Overflows from gullies

Where waste pipes and downpipes discharge into gullies, the first signs of trouble may be when the gully overflows and the surrounding area is flooded as a result. The gully trap has probably become blocked, either by blown leaves or other debris, or by a build-up of grease and scum on the sides of the trap. Raise the gully grid if one is fitted (and get a new one if it's broken or missing). Then scoop out any debris with a rubber-gloved hand or an improvised scoop, scrub the gully out with caustic soda and flush it through with plenty of clean water before replacing the grid.

Blockages below ground

A blockage in the underground drains may be shown up by a WC which, when flushed, fills with water almost to the rim and then very slowly subsides, or by dirty water seeping from under a manhole cover. You'll need a set of drain rods to clear any underground blockage. It is best to hire these from a local

CLEARING BLOCKED GULLIES

1 *Both surface-water and yard gullies are easily blocked by wind-blown debris such as waste paper and dead leaves. First lift off the gully grating.*

2 *Try to scoop out as much debris as possible from the gully trap, either by hand or with an improvised scoop such as an old tin can.*

3 *If the blockage is cleared and the water flows away, scrub out the sides of the gully with a brush and detergent. Clean the gully grating too.*

4 *Finally, hose the gully out thoroughly with running water. If you are unable to clear the blockage, you may have to rod the drain run from a nearby manhole.*

tool hire firm if and when the emergency arises. A drain that blocks sufficiently frequently to justify the purchase of a set of rods undoubtedly has a major defect that needs professional advice and attention.

Raising the manhole covers will give you an indication of the position of the blockage. If, for instance, the manhole near your front boundary is empty, but the one beside the house into which the soil pipe and yard gully discharges is flooded, then the blockage must be between these two manholes. Screw two or three lengths of drain-rod together, add the appropriate accessory to one end and then lower it into the flooded manhole. Feel for the drain half-channel at its base and push the rod end along it and into the drain towards the obstruction. Screw on extra rods as necessary until you reach and clear the blockage. You may find it easier to push the rods into the drain — and to extract them

again — if you twist them as you do so. *Always* twist in a clockwise direction. If you twist anti-clockwise the rods will unscrew and one or more lengths will be left irretrievably in the drain.

Many older houses have intercepting traps. These traps, which were intended to keep sewer gases out of the house drains, are the commonest site of drain blockage. You can see if your drains have an intercepting trap by raising the cover of the manhole nearest to your property boundary before trouble occurs and looking inside. If there is an intercepting trap the half-channel of the gully will fall into what appears to be a hole at the end of the manhole; actually it is the inlet to the trap. Immediately above this hole will be a stoneware stopper. This closes the rodding arm giving access to the length of drain between the intercepting trap and the sewer.

A blockage in the intercepting trap is

RODDING BLOCKED DRAINS

1 *Raise manhole covers carefully. If the hand grips are missing, use an old brick bolster to lift one edge, and then slide in a piece of wood.*

2 *With the wood supporting one end of the cover, grasp it securely and lift it to one side. Bend from the knees so you don't strain your back.*

3 *Select one of the drain rod heads (a rubber disc is being fitted here) and screw it securely onto the threaded end of the first drain rod.*

4 *Screw a second rod onto the end of the first, and lower the head into the half-channel in the bottom of the chamber. Push the rods towards the blockage.*

5 *Screw on further rods as necessary and work the head in and out to clear the blockage. Never turn the rods anticlockwise, or they may unscrew and be lost.*

6 *When you have cleared the blockage, hose down the sides and base of the manhole with running water, and let water run through the drain for a while.*

indicated when all the drain inspection chambers are flooded. It can usually be cleared quite easily by plunging. To do this, screw a drain plunger (a 4in or 100mm diameter rubber disc) onto the end of a drain rod. Screw on one or two other rods as necessary and lower the plunger into the flooded manhole. Feel for the half-channel at its base and move the plunger along until you reach the inlet of the intercepting trap. Plunge down sharply three or four times and, unless you are very unlucky, there will be a gurgle and the water level in the manhole will quickly fall.

Very occasionally, there may be a blockage between the intercepting trap and the sewer, and the point must be made that this length of drain is the householder's responsibility, even though much of it may lie under the public highway. To clear such a blockage the stoneware cap must be knocked out of

the inlet to the rodding arm (this can be done with the drain rods but it isn't the easiest of jobs) and the rods passed down the rodding arm towards the sewer.

Intercepting traps are also subject to a kind of partial blockage that may go unnoticed for weeks or even months. An increase in pressure on the sewer side of the trap – due to a surge of storm water, for instance – may push the stopper out of the rodding arm. It will fall into the trap below and cause an almost immediate stoppage. However this will not be noticed because sewage will now be able to escape down the open rodding arm to the sewer. The householder usually becomes aware of a partial blockage of this kind as a result of an unpleasant smell, caused by the decomposition of the sewage in the base of the manhole.

The remedy is, of course, to remove the stopper and to replace it. Where the trouble

recurs it is best to discard the stopper and to lightly cement a glass or slate disc in its place. In the very unusual event of a stoppage between the intercepting trap and the sewer, this disc can be broken with a crowbar and replaced after the drain has been cleared – see *Ready Reference*.

After any drain clearance the manhole walls should be washed down with a hot soda solution and a garden hose should be used to flush the drain through thoroughly.

Blocked gutters

Roof rainwater gutters may become obstructed by leaves or other objects. An overflowing gutter isn't an instant catastrophe but, if neglected, it will cause dampness to the house walls. An inspection, removal of debris and a hose down of gutters should be a routine part of every householder's preparations for winter.

CHAPTER 5
Insulating

CONDENSATION causes and cures

Condensation in buildings is a bigger problem now than ever before – the result of changes in building methods and our way of life. To tackle it, you need to know what it is and why it happens.

The air around us contains water vapour, and the amount it can carry depends on the temperature – the higher the temperature, the greater the amount of water vapour. If the air becomes cooler it cannot carry as much vapour, and the excess may be released in the form of water droplets. In the atmosphere this produces clouds and rainfall; in confined spaces like the home it produces condensation.

You can see this happening quite easily in a kitchen when you're cooking. A lot of water vapour is created by boiling pans, and this remains suspended in the air in the kitchen as long as the temperature is high. But if the air meets a cold surface – a window, for example – its temperature drops, and the excess water vapour turns back into water, or condenses. Condensation occurs particularly in bathrooms, but can be found throughout your home at some time or another.

Condensation is always a menace, and can lead to corrosion and rot as can any unwanted water. If it forms only a thin film of moisture, this may quickly evaporate when the room heats up, but too often the water seeps into cracks and crevices in the house's structure and starts to cause problems.

The problem of moisture

Dense materials, like glass and glazed tiles, are not harmed by moisture and can be easily wiped off. But if it runs off the surface it can carry with it dirt, which can stain nearby materials. Metal surfaces do not absorb moisture, but moisture combined with oxygen in the air will cause iron to rust. If mineral salts are present, or if dissimilar metals are in contact, corrosion may take place.

Some materials, like fibreboard and plasterboard, lose their strength when wet and may swell and sag. But more damaging is the risk of mould and rot. Mould spores are almost always present in the air, and on the surface of many materials. To flourish, they need moisture, and food which is supplied by general dirt. Condensation provides the moisture. Textured surfaces collect more dirt than smooth surfaces, and are more likely to develop mould growth.

Mould first appears in spots or small patches and spreads to form a furry layer – usually grey-green, black or brown in colour. Though unsightly it can easily be cleaned off in the early stages. It may do little harm, but will reappear unless a fungicide is used.

Fungal attack on timber, particularly dry rot, is more serious, causing lasting damage. Once established, dry rot can actually produce the moisture needed for further growth and it can spread extensively through other materials such as brick.

Moisture has another unwanted effect. Many materials, such as sheeps' wool and plastic foam, gain heat insulating qualities through the small pockets of air in them. If this air is replaced by water, then this insulating power is lost. If this happens within a brick wall – so-called 'interstitial' condensation – the wall's resistance to heat flow is decreased and the wall gets colder, producing still more condensation.

How water vapour is created

We can't avoid producing water vapour indoors. For example, during eight hours of sleep, every human body gives off a quarter litre (½ pint) of water. When we are active we make much more. One of the worst offenders in the home is the flueless room heater, which gives out one litre (1¾ pints) of water vapour for every litre of oil burnt.

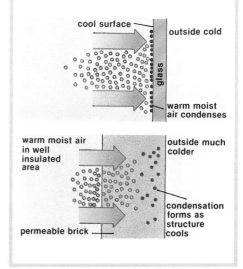

WHAT CAUSES CONDENSATION

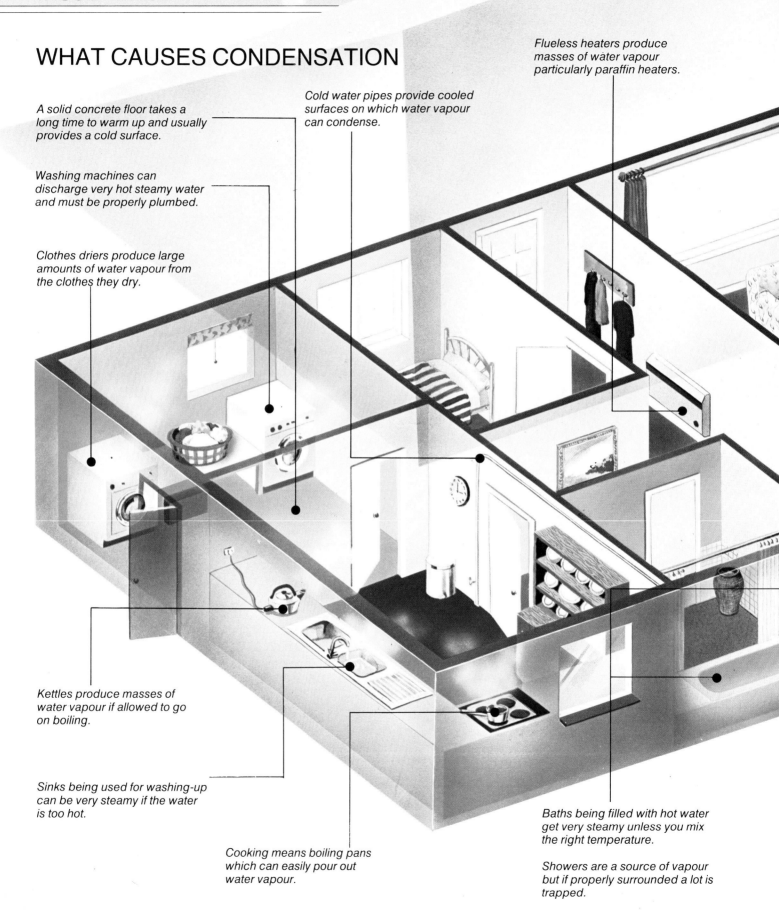

A solid concrete floor takes a long time to warm up and usually provides a cold surface.

Washing machines can discharge very hot steamy water and must be properly plumbed.

Clothes driers produce large amounts of water vapour from the clothes they dry.

Cold water pipes provide cooled surfaces on which water vapour can condense.

Flueless heaters produce masses of water vapour particularly paraffin heaters.

Kettles produce masses of water vapour if allowed to go on boiling.

Sinks being used for washing-up can be very steamy if the water is too hot.

Cooking means boiling pans which can easily pour out water vapour.

Baths being filled with hot water get very steamy unless you mix the right temperature.

Showers are a source of vapour but if properly surrounded a lot is trapped.

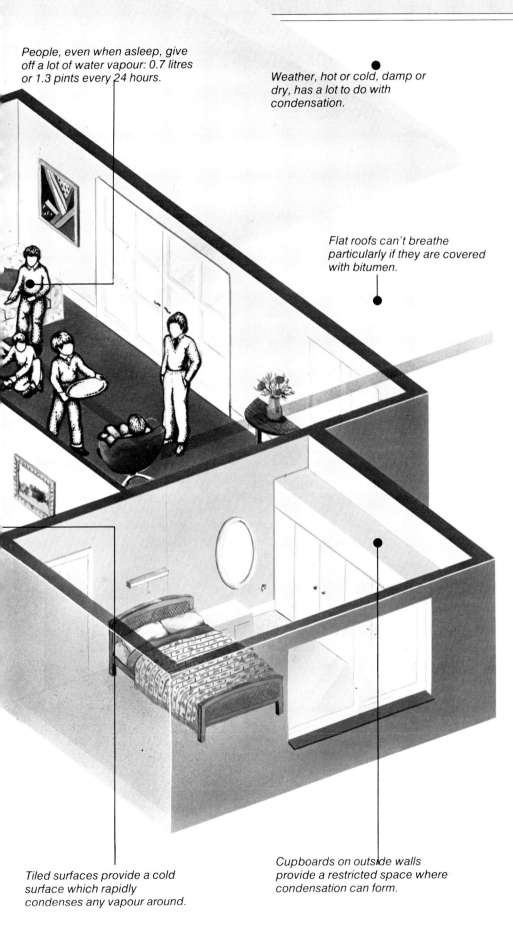

People, even when asleep, give off a lot of water vapour: 0.7 litres or 1.3 pints every 24 hours.

Weather, hot or cold, damp or dry, has a lot to do with condensation.

Flat roofs can't breathe particularly if they are covered with bitumen.

Tiled surfaces provide a cold surface which rapidly condenses any vapour around.

Cupboards on outside walls provide a restricted space where condensation can form.

HOW TO CURE CONDENSATION

Mechanical ventilators
Powered by an electric motor, these are the sophisticated development of wind-operated vents and obviously much more efficient. If one is installed in a room where there is a central heating or hot water boiler there should be a vent in the inside door to ensure that noxious gases are not drawn into the room.

Inner wall insulation
Lining rooms with polystyrene sheet is a cheap form of wall insulation and reduces heat loss. It also reduces the condensation threat but can lead to interstitial condensation inside the cavity itself.

Cavity wall insulation
This reduces heat loss from the house and therefore your heating bills. It also cuts down the incidence of cold outside walls, reducing the likelihood of condensation.

Vented clothes driers
Clothes driers produce masses of water vapour and should always be vented direct to the outside of the house. This can be done via a flexible hose put out of a window, but ideally should be through a vent pipe placed in the wall exiting via a protective cowl.

Self-closing doors
Where there are heavy sources of water vapour, as in the kitchen, it is best to contain them rather than let the vapour spread to other rooms where quite often they are likely to condense. A self-closing door is the answer here.

Cooker hoods
These are designed to vent hot air and gases coming up from the cooker. Those which simply filter the air are really only good for getting rid of kitchen smells, but those which can be vented to the outside air, either directly through the wall or via a fan controlled duct, can cut down condensation risk.

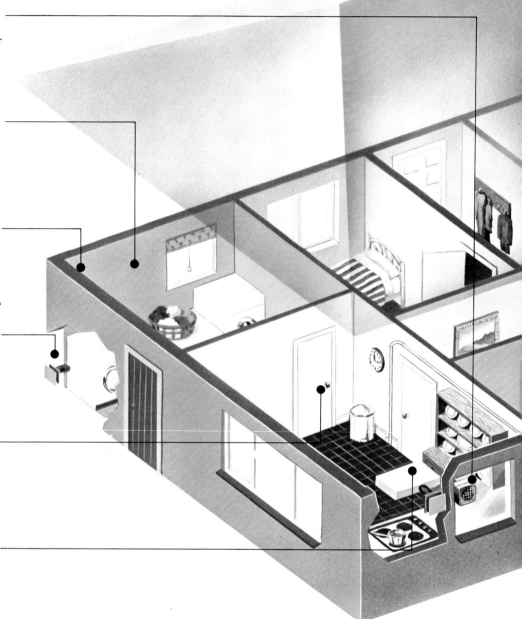

Having a bath or shower can produce two litres (3½ pints) of water vapour. Another offender is damp. This can penetrate an outside wall or a solid ground floor lacking damp-proofing and later evaporate because of indoor warmth, so adding more water vapour to the air.

Because it is impossible to prevent the creation of water vapour, the main aim then becomes to get rid of it before it can give trouble by forming condensation. Ventilation is the answer. This can be done by opening windows, installing extractor fans, venting exhaust air from clothes driers to the outside air and the use of balanced flue gas heaters.

Water vapour moves about. It doesn't only condense on cold surfaces in the room where it is produced; it can penetrate all parts of the home, and is likely to condense in any colder area it reaches. It also rises by convection to cooler bedrooms and the space under the roof.

Warm, moist air gets into the roof space through ceiling cracks, holes used by pipes and electric wiring and gaps around the trap door. It doesn't matter how small the gap – it can still get through as it's a gas. It also passes through porous plaster or plaster-board ceilings unless they incorporate a moisture barrier.

Unless there is sufficient ventilation for it to escape to the outside air, it will condense on the roof covering and roof timbers. The severity of the condensation depends on the roof construction, how well the loft is insulated and ventilated, and how easily moist house air can get into it. However, it can very quickly build up in a poorly ventilated loft, saturating the insulation and

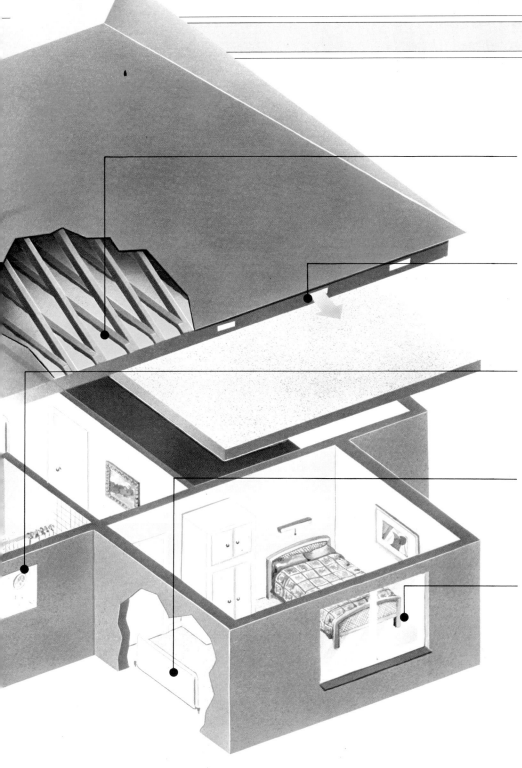

Loft insulation
Loft insulation is yet another way of retaining heat inside the main part of the house and also contains the risk of condensation, but it must be coupled with the provision of proper loft ventilation, or condensation may become a problem in the loft.

Loft ventilation
This is vital to protect the timbers in your roof from rot attack. The better the loft insulation the greater the temperature contrast between the loft and rooms below, and the greater the risk of condensation.

Wind-operated vents
These small plastic vents set into the window frame usually blow round in the wind, and even a small breeze can make them work. They simply provide ventilation which disposes of unwanted water vapour. While not that effective they are very cheap to install.

Central heating
Usually installed as the source of heat, central heating will also reduce the risk of condensation as the water vapour is not allowed to cool and the temperature differential between different parts of the house is reduced. But effective central heating is rather expensive to run for long periods these days.

Double glazing
This is a highly effective way of retaining heat as 20% is lost through windows which are single glazed. It also ensures that the inner pane of glass is not cold, which is usually the case with single glazing, and thus eliminates a major source of condensation.

making it quite useless. In the end it can soak through the ceiling too.

Loft insulation (covered on pages 140-144) certainly makes a house warmer, but means that the roof structure will be colder. This exaggerated difference in temperature enables the water vapour to pass more easily from the house itself to the roof space. Tiles on loosely laid felt will 'breathe' and allow the moisture to disperse, but fully-lined roofs tend to trap moist air. Even worse are flat roofs having a lead, bituminous felt or asphalt covering; these cannot breathe at all.

Vapour inside the walls
The better draught-proofed, and more airtight a house, the more likely it is that moist air will force its way into the structure during the winter, possibly leading to condensation.

While 'superficial' condensation is a nuisance and can spoil decoration, it is visible, and serves as a warning to the householder to provide better ventilation. But interstitial condensation can cause serious and lasting damage to a building and, unless it is so severe that damp shows through on a ceiling or outside wall, it can go

unnoticed for many years. In older draughty houses, risk of 'interstitial' condensation is slight, though superficial condensation will sometimes occur in unheated rooms. Risks increase when fireplaces are blocked up, windows double-glazed, external doors draught-proofed, and lofts and external walls better insulated. Builders of new, well-insulated air-tight houses should guard against moist air getting into walls and the loft by using air barriers, called vapour checks, and by ensuring that any air leaking through is easily vented to the outside.

INSTALLING DRAUGHT EXCLUDERS

Why put up with uncomfortable draughts when you can buy a range of easy-to-install excluders to provide an effective seal against the weather? Here's how to fit some of the more common types.

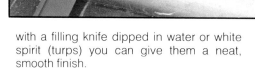

There's nothing more unpleasant than sitting in a draught. Yet while many of us will complain about feeling shivery, it's surprising how many people are prepared to put up with a cold stream of air blowing round their ankles. However, apart from making your home more comfortable to live in, draught-proofing could also save you a considerable amount of money which will more than pay for the cost of the work. The equation is simple: *draughts = higher heating bills.*

Tracking down the draught
How many times have you heard the expression: 'There's a draught coming from somewhere'? Usually the reason is put down to an interior door that hasn't been closed properly or which has a large gap under it. But in fact, in most instances this isn't to blame. The draught has to come from somewhere, yet in most cases it's coming through ill-fitting window casements, sashes and doors. Fortunately, however, there's a tremendous range of products on the market to deal with virtually every situation and you should choose the type best suited to your needs.

When it comes to installing these devices, carry out the work systematically and don't just block up a few draughts and leave others. You've got to seal the outside of the house and when you've done that it won't matter if you leave an interior door open – it won't on its own cause a draught. However, don't get over-enthusiastic and block up airbricks and ventilators as it's important to maintain a circulating supply of air in the house – especially where fuel-burning appliances are in use.

Checking frame fit
If a window or door frame has been correctly installed there shouldn't be a gap between the frame and the wall outside. If there is, say as a result of settlement or a poorly seasoned frame drying out, you may well get a draught through here (as well as penetrating damp). The answer is to use either flexible crack fillers or mastics, which are most easily applied with a caulking gun. Mastics don't set, so they can cater for slight movements in the frame, and by running over the surface

with a filling knife dipped in water or white spirit (turps) you can give them a neat, smooth finish.

Using foam strip
Foam strip is probably the most common method of draught-proofing and is easily available in a variety of forms and thicknesses. It's also cheap, but not very long-lasting. However, all you have to do when it wears out is to peel it off and stick on a new strip. Invariably some of the adhesive backing will be left behind when you do this, but it can be removed from the frame by rubbing with a cloth soaked in white spirit (turps).

The strip has to be stuck on the rebate of the frame so that the door or window compresses it when closed and does not slide across its surface. For this reason on the hinge side of the frame you have to position the strip on the *side* of the rebate.

Weatherstrip
Being made of metal or plastic, these excluders are more substantial than foam strip. They work on a hinge principle – some are in the form of a flap, others have a V profile – which bridges the gap between the frame and the window or door. The strip can either be fitted to the frame (in the same places you would fit foam strip) or to the window or door itself. If you are installing it round a door then you can't run it down the lock/handle edge:

you'll have to use the frame for this part. Generally speaking fixing to a door is more tricky and you may find it easier to take the door off the hinges first. Weatherstrip can be fitted to the bottom edge, but check that it doesn't drag across a carpet as the door is opened and closed.

Rigid and flexible strip
In contrast to the previous excluders, these strips are fitted to the inner face of the door or window frame on the outside, not in the rebate. They consist of a plastic or aluminium holder with a flexible insert (either a PVC flap or tube) against which the door presses when it's closed. For this reason it's best to position the strip with the door shut so you can see that the flexible strip touches the door along its entire length. You can then open the door to make nailing easier.

Dealing with door bottoms
This is probably going to be where you get most draughts because for a door to operate without sticking there's got to be a small gap between the bottom edge and the sill. But there are a number of devices specially designed to seal this gap when the door is closed. They range in sophistication from a simple flap fitted to the door to two-part sealers which are fitted to the door and sill.
Simple excluders These consist of a brush or PVC strip set in a plastic, aluminium or

DRAUGHT-PROOFING WOODEN FRAMES

1 If fitting a metal spring strip, there needs to be at least a 2mm ($^1/_{16}$in) gap between the frame and door or window. Check this with a coin.

2 Measure accurately between the door jambs and also down the side, then cut the metal strip to length. Normally it's thin enough to cut with scissors.

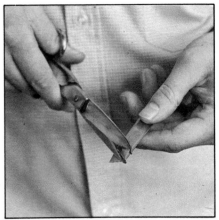

3 So that the spring flaps of the strip complete the seal at the corners, mitre the edges – 45° for the top ends and 20° for the sides is about right.

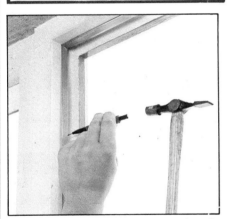

4 Fix the top strip into position with nails at each end, and then at 100mm (4in) intervals. Next nail the side strips in place down the rebates.

5 Some strip systems have to be nailed to the outside of the door frame. Again you have to mitre the corners of the rubber strip to continue the seal.

6 When the door is closed it presses against the rubber seal, so cutting out any draughts. But you may have problems if the door is badly warped.

7 If you're using foam strip on outward opening windows or doors measure the inside of the rebates to see roughly how much strip you're going to use.

8 Press the end of the strip into the corner of the frame, then work along the rebate unrolling the strip as you go. Keep it taut for easier application.

9 If the window frame has warped so that in places it doesn't press against the foam, you can apply a second strip of sealer over the first.

DRAUGHT-PROOFING DOOR BOTTOMS

1 If you're using a door brush, mark the width of the door on the plastic holder, slide back the brush and cut the holder to length with a hacksaw.

2 Push the brush back so that it's flush with the far end, then use the cutting edges of a pair of pliers to cut the strip to the same length as the holder.

3 Position the excluder so that the brush rests on the floor. Fix the outside screws first so you can adjust the bar if the floor is uneven.

4 With this automatic device, make sure that the spring gear and striking bar are on the door opening side. Then cut the bar to length and screw it in place.

5 The spring mechanism means that the bar is raised when the door is opened. Cut the vinyl strip to length and slide it into the groove.

6 Screw the striking plate to the inside of the door jamb. You may have to chisel a bevel on the jamb so the excluder can swing through it when the door is closed.

7 As the door is shut, the striking bar hits the striking plate, forcing the vinyl flap down against the spring and onto the threshold to complete the seal.

8 There are various forms of threshold sealer. With this type, cut the aluminium holder to the width of the door jambs, leaving screw holes at each end.

9 When the holder is screwed in place, cut the vinyl strip about 12mm ($1/2$in) longer than the threshold. Then press the strip into the channel.

wooden batten. They are usually sold in 900mm (36in) lengths but most can be cut down to size. To fit them you just have to nail or screw them to the bottom edge of the opening side of the door (see step-by-step photographs). Where a door has a high sill you'll have to use a type that closes against the sill itself rather than rests on the floor.

Hinged excluders One of the main problems with the simple flat excluders is that they drag across the floor when the door is opened. So to get round this you could install a hinged type instead. These also vary in complexity, but all of them have some form of springing device which lifts a flexible PVC strip clear of the sill when the door is opened. You'll also have to fit a striking plate or a stud to the bottom of the door frame which will force the flap down over the gap when the door is closed. A further advantage of these excluders is that they automatically compensate for uneven sills and they can also deal with large gaps (see step-by-step photographs).

Threshold excluders The types used for internal doors are simply screwed to the floor (see step-by-step photographs), but if the gap is too wide you'll have to make some modifications. This may mean mounting the excluder on a strip of wood, fitting a replacement sill or lowering the door on its hinges. If the gap is too narrow for the excluder to be fitted you may have to trim a little off the bottom of the door. Use a plane rather than a saw, and chamfer the door so that it squeezes the flexible part of the excluder as it closes.

Threshold excluders for external doors are more complicated and consist either of a complete replacement sill containing a simple threshold excluder, or a face sealing/combination-type excluder. The replacement sill is no more difficult to fit than a simple threshold excluder, though the ends should be sealed with mastic or putty to stop water getting under them.

In contrast, the second type needs considerable care when it's being installed. Instructions vary, but it is important to ensure that where there are two parts they meet accurately, and that the weather is kept out of the seal, which means screwing a weatherbar along the bottom outside face of the door. Some types even require the door or frame to be shaped to fit the excluder.

Ready Reference

FITTING DRAUGHT-PROOFING

Different types of excluder have to be fitted to different parts of a door or window frame, as shown below.

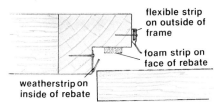

flexible strip on outside of frame

foam strip on face of rebate

weatherstrip on inside of rebate

TIP: USE A NAIL PUNCH

To prevent damaging the excluder and frame use a nail punch to drive the fixing pins.

SILICONE SEALANTS

As an alternative to strip excluders use silicone sealant to make a tailor-made gasket. It's ideal for metal frames and badly warped doors and windows.

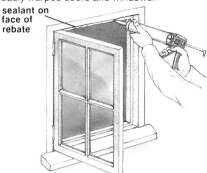

sealant on face of rebate

● clean and make good any paintwork
● apply a thin bead of silicone to the face of the frame's rebates and to the side of the rebate on the hinge side
● coat the closing faces of the door or window with special release agent (petroleum jelly, liquid detergent or sticky tape will also do) so they don't stick to the silicone when the door is shut to mould the seal
● leave silicone overnight to cure
● clean up the seal with a sharp knife.

METAL WINDOWS AND FRAMES

These tend to fit better than wooden ones, but if you need to draught-proof them use foam strip or silicone sealant.

LETTERBOXES

Fit a hinged flap over the opening on the inside to seal out draughts. Alternatively fit a brush type excluder.

For further information on draught-proofing materials see FACTFINDER 55.

DRAUGHT-PROOFING SASH WINDOWS

Sash windows are the most difficult type of window to draught-proof. Usually you'll have to use a combination of excluders to make an effective seal.

outside

inside

foam strip, sprung strip or V seal fixed to top of sash or frame

spring strip or V seal fixed to side of frame or sash

self-adhesive brush strip, V seal or spring strip

flexible or rigid seal fixed to sash

flexible strip fixed to sash bottom

foam strip, sprung strip or V seal fixed to bottom of sash or frame

FITTING SECONDARY GLAZING

Secondary double glazing – the fitting of fixed, hinged or sliding panes to the inside of existing windows – cuts heat loss and draughts dramatically. If you install it yourself, it need not be prohibitively expensive either.

There are two basic types of double glazing available to the homeowner. Primary double glazing involves the fitting of a sealed glazing unit – two linked panes of glass separated only by a hermetically sealed gap – into an existing or replacement window frame. These sealed units are factory-made, but can be installed by the do-it-yourselfer (see pages 132-135).

Secondary double glazing is the term used to describe the installation of a completely independent second layer of glass (or other glazing material) some distance away from the existing single glazing, either to the inside of the window frame or to the window reveal surrounding it.

The fitting of this form of double glazing is well within the scope of the do-it-yourselfer and offers some advantages over primary double glazing. It is cheaper and quicker to install, since instead of having to order sealed units from a specialist manufacturing company you need only visit your local DIY shop and collect the necessary kit of component parts.

Sealed units have no draughtproofing abilities when installed in old badly-fitting opening windows, whereas secondary double glazing seals the entire frame, acting as both a thermal barrier and draught-proofer.

It is worth noting, however, that primary double glazing is more effective as a thermal barrier and is also less obtrusive, being no more visible than a single pane of glass.

Types of secondary double glazing

An extremely wide variety of secondary double glazing systems exist to cater for virtually all situations (and pockets). Glass is by no means the only material used for glazing. Other products used are clear polythene film in varying degrees of strength and clarity, or other transparent rigid plastics.

Methods of framing the glazing also vary enormously, with just double-sided adhesive tape being used for some systems and rigid or flexible PVC or aluminium extrusions for others.

Yet more choice comes with installation methods, where there are fixed, hinged or sliding systems (vertical or horizontal).

Which type to choose

When deciding on a secondary double glazing system, several factors should be considered carefully. Cost naturally plays an important part. If you live in rented accommodation and don't expect to stay for long, or simply want the cheapest form of double glazing for financial reasons, then the chances are that you will find clear polythene sheeting will serve your purposes. Attached to the existing window frame with double-sided adhesive tape, the polythene will prevent draughts very successfully, but in its most basic form it is not totally clear, is easily damaged, and seldom looks very tidy.

This type of double glazing, although inexpensive and effective, does have one major disadvantage; once fixed, it is there for good – or at least until completely removed and discarded at the end of the winter.

Double glazing of this nature is classed as fixed, but there is another 'fixed' variety which is less permanent and which can be temporarily removed and later replaced successfully. This type generally consists of a sheet of glass or rigid plastic sheet fitted into either a plastic or aluminium frame and then secured to the existing window frame using turnbuttons or shaped studs which hold it firmly in place.

One drawback with fixed systems is that they do not allow for ventilation, and this can be very important. In situations where ventilation is necessary or you simply want easily openable windows, you will have to decide whether to purchase a double glazing system which incorporates sliding panels or hinged ones. And one factor which could help you make this choice is the sort of existing window you have.

Sliding double glazing systems need to have their outer tracks or channels secured to the sides, top and bottom of the window reveal. If your window has no reveal, or this is less than about 40mm (1½in) deep, then you will be unable to fit a sliding system unless you choose a type that is attached to the window frame itself.

Hinged systems are fixed to the existing window's surrounding wooden frame. In some cases, notably on metal windows, catches and stays project into the room past the frame and could prevent a hinged panel closing. The space between old and new panes can, however, be increased to allow for such projections by fitting an additional

FITTING SLIDING TRACK

1 *Measure the height and width of the opening at each side, and write down the smaller measurement in each case if the figures differ.*

2 *Mark the length required on each of the track sections, cut them with a hacksaw, and file the ends smooth. Then drill holes for the fixing screws.*

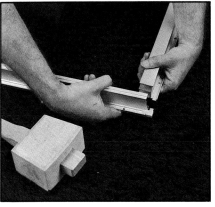

3 *Assemble the track sections on a flat surface. Insert the corner pieces and use a mallet to tap the sections together gently but firmly.*

4 *Lift the assembled frame into place against the window frame, offering up the top track first. Then secure it with just one screw at top and bottom.*

5 *Check that the frame is square by measuring diagonals, and that the top and bottom tracks are level. Add more screws to secure the frame.*

6 *Where screws have to be driven into inaccessible corners, use a short piece of clear plastic tubing to hold the screw on the blade as you drive it.*

timber framework to the face of the existing one, or within the reveal itself.

The width of the frame, whether old or newly-installed, must be sufficient to accommodate the hinge posts and panel surround of the hinged system you have chosen. It is therefore essential, before buying the materials for a hinged system, to check the minimum window frame dimensions recommended by the makers of that system. It is not uncommon for wooden window frames, particularly those around metal windows, to be too narrow for face fixing. Here again the problem can be overcome by fitting a new frame of sufficient width inside the reveal.

An additional inner frame can also be used to increase the gap between panes, as would be necessary if the double glazing were being installed for sound insulation. Where the aim is to reduce noise penetration the ideal gap between panes should be about 200mm (8in). A gap of around 25mm (1in) is the optimum for good thermal insulation when installing secondary double glazing.

Preparing for installation

Once you have chosen the basic variety of double glazing which suits your home and taste, you must study the manufacturers' literature with great care. This will tell you what thickness of glass should be used, the most common being 4mm (32oz). It will also detail existing frame size requirements, and indicate the maximum size that any one glazing panel should be. Information will also be provided, particularly with hinged or sliding systems, on how to measure the required sizes for each pane of glass so that this can be ordered in advance.

Some preparatory work may well be needed on the existing window frames. An additional sub-frame may have to be fitted, if, as described earlier, the present frame is not wide enough or has window fittings projecting past it. Use prepared timber painted to match the existing frame. Either secure it directly to the old frame with screws, or fix it to the window reveal with screws driven into wallplugs.

Clean and make good any defects on the old frame. Use draught excluders on badly-fitting opening windows to prevent as much air as possible from outside entering the space between the two glazing panes. It is the movement of air in the cavity that transfers warm air from the inner pane to the outer, and cold air from the outside pane to the inside one. Although the secondary double glazing will stop the draughts, it will be no more use than a single pane of glass at preventing heat loss if there is a howling gale blowing between the panes.

Plan your double glazing so that new

MAKING UP SLIDING PANELS

1 Follow the instructions for measuring and ordering the glass. Then mark each length of edge section to the correct dimension.

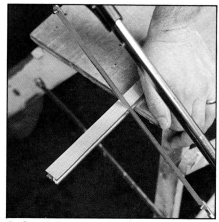

2 Carefully cut each edge section to length with a hacksaw, making the cut as square as possible and filing away any burr that's left.

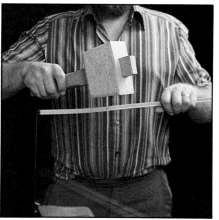

3 Measure and cut the lengths of glazing gasket using a fine-toothed saw. Then tap them into place along the appropriate edges of the glass with a mallet.

4 Tap the top and bottom edge sections into place over the gaskets, add the handle to one of the side sections and then tap the side sections into place.

5 With the pane completely framed by the four edge sections and their gaskets, drive in small self-tapping screws to lock the corner blocks in position.

6 Move the handle along the groove in the side section to the desired position and then use a screwdriver blade to form a notch in the aluminium.

7 Now use a mallet to tap the handle along the groove and over the burr formed by the screwdriver to lock it in place. Repeat on the other panel.

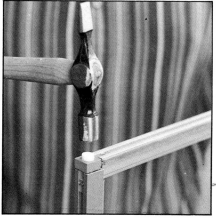

8 Tap the small PTFE slides into the recesses in the two bottom corner blocks of each panel. These help the panels to slide smoothly in the tracks.

9 Offer up first the inner and then the outer sliding panels to their respective tracks, and check that they slide from side to side without binding.

panels match as closely as possible the layout of your existing windows, with vertical divisions kept in line with mullions and opening sections (whether hinged or sliding) aligned with opening windows.

Measure your window opening carefully before ordering any glass. Problems can arise, particularly with sliding systems, if the window opening or frame is not square. If the two diagonal measurements of the opening are not equal, then the opening is definitely out of true, so for all calculations use the shortest width and height measurements.

Fitting the systems

1: Polythene film To fit this very basic form of fixed double glazing you will need just a roll of double-sided adhesive tape, a roll of clear polythene, a tape measure and pair of scissors or handyman's knife.

Stick the tape, without removing the backing paper, to the face of the outer window frame all round the perimeter. Measure the size of the opening and cut a piece of polythene to suit. Remove the backing paper from the top piece of tape and attach the edge of the polythene gently to it. Allow the sheeting to hang down. Check that it fits squarely before removing the backing paper from the other three pieces of tape and securing the polythene to it, keeping it stretched taut all the time.

Strong, less creasable polythene, classed as semi-rigid, can be fixed in a different way by cutting it to the exact size first, then attaching the sticky tape to it rather than the window frame. With the backing paper removed from the top edge only, the sheet is aligned to the head of the window frame, then stuck in place, followed by the other three edges.

2: Non-opening removable panels The most recent version of this form of double glazing uses a PVC extrusion stuck to the window frame, with a second extrusion holding the plastic sheeting in place. The work required involves cutting the PVC extrusion to size and fitting it around the existing frame. Either butt or mitred joints can be made at the corners. The plastic sheeting is then cut to size to fit in the profile. The clip-on extrusion is finally cut to size and snapped into place.

Other variations of this non-opening type of double glazing usually consist of plastic 'U' channelling fitted around pre-cut panes of glass. The glass, now with protected edges, is secured to the window frame with turnbuttons or clips spaced every 300mm (12in) around the perimeter to press the panel firmly against the frame and so exclude draughts. The glass for this type must be cut to size, allowing for the space taken up by the fixing clips on the frame. The panels can be removed and stored elsewhere at the end of the winter season.

Rather stronger non-opening panels can be made using aluminium framing instead of plastic 'U' channel, but these are generally a fixed version of hinged panels described next.

3: Hinged panels The most common hinged secondary double glazing systems are constructed using glass with an aluminium extrusion frame. The frame incorporates one channel with a plastic glazing gasket for the glass, a draught-proofing insert of either plastic or nylon fibre bristles which press against the window frame, and a second channel into which hinge fittings, turn-buttons and corner joins are fitted. Glass of the specified thickness is cut to size. Some makes can be fitted with more than one thickness of glass, this being determined by the overall panel size. A different size of glazing gasket is used for each thickness.

Once the glass is cut, the glazing gasket can be fitted to it, and the aluminium extrusions cut to length using a hacksaw. Straight cuts are made since the special corner joins eliminate the need for mitred corners.

The panel is then assembled, special care being needed to ensure that the glazing gasket is correctly seated in its channel and that all hinge fittings are properly inserted in the outer edge of the aluminium frame.

Hinge posts are then screwed to the window frame and the panel is lifted into place. Turnbuttons are finally fixed round the other three edges of the hinged panel to ensure that the panel is held tightly against the window frame when closed.

4: Sliding panels Made from either aluminium or PVC extrusions, sliding double glazing units are generally quick and easy to assemble and fit. Normally sold in two-part kit form with everything but the glass provided, the biggest problem is often deciding which part belongs where, so the first step is to identify the different sections. One part of the kit will contain all the vertical sections – the frame uprights and glass edging – and the other, the horizontal sections – the top and bottom sliding tracks and more glass edging.

The outer frame is fitted to the window reveal. This will usually involve drilling holes into the reveal sides, top and bottom and plugging the holes to take screws. Great care must be taken to ensure that the top double channel (the deeper one) is fitted directly above and in line with the bottom channel.

With the frame secured, the panes of glass can be fitted with their edge profiles, and the panels are then lifted into position in the sliding channels.

Provided that you have measured the glass correctly according to the instructions given by the double glazing manufacturer, you should find that the panels slide easily and that all nylon fibre draught excluders built into the system align perfectly.

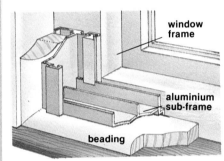
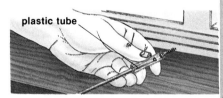

INSTALLING SEALED UNITS

Fitting sealed double glazing units will provide good heat and sound insulation as well as reducing draughts. They are easy to install in either existing or replacement window frames.

It is well known that double glazing offers considerable benefits for the homeowner. It can considerably reduce draughts from around the window area, not only those which enter through badly fitting frames but also down-draughts caused by warm air close to a cold, single pane of glass being quickly cooled and so falling. Eliminating these down-draughts makes for a more comfortable environment and prevents that 'chilly' feeling even though the room is heated. Some forms of double glazing can, to some extent, also reduce the penetration of noise from outside the building, but the major advantage is that the use of two panes instead of one can help reduce heat losses through glazed areas, providing a potential for saving energy and, hence, cutting fuel costs.

By far the most efficient method of achieving such thermal insulation is by the fitting of sealed double glazing units in place of single panes of glass in the window frame. This is known as primary double glazing.

Each sealed unit comprises two sheets of glass separated by a metal, glass or rigid plastic spacer which is fitted around the edges. The air between the two panes is dehydrated so that it contains no moisture, and the entire unit is sealed hermetically so that none can enter. As long as the seal remains unbroken condensation cannot form between the two sheets of glass.

The space between the panes normally varies between 6 and 12mm (¼ and ½in), the wider gap providing the best thermal insulation properties. The glass itself will vary in thickness from 3mm (⅛in) upwards depending on the size of the pane and the position of the window, many different types being available including float, laminated, toughened, standard sheet, tinted and obscured.

All sealed double glazing units are factory made by specialist companies and cannot be assembled at home. However, they can be fitted by the non-professional glazier in much the same way as normal replacement panes of glass (see techniques covered on pages 94-96) either to existing window frames or into completely new replacement windows.

Local glass merchants are becoming increasingly involved in the supply of sealed double glazing units in a wide range of standard sizes or in made-to-measure form to suit individual requirements, and it is now common practice for complete replacement windows, made from wood, aluminium or UPVC, to be supplied with sealed glazing units fitted as standard.

Fitting to existing frames

There are several factors you should consider in deciding whether or not to replace single panes of glass with sealed double glazing units.

Your existing window frames must be in excellent condition as there is little point in fitting sealed units into frames which may themselves have to be replaced within a few years. If the frames are more than 30 years old they are not likely to be of a standard size and so they would need specially-made sealed units. These would not be reusable in a new standard replacement frame and so this would have to be made specially, too.

Standard size sealed units are, in effect, mass-produced and so are cheaper than specially made ones. They are obtainable virtually 'off the shelf' from many suppliers, particularly for use in wooden-frame windows.

The rebate in the existing frames must be deep enough to accommodate the thickness of the sealed units and still allow them to be puttied in place or fixed with a glazing bead. You are likely to be changing from a single glazing thickness of 3 or 4mm (about ⅛in) to at least 12mm (½in), rising to 18mm (¾in) if you want units with a 12mm gap. For the latter, therefore, you would need a rebate measuring some 30mm (1¼in) from front to back, and not all old frames have this.

It is possible, however, to overcome the problem of too narrow a glazing rebate by using what are known as 'stepped' sealed units. These have one sheet of glass smaller than the other, the larger pane being fitted exactly in the same position as the original single pane with the smaller one on the inside, overlapping the back of the glazing rebate. Such stepped units are readily available to fit standard modern window sizes, or they can be made specially. They can be used in wooden frames but not in steel, which are generally unsuitable for sealed unit double glazing.

The same can be said of any windows incorporating a large number of small panes, such as Georgian styles. The cost of replacing all the individual panes with sealed units

PREPARING THE FRAME

1 Chop out all the old putty with a glazier's hacking knife or an old chisel. Take care not to damage the wooden window frame.

2 The glass will be held in place by small sprigs driven into the glazing rebate. Remove them with pincers or pliers. If straight they can be reused.

3 Have a helper tap around the edge of the window inside to free it. Wear gloves, or use a towel, to hold the glass and to avoid cuts.

4 With the old glass removed, chop away all remaining traces of putty from the rebate, being careful not to damage it in the process.

5 Brush all the dust and debris from the rebate and then prime any areas of exposed wood, allowing the primer to dry thoroughly.

6 When the primer has dried, apply a layer of bedding putty to the glazing rebate, working it well into the angle with your thumb.

would be extremely high, even if the glazing bars were of a suitable size. However, if you wish to keep this appearance, complete sealed units are available that reproduce the Georgian or leaded-light look quite effectively.

If you are quite satisfied that sealed units can be fitted to your existing frames, the first step is to measure the rebate so you can order the correct size. Take great care to get the correct dimensions because, once made, the size of the sealed unit cannot be altered. With standard sizes this is not so much of a problem, but if you are having the units specially made it could prove to be an expensive mistake if you get it wrong. The height and width of the rebate should each be measured in at least two places. If there is a difference between any of the measurements, work with the smaller size. Deduct a further 3mm (1/8in) from both the selected height and width to allow for clearance

around the unit, and this will be the size you should order.

Once you have the new sealed units, remove the putty from the window frame using an old chisel or similar tool and taking care not to damage the wood. Pull out the glazing sprigs with a pair of pincers and carefully lever the glass from the frame. Wear thick gloves or wrap a towel round the edge of the pane to prevent cuts as you lift it clear. If the glass is stuck fast to the old bedding putty, you may find that it can be tapped out from inside by a helper. Only gentle taps should be used to avoid breaking the glass accidentally. If all else fails, break the glass from the inside with a hammer (making sure there is no-one outside who might be injured by the flying fragments) and pull out any remaining glass with a gloved hand or pair of pliers. Clean out the remains of the putty and brush any dust or dirt from

the rebate. Reprime any areas of exposed wood and allow the primer to dry before fitting the new unit.

Line the rebate with a bedding layer of fresh putty, inserting rubber spacing blocks at intervals along the bottom and at each side. These should be cut to a thickness that will centralise and square the double glazing unit in the frame.

Offer up the new unit bottom edge first and gently press it into place with the palms of your hands so that the bedding putty oozes out round the inside edges of the sealed unit. Apply pressure only to the edges of the unit to prevent the glass breaking where it is unsupported in the middle. Check inside that there is about 3mm (1/8in) of putty between the inner face of the glazing unit and the rebate.

Next, very carefully tap in the glazing sprigs, using a cross-pein hammer. Use at least two sprigs per side and slide the head of the hammer across the glass to avoid breaking it. Drive each sprig in squarely so that it does not pinch the glass until only 6mm (¼in) remains visible. If you can't obtain proper glazing sprigs, you can use 19mm (¾in) panel pins with their heads nipped off.

Apply a finishing fillet of putty all round the rebate, pressing it into place with your thumb so that it covers all the edges of the glass. Smooth this off to an angle with a putty knife, making sure it does not project above the level of the rebate otherwise it will be visible from inside the room. Mitre the corners carefully and clean off any excess putty from both inner and outer panes of the unit. Leave the putty to harden for two weeks before applying a coat of primer and finally a finishing coat of paint. The latter should overlap onto the glass by 3mm (⅛in) to ensure a watertight seal.

If stepped double glazing units are to be fitted, a rebate for the stepped portion of the unit can be made by pinning lengths of beading around the inside of the window frame. Extra putty will be needed around this stepped rebate to provide a bed and surround for the inner pane of glass.

New wooden window frames

The increasing use of sealed double glazing units has led to most manufacturers supplying new wooden frames with glazing rebates of sufficient depth to take standard sealed units up to a maximum thickness of about 20mm (⅞in). By choosing your supplier carefully you will be able to order both frames and glazed units at the same time. You won't need to measure for the glass if the frame is one of the many standard sizes available.

If you need to have frames made, you should make it clear to the supplier that you will be fitting sealed double glazing units. He will then make allowance for this when making up the frames.

Normally, the glass is fitted using wooden glazing beads to hold it in place and putty or a similar glazing mastic to provide a seal between the unit and the frame. Acrylic putty is coming into use now and is ideal for double glazing units.

Aluminium and UPVC replacement windows

Although they are still available, it would be difficult to find either aluminium or UPVC replacement windows which are intended for use with single pane glazing. Invariably, such windows are designed to be fitted with sealed units having a 6 or 12mm (¼ or ½in) gap. It is common for companies specialising in these windows to operate a supply-and-fit service. However, most will also work on a

FITTING THE UNIT

1 Rubber spacing blocks should be set into the putty to centralise the unit in the frame. These can be cut from an ordinary hard pencil eraser.

2 Offer up the sealed double glazing unit, positioning the bottom edge first by setting it on the rubber blocks. Then push the unit into place.

5 Apply a fillet of putty to cover the sprigs and edge of the glazing unit, trimming it off with a putty knife. Remove excess putty from the glass.

6 Carefully mitre the putty at the corners of the glazing rebate with the putty knife. Alternatively, a straight-bladed filling knife could be used.

supply-only basis. This means that they will provide you with all the component parts ready for you to install yourself.

When doing your own fitting, the only measurements you need to give the supplier are the height and width of the opening into which the window is to be fitted. If the existing outer wood frame is in excellent condition, particularly at the bottom of the jambs and along the sill, you can normally fit the new window in exactly the same place as the old one, with no trouble at all.

If the outer frame is in poor condition and a new one is required, then the window supplier will be able to provide this as well. In this case, the only dimensions he needs are those of the opening in the wall. From these he will be able to calculate all the other sizes. You will, of course, need to specify the style of window, the type of glass, whether or not the glass has to be leaded or fitted with a grille to

simulate a Georgian style window, or be made non-standard in any other way.

The sealed double glazing units fitted in replacement aluminium or UPVC windows are the same as those used in wooden framed windows but the installation method is somewhat different. The glazing unit is always fitted 'dry', rubber or PVC gaskets being used to provide a seal to the frame. No mastics or sealants are required at the glazing stage. There are two basic glazing methods in common use. One of them involves making up the frame around the glazing unit. Each frame section, complete with gaskets on either side, is pushed over the sealed unit and then the four corners are screwed together tightly to hold it in place.

The other method is to make up the frame, which has an integral glazing rebate, insert the glazed unit and secure it in place with a 'snap-in' glazing bead. Provided that the

3 Once the unit is in place in the rebate, use firm hand pressure around the edges to bed it properly in the putty. Don't apply pressure to the centre.

4 If the old glazing sprigs are in good condition, re-use them; use new ones otherwise. Slide the hammer across the glass to prevent breakage.

7 Trim the putty which oozes out of the back of the rebate (when the glazing unit is pressed in place) flush with the edge of the frame.

8 Allow the putty to dry for 14 days before applying the first undercoat of paint. The final top coat should lap onto the glass by 3mm (1/8in).

Ready Reference

TYPES OF SEALED UNIT

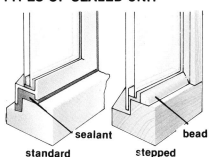

standard   stepped

sealant   bead

There are two types of sealed unit – standard and stepped. The former comprises two similar sized panes of glass held apart by a metal, glass or rigid plastic spacer. It is designed to fit in the glazing rebate in place of a single pane of glass. Where the rebate is too narrow, such as on old wooden windows, a stepped unit may be used.

GLAZING WITH WOOD BEADS

In some cases, glass is secured in the rebate by means of wooden beading pinned round the edge. With this kind of fixing, the glazing unit should be bedded in putty or a sealant before refitting the beading. It may be necessary to use a narrower bead than that fitted originally.

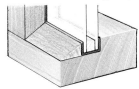

SETTING SPACING BLOCKS

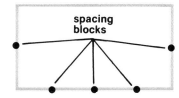

spacing blocks

To keep the glazing unit central and square in the rebate while the putty hardens, rubber spacing blocks should be set at regular intervals along the base of the rebate and at the sides. Set them out as shown. The number along the bottom depends on the width of the unit.

TIP: CLEANING WINDOWS

When fitting a sealed unit to a window on an upper floor, clean off all labels and finger marks from the outside before dismantling your access tower.

---

glazing bead is on the inside (which is becoming standard practice) the sealed unit can be replaced easily if damaged, and the glazing is secure. No potential intruder can prise off the bead and remove the glass from the outside. Gaskets are incorporated in the glazing rebate and glazing bead to ensure a watertight and airtight seal.

Condensation and safety

Obviously, the fitting of sealed double glazing units to old window frames can only be of value if those old frames are in good condition and are not so badly fiting that they let in draughts. This should be checked very carefully beforehand and, if necessary, the frames should be replaced.

Condensation will never appear in the space between the two panes of glass as long as the hermetic seal remains undamaged. Consequently, care should be taken during installation to ensure that the seal is not broken accidentally. Sealed units, may, however, develop condensation on the room side of the inner pane, although this is likely to be far less troublesome than on single glazed windows. The units should never be considered as a complete cure for a condensation problem. Their value lies in their thermal insulation properties and the elimination of down-draughts.

When ordering sealed double glazing units seek the advice of your local glass merchant. He will be able to tell you what thickness of glass should be used and, even more important, the type of glass. New regulations concerning glass for use in particular situations, such as in windows at low level and in doors, have come into force. They are intended to ensure your safety and so should be followed carefully, hence the need for expert guidance.

INSULATING TANKS AND PIPEWORK

Worried by the thought of your next heating bill? Concerned by the prospect of your pipes freezing in winter? Proper insulation could well be the answer – and what's more it's cheap and easy to install.

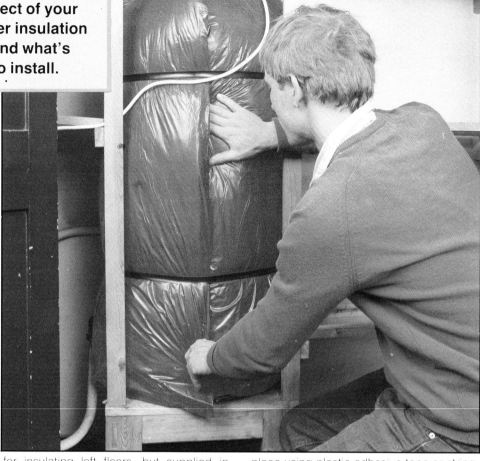

Insulation is important because it reduces heat loss, and when properly applied to your water system it benefits you in a number of ways. Firstly, it saves you money by slowing down the rate at which heat is lost from the pipes and tanks of your hot water system. Secondly, by reducing the heat loss from your cold water system (and even the coldest water contains *some* heat) it tends to keep your cold water warmer in winter, thereby minimising the risk of frozen pipes. Warmer cold water in winter also means that it takes less energy to heat it up to the desired temperature when it enters your hot water tank. In this respect too insulation saves you money.

So for all the above reasons you should consider properly insulating your pipes and tanks. The cost of the materials you will need is small and the potential savings great. And if you have already insulated your loft floor then this is one job you really must attend to. It has to be done because the temperature of your loft in winter will now be only marginally higher than that of the air outside, which means that the danger of any exposed pipework freezing in cold weather is greatly increased. Ideally you should therefore insulate your pipes and tanks before you tackle the loft floor. And don't forget that the risk of frozen pipes also applies to pipes in the cellar, and anywhere else where they might be subject to extremes of cold.

Before purchasing the insulation material for your pipes and tanks, work out how much you are likely to need. Most tanks will have their capacity and/or their dimensions marked on them somewhere – if yours don't then measure them yourself. You will also need to calculate the combined length of the pipes you intend insulating and establish what their diameter is – though this last measurement is only important if you plan to use split sleeve insulation (see below). As you'll want the insulation on your tanks to overlap that which you fit to any pipes that run into them, it's best to start by insulating your pipework.

Insulating pipes

Two types of pipe insulation are commonly available. The first is made out of a glass fibre or mineral wool material similar to that used for insulating loft floors, but supplied in bandage form (75 to 100mm/3 to 4in wide and 10mm/³⁄₈in thick) generally with a flimsy plastic backing. The second type comes in the form of split sleeves which are made from some sort of foamed material – usually plastic. Both types of pipe insulation have their advantages and disadvantages (see below) and both types are cheap. And since there is no reason why they can't be used side by side on the same pipe system, you'll almost certainly find that the easiest way to insulate your pipework is by using lengths of both.

Fitting bandage insulation

The bandage type is fitted by wrapping it around the pipe in a spiral, with each turn overlapping the previous one by at least 10mm (³⁄₈in). It doesn't matter which way round the plastic backing goes. Make sure that the bandage is sufficiently tight to prevent air circulating between the turns, but don't pull it too tight or you will reduce its effectiveness. When starting or finishing each roll, and at regular intervals in between, hold it in place using plastic adhesive tape or string. Tape or tie the bandage, too, on vertical pipe runs and on bends as these are places where the turns are likely to separate. And don't forget to lag any stop-valves properly – only the handle should be left visible.

Apart from being rather more time consuming to install than split-sleeve insulation the main drawback with the bandage type is that it is difficult to wrap round pipes in awkward places, such as those that run under floorboards. For pipes like these you will generally find that sleeves are more suitable since once fitted they can be pushed into position.

Fitting split-sleeve insulation

Split-sleeve insulation normally comes in 1m (3ft 3in) or 2m (6ft 6in) lengths. It is available in a variety of sizes to fit piping from 15mm (½in) to 35mm (1½in) in diameter. The thickness of the insulating foam is generally around 12mm (½in). Make sure that you buy the right size sleeve for your pipes – if the sleeves don't fit snugly round your pipework they won't provide satisfactory insulation.

INSULATING PIPEWORK

1 Start by wrapping the bandage twice round the end of the pipe next to the tank. Hold the turns in place securely with string or tape.

2 Wrap the bandage round the pipe in a spiral. Make sure that each turn overlaps the previous one by at least 10mm (³/₈in). Don't pull the bandage too tight.

3 Whenever you finish a roll of bandage and start a new one allow a generous overlap to prevent air circulating between the turns of the join.

4 Finish off the pipe in the same way that you started, with an extra turn of bandage. Lastly, check the pipe to make sure all the insulation is secure.

5 Fitting split-sleeve insulation is simple. You simply prise apart the split and slip the sleeve over the pipe. Use tape to keep the sleeve in place.

6 At bends, where the sleeve tends to come apart, tape the split lengthways. Tape the sleeves, too, whenever you join one to another.

7 At tees, first cut a 'notch' from the main pipe sleeve. Then shape the end of the branch pipe sleeve to fit and slot it into place. Tape the join.

8 Use split sleeve insulation on pipes that would be hard – or impossible – to fit with bandage. Slip the sleeve over the pipe and slide it into position.

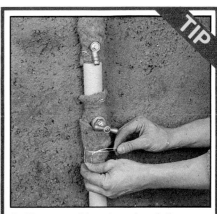

9 Sleeve and bandage insulation can – and sometimes must – be used together. A stop-valve, for example, can only be properly lagged with bandage.

INSULATING COLD TANKS

1 *Proprietary jackets will fit most cold water tanks. Start by flopping the jacket over the tank and pulling it roughly into position.*

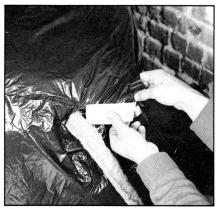

2 *Rather than cut into the jacket's 'envelopes', try to accommodate a pipe by parting the seam between them. All cuts must be sealed with tape.*

3 *When installing blanket insulation start with the side of the tank. If you're using glass fibre blanket wear gloves and a face mask.*

5 *The tank must have a firm lid to prevent the water inside being polluted. Don't tie the lagging to the lid in such a way that it is impossible to undo.*

6 *Expansion tanks need insulating too. If using sheet polystyrene, remember to cut the panels so that they overlap when fitted to the tank.*

7 *Use tape, string, or glue to hold the side panels together. Fill the gaps left as a result of making cut-outs with wedges of waste polystyrene.*

Both flexible and rigid sleeves are available, but as the rigid type isn't much use for pipework that bends frequently, you'd probably be better off using the flexible variety.

Fitting the sleeves is very straightforward. You simply prise apart the slit that runs along the length of the sleeve and slip the insulation over the pipe. It's advisable to tape the sleeve at intervals, and you must do so at joins. At bends, where the sleeves will tend to come apart, you should tape the split lengthways.

Once sleeve insulation has been fitted, it can easily be slid along a length of pipe to protect a part of it that may be hard to get at. However, you should bear in mind that it won't be able to get beyond any pipe clips, very sharp bends or bulky joints it may encounter. You'll find that most flexible sleeves will readily slide round curves and even 90° bends made using soldered fittings, but whenever you run up against problems in the form of bulky compression elbows or

tee connectors the sleeves will have to be cut accordingly. However, in some circumstances you might well find that bandage insulation provides the better solution.

To fit round a 90° elbow the sleeve should be cut in two and the sleeve ends then cut at an angle of 45° before being slipped over the pipe. You should then tape over the resulting join. For the most convenient method of dealing with a tee fitting see the step-by-step photographs.

Insulating cold water storage tanks

When it comes to insulating your cold water storage tank and central heating expansion tank (if you have one), there are a number of options open to you. If your tank is circular you could cover it with a proprietary jacket consisting of a number of polythene or plastic 'envelopes' filled with insulant; or you could simply wrap it up in a layer of mineral wool or glass fibre blanket similar to – or even the

same as – that which is used to insulate loft floors. If, on the other hand, your cold water tank happens to be rectangular then you could construct a 'box' for it yourself out of expanded polystyrene, or buy a proprietary one ready-made.

A proprietary jacket couldn't be easier to fit: you simply pull it into position and then tie it in place – tapes are sometimes provided by the manufacturer. If you have to cut into the jacket to accommodate a pipe, make sure that you seal it up again with plastic adhesive tape to prevent moisture getting in and the insulating material from escaping.

Expanded polystyrene kits are also extremely easy to fit. Apart from having to fix the pieces of polystyrene together with tape, string or polystyrene cement, the only work you will have to do is to make cut-outs for the pipework. More work will be required should you decide to make your tank kit out of sheet polystyrene (see step-by-step photographs)

4 If the blanket isn't as wide as the tank is deep, a second layer, which should overlap the first, will be necessary. Use string to hold the blanket in place.

8 Make a lid for your tank by gluing together two panels of polystyrene. The smaller (inner) panel should just fit inside the tank.

HOT TANKS

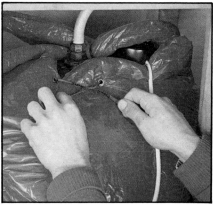

1 When using a proprietary jacket to insulate a hot water cylinder, start by securing the polythene 'envelopes' round the hot water supply pipe.

2 The sides of the jacket are held in place with straps. Take care not to cover the capping and wiring of any immersion heater.

Ready Reference

SLEEVING SIZES
To be effective, split-sleeve insulation must be the right size for your pipes. If they are modern – which usually means copper – most of your pipes will be 15mm (½in), though the main distribution ones are likely to be 22mm (¾in). Check any pipes that you aren't sure of.

TIP: PROBLEM PIPES
There are two areas where you must take extra care:
● when insulating a pipe that runs close to a wall – especially an outside wall – make sure that you protect the *whole* surface. To insulate only the more accessible side of the pipe would be worse than useless: the pipe would still be exposed to the cold wall but denied the heat of your house
● if the expansion pipe of the cold water tank you are insulating stops short of the lid then you'll have to devise some means of catching any outflow. The easiest way to do this is to use a plastic funnel. Bore a hole to accommodate the funnel through the lid and the insulation material, and fix it in place with plastic adhesive tape.

TIP: GOING AWAY
Insulation alone may not be sufficient to protect your pipes and tanks from the cold if you leave your house unoccupied for more than a few days in winter. So in your absence make sure that the heating is switched on briefly each day. If you can't trust your thermostat, ask a neighbour.

– but it would of course be a lot cheaper.

If you decide to use insulation blanket to lag your tank then try to buy the sort that is bonded with paper as you will find it much easier to handle. Buy a roll that is as wide as your tank is deep if you can, as this will save you the trouble of having to go round the side of your tank twice. The thickness of the blanket isn't critical, but blanket 50mm (2in) thick will give your tank adequate insulation and be easier to work with than a thicker one. However, it could well be that you have an odd roll or two of blanket left over from some previous insulation job; if you do, then use that rather than going to the expense of buying additional rolls.

The top of the tank to be insulated must have a firm covering to prevent the water inside being contaminated by fibres from the blanket you are fitting. So if it doesn't already have a lid, cut one out of hardboard, polystyrene or some other sheet material.

Lagging a tank with blanket insulation is simply a matter of common sense. You cut the blanket to size, drape it round the side of the tank, and having cut slits to enable the blanket to fit round the pipes, secure it with string. The lagging on the lid should overlap the side lagging by about 150mm (6in); and as you'll need to inspect the inside of your tank from time to time make sure it's easily removable.

Under normal circumstances the bottom of your tank should not be insulated, nor should the loft floor directly below. The reason for this is that it allows heat from the house to rise up through the floor and slightly increase the temperature of your cold water. The only circumstance in which you do insulate these places (and this applies regardless of what form of insulation you are using) is when, in order to increase the water pressure for a shower on the floor below, the tank has been raised more than a foot or so above the joists.

Insulating hot water tanks
Although you could in theory lag your hot water tank by adapting any of the methods that are used for cold water tanks, in practice you will nearly always find that you have no choice but to use a proprietary jacket. The fact that most hot water tanks are situated in airing cupboards means that blanket insulation is out of the question, and unless your tank is a rectangular one (which these days are very rare) you won't be able to use polystyrene.

Proprietary jackets for hot water tanks are made of the same materials as those used on cold water tanks and are just as easy to fit. The system used to fasten the jacket to the tank varies, but basically at the top you secure the 'envelopes' round the hot water supply pipe with a loop of cord, while further down you hold them in place with straps. The base of the tank is left uninsulated, as is the capping and wiring of any immersion heater.

INSULATING YOUR ROOF

About a quarter of the heat lost from an uninsulated house goes through the roof, and so some kind of roof insulation should be your first priority for saving money on heating bills.

Houses leak heat like a sieve. Up to 75 per cent of the warmth generated within the house finds its way to the outside world through the roof, walls, windows and doors, and this represents an enormous waste of energy and money.

Insulation reduces the rate at which heat passes through the various parts of your house's structure, by trapping 'still' air within the insulating material itself. Still air doesn't conduct heat much and so wrapping your house in suitable insulation serves the same purpose as putting a tea-cosy on a tea pot: the tea stays hot for far longer. The converse is true during the summer: the insulation bars the heat of the sun.

About a quarter of all the heat lost from an average house goes through the roof, and this is a particularly easy area to insulate effectively. What you do is to put your insulation in one of three places: on the highest ceiling; on the loft floor; or on the inside of the roof itself. Insulating the loft floor is the simplest and most effective of these: you should insulate the ceiling where there's no loft or the roof slope where the loft space has been converted into living accommodation.

Why you should insulate

The savings you can make by insulating your loft depend on whether there's any insulation there already (it's the first layer that's most effective), how much you put in, and whether you can control or alter your heating system to take advantage of the insulation. The last point is particularly important: if you install loft insulation and leave central heating controls as they are with a thermostat in, say, the living room, the most noticeable effect will be warmer rooms upstairs rather than dramatically decreased fuel bills. If, however, you can lower the tempertures in upstairs rooms, or keep them the same as before, by fitting thermostatic radiator valves or by turning radiators down (or off), your house will lose less heat and your fuel bills will be lower.

Types of insulation

There are four main types of loft insulation you can use: blanket, loose-fill, sheet (see *Ready Reference*) and blown fibre. You can install any of the first three yourself but blown fibre must be installed by a contractor.

The most extensively used loft insulation material is rolls of glass fibre or mineral fibre blanket, which you lay between the joists of the loft floor. You can choose from either of two thicknesses: 80mm (just over 3 in) and 100mm (4in).

Although you'll benefit in terms of warmer rooms by installing thicker insulation, the more you put in, the less cost effective it becomes. From a practical point of view thicknesses greater than 125mm (5in) will probably take the insulation over the top of the joists, making walking about or storing things in the loft rather difficult.

To save storage and transportation space the material is compressed when rolled up and packaged but it regains its original thickness quite quickly when unwrapped. The most common width of roll is 400mm (16in). Lengths vary from brand to brand, but they're usually about 6 to 8m (20 to 25ft) long. Some glass fibre insulation is available in 600mm (2ft) wide rolls for use in lofts with wider-than-usual joist spacings.

The 400mm (16in) width is the most suitable size for most houses and allows a little to turn up where it meets the joists. Joists are usually 400mm (16in) apart but they might be as much as 450mm (18in) or as little as 300mm (1ft). If you have narrow-spaced joists the 600mm (2ft) width is probably the best to use: you can cut a roll in half with a panel saw while it's still in its wrapper.

Working out how much insulation you'll need is simply a matter of multiplying the length of the loft floor by the width to calculate how many square metres there are, and then checking the chart in *Ready Reference*.

Remember that the 100mm (4in) thickness of blanket insulation comes in shorter length rolls than the 80mm (3in) thickness. An 8m (26ft) roll, 400mm (16in) wide, covers 3.2 sq m (35 sq ft). For blanket insulation, ignore the joists in your calculation; for loose-fill and sheet insulation, include the joist size, otherwise you could end up with 10 to 15 per cent too much. Loose-fill insulation comes in bags, typically containing 110 litres (4 cu ft). This is enough for 1.1 sq m (12 sq ft) laid 100mm (4in) deep. By far the most effective material is called vermiculite, which is made from a mineral called mica, though you might also find expanded polystyrene granules, loose mineral wool or cellulose fibre being sold as loose-fill insulation.

Thickness for thickness, vermiculite is more than twice the price of glass fibre blanket and it's not as effective. To get the same insulating effect as 80mm (3in) of glass fibre, you'd need 130mm (about 5in) of vermiculite, which might well come over the top of the ceiling joists.

Another disadvantage of loose-fill insulation is that it can blow about in a draughty loft:

WHERE TO INSULATE

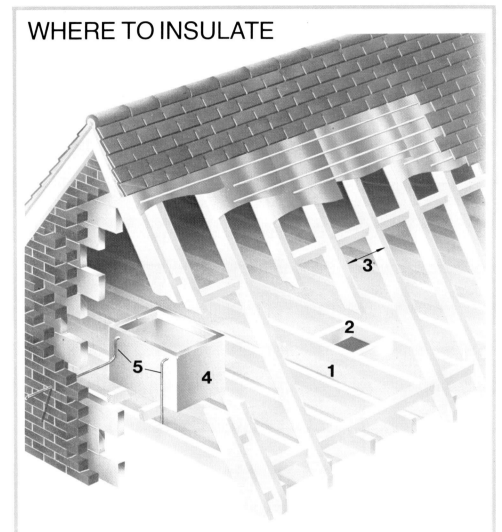

Use blanket insulation between the joists (1) or lay loose-fill or sheet materials; insulate the loft hatch (2) by sticking on a sheet of polystyrene; clad the rafters (3) with plasterboard or fix blanket insulation between them; lag the cold water tank (4) with a proprietary jacket or tie blanket or sheet insulation around it; lag pipes (5) with foam tubes or mineral fibre rolls.

this is most likely to be the case round the outside edges of the roof, by the eaves, where there are always some gaps. However, it's good for unevenly-spaced joists where other types of insulation might leave gaps.

To lay loose-fill insulation, you simply empty out the bags between the joists and spread it to an even thickness.

Sheet insulation isn't used much for loft insulation, though it's sometimes used for insulating between rafters, over solid walls and on flat roofs. The best type of rigid sheet for loft insulation is expanded polystyrene. It comes in various thicknesses in sheets from 1200 × 2400mm (4 × 8ft). You'll have to cut it up to get it through the loft hatch, and then cut each strip to the precise width required to match the joist spacing.

Other sheet materials such as fibreboard or chipboard can be laid across the joists, with loose-fill or blanket insulation sandwiched underneath. You can walk on chipboard, so it's also suitable for use as a floor, but fibreboard won't support your weight.

Blown fibre insulation costs little more than installing glass fibre blanket but it must be installed by a contractor. The three common materials are mineral fibre, pelleted glass fibre and cellulose fibre. It's easy and quick to put in, and will cover all the nooks and crannies that are difficult to reach by other methods.

Preparation

Lofts are usually dark, dirty places, so it's advisable to wear some really old clothes, preferably ones you can throw away afterwards.

Blanket insulation, especially glass fibre, can cause irritation to the skin, so you must wear rubber gloves when handling it. Remove your wrist-watch and roll up your sleeves. It's

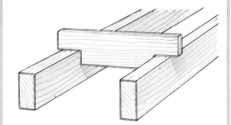

LAYING BLANKET INSULATION

1 *Clean up any dust and dirt from the loft floor. Use a cylinder vacuum cleaner with a nozzle attachment so that you avoid disturbing the dust.*

2 *Starting from the eaves, unroll the insulation between the joists. Leave a small gap at the eaves to allow air to circulate in the loft space.*

3 *If the headroom at the eaves is limited, unroll the blanket and push the end gently into the eaves with a broom. Take care not to tear the insulation material.*

6 *Once you've unrolled the blanket, return to the other end and press it down. Where you're joining one roll to another, butt the ends together.*

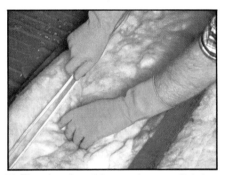

7 *The electric cables serving your lighting system are probably lying loose on the loft floor. Never cover them with insulation: lay them on top instead.*

8 *An even better solution is to attach loose cables to the side of a joist, if there's enough slack. Use cable clips to hold them in place.*

also sensible to wear a simple mask to cover your nose and mouth as the insulation material is not only unpleasant but dangerous to inhale. Loose-fill is a dusty material and you'd be wise to wear a pair of protective goggles — as well as a mask – when laying this. You can buy a mask, with replacement lint filters, and the goggles, all of which are available from most DIY stores.

You'll need a good light to work by; a fixed loft light is best, but if there isn't one, you could rig up an inspection lamp or even a table lamp. Don't, however, use a torch: you'll have enough to contend with without having to carry and aim a light. Don't use a naked flame because the risk of fire is high in the enclosed space of the loft.

Be careful where you tread. The space between the joists – the ceiling of the floor below – is only plasterboard or, in older houses, lath and plaster, and neither will support your weight. Rather than balancing on the joists – especially when you're carrying rolls or bags of insulation – it's better to have a short plank or piece of chipboard to stand on, but make sure that both ends are resting on a joist without overlapping, or it could tip up under

your weight, with disastrous consequences.

Before you start to lay the insulation you should remove any boxes or other items you have stored in the loft to give you plenty of room to manoeuvre: if there's too much to take down from the loft you can shift it up to one end of the loft, lay the insulation in the free area, then move the boxes back again and lay the other half.

Clean up the spaces between the joists using a vacuum cleaner with a nozzle attachment to enable you to reach awkward corners. If you don't have one you can use a soft-bristled broom or a hand-brush and a dust-pan, but you'll stir up a lot of dust in the process.

Use small pieces of the insulation material to block up any holes made in the ceiling for pipework to and from storage tanks.

Laying the insulation

Laying the blanket type of insulation is simplicity itself: all you do is to start at the eaves and unroll the blanket between the joists. On widely-spaced joists it'll just lie flat on the loft floor but if the joist spacing is narrow, or irregular, you can tuck it down and allow it to curve up the sides of the joists. Cut or tear

LAYING LOOSE-FILL

Right: Stop the loose-fill insulation from falling into the wall cavity at the eaves by placing a few bricks or a chipboard panel between the joists.

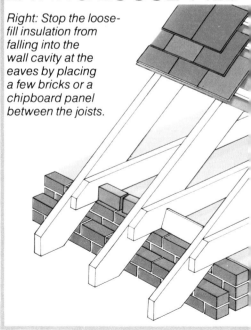

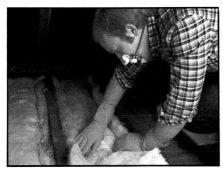

4 The blanket can either lie flat between the joists or, if the joist spacing is narrow or irregular, you can allow it to curve a little way up the sides.

5 Continue to unroll the blanket between the joists. As the loft floor won't support your weight, work from a plank or board placed across the joists.

9 When you've secured the cables to the side of a joist you can lay your blanket in the usual way; if it still covers the cable, you should cut it away.

10 Where there are cross beams, lay the blanket over the top, cut it with a sharp knife and push the ends under the obstruction. Butt the ends together.

INSULATION

Left: Empty out the bags of loose-fill between the joists; stand on the footboard across the joists.
Right: Use a timber spreader to even out the insulation to the correct level.

Ready Reference

LAGGING THE TANK

Your cold water storage tank must be insulated to prevent the water freezing in cold weather. You can use:
● sheets of expanded polystyrene 50mm (2in) thick, cut to fit the sides and top of the tank, and held in place with wire, tape or string. Make cut-outs for the pipes serving the tank

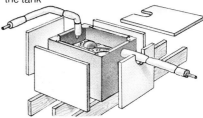

● lengths of blanket insulation tied to the sides and top of the tank. Make a removable cover in two halves from chipboard to fit round the expansion pipe

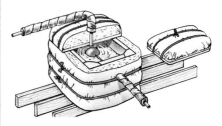

● a proprietary lagging kit consisting of pre-wrapped insulated pads, which you strap on to the tank
● panels of chipboard forming a box to contain loose-fill insulation.

LAGGING THE PIPES

You can lag pipes in the loft space with:
● mineral fibre rolls, wrapped on diagonally like bandages and secured with wire, adhesive tape or string or

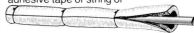

● strips of blanket insulation wrapped on and tied in place or
● proprietary foam tubes slit down their length so they can be slipped on the pipe.

You needn't lag the pipes if they're contained within loose-fill insulation or they'll be covered with blanket insulation.

See techniques on pages 136-139.

small pieces of blanket from the roll to fit very small nooks and crannies.

Butt up new rolls and allow for extra material at beams and pipes that are set at right angles to the joists. Cut the insulation and tuck it under the obstruction, then butt up the next piece to it.

Don't insulate under the cold water tank, which will be mounted on timber bearers at right angles to the joists: heat rising through the ceiling immediately beneath the tank will help to prevent the water freezing in very cold weather. The tank itself should be insulated (see *Ready Reference*), with glass fibre blanket or expanded polystyrene sheets all round and on top, or you can use a proprietary tank lagging kit, available from DIY stores.

If your tank is mounted high above the loft floor — usually to enable you to get a sufficient head of water for a shower unit – you can insulate underneath it. The whole tank should, in this case, be lagged.

Cut a square of blanket to cover the top of the loft hatch cover and tack it in place, leaving an overlap to stop draughts getting into the loft space.

If you're laying one of the loose-fill materials you'll have to stop it from falling into the wall cavity at the eaves. Place a few bricks on edge, or a panel of chipboard, between the joists near the eaves, to contain the granules.

Empty out the bags between the joists, starting at the eaves, and use a specially shaped timber spreader (see *Ready Reference*) to spread it to the correct thickness.

The loft space will be much colder after you've insulated it, so it's particularly important that you lag any water pipes that pass through the loft (see *Ready Reference*).

Insulating pipework

If the pipes lie within your loose-fill or under your blanket insulation there's no need to lag them separately, but if they're positioned above you'll need to wrap them with pieces of blanket insulation, ready-made mineral fibre rolls, or proprietary pre-formed pipe insulation.

To prevent electric cables overheating you shouldn't cover them with insulation. Attach them to the side of a joist or, if you're using blanket material, lay them on top. If your wiring is the old rubber-insulated sort you'd be wise to replace it.

Another point to watch now that the loft will be much colder is the greater risk of condensation (see details on pages 119-123) in the loft space. This can be a serious problem, which can rot the roof timbers and soak the insulation, making it useless. The way to avoid this is to ensure there's sufficient ventilation in the loft space by leaving gaps at the eaves equivalent to 10mm (3/8in) all the way round. Don't fill the gaps with insulation. At the same time, make sure that the gaps around pipes and the loft hatch are well sealed to keep moisture out.

INSULATION ALTERNATIVES

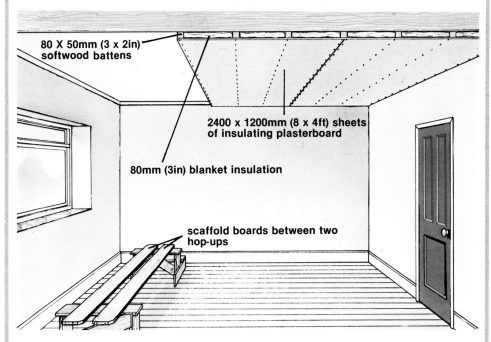

80 X 50mm (3 x 2in) softwood battens

2400 x 1200mm (8 x 4ft) sheets of insulating plasterboard

80mm (3in) blanket insulation

scaffold boards between two hop-ups

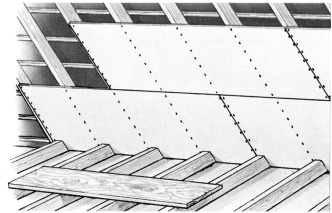

If your house has a flat roof you won't have a loft so you'll have to insulate the underside of the ceiling instead (above). To do this, you can nail up sheets of insulating plasterboard directly to the joists, which have an insulating layer and a vapour check that prevents moisture penetrating the surface. Or you can nail battens to the ceiling joists and sandwich blanket insulation between the false and the real ceiling.

You need to insulate the rafters only if you're converting your loft into a habitable room. You can use most of the materials that you use on the loft floor but the easiest to use are the sheet materials, which you can secure across the rafters (above) and the blanket materials, which can be pushed between the rafters and held in place with timber battens (left). You can also buy insulation blanket with a paper cover which you pin or staple to the rafters.

CHAPTER 6

Fitting and Fixing

ADHESIVES

To get the best results you have to pick the right adhesive for the materials you want to join, and then use it in the correct way. But the range available can make your choice extremely confusing.

The idea of an adhesive is easy to grasp: it sticks things together. In practice, however, there's a lot you need to know about the different types of adhesive on the market: how each works, what it will (and will not) stick together, how long it takes to set, whether the bond is heat-proof or waterproof, and so on. Equipped with this information, you can then begin to make the correct choice of adhesive type for the job you want to do.

Here you will find a brief description of the major types of adhesive, and a table that tells you which type to use to stick various materials together. Remember that adhesives should always be used exactly as directed by the manufacturer for the best results. They should also be treated with respect as they can damage the skin; furthermore, their fumes may be dangeous to inhale and highly inflammable.

1 Animal and fish glues
Also known as 'scotch' glues, these are the traditional woodworking adhesives, and come in either liquid form, or as solid chunks or sheets that you have to melt down. They are capable of producing a very strong bond, but have no gap-filling ability, so that woodworking joints must fit very tightly. They dry rather slowly, and are seriously weakened when exposed to dampness, however slight. They have now been almost completely replaced by modern synthetic adhesives.

2 PVA adhesives
PVA (polyvinyl acetate) adhesive is a white liquid which dries clear in under an hour, producing a strong bond within 24 hours. It is now the most important woodworking adhesive indoors,

but can be used on most dry, porous surfaces. It is widely employed within the building trade as a bonding agent for concrete, and a masonry sealant. However, PVA adhesives do have limitations. They are not very good at filling gaps, so woodworking joints must have a good fit, and must be cramped until dry. The bond doesn't stand up well to stress, and is weakened by exposure to moisture. PVA adhesives also have a tendency to stain some hardwoods.

3 Casein adhesive
This woodworking adhesive comes as a powder that you mix with water, and dries to a pale yellow colour. It stands up to low temperatures and dampness better than PVA, and gives a stronger bond. However, it is weakened by water – though its strength returns as it dries out again. It can also take up to 6 hours to set so joints must be cramped. It stains many hardwoods.

4 Resorcinol Formaldehyde adhesive
An excellent woodworking adhesive, giving a strong, rigid, extremely water-resistant bond. The snag is that it comes in two parts which must be mixed together, so some wastage is inevitable. It stains most hardwoods rather badly.

5 Urea-Formaldehyde adhesive
Another two-part woodworking adhesive, urea-formaldehyde – often referred to simply as 'urea' – is the usual choice for exterior

woodwork. As well as giving a very strong bond, and having the ability to bridge gaps, it stands up very well to just about everything the weather can throw at it. These qualities also makes it useful in many indoor situations. Unfortunately, it dries rather slowly and joints must be cramped for up to 6 hours. When used on hardwoods it may stain.

6 Contact adhesives
Normally based on synthetic rubber, these get their name from the way in which they are used. You apply a thin coat to both the surfaces to be joined, allow it to become touch dry, and then achieve an instantaneous bond by bringing the surfaces into contact with each other. The resulting bond will resist being pulled apart, but in time some sideways slippage may occur. For this reason, contact adhesives are not suitable for general woodwork and repairs.

Their main use is for sticking down sheet materials such as plastic laminate and cork tiles. Obviously, the fact that the adhesive bonds on contact can cause problems where accurate positioning is required, as you cannot make minor adjustments once the surfaces have been brought together. But some contact adhesives are available which have a delayed action, and so overcome this problem to a certain extent. The petroleum-based solvent used in most brands gives off vapour which is dangerous and unpleasant to inhale, and also highly inflammable. You must be sure to work in a well ventilated area, and, if this not possible, use a water-based contact adhesive instead.

7 Latex adhesives
In many ways these are similar to water-based contact adhesives, except that they use natural rubber (latex), and can either be

used as a contact adhesive, or as an ordinary adhesive where you bring the surfaces together while the adhesive is wet. They are a little too expensive to be used on large areas and so are generally used for such tasks as joining fabrics, sticking down carpet, and so on – situations in which the flexible, washable (but not dry-cleanable) bond they produce is a major advantage.

8 PVC adhesives
These stick flexible PVC. The strong, flexible bond they provide makes them the ideal choice for repairing rainwear, shower curtains, beach balls, and things of that sort.

9 Cyanoacrylate adhesives
These are the adhesives ('super glues') once claimed to stick anything to everything in seconds. A cyanoacrylate adhesive will quickly bond a wide variety of materials, but it has limitations. It's expensive, and although you need very little of it, this makes it impractical to use for anything more than small repairs. Surfaces must be scrupulously clean, and a perfect fit, as it has no gap-filling ability whatsoever. Another point to remember is that when used in industry, cyanoacrylate is specially formulated to stick two specific materials together with a very stong bond. Choose two different materials and you have to use a different formula. What the handyman can buy is a compromise formula, and there are therefore some materials that it doesn't stick very well. Glass is perhaps the best example. Ordinary cyanoacrylate is degraded by the ultra-violet radiation in sunlight and glass leaves it exposed and vulnerable. As a result, a special formulation for glass has been brought out to overcome this problem.

Another problem is that cyanoacrylate reacts in a rather odd way with water. The presence of moisture actually speeds up the setting process, but, once set, exposure to water breaks down the bond. Finally, an unfortunate side-effect is that cyanoacrylate adhesive has the alarming ability to stick people to themselves or to their surroundings, so it needs to be used with great care. It is not, however, as dangerous as sometimes suggested: a lot of patient work with hot soapy water often does the trick.

In summary, a cyanoacrylate adhesive isn't as 'super' as it might appear, but it is worth keeping a tube handy for repairs where other adhesives have failed.

10 Epoxy resin adhesives
These are less convenient than cyanoacrylates as they come in two parts, a resin and a hardener, which must be carefully mixed. But epoxy resin adhesives come closer to the 'stick-anything-to everything' ideal. The strong, heat-resistant, oil-resistant, water-resistant bond that they provide makes them a good choice for small-scale repair work involving metal, china, and some plastics, as well as a variety of other materials. The surfaces must be clean, but since the resin will bridge small gaps without losing strength, a perfect fit is not essential. In fact, for repair work, epoxies have only two major snags. One is that they dry to a pale brown colour, which tends to highlight the join, though it is possible to colour the adhesive with dry pigment. The second is that they need a setting time of up to 48 hours. This can be overcome by using a fast-setting formulation, which generally holds within five or ten minutes, but still

requires at least 24 hours to achieve full strength. Of course, epoxies can be used for large-scale jobs too. The reason why they tend not to be is that they are simply too expensive to use in

11 Acrylic adhesives
This is a two-part adhesive with a difference. It will join the same sorts of material as an epoxy, achieving a bond of only slightly less strength in as little as 5 minutes. You don't have to pre-mix the adhesive and catalyst before you apply them. Instead, you can apply the catalyst to one surface, the adhesive to the other. And most important of all, the surfaces need not be clean. Even oily surfaces can be joined successfully. But it's expensive, and it is not yet widely available.

12 Plastic solvent adhesives
Although between them, epoxies, acrylics, PVC adhesives, and cyanoacrylates allow you to stick many plastics to themselves, some require a special solvent adhesive. This works by chemically 'melting' a layer of plastic on each of the surfaces to be joined, so that they merge together and produce a 'welded' joint rather like the join in a plastic model kit assembled with polystyrene cement. They work quickly, and give strong results. However, you must be sure to match the solvent to the

particular type of plastic, and only two solvents are commonly available. These are UPVC solvent adhesive (for unplasticised polyvinyl chloride; used mainly for joining lengths of UPVC drain pipe) and polystyrene cement, mentioned above.

13 Cellulose adhesive
Adhesives based on cellulose aren't very strong, but they are fairly waterproof and heatproof, transparent when they dry and they do set quickly. They are most useful as an alternative to epoxy resin adhesives, or to cyanoacrylates, when repairing china and glass.

14 Vegetable gums and pastes
Based on either starch or dextrine, two plant extracts, these are useful only for sticking paper and card, and even here, these days, they tend to be restricted to the 'suitable for children' market.

15 Specialist adhesives
In addition to the general-purpose adhesives we have mentioned so far, you'll find a number of specialised adhesives, such as tile and wallpaper adhesives.

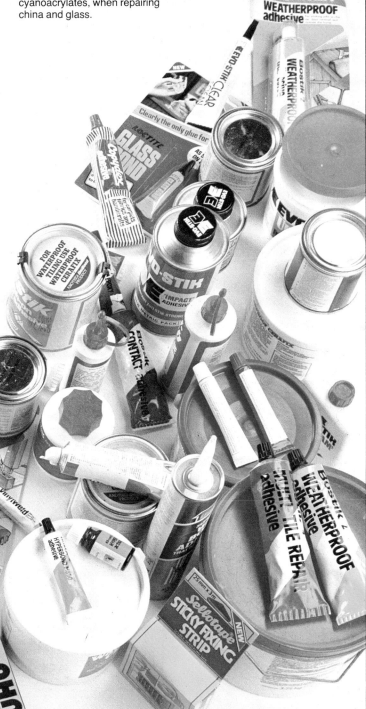

Choosing the right Adhesive...

KEY TO ADHESIVE TYPES

H Clear household	7 Latex	14 Vegetable gum
1 Animal and fish	8 PVC	**Specialist adhesives**
2 PVA	9 Cyanoacrylate	15 Wallpaper
3 Casein	10 Epoxy	16 Flooring
4 Resorcinol formaldehyde	11 Acrylic	17 Ceramic tile
5 Urea formaldehyde	12 Plastic solvent	18 Expanded polystyrene
6 Contact	13 Cellulose	

To stick ▽ to this ▷	Wood	Wallpaper	Rubber	Plastic (soft)	Plastic (hard)	Plastic laminate	Plastic flooring	Plasterboard	Paper & cards	Metal	Man-made boards	Leather	China & glass	Fabrics	Expanded polystyrene	Cork tiles	Ceramic tiles	Carpet
Ceramic tiles	9 10 11	—	—	—	6 9 10 11	6	16	—	—	9 10 11	—	—	—	—	—	6	17 10	6 7
Cork tiles	6 2	15	—	—	—	6	16	—	H 2 7	—	2	—	—	7	—	6	—	7
Expanded polystyrene	18	15	—	—	—	6	—	—	—	—	2	—	—	7	18	18	—	—
China & glass	10 11	—	6 9	—	9 10 11	—	—	—	H	H 9 10 11	—	H 9 10 11	H 9 10 11 13	6 7 H	—	H	—	—
Man-made boards	1 2 3 4 5	15	9 10 11	—	9 10 11	6	16	8	H 2 7 15	6 10 11	1 2 3 4 5	6	9 10 11	6 7	18	6 16	17	6 7
Metal	9 10 11	15	9 10 11	—	9 10 11	6	—	H	9 10 11	10	6	9 10 11	6	—	6	6 9 10 11	9 10 11	6
Paper & cards	2	15	—	H	—	—	—	—	H 1 2 7 14 15	—	—	H	H	7	—	—	—	—
Plasterboard	2	15	—	—	—	6	16	2 15	—	—	6	6	—	2 15	18	6	17	6
Plastic flooring	—	—	—	—	—	—	16	—	—	—	—	—	—	—	—	16	17	6
Plastic (hard)	—	—	9 10 11	9 10 11 12	9 10 11 12	—	—	H	—	9 10 11	—	—	—	—	—	—	—	—
Plastic (soft)	—	—	9 10 11	8 9 10 11 12	9 10 11	—	—	—	—	—	—	—	—	—	—	—	—	—
Masonry	5 10	15	6	—	9 10 11	—	16	6	H 7 15	9 10 11	6 2	—	—	6 7	18	16	10 11 17	6 7
Wood	1 2 3 4 5	15	6 9 10 11	9 10 11	9 10	6	16	2	1 2 7 14 15	9 10 11	1 2 3 4 5	6	9 10 11	6 7	18	6 16	10 11 17	6 7

SIMPLE JOINTS

It's often thought that only elaborate joints give good results in woodwork. It isn't true. There are simple ways to join timber, and one of the simplest is the butt joint. It's easy to make, can be used on natural timber or man-made boards, and it's neat. What's more, given the right adhesive and the right reinforcement, a butt joint can also be strong enough for most purposes.

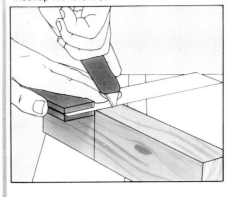

The great thing about butt joints is their simplicity. You can use them on any kind of timber or man-made board, provided it isn't too thin – not under 6mm (¼in). The only problem you will run into is where you are joining chipboard. A special technique is needed here to get the screws to grip, as is explained later.

Although it is possible to simply glue two pieces of wood together, unless you add some kind of reinforcement the result won't be very strong. So in most cases, the joint should be strengthened with either screws or nails. The question is which? As a rule of thumb, screws will give you a stronger joint than nails. The exception is where you are screwing into the endgrain of natural timber. Here, the screwthread chews up the timber to such an extent that it has almost no fixing value at all. Nails in this case are a much better bet.

Choosing the right adhesive
Even if you are screwing or nailing the joint together, it ought to be glued as well. A PVA woodworking adhesive will do the trick in most jobs, providing a strong and easily achieved fixing. This type of adhesive will not, however, stand up well to either extreme heat or to moisture; the sort of conditions you'll meet outdoors, or in a kitchen, for example. A urea formaldehyde is the glue to use in this sort of situation. It isn't as convenient – it comes as a powder that you have to mix with water – but your joints will hold.

Choosing the right joint
There are no hard and fast rules about choosing the best joint for a particular job. It's really just a case of finding a joint that is neat enough for what you're making, and strong enough not to fall apart the first time it is used. And as far as strength is concerned, the various kinds of butt joint work equally well.

Marking timber
Butt joints are the simplest of all joints – there's no complicated chiselling or marking out to worry about – but if the joint is to be both strong and neat you do need to be able

to saw wood to length leaving the end perfectly square.

The first important thing here is the accuracy of your marking out. Examine the piece of wood you want to cut and choose a side and an edge that are particularly flat and smooth. They're called the face edge and face side.

Next, measure up and press the point of a sharp knife into the face side where you intend to make the cut. Slide a try-square up to the knife, making sure that its stock – the handle – is pressed firmly against the face edge. Then use the knife to score a line across the surface of the timber. Carry this line round all four sides of the wood, always making sure that the try-square's stock is held against either the face edge or the face side. If you wish, you can run over the knife line with a pencil to make it easier to see – it's best to sharpen the lead into a chisel shape.

Why not use a pencil for marking out in the first place? There are two reasons. The first is that a knife gives a thinner and therefore more accurate line than even the sharpest pencil. The second is that the knife will cut through the surface layer of the wood, helping the saw to leave a clean, sharp edge.

Sawing square

One of the most useful – and easiest to make – aids to sawing is a bench hook. It'll help you to grip the wood you want to cut, and to protect the surface on which you are working. You can make one up quite easily, by gluing and screwing together pieces of scrap timber (see *Ready Reference*).

You also need the ability to control the saw, and there are three tips that will help you here. Always point your index finger along the saw blade to stop it flapping from side to side as you work. And always stand in such a way that you are comfortable, well balanced, and can get your head directly above the saw so you can see what you are cutting. You should also turn slightly sideways on. This stops your elbow brushing against your body as you draw the saw back – a fault that is often the reason for sawing wavy lines.

Starting the cut

Position the piece of wood to be cut on the bench hook and hold it firmly against the block furthest from you. Start the cut by drawing the saw backwards two or three times over the far edge to create a notch, steadying the blade by 'cocking' the thumb of your left hand. Make sure that you position the saw so that the whole of this notch is on the waste side of the line. You can now begin to saw properly using your arm with sort of piston action, but keep your left (or right as the case may be) hand away from the saw.

As the cut deepens gradually reduce the angle of the saw until it is horizontal. At this point you can continue sawing through until you start cutting into the bench hook. Alternatively, you may find it easier to angle the saw towards you and make a sloping cut down the edge nearest to you. With that done, you can saw through the remaining waste holding the saw horizontally, using the two angled cuts to keep the saw on course.

Whichever method you choose, don't try to force the saw through the wood – if that seems necessary, then the saw is probably blunt. Save your muscle power for the forward stroke – but concentrate mainly on sawing accurately to your marked line.

Cleaning up cut ends

Once you have cut the wood to length, clean up the end with glasspaper. A good tip is to lay the abrasive flat on a table and work the end of the wood over it with a series of circular strokes, making sure that you keep the wood vertical so you don't sand the end out of square. If the piece of wood is too unmanageable, wrap the glasspaper round a square piece of scrap wood instead and sand the end of the wood by moving the block to and fro – it'll help in keeping the end square.

DOVETAIL NAILING

This is a simple way of strengthening any butt joint. All you do is grip the upright piece in a vice or the jaws of a portable work-bench, and glue the horizontal piece on top if it – supporting it with scrap wood to hold the joint square – and then drive in the nails dovetail fashion. If you were to drive the nails in square, there would be more risk that the joint would pull apart. Putting them in at an angle really does add strength.

The only difficulty is that the wood may split. To prevent this, use oval brads rather than round nails, making sure that their thickest part points along the grain. If that doesn't do the trick, try blunting the point of each nail by driving it into the side of an old hammer. This creates a burr of metal on the point which will cut through the wood fibres rather than parting them.

Once the nails are driven home, punch their heads below the surface using a nail punch, or a large blunt nail. Fill the resulting dents with wood stopping (better on wood than ordinary cellulose filler) and sand smooth.

1 *Drive nails at angle: first leans to left; next to right, and so on.*

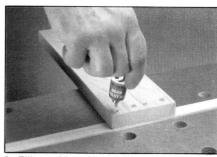

3 *Fill resulting dents with stopping compound to cover up nail heads.*

THE OVERLAP

This is the simplest of all and is one you can use on relatively thin timber. The example shown is for a T-joint, but the method is the same if you want to make an X-joint.

Bring the two pieces of wood together as they will be when joined, and use a pencil to mark the position of the topmost piece on the one underneath. To reinforce the joint, countersunk screws are best, so mark their positions on the top piece of wood, and drill clearance holes the same diameter as the screw's shank – the unthreaded part – right the way through. The screws should be arranged like the spots on a dice (two screws are shown here, but on a larger joint where more strength is needed five would be better) to help stop the joint twisting out of square. Enlarge the mouths of these holes with a countersink bit to accommodate the screw heads, and clean up any splinters where the drill breaks through the underside of the wood.

Bring the two pieces of wood together again using a piece of scrap wood to keep the top piece level. Then make pilot holes in the lower piece using either a bradawl or a small drill, boring through the clearance holes to make sure they are correctly positioned. Make sure the pilot holes are drilled absolutely vertically, or the screws could pull the joint out of shape. Finally, apply a thin coating of adhesive to both the surfaces to be joined (follow the adhesive manufacturer's instructions), position the pieces of wood accurately and, without moving them again, drive home the screws.

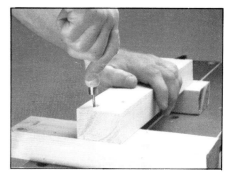

3 *Reassemble joint and bore pilot holes in bottom piece with bradawl.*

2 With nail punch or large blunt nail, hammer nail heads below surface.

4 When stopping is dry, sand flush with surface of surrounding timber.

CORRUGATED TIMBER CONNECTORS

Another simple way of holding a butt joint together is to use ordinary corrugated timber connectors. Simply glue the two pieces of wood together, and hammer the connectors in across the joint. Note that they are driven in dovetail fashion – the fixing is stronger that way.

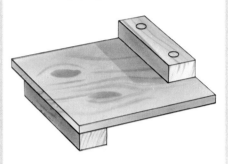

For strength, hammer in connectors diagonally rather than straight.

Ready Reference

MAKING YOUR OWN BENCH HOOK

This a very useful sawing aid to help grip the wood when cutting. Hook one end over the edge of the workbench and hold the wood against the other end. Make it up from off-cuts and replace when it becomes worn.

You need:
● a piece of 12mm (½in) plywood measuring about 250 x 225mm (10 x 9in)
● two pieces of 50 x 25mm (2 x 1in) planed softwood, each about 175mm (7in) long. Glue and screw them together as shown in the sketch. Use the bench hook the other way up if you're left-handed.

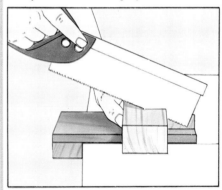

TIP: SAWING STRAIGHT

● hold wood firmly against bench hook and start cut on waste side of cutting line with two or three backward cuts
● decrease angle of the saw blade as cut progresses
● complete cut with saw horizontal, cutting into your bench hook slightly

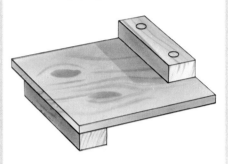

TIP: TO SMOOTH CUT END

● rub with a circular motion on glasspaper held flat on the workbench, so you don't round off the corners
● on large pieces of wood, wrap glasspaper round a block of wood and rub this across the cut end

1 Bring pieces squarely together. Mark position of each on the other.

2 Drill and countersink (inset) clearance holes for screws in uppermost piece.

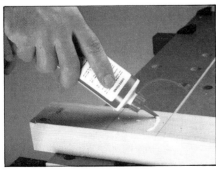

4 Apply woodworking adhesive to both pieces and press them together

5 Carefully drive in screws. If they're tight, remove and lubricate with soap.

FIXING INTO CHIPBOARD

Because neither nails nor screws hold well in chipboard, how do you hold a butt joint together? The answer is that you do use screws, but to help them grip, you drive them into a chipboard plug. Chipboard plugs are a bit like ordinary wall plugs. In fact, you can use ordinary plugs, but you have to be careful to position the plug so that any expanding jaws open across the board's width and not across the thickness where they could cause the board to break up.

The initial stages of the job are exactly the same as for the overlap joint – marking out, drilling the clearance holes, and so on. The difference is that instead of boring pilot holes in the second piece of wood, you drill holes large enough to take the chipboard plugs. Pop the plugs into the holes, glue the joint together and drive home the screws.

Incidentally, if you can't use any sort of plug at all – for example, when screwing into the face of the chipboard – the only way to get the screw to hold properly is to dip it in a little woodworking adhesive before you drive it home.

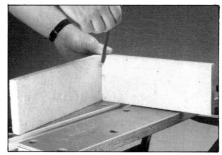

1 *Bring pieces together and mark position of overlap with a pencil.*

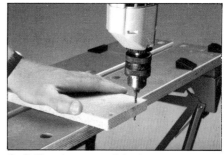

2 *Drill and countersink clearance holes in overlapping piece.*

3 *Mark screw positions through holes onto end of second piece.*

4 *Drill chipboard to take plugs, then glue and screw joint together.*

REINFORCING BLOCKS

The joints described so far are fairly robust, but if a lot of strength is needed it's worth reinforcing the joint with some sort of block. The simplest is a square piece of timber.

First drill and countersink clearance holes through the block and glue and screw it to one of the pieces you want to join so that it's flush with the end. To complete the joint, glue the second piece in position, and drive screws through into that. You can arrange for the block to end up inside the angle or outside it. Choose whichever looks best and is easiest to achieve.

With the block inside the angle, you'll have a neat joint and the screw heads won't be openly on display. However, in most cases it means screwing through a thick piece of wood (the block) into a thin piece (one of the bits you want to join), so it's not as strong as it might be. If greater strength is needed work the other way round, driving the screws through the pieces to be joined, into the block. You can neaten the result to a certain extent by using a triangular rather than a square block.

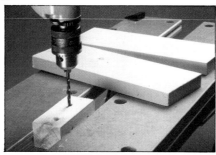

1 *Drill and countersink clearance holes through reinforcing block.*

2 *Glue and screw block in place level with end of one piece of wood.*

3 *Glue second piece in place and drive screws into it through block.*

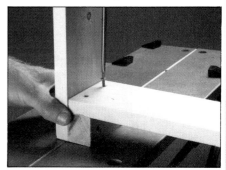

4 *In some cases this joint looks better with block outside angle.*

JOINTING BLOCKS

Made from plastic, these are just sophisticated versions of the wooden blocks you can make yourself, and they're used in similar situations. Their only real advantage is that they tend to give a neater result when you're working with veneered or melamine covered chipboard, but only because they come in the right colours. There are basically two kinds to choose from.

The simplest is just a hollow triangular 'block' that comes with a snap-on cover to hide the screws. More complicated versions come in two parts. You screw one half of the block to each piece of wood, and then screw the two halves together using the machine screw provided. It's essential here that both halves of the block are positioned accurately, and since the blocks vary from brand to brand in the details of their design, you should follow the manufacturer's instructions on this point.

1 *Screw half of block to one piece of wood and mark position on other.*

2 *Next, screw second half of block in place on second piece of timber.*

3 *Finally, connect both halves of block using built-in machine screw.*

4 *Treat blocks that come in one piece as wooden reinforcing blocks.*

ANGLE IRONS

If still greater strength is needed, use either an angle iron or a corner repair bracket to reinforce the joint. These are really just pieces of metal pre-drilled to take screws and shaped to do the same job as a reinforcing block (the angle irons) or to be screwed to the face of the two pieces of timber across the joint (the flat T-shaped and L-shaped corner repair brackets).

In either case, bring together the pieces of wood to be joined, position the bracket, and mark the screw holes. Drill clearance and pilot holes for all the screws, then screw the bracket to one of the pieces before glueing the joint together and screwing the bracket to the second piece. They don't look very attractive, so use where appearance isn't important, ie, at the back of a joint, or where the joint is going to be concealed in some other way.

1 *Corner joints strengthened with plywood and an angle repair iron.*

2 *T-joints can be simply made with angle irons or repair brackets.*

SKEW NAILING

There'll be some situations where you cannot get at the end of the wood to use dovetail nailing. Here you must use skew nailing instead. This means glueing the two pieces securely together and then driving a nail into the upright piece of wood at an angle so it also penetrates the horizontal piece. Put a couple of nails into each side of the upright so that they cross. To stop the upright moving, clamp a block of wood behind it or wedge it against something solid.

Stop movement while driving nails with scrap wood block and G-cramp.

WALL FIXINGS

There's a huge variety of wall fixings available. Some are designed for solid walls, some for hollow walls. Choosing the right one will ensure that whatever you're fixing stays there.

Two things will decide which type of wall fixing you need: the first is the strength of fixing you require – book shelves, for instance, are going to need a much stronger fixing than a picture frame – and the second is the kind of wall you're fixing to.

Whether you're fixing in solid walls (either plaster covered brick, stone, concrete, or some other kind of building block) or in hollow ones (plasterboard, lath and plaster, or wood panels fixed to a timber framework), screws are normally used. However, on their own, screws don't grip in masonry, so you have to use some sort of plug.

Hints

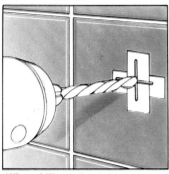

When drilling in hard shiny surfaces — ceramic tiles, for example — you often find that the drill bit wanders out of position as soon as you turn on the drill. To avoid this, cover where you want the hole with sticky tape.

Sticky tape is also handy for making sure you don't drill too deeply. Just wrap it round the drill bit the length of the plug in from the tip, to form a little flag. When the flag touches the wall, you know you've drilled far enough.

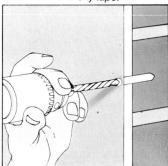
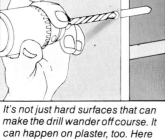

It's not just hard surfaces that can make the drill wander off course. It can happen on plaster, too. Here the answer is to make a shallow dent by turning the bit by hand. The dent should then keep the tip of the drill just where you want it.

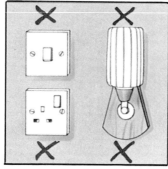

Take care when drilling into walls not to go through electric cable. The main danger areas to avoid are above and below light switches or power sockets, and anywhere near wall lights. Also avoid areas near pipes.

The screw used is important for a strong fixing. Choose one that will penetrate at least 25mm (1in); more if it is to carry a lot of weight. The screw gauge also matters. The higher the gauge number, the thicker the screw, and the stronger the fixing. A No 6 is for light fixings only. A No 8 will do for most other jobs, but for a very sound fixing indeed, use either a No 10 or No 12.

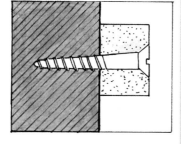

Fixings in solid walls

Drill a hole, insert a wall plug, and then drive the screw into that. As the screw penetrates, the plug expands and presses against the sides of the hole. So long as you don't overtighten it (in which case the screw thread will destroy the plug) the screw will then be very firmly embedded indeed.

You must, though, ensure that the plug expands in solid masonry, rather than in the plaster coating, or in any mortar joins.

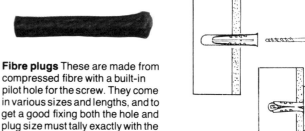

Fibre plugs These are made from compressed fibre with a built-in pilot hole for the screw. They come in various sizes and lengths, and to get a good fixing both the hole and plug size must tally exactly with the size of screw. Refer to the manufacturer's recommendations here.

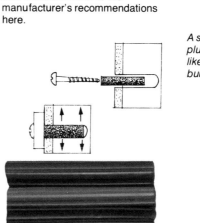

Strip plastic plugs Similar to fibre plugs, these are sold in 300mm (12in) lengths so you can cut off just the amount you need. Again, you must match the size of plug and the hole to take it, with the size of screw, and to help you the plug sizes are colour coded. White is for screw gauges 4 and 6 and needs a hole drilled with a No 8 masonry bit; red is for gauges 6 and 8 and needs a No 10 bit; green is for gauges 8, 10, and 12, and needs a No 12 bit; and blue is for gauges 10, 12, and 14, and needs a No 16 bit.

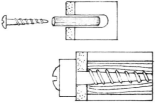

Standard wall plugs Also made from plastic, these give a stronger fixing than strip plugs. Designs vary, but all have slits or opening jaws to increase the degree to which the plug can expand, as well as fins and barbs to increase grip. The other advantage of this sort of plug, is that, with most brands, one size of plug can take several sizes of screw, without reducing the fixing's strength.

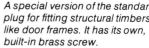
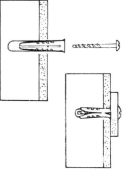

A special version of the standard plug for fitting structural timbers like door frames. It has its own, built-in brass screw.

Breeze block plugs One thing ordinary plugs are not good at is gripping in soft or crumbling masonry, notably breeze block and aerated concrete block. Here a special plug is required. It consists of a central core surrounded by tough, flexible fins arranged in a sort of spiral. To use it, drill a hole a little larger than the central core, and hammer the plug in. The fins compress, then force themselves against the sides of the hole to hold the plug even if the masonry does give way.

Rawlbolts The thing to use if you need a really heavy-duty fixing – for example, fixing a lean-to roof to the side of a house. Rawlbolts work in much the same way as a standard plug, but are made from metal, and come ready-fitted with a bolt. Various sizes are available, and you can choose between a number of types of head, including a threaded stud to take a nut, a hook, an eye, and a normal hexagonal bolt head.

Wooden pegging The solution to the problem of fixing into mortar joints – take a piece of wood, preferably hardwood, roughly 19mm (¾in) in diameter, taper one end, and then drive it into a 12mm (½in) hole with a mallet. You can then screw into it in the same way as any other piece of timber.

Masonry nails Masonry nails are used like any other nail. They are just specially hardened, and designed to penetrate and hold in masonry. They come in sizes to suit most jobs – choose a length that will penetrate the wall by about 19mm (¾in) – and, in spite of their tendency to shatter if you don't hit them squarely, they do offer a fast way to get a fixing. However, the result is not neat, so reserve them for rough constructional jobs, where looks are not important.

Plugging compound For a relatively light fixing in crumbling walls, use a plugging compound; a fibrous material that you mix with water and pack into the hole using the tool provided. Once the hole is full, make a starting hole with the pointed end of the tool, and carefully drive in the screw. As the compound dries, it "cements" the screw in place.

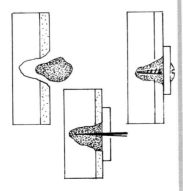

Fixings in hollow walls

Here, getting the screw to grip is even more of a problem than with a solid wall. After all, the screw has nothing to bite on but air. There are a number of ingenious solutions, but virtually all have a snag; remove the screw, and the fixing device is lost inside the cavity.

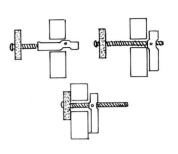

Petal anchors Made from plastic, these are twisted onto the end of the screw and pushed through the hole into the cavity beyond. As the screw is tightened, the anchor's petals open out against the back of the plasterboard, or whatever, thus preventing both anchor and screw from pulling out.

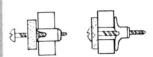

Expanding plugs Designs vary, but all work in the same sort of way. You push them into the hole, insert a screw – some have a built-in machine screw – and tighten up. The plug bulges out inside the cavity until it is too large to come back through the hole.

Gravity toggles The toggle is essentially a small metal hinged device fitted to the end of a machine screw (supplied). When pushed through the hole, it flops down inside the cavity, bridges the hole, and so allows the screw to be tightened. This bridging action is ideal for lath and plaster walls.

Spring toggles These use the same principle as gravity toggles. The difference is that two sprung metal wings are used to do the bridging job.

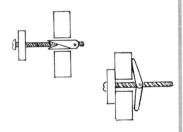

Screwing into the framework

The only way to make a really strong fixing in hollow walls is to screw directly into the wall's internal timber framework. This consists of upright "studs" spaced about 400mm apart, and horizontal "noggins" put in mainly where there is a horizontal join between plasterboard sheets. The former offer the strongest support for a fixing.

To locate them, tap the wall until it sounds reasonably solid, then drill a series of tiny test holes until you strike wood. If the studs aren't where you need them, span two with a stout piece of timber screwed in place on the surface, and make the fixing into that.

SHELVING THE BASICS

There are lots of ways of putting up shelves. Some systems are fixed, others adjustable – the choice is yours. Here's how both types work, and how to get the best from each.

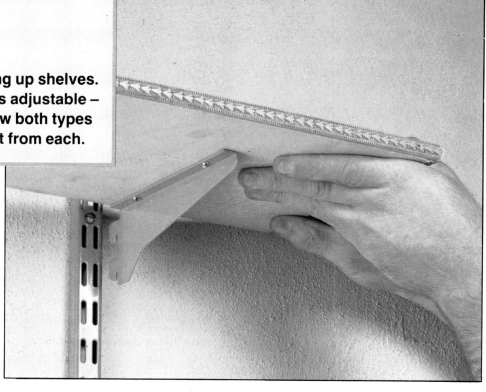

Deciding how much shelving you'll need is always tricky – because, the more shelves you have, the more you'll find to go on them! So it's always wise to add an extra 10 per cent to the specification when you start planning.

Think carefully about what you want to store and display, and try to categorise it by size and weight. The size part is fairly easy. Concentrate first on the depth (from front to back) and length; a collection of paperback books, for instance, might need 3.5m (10ft) of 150mm (6in) deep shelves. Having the shelves a bit deeper than you really need is always worthwhile, and if you add 10 per cent the length should look after itself.

Next, the heights in each grouping will tell you roughly how far apart the shelves must be. Most paperbacks are 175mm (7in) high – allow an extra 25mm (1in) for easy access and removal.

Finally, weight. The trouble here is that, even if you weigh what you'll be storing, you can't translate the result into shelf, bracket and fixing materials or sizes. Instead, think in terms of light, moderately heavy and very heavy. Items such as the TV and stereo, while not especially weighty, are best treated as very heavy, because it would be nothing short of disastrous if a shelf did give way under them!

Shelf design
Where you put the shelves affects the amount of storage you can gain, how you build them, and the overall look of the room itself. This last may not be important in a workshop, for instance, but in a living room, where the shelves may well be the focal point, a bad decision can be serious.

The obvious spot for shelving is against a continuous wall. This offers most scope to arrange the shelves in an interesting and attractive way. An alcove is another possibility. Shelving here is neat, and easily erected; it is a very good way of using an otherwise awkward bit of space. A corner has similar advantages if you make triangular shelves to fit – though they're really only suitable for displaying plants or favourite ornaments.

Planning it out
If appearance matters and you're putting up a lot of shelves, a good way to plan is by making a scale drawing of the whole scheme to see how it looks. Then check for detail. If your TV has an indoor aerial, make sure you have room to adjust it. With stereo systems, ensure the shelf is deep enough to take all the wiring spaghetti at the back. And do think about the heights of the shelves from the floor (see *Ready Reference*).

Finally, make sure you provide adequate support for the shelves and the weight they'll be carrying. There is no very precise method of gauging this, but you won't go wrong if you remember that for most household storage a shelf needs support at least every 750mm (30in) along its length. This will usually be enough even with chipboard, which is the weakest of shelving materials. But bowing may still be a problem, so for items in the 'very heavy' category it's advisable to increase the number of supports by reducing the space between them.

Which material?
Chipboard is usually the most economical material, and if properly supported is strong enough for most shelving. It can be fairly attractive, too, since you can choose a type with a decorative wood veneer or plastic finish. These come in a variety of widths – most of them designed with shelving in mind.

Natural timber, though more costly and sometimes prone to warping, is an obvious alternative. You may have difficulty obtaining some timber in boards over 225mm (9in) wide, but narrower widths are readily available. For wider shelves, another way is to make up the shelf width from narrower pieces. An easy method is to leave gaps between the lengths and brace them with others which run from front to back on the underside, forming a slatted shelf.

Blockboard and plywood are also worth considering.

Both are a lot stronger than chipboard and have a more attractive surface which can be painted or varnished without trouble. However, in the thicknesses you need – at least 12mm (½in) – plywood is relatively expensive; blockboard is cheaper, and chipboard cheaper still. All these man-made boards need to have their edges disguised to give a clean finish. An easy yet effective way to do this is just to glue and pin on strips of timber moulding or 'beading'. Also remember that the cheapest way to buy any of these boards is in large sheets (approximately 2.4m x 1.2m/8ft x 4ft), so it's most economical to plan your shelves in lengths and widths that can be cut from a standard size sheet.

Shelves needn't be solid, though. If you want them extra-thick, for appearance or strength, you can make them up from a timber frame covered with a thin sheet material. Hardboard is cheap, but thin plywood gives a more attractive edge; alternatively use a timber edging strip.

BRACKET SHELVING

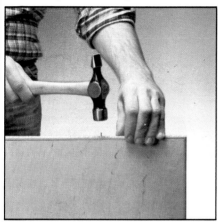

1 If your shelves are of man-made board, a good way to give them neat edges is to pin on decorative 'beading', mitred at the corners.

2 Begin by screwing the shorter arm of the bracket to the shelf. Position it squarely and in such a way that the shelf will lie snugly against the wall.

3 Using a spirit level as a guide, mark a pencil line along the wall at the height where you want the top of the shelf to be positioned.

4 Hold the shelf, complete with brackets, against this line, and mark with a pencil through the screw holes in the brackets, so you know where to drill.

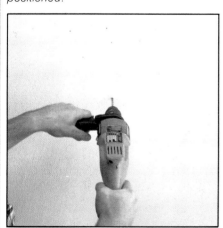

5 Drill holes in the wall with a power drill, using a masonry bit if necessary, and being sure to keep the drill straight. Then insert plastic plugs.

6 Hold the shelf in position, insert one screw in each bracket and tighten it halfway; then insert the others and tighten the whole lot up.

Ready Reference

PLANNING SHELVES

When you design storage, plan ahead and think about *how* you're going to use it.

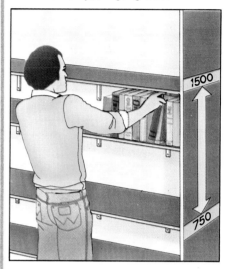

Height. Keep everyday items well within reach. That means between 750 and 1500mm (30 and 60in) off the ground.
Depth. Shelves that are deepest (from front to back) should be lower, so you can see and reach to the back.
Spacing. An inch or two over the actual height of the objects means you can get your hand in more easily.

HOW TO SPACE BRACKETS

Space brackets according to the shelf thickness. Heavy loads (left) need closer brackets than light loads (right).

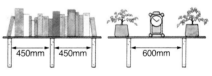

12mm (½in) chipboard

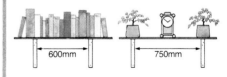

12mm (½in) plywood
19mm (¾in) chipboard

19mm (¾in) plywood

157

ADJUSTABLE SHELVING

1 Metal uprights come in a range of sizes, but occasionally they may need shortening. If so, you can easily cut them down with a hacksaw.

2 After using your level to mark the height for the tops of the uprights, measure along it and mark out the spacings between them.

3 Hold each of the uprights with its top at the right height, and mark through it onto the wall for the position of the uppermost screw hole only.

4 Remove the upright, drill the hole and plug it if necessary. Then replace the upright, and fit the screw – but don't tighten it completely.

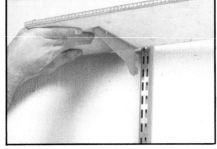

5 With the upright loose, hold a level against it and adjust it till it's vertical. Then mark through it for the other screw positions.

6 Hold the upright aside and drill the other holes. Plug them, insert the screws and tighten them all up – not forgetting the topmost one.

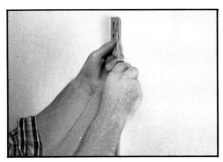

7 Now you can screw the bracket to the shelf, aligning it correctly and taking particular care over how it lines up at the back edge.

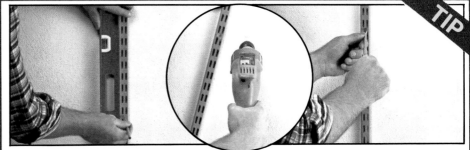

8 One type of adjustable system uses brackets with lugs at the back. It's easiest to let these lugs project behind the shelf when screwing on brackets.

9 The lugs simply hook into the slots in the uprights. Changing the shelf height is just a matter of unhooking them and moving them up or down.

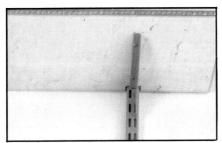

10 If you want the back edge of the shelf right against the wall, notch it with a tenon saw and chisel to fit round the upright. Inset the bracket on the shelf.

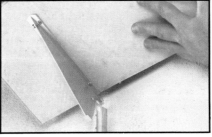

11 The channel system is different. First of all, you engage the bracket's upper lug in the channel and slide it down, keeping the lower one clear.

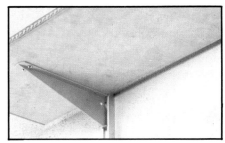

12 When you reach the position you want, level the shelf and the bracket, so as to slide its lower lug into one of the pairs of slots down the upright.

Fixing shelves

The simplest method of fixing shelves is directly to the wall, using brackets. L-shaped metal brackets of various sizes and designs are available everywhere – some plain and functional, some with attractive lacquered or enamelled finishes. It's just a question of choosing ones about 25mm (1in) less than the shelf depth, spacing them the right distance apart and screwing them to both shelf and wall.

If you're filling up your shelves with books, the support brackets won't be seen. But if you're using the shelves for ornaments, the brackets will be visible, so choose a style that blends. Alternatively, you can make up your own brackets from two pieces of timber butt-jointed into an L shape and braced with a diagonal strut or triangular block.

The fixing technique is the same either way. First you draw a line on the wall where the shelf is to go, using a spirit level. Next, fix the brackets to the shelf and put the whole assembly up against the line. Mark on to the wall through the pre-drilled screw holes in the brackets; then take the shelf away and drill holes in the wall, filling each with a plastic plug. Lastly, drive in one screw through each bracket; then insert the rest and tighten them all up.

Because the accuracy of this method relies largely on your ability to hold the shelf level against your line, you may find it easier to work the other way round. By fixing the brackets to the wall along the guide line, you can then drop the shelf into place and screw up into it through the brackets. This works, but you must position the brackets with great care, and avoid squeezing them out of position as you screw them into the wall. That isn't always easy. For one thing, many brackets don't have arms which meet at a neat right angle. They curve slightly, which makes it hard to align the top of the shelf-bearing arm with the line on the wall.

Making a firm fixing

Remember that the strength of all brackets depends partly on the length of their arms (particularly the one fixed to the wall) and partly on the strength of your fixing into the wall. The longer the wall arm in proportion to the shelf arm, the better; but it's also important to use adequate screws – 38mm (1½in) No 8s or 10s should do – and to plug the wall properly. In a hollow partition wall you really must make sure you secure the brackets to the wall's wooden framework and not just to the cladding. Even if you use plasterboard plugs or similar devices (see pages 154-155), a lot of weight on the shelf will cause the brackets to come away from the cladding and possibly damage the wall.

Of course, there is a limit to how much weight the brackets themselves will take.

Under very wide shelves they may bend. With shelves that have heavy items regularly taken off and dumped back on, and shelves used as desk-tops, worktops and the like, the movement can eventually work the fixings loose. In such cases it's best to opt for what's called a cantilevered shelf bracket. Part of this is set into the masonry to give a very strong fixing indeed. Details of its installation vary from brand to brand, but you should get instructions when you buy.

Alcove shelving

All proprietary brackets are expensive. However, for alcove shelving there's a much cheaper alternative, and that is to use battens screwed to the wall. All you do is fix a 50 x 25mm (2 x 1in) piece of softwood along the back of the alcove, using screws driven into plastic plugs at roughly 450mm (18in) centres. Then screw similar ones to the side walls, making sure that they line up with the first. In both cases, getting the battens absolutely level is vital. In fact, it's best to start by drawing guidelines using a spirit level as a straight edge.

A front 'rail' is advisable where the shelf spans a wide alcove and has to carry a lot of weight. But there's a limit to what you can do. With a 50 x 25mm (2 x 1in) front rail and battens, all on edge, 1.5m (5ft) is the safe maximum width.

A front rail has another advantage because, as well as giving man-made boards a respectably thick and natural look, it also hides the ends of the side battens. So does stopping them short of the shelf's front edge and cutting the ends at an angle.

The shelf can be screwed or even just nailed to the battens to complete the job.

Movable shelves

Unfortunately, both brackets and battens have one big drawback: once they're fixed, they're permanent. So you might consider an adjustable shelving system which gives you the chance to move shelves up and down. Such systems consist of uprights, screwed to the wall, and brackets which slot into them at almost any point down the length.

There are two main types. In one, brackets locate in vertical slots in the uprights. The other has a continuous channel down each upright. You can slide brackets along it and lock them at any point along the way, where they stay put largely because of the weight of the shelf. With both types, brackets come in standard sizes suitable for shelf widths, and there's a choice of upright lengths to fulfil most needs.

Many proprietary shelving systems of this sort include a number of accessories to make them more versatile. These include book ends, shelf clips and even light fittings.

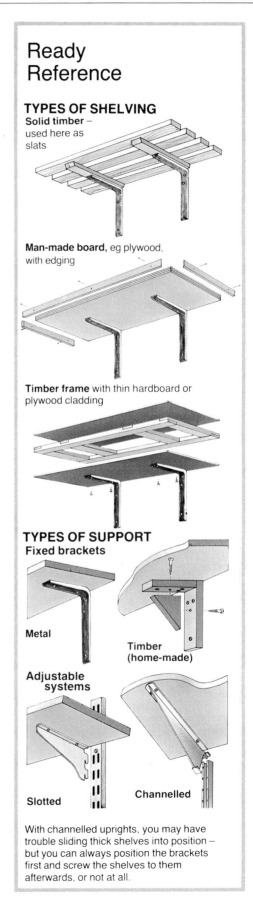

Ready Reference

TYPES OF SHELVING
Solid timber – used here as slats

Man-made board, eg plywood, with edging

Timber frame with thin hardboard or plywood cladding

TYPES OF SUPPORT
Fixed brackets

Metal

Timber (home-made)

Adjustable systems

Slotted

Channelled

With channelled uprights, you may have trouble sliding thick shelves into position – but you can always position the brackets first and screw the shelves to them afterwards, or not at all.

BUILDING SHELVING UNITS

Self-supporting shelves, unlike the wall-mounted type, can be moved wherever and whenever you like – without leaving screw holes to be plugged. Here's how to make them rigid and roomy.

Apart from their most obvious advantages over built-in units, freestanding units don't have to be tailored to fit any irregularities of walls and alcoves. But, because they aren't fixed in position, you have to devote a bit more time and thought to making them rigid.

This is often a matter of making a straight-forward box, although frame construction is another possibility. Either way, it is important to remember that the shelves themselves won't add much stability, particularly if they're adjustable. You need additional stiffening to compensate the tendency for the whole unit to fold up sideways into a diamond shape.

The basic box
Always keep your materials in mind. The options are, of course, solid timber or man-made boards. Plywood is probably the best all-rounder, but it's quite expensive. Chipboard is cheap, and chipboard screws make a strong butt joint. In solid timber and block-board, you're restricted by the fact that you shouldn't screw or nail into end grain.

Dowels or plastic jointing blocks are good for assembling most of the structure, but dowels are less than ideal for corners, because a dowel joint isn't all that rigid. A timber strip glued and screwed into both surfaces, can add some necessary reinforcement; but shelf units often rise above eye level, and you'll have to be careful that it's not unsightly as well.

A barefaced housing joint is one remaining possibility – that is, apart from those afforded by power tools. A circular saw or router makes it a lot easier, for example, to cut rebate joints or mitres.

An additional point is that plastic facings such as melamine laminate won't accept glue, so that some form of screw fastening is virtually your only way of fixing other components to them.

Stiffening the unit
The simplest way of making a unit rigid is to pin a back panel to the rear edges of the box and perhaps even to the back edges of the shelves as well.

However, there may be occasions (for example, if the unit is to stand in the middle of a room) when you want a more open, airy look than is possible with this unmodified form of construction. In such cases the answer is to add bracing to the actual box components themselves. Even if you are incorporating a back, the extra stability such bracing provides won't come amiss – especially on large units.

The principle works as follows. Flat boards bend under stress. You can counter this by fixing lengths of reinforcing timber along them, preferably on edge. Every board thus dealt with helps to keep the whole structure stable.

You can even stiffen the open (front) face of the cabinet, by running bracing members across it, provided these are firmly jointed to the cabinet sides – say with dowels, plastic jointing blocks or steel angle repair brackets. A recessed plinth does this job and the type of plinth that's made up separately stabilises the cabinet by stiffening its bottom.

Frequently the neatest way of stiffening the front is to place such reinforcement along the shelves – either underneath them (inset if you like) or fixed to their front edges.

Rectangular-sectioned timber such as 50x25mm (2x1in), or a metal L-section, is ideal here. The procedure has the added advantage of strengthening the shelves, and you can treat intermediate shelves in the same way – not just the top and bottom panels.

Supporting the shelves
You can fix shelves into the unit by any of the methods appropriate for box construction using hand tools. The strongest and most professional of these is to house the shelves into the uprights

A stopped housing makes the neater joint here, since it means the front edge of each upright is unbroken by the ends of the shelves, but a through housing is quite adequate. The other invisible fastening for fixed shelves is dowels. Screws will leave plastic caps showing on the outsides of the side panels.

The choice between these methods depends largely on your materials. A plastic-faced upright panel means the dowel joints can't be glued, so you rely even more than usual on the main box for strength. Timber shelves,

A STURDY SHELF UNIT

This unit's top and sides are made of plastic-faced chipboard; the softwood shelves are planed down in the width to match.

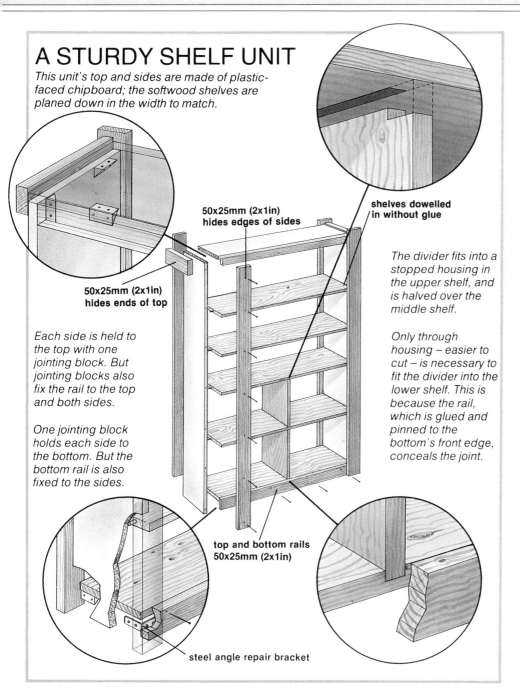

50x25mm (2x1in) hides edges of sides

50x25mm (2x1in) hides ends of top

shelves dowelled in without glue

Each side is held to the top with one jointing block. But jointing blocks also fix the rail to the top and both sides.

One jointing block holds each side to the bottom. But the bottom rail is also fixed to the sides.

The divider fits into a stopped housing in the upper shelf, and is halved over the middle shelf.

Only through housing – easier to cut – is necessary to fit the divider into the lower shelf. This is because the rail, which is glued and pinned to the bottom's front edge, conceals the joint.

top and bottom rails 50x25mm (2x1in)

steel angle repair bracket

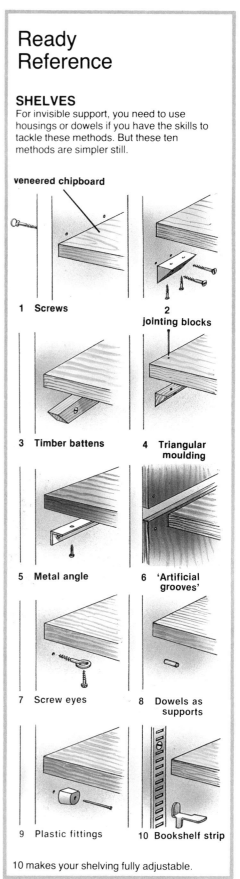

Ready Reference

SHELVES

For invisible support, you need to use housings or dowels if you have the skills to tackle these methods. But these ten methods are simpler still.

veneered chipboard

1 **Screws**

2 **jointing blocks**

3 **Timber battens**

4 **Triangular moulding**

5 **Metal angle**

6 **'Artificial grooves'**

7 **Screw eyes**

8 **Dowels as supports**

9 **Plastic fittings**

10 **Bookshelf strip**

10 makes your shelving fully adjustable.

on the other hand, can't be screwed in directly because you'd be going into the end grain.

Plastic jointing blocks are an obvious and fairly unobtrusive possibility. Timber battens, glued and pinned, or screwed and if possible glued, to shelves and uprights are tough; they can also be quite neat if you chamfer their front ends, cut them off at an angle, or hide them with a front rail. A triangular-sectioned timber 'stair rod' moulding, or an L-sectioned strip of steel or aluminium, is neater still.

You can create artificial housings by using pieces of timber or board, the same width as the uprights, pinned and glued to their inside faces, and leaving just enough space for the shelves to fit between them. This means you can make the uprights themselves a bit thinner.

A rather different approach is to let the shelf ends rest on small supports sticking out of the uprights. These might be screw eyes (with screws driven up through them into the undersides of the shelves to fix them in place if necessary); they could be 6mm (¼in) diameter dowels. You can also get several sorts of plastic studs which screw in, nail in or push into drilled holes. Some are specially designed for glass shelves. And sometimes the hole is filled by a bush which

ASSEMBLING THE CARCASE

1 After cutting all the shelves to the same length, mark and cut housings for the divider halfway along the shelves above and below it.

2 Use one of the housings as a guide to mark the position of the halving to be cut in the shelf which the divider crosses.

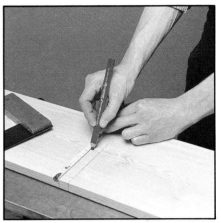

3 Measure halfway across the shelf for the depth of the halving. Then cut the divider to length, and measure and mark it out likewise.

4 Cut the matching halvings in the divider and the shelf it crosses; use a tenon saw across the grain and then a chisel to chop out the waste.

5 Align both uprights exactly and mark on them the height of each shelf (at a point which is halfway across the shelf's thickness).

6 Use a combination square at the same setting to mark the exact dowel positions on both the uprights and on all the shelf ends.

7 Drill all the dowel holes, glue the dowels into the shelf ends, and fit all but the top and bottom shelves to the uprights when the adhesive sets.

8 Screw the top and bottom shelves into position with plastic jointing blocks, or any other appropriate jointing technique.

9 Insert the divider into the unit from the back, using scrap wood to prevent damage to its rear edge as you tap it into position.

ADDING REINFORCEMENT

1 *Fix a stiffening rail across the top, screwing it to the uprights and the underside of the top shelf with jointing blocks.*

3 *Use steel angle repair brackets to hold the plinth firmly to the uprights and thus help to keep the whole unit rigid as well.*

5 *Glue and pin further lippings to both long edges of each upright to enhance the unit's appearance and give it extra rigidity.*

2 *Glue and pin the plinth rail to the front edge of the bottom shelf (which is cut narrower than the other shelves to allow for this).*

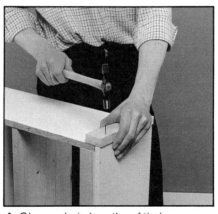

4 *Glue and pin lengths of timber, as long as the uprights are wide, to the ends of the top shelf in order to conceal them.*

6 *Lastly, fill all nail holes with wood stopping of the appropriate shade, and varnish the timber parts to improve their looks and durability.*

will accept a number of different types of stud.

Lastly, there's a very neat way to make the shelves in a freestanding unit fully adjustable. This is to use 'bookshelf strip' – metal strips with continuous rows of slots, into which you clip small metal lugs; the shelves rest on these. The strips (of which you'll need two each side) can be simply screwed to the insides of the uprights, or fitted into vertical grooves if you've got the power tools to cut them.

A home-made version of this system uses removable dowels in regular vertical rows of drilled holes.

Installing dividers

For the distances you can safely span with various thicknesses of various materials, see page 157. Really wide shelves may need extra support in the middle. Vertical dividers will provide this, and can also add to looks and usefulness. They're usually housed or dowelled in at top and bottom, and halved over intermediate shelves.

Alternatively, a square- or rectangular-sectioned timber upright, fixed to the front edges of the shelves, will help matters. It can be glued and pinned to the shelves, dowelled in or notched over them.

Frame shelving

If you only think in terms of box construction, you limit the scope of your projects. A shelf unit's sides can just as well be open frames as single slabs. This gives a lighter look, and also avoids the problems of using man-made boards. But you do need to pay even more attention to making the structure rigid. You'll certainly need extra strengthening pieces running from side to side.

Shelves can be supported in most of the ways already mentioned – with the additional possibility of placing them on the cross pieces in the frames themselves. These cross pieces can even be pieces of broom-stick – in other words, each upright is in effect a ladder, with the shelves resting on the rungs.

Box modules

In fact, as far as freestanding shelves are concerned, the possibilities are limitless. One more example may help to demonstrate this. There's no reason why you shouldn't make your 'shelving' up as a stack of completely separate open-fronted boxes. They needn't even be the same depth from front to back. Such a system lets you rearrange its shape completely at will. Its main disadvantage is that most of the panels are duplicated, so the cost of materials goes up. But moving house is easy: each box doesn't even need packing!

As long as you make the structure rigid, the choice of design is yours.

FITTING CURTAIN TRACKS

The precise method you use to fit curtain track will depend on the type you are installing. For a successful result, follow the manufacturer's instructions carefully, but here's a general idea of what's involved.

There is a wide variety of curtain tracks available, ranging from simple plastic or metal track which provides a neat inconspicuous method of hanging curtains to decorative metal rods or wooden poles which are designed to be a feature of the window treatment.

Curtain track has a series of small-wheeled runners, from which the curtains hang by means of hooks slotted into their heading tape. Rods and poles usually have rings which slide along them to carry the curtains, but some, too, have runners concealed in the bottom of the rod or pole. In addition, small curtains may be hung on wire threaded through the hem at the top and stretched between two hooks. Nets, in particular, are often supported in this way. Check with your supplier on types of track available.

Track is fixed by a series of small brackets through which you drive screws. Usually, there is a hole in both the back and the top of the bracket, so that they are suitable for back or top fixing. Poles or rods usually have only two, much larger and stronger, brackets which are fixed near each end. They are suitable only for back fixing. Pole and rod brackets are much more decorative than those of track and are meant to be seen as part of the design. Long poles or rods (usually those over 1200mm/48in) may require an intermediate bracket; check with the manufacturer's instructions about this.

Curtain wire must be fixed inside the window opening or reveal. Poles and rods should be fixed above and outside the reveal, as they are not seen to advantage otherwise. Track can be fitted inside or out, depending on the look you want.

Fixing inside the reveal

There are two advantages to hanging curtains inside the reveal. One is that because the curtains are shorter you need less fabric; it could be much less. The other is that it is normally much easier to make a fixing inside the reveal. Most windows have frames of timber (even steel and aluminium frames are usually set in a timber surround) and the track or wire can be fixed to this. All you need to do is make a pilot hole for the fixing screw or

hook and then drive it home; this will be even easier if you drill the holes with an electric or hand drill first.

There's also the fact that radiators are often sited underneath a window and you will restrict the emission of heat if you cover them up with curtains hung outside the reveal.

There are exceptions as to this ease of fixing however. Normally these involve steel windows which are fixed direct to the brickwork of a window opening, so there is no timber surround. Frames like this may incorporate a device for supporting curtain fittings; there may, for example, be integral hooks from which wire can be stretched. But otherwise, there are two courses open to you. With one, you can drill holes in the steel and fix to the frame with nuts and bolts, incorporating rubber or plastic washers to ensure weathertightness. This is a rather labourious job and you may instead decide to adopt the alternative method of fixing to the top of the reveal. This involves cutting into the lintel, which may be a straightforward or rather complicated business, depending on the material from which the lintel is constructed. If you are in any doubt, you should seek professional advice.

Fixing outside the reveal

You may decide that you do not like the idea of short-length curtains fitted inside the reveal; and that you would prefer the elegant look

which floor-length curtains can give. If you opt for full-length curtains outside the window opening, the installation normally becomes a little more complicated because you will be involved in making fixings into a wall.

If you want the track, rod or pole to be situated immediately above the reveal you will have to take the lintel which supports the brickwork above into account. In some cases, especially in Victorian houses or even older ones, the lintel may be a timber one. Making fixings into this is just as simple as making them into a timber frame. However, many old houses have lintels of solid stone and in more modern houses the lintel will probably be of reinforced concrete (and in high-rise flats the walls may be of this material).

The age of your house will give you some idea as to what type of material is used for the lintels, but how can you be sure? In some cases you can see the lintel from outside the house and you will be able to tell just by looking. But if the lintel is concealed you will have to determine the type of material used by other means. You should make a test boring with a drill and bit. You will soon know whether it is stone or concrete on the one hand or timber on the other. (Don't worry about this test hole being unsightly; you can cover it up later on.)

Boring into stone and concrete is a different matter from drilling into ordinary masonry. You will get along better with an electric,

FITTING TRACK INSIDE A REVEAL

1 *Carefully measure the width from one side of the reveal to the other. Make your measurement at the position you intend to fix the track.*

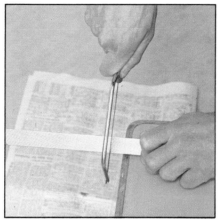

2 *Most tracks can be easily cut to size. Mark off the required length on the track and then cut through it; a fine-toothed hacksaw is suitable for this.*

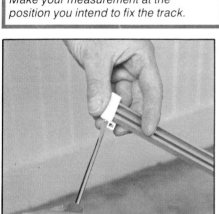

3 *Fit one endcap at the end of the track and slide on the runners. Then fit the second endcap at the other end (don't overtighten these caps).*

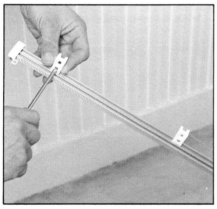

4 *Screw on the fixing brackets. Follow the manufacturer's instructions regarding the position for the end brackets and also the spacing of the rest.*

5 *Hold the track up (here to the top of the reveal), keeping it straight and level, and use a bradawl to make pilot holes for the screws.*

6 *Use an electric drill to bore deeper holes at the positions marked and then replace the track and screw it firmly into place.*

Ready Reference

FIXING TRACK

Track requires a lot of support brackets. The exact number varies according to the height of the curtains and the weight of the fabric; they can be spaced at intervals as close as 300mm (1ft) and seldom wider than 450mm (18in). Check with the instructions.

TIP: FIT A BATTEN

Where the plaster on walls or ceiling is not particularly sound or where you want to avoid a lot of drilling into a resistant surface like reinforced concrete, you can fix the track brackets to a wooden batten which will require fewer fixings than the track itself. For this:
● fix the batten with masonry pins or nails which you drive into the wall with a hammer, avoiding drilling and plugging (some masonry nails will go into concrete)
● hide the batten if you wish with a pelmet, cover it with the paint you've used on the walls or cover it with wallpaper so it will hardly be noticeable, or
● hack out a trench for the batten in the masonry, using cold chisel and a club hammer, and fix the batten direct to the masonry beneath (you could use an epoxy resin adhesive for this); then cover it up using plaster or filler.

● on a ceiling you can screw the batten to the joists (don't cut out a trench for the batten or you may cause damage).

TIP: NUMBER OF RUNNERS

Don't use more runners than there are hooks in the curtains or the excess ones will cause the curtains to jam.

TIP: SECURE END BRACKET

For cord-operated track where the cord hangs at one side, the bracket which bears the weight of frequent pulling should be extra secure.

FITTING A ROD ABOVE THE REVEAL

1 *With an extendable rod like this one place it up against the wall above the reveal to work out where it will look best and how far to extend it.*

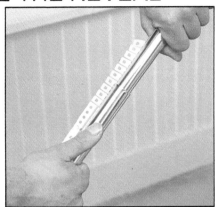

2 *To extend the rod to the required length you simply pull it outwards. Place it back up against the wall to check that it's the right length.*

3 *Longer rods require a central fixing support bracket. Use a pencil to mark off fixing points for this through the screw holes at top and bottom.*

4 *Measure on the rod to work out where the fixing brackets will come and then transfer this measurement to the wall at both ends.*

5 *It's important that you get the rod truly horizontal, so check with a spirit level, and if necessary, adjust the pencil marks you've made.*

6 *Use an electric drill to bore holes at the positions you've marked. You can then fit wall plugs into the holes ready to take the screws.*

7 *Screw the brackets firmly to the wall using a screwdriver. Screws in a finish to match the brackets will normally be supplied with the rod.*

8 *Where you are using a centre support as well as the end brackets, fix one half of the support to the wall; then fix the matching part on the rail to it.*

9 *At the ends, loosen the rosette screw, leave one runner between the bracket and the rod end and slot the rod in place. Then re-tighten the rosette screw.*

THE FINAL STAGES

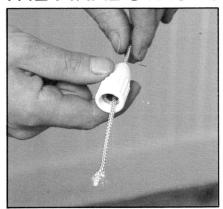

1 *Work out how long you wish the draw cords to be. Cut them if required, then thread them through the acorns supplied and tie knots to secure the ends.*

2 *You can then go ahead and hang the hooks attached to the curtains on the runners, including the master runners in the middle of the rod.*

rather than a hand drill and best of all would be a hammer drill. A two- or multi-speed drill that allows you to work very slowly will make the job easily manageable.

If you don't have a slow-speed hammer drill, then you can adopt the following procedure when dealing with concrete which consists of sand, cement and aggregate with, in the case of reinforced concrete, iron bars in the middle. A bit in a rotary electric drill will cut easily into sand and cement; difficulties will arise when it meets a stone for it will then bore no further. So you should bore in the normal way with your drill and when it seems to stop making progress (a sign that it has come up against a stone) remove it and insert in the hole a percussion bit or jumping bit. To remove the obstruction, strike this a sharp blow with a club hammer and it should cut through or dislodge the flint. Then carry on drilling in the normal way. Any reinforcing bars should be too far from the surface for you to come up against them.

An alternative solution is to aim to avoid the lintel altogether. For this you fix the rod, pole or track slightly higher up. You will then be dealing with bricks, or in the case of a modern house, building blocks, which are very easy to cut into. In fact the problem with building blocks is that they are soft and it is not always easy to get a sufficiently firm fixing in them. However you should be alright with curtains; the fixing has to withstand a certain amount of force when the curtains are drawn but they need nothing like the support of, say, wall-mounted kitchen cabinets.

One question which will concern you here will be the height of the lintel. Once again, you may well be able to see it from outside and you can then measure it. When it is concealed, working out its height is a more

difficult matter, but in general, 150mm (6in) is normally the minimum thickness for a lintel and 300mm (1ft) the maximum. So if you fix your track, pole or rod more than 300mm (1ft) above the top of the reveal it should be clear of the lintel. There are, of course, exceptions to this rule but it is generally the case. Again, you could make a test boring first to make absolutely certain.

If you are using curtain track you could decide to fit it even higher than this, right at ceiling level in fact. Floor-to-ceiling curtains look very striking in any room. You could go further and install curtains to cover an entire wall, even though the window may be comparatively small. It's an expensive treatment but can be a really attractive one, giving the illusion that you have enormous picture windows. It will also make the room much warmer and cosier in winter since the curtains will provide extra insulation.

If you do position the track at the top of the wall and there is no cornice, you can avoid drilling into the wall. Instead, you can top-fix the track to the ceiling by driving screws through the plaster and into the joists above. First, of course, you will have to locate the joists. Sometimes you can actually see them bulging through the plaster. Or in an upstairs room you can look for them in the loft; in a downstairs room, look in the room above. The fixing nails of the floorboards (assuming they are not hidden beneath a floorcovering) will show you their position. Or again, you can test out their position by tapping the ceiling with your knuckles. There will be a distinct difference between the hollow sound when you strike the ceiling between the joists and the solid feel as you hit the part immediately below one. If all else fails you will, once again, have to make a series of test borings.

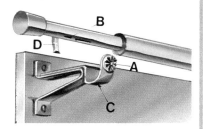

FITTING LOCKS ON WINDOWS

Burglary is a growth industry these days, and windows are particularly vulnerable to attack. But fitting security bolts and latches takes only a few minutes and is a relatively inexpensive job.

Just because you have locks on the outside doors and you are careful to shut all the windows before you go out doesn't mean that your house is safe against a burglar. Such action may deter the thief acting on the spur of the moment, but it won't prevent the committed house-breaker from trying to get in, particularly if he thinks the pickings are worth the risk.

Fortunately, there is a wide range of security bolts and locks available from good stockists to prevent easy access. And the fact that some of these devices are visible from the outside may instantly put off a would-be burglar. You can buy bolts for specific situations – say, for a sliding metal frame, a wooden casement window or a sliding sash window. Some can be used in more than one position, but it's important to follow the manufacturer's instructions closely on where to fit them. There are multi-purpose locks which can be fitted in several ways, but these tend to be more expensive.

Of all the window types, louvre windows still present the greatest security risk. Even if they are closed, it is still relatively simple for a burglar to remove some of the glass slats to gain access to your home. One solution is to glue the glass panes into their holders on either side of the frame, but there is the disadvantage that if you accidentally break a slat it becomes difficult to fit another.

The surest method of all is to fit a grille on the inside of the window. This may seem like drastic action. However, if the window is concealed from general view, this may be the only means of keeping a determined thief out unless a burglar alarm is installed.

Fitting a grille could make your home look like a prison. Fortunately, ornamental designs are available to lessen the impact. Normally you have to order the grille to the size of your window. It is installed by being mortared into the surrounding brickwork – inevitably this will cause some damage to the decoration. Some grilles are hinged and incorporate a lock to secure them in position. This enables the grille to be moved aside so that the glass can be cleaned, and, more importantly, in the event of a fire, you are still able to use the window as an escape route.

PROTECTING YOUR HOME

Railings (1), and a locked side gate, will hamper access to the back of the house. Lock a garage side door (2) with a rim lock or padlock. Use anti-vandal paint on a down-pipe (3). Fit grilles behind louvre windows (4) and special locks on sash windows (5).

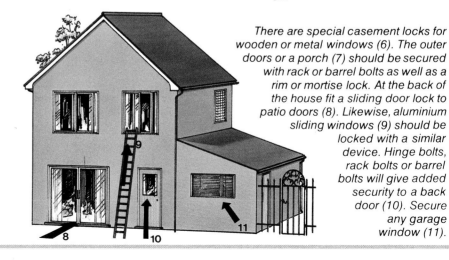

There are special casement locks for wooden or metal windows (6). The outer doors or a porch (7) should be secured with rack or barrel bolts as well as a rim or mortise lock. At the back of the house fit a sliding door lock to patio doors (8). Likewise, aluminium sliding windows (9) should be locked with a similar device. Hinge bolts, rack bolts or barrel bolts will give added security to a back door (10). Secure any garage window (11).

FITTING A PUSH-LOCK

1 *Mark the position of the lock on the fixed and opening sections of the frame. Use the plastic wedge to ensure the lock sits square to the casement.*

2 *Separate the lock from the backplate and screw the backplate to the casement. This is deep enough to receive the bolt so you don't need to drill a hole.*

3 *Push the lock over the backplate and position the wedge, then screw the lock against the side of the frame. Cover the screw holes with plastic plugs.*

4 *A special key is needed to unfasten the lock. Keep it accessible, but out of reach of the window so the frame can be opened quickly in an emergency.*

The simplest security devices, particularly from the point of view of fitting, are those which give added support to the latch and stay already attached to the window. Stay bolts, for example, are available in various designs; some just clamp on, others have to be screwed in place (see *Ready Reference*), replacing the existing stay catch entirely. And if you don't want to go to the trouble of replacing the latch with a lockable version you can always fit a cockspur lock underneath the catch instead (see *Ready Reference*).

Fitting the devices
The step-by-step photographs show how different windows can be secured using various security devices. However, there is little point in fitting a bolt if the frames are rotten or unsound, as the bolt can easily be prised off by any burglar using force.

Most devices can simply be screwed into position on the surface of the opening or fixed frame. But some bolts, for example the rack bolt, have to be concealed within the frame itself, like a mortise lock. For added security it's often advisable to fit two bolts, one at the top, the other at the bottom.

When fitting any of these devices it's important that they can't be removed even if the glass is broken or a hand slipped through a fanlight inadvertently left open. So use clutch-head screws which are almost impossible to remove once they have been driven into place. Alternatively, you may have to drill out the heads of Supadriv screws so they can't be taken out. On metal frames you'll first have to drill pilot holes before you can drive in the screws, but do make sure you avoid the glass. On old galvanised frames, prime any holes with a rust inhibitor before driving in the screws, otherwise your fitting can be forced out by a burglar

TIP: KEEP KEYS HANDY
Security devices are for keeping burglars out and not you in. In the event of a fire you should be able to unlock them easily and quickly. So keep keys near the window, but out of reach of a burglar's arm stretching through a broken pane.

WINDOW STAY LOCKS
Window stays allow a window to be fastened in the open position. Some stay locks prevent the stay being lifted off the catch and the window being fully opened for access. However, they do not prevent the stay from being cut through. Their main advantage is in preventing young children from climbing out of the window.

Types of stay

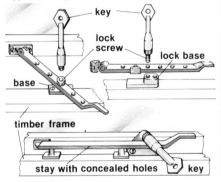

COCKSPUR LOCKS
When set in the closed position, cockspur locks prevent the latch from being opened. There are three main types:
● vertical sliding (A)
● sliding wedge (B)
● pivoting (best on aluminium frames – C).

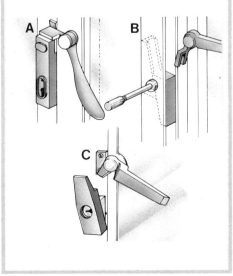

METAL FRAMES

1 Mark and drill fixing holes on the opening frame. Use a depth gauge on the drill bit to prevent overdrilling. Then screw the lock in place.

2 Set the locking staple on the fixed frame and close the lock to keep it in place. You can then mark the fixing holes with a pencil.

3 Unfasten the bolt and push the locking bar to one side. Drill the fixing holes and screw the staple into place, covering the self-tapping screws with plastic plugs.

SECURING SASH WINDOWS

1 There are various types of acorn stop. For the simplest, drill a hole no more than 75mm (3in) above the bottom rail of the outer sash and fit the backplate.

5 Mark the position of the backplate on the outer sash and use a chisel to cut a recess so the plate will sit flush with the surface of the rail.

9 A special 3-stage sash lock is also available. To fit it, hold the striking plate against the outer frame and mark where the recesses have to be cut.

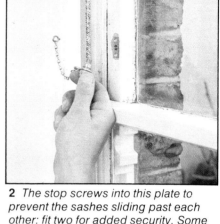

2 The stop screws into this plate to prevent the sashes sliding past each other: fit two for added security. Some stops can be locked in place.

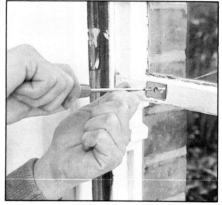

6 Next, screw the backplate into position. With some dual screws there may be a small threaded barrel which you screw in instead of the backplate.

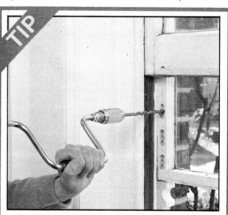

TIP

10 It's easier and more accurate to use a brace and bit, rather than an electric drill, to cut the recesses so that the striking plate sits flush.

3 When fitting dual screws, check that the rails of the sashes are thick enough to take the barrels. Site the locks about 100mm (4in) in from the side edges.

4 Drill a 10mm (3/8in) diameter hole through the inner sash and for 15mm (5/8in) into the outer one. Mark the bit with tape as a guide.

7 Close the frame, then screw the large threaded barrel of the bolt into the inner sash. Make sure you stop when it is flush with the rail surface.

8 To secure the lock you have to screw a bolt through the large barrel on the inner sash and into the locking plate on the outer sash using a key.

11 Use a sharp chisel to square up the edges and clear out the waste in each recess. Then screw the striking plate into position.

12 Screw the locking unit to the top edge of the inner sash with clutch head screws. The locking bar is wound into the striking plate with a special key.

Ready Reference

SLIDING WINDOW LOCKS

The clamp-on type has jaws which are opened and closed with a special key. The lock is placed over the track and against the frame of the closed window and is then locked in position.

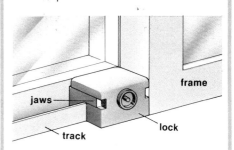

TIP: FIT A DEPTH STOP

When drilling holes in metal (and particularly aluminium) frames, fit the twist drill with a depth stop so there is no risk of drilling into the glass of the window and cracking it, or of breaking the weatherstrip or sealing strip.

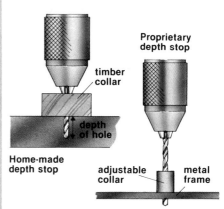

TIP: NARROW STILES

Rack bolts are often too bulky to fit into frames with narrow stiles, but special surface-mounted locks are available. When closed they draw the sash tightly into the frame so the sash can't be levered out. They also help to cut down draughts.

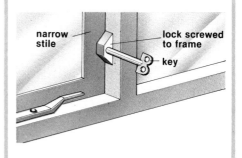

FITTING A RACK BOLT

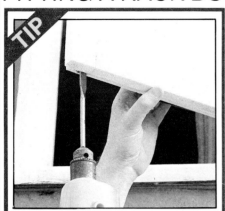

1 Mark and drill the hole in the frame to accommodate the bolt – vertically, if the frame sides are narrow. Repeat the operation for the keyhole.

2 Next screw the bolt into place. You may have to recess it slightly so that the bottom plate doesn't foul the moving frame when it's being closed.

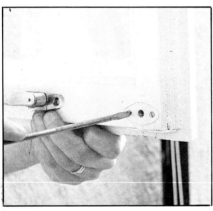

3 Screw the keyhole plate into position. Coat the bolt with chalk, shut the window and then try to close the lock so the bolt marks the frame.

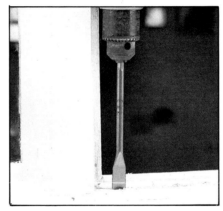

4 This will leave a chalk mark on the fixed frame. You can now drill a hole to receive the bolt. When doing this it's important to keep the drill upright.

5 Screw the backplate over the hole to prevent wear. Again you may first have to recess it so that it doesn't obstruct the frame when it's being closed.

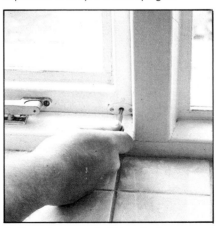

6 For extra security fit two bolts – one at the top, the other at the bottom of the opening edge of the frame. Don't forget to remove the key after locking the bolt.

LOCKING LATCHES

1 Remove the old latch and catch and fill the fixing holes. Sand the newly exposed woodwork, then prime and paint it the same colour as the frame.

2 With the window closed, screw the new catch to one window frame midway between top and bottom. Then position the catch in relation to this.

3 When the latch is in the closed position you can insert a special key and wind the locking bar into the backplate to secure the casement.

FITTING LOCKS ON DOORS

There's little point in going to the time, trouble and expense of fitting security devices to windows if you don't carry out a similar operation on doors as well.

A door sitting solidly in its frame may appear an impressive barrier to a would-be burglar, but if it's only fitted with a traditional mortise or rimlock then it's far more vulnerable than you may think. Modern locks, admittedly, are hard to pick; however, a burglar isn't going to waste time trying to do this. He wants quick access, and brute force rather than stealth is often his best means of getting in. Consequently, he may try to force open an outside door either by kicking it or by using a crowbar to lever it free. If the door isn't properly protected, it will only take a few seconds before he's inside.

Attacking the weak points
Your main entry/exit door is the most difficult to make secure. The best protection is offered by a mortise deadlock fitted into the edge of a substantial door. A rimlock is less resistant to forcing, because it is merely screwed to the face of the door.

Check that all fixings – including the hinges – are secure, and that the woodwork is in good condition. Also make sure that the lock cannot be reached by a hand pushed through the letterbox.

For added protection of this door when you're in the house, the simplest device to fit is a door chain. There are various types, but all depend on a secure fixing if they are to be effective. The plate close, into which the chain is hooked, is screwed to the opening edge of the door, and the chain staple is screwed to the fixed frame – see step-by-step photographs overleaf. With aluminium doors, it helps to improve the strength of the fixing if a block of wood can be slipped into the door frame section, perhaps through the letterplate opening or lock cut-out. This will give the self-tapping securing screws more to grip on. Also, fix the chain staple to the timber part of the door frame and not to the aluminium sub-frame.

Security for other doors
The best protection for other doors is given by substantial bolts. These can be surface-mounted, but make sure that the fixings are secure and that they cannot be reached if glass in the door is broken.

Better protection is offered by rack bolts mortised into the door edge at the top and bottom. But it's best not to use these on thin doors as they can weaken the stile. And don't set them into the mortise and tenon joints at the corner of the door as this will also weaken the door structure. As an alternative, you can fit flush or barrel bolts.

Protecting the hinges
The other area frequently forgotten is the hinge side of the door, which is most vulnerable to being kicked in if the door opens outwards. Hinge bolts, however, help prevent this and can be fitted to front doors as well as other external doors. The stud type (see step-by-step photographs) are best set 25mm (1in) inside the top and bottom hinges, but on heavier doors it's best to use the tongue type. The male part is fixed to the edge of the door and a recessed plate is set in the frame.

Patio doors
At one time sliding patio doors had a poor security record, notably because burglars had the audacity to lift the sliding sash clear of the track. This isn't possible with modern designs, which also incorporate a locking device. However, there are purpose-made patio door locks available to give added security (see *Ready Reference*).

Ready Reference

SECURING FRENCH DOORS
Because the doors lock against each other they are awkward to secure. Fit hinge bolts on the outside edges, and rack or barrel bolts which should lock into the top frame and the floor.

PATIO DOOR LOCK
This is screwed to the bottom edge of the inside frame and a bar is pushed into a predrilled hole in the outer one.

PREVENTING FORCED ENTRY

One of the most unpleasant situations anyone can experience is to answer a knock at the door to be faced with someone barging his way in uninvited.

Once the door has been opened, a rim or mortise lock is totally ineffective at keeping an intruder out. But to prevent this happening you can fit one of a variety of door chains so you can identify who is at the door without having to open it more than just ajar.

Most chains can be hooked in position when you are in the house, but there is a type that you can lock in place from the outside to give added protection to the door locks.

Don't forget that you can also fit a door viewer to a solid timber door and this will enable you to see who is on the other side without them seeing you.

1 Set the door chain centrally on the opening edge of the door. First mark the fixing holes of the plate close that has to be attached to the door itself.

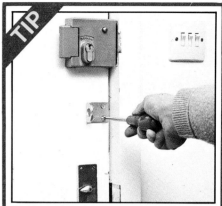

2 Use a bradawl to mark small starting holes in the door and then screw the plate in position. If the timber is soft, resite the plate.

3 Partly drive in the bottom screw of the staple that holds the chain in place on the frame. Slip the chain over the staple and fasten both fixing screws.

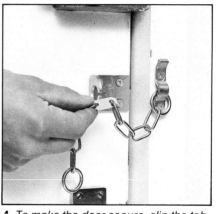

4 To make the door secure, slip the tab on the linkage through the slotted ring on the plate close and draw the chain back to lock against the plate.

5 A door viewer should be fitted centrally at eye level to a solid timber door. It allows you to see who is on the other side without them seeing you.

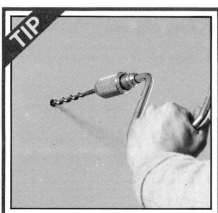

6 Next drill a 12mm (1/2in) hole through the door. If using an electric drill hold a wood block at the back of the hole to prevent splitting.

7 Push the barrel through the hole from the outside of the door so the flange surrounding the lens of the viewer presses tightly against the door.

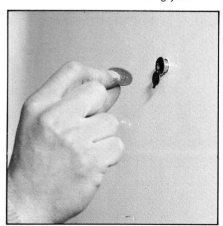

8 On the inside, screw the eyepiece, which has a swivel cap over the end, to the barrel using a coin. This will hold the viewer firmly in place.

SECURING DOOR EDGES

1 Rack bolts for doors have a longer barrel than their window counterparts. First mark the position of the barrel and the keyhole on the edge of the door.

2 Drill the barrel hole and keyhole, then cut a recess so that the plate of the bolt sits flush with the door edge. Check that the barrel hole is deep enough.

3 Screw the bolt and keyhole plate into place. Chalk the end of the bolt, close the door, then use the special key to try to lock the bolt.

4 Where the bolt makes a chalk mark on the frame, drill a suitably-sized receiver hole. This should be protected by a metal plate recessed into the frame.

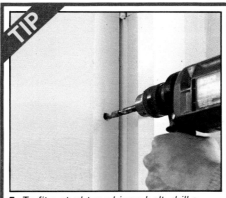

5 To fit a stud-type hinge bolt, drill a 10mm (³/₈in) diameter hole about 38mm (1¹/₂in) into the closing edge of the door. Tape the bit to act as a depth stop.

6 Drive the ribbed part of the bolt into the hole with a hammer. Then partially close the door so that the bolt makes a mark on the door frame.

7 Measure how far the stud protrudes from the door edge and then drill a 12mm (¹/₂in) diameter hole in the door frame to slightly more than this depth.

8 This hole in the frame is covered with a mating plate; you will probably have to recess this to ensure that the door can close properly without sticking.

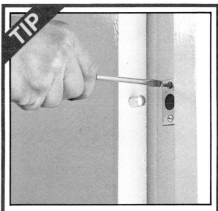

9 Screw the mating plate into the recess, making sure you drive the screws squarely into the countersunk holes so they don't foul the door.

CHAPTER 7
Plumbing

REPLACING TAPS

Changing the old taps on your basin is a bright and practical way of making your bathroom more attractive. It may also be a good idea if they are old and inefficient.

There may be a number of reasons why you wish to replace the taps supplying your sink, basin or bath. They may continually drip or leak, where new taps would give efficient, trouble-free service. Perhaps you want the advantages that mixers have over individual taps or perhaps it is simply that the chromium plating has worn off leaving the taps looking incurably shabby.

It is more likely, however, that appearance, rather than malfunction, will be your reason for changing. There are fashions in plumbing fittings as in clothing and furniture. Taps of the 1950s or 60s are instantly recognisable as out-of-date in a bathroom or kitchen of the 1980s. Fortunately, fashions in sinks, basins and baths have changed rather less dramatically over the past three decades. There is probably no more cost-effective way of improving bathroom and kitchen appearance than by the provision of sparkling new taps or mixers.

Choosing taps

When you come to select your new taps you may feel that you are faced with a bewildering choice. Tap size, appearance, the material of which the tap is made, whether to choose individual taps or mixers and – for the bath – whether to provide for an over-bath shower by fitting a bath/shower mixer: all these things need to be considered.

Size is easily enough dealt with. Taps and mixers are still in imperial sizes. Bath tap tails are 3/4in in diameter, and basin and sink taps 1/2in in diameter. There are, however, a few suppliers who are beginning to designate taps by the metric size, not of the taps themselves, but of the copper supply pipes to which they will probably be connected. Such a supplier might refer to bath taps as 22mm and sink and basin taps as 15mm.

Most taps are made of chromium-plated brass, though there are also ranges of enamelled and even gold-plated taps and mixers. Although taps and mixers are still manufactured with conventional crutch or capstan handles, most people nowadays prefer to choose taps with 'shrouded'

heads made of acrylic or other plastic. In effect, these combine the functions of handle and easy-clean cover, completely concealing the tap's headgear. A still popular alternative is the functional 'Supatap', nowadays provided with plastic rather than metal 'ears' for quick and comfortable turning on and off.

There is also a very competitively priced range of all-plastic taps. These usually give satisfactory enough service in the home, but they cannot be regarded as being as sturdy as conventional metal taps, and they can be damaged by very hot water.

So far as design is concerned the big difference is between 'bib taps' and 'pillar taps'. Bib taps have a horizontal inlet and are usually wall-mounted while pillar taps have a vertical inlet and are mounted on the bath, basin or sink they serve.

Taking out old basin taps

When replacing old taps with new ones the most difficult part of the job is likely to be – as with so many plumbing operations – removing the old fittings. Let's first consider wash basin taps.

You must, of course, cut off the hot and cold water supplies to the basin. The best way of doing this will usually be to tie up the float arm of the ball valve supplying the cold water storage cistern so as to prevent water flowing in. Then run the bathroom cold taps until water ceases to flow. Only then open up the hot taps. This will conserve most of the expensively heated water in the hot water storage cylinder.

If you look under the basin you will find that the tails of the taps are connected to the water supply pipes with small, fairly accessible nuts, and that a larger – often

Ready Reference

EQUIPMENT CHECKLIST

For replacing existing taps, you will need the following tools and equipment:
- new taps of the right type and size
- an adjustable spanner
- a basin wrench ('crowsfoot')
- an adjustable wrench
- penetrating oil
- plastic washers (see below)
- plumber's putty
- PTFE tape

You may also need tap tail adaptors (if the new taps have shorter tails than the old ones) and new tap connectors (if your new taps have metric tails instead of imperial ones).

WHAT ABOUT WASHERS?

With ceramic basins, use a plastic washer above and below the basin surface (A) so you don't crack the basin as you tighten the back-nut. You can use plumber's putty instead of the upper washer.

On thin basins, use a special top-hat washer between basin and back-nut (B).

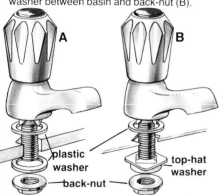

The lugs at the top of the tap tail are meant to stop tap turning in square tap holes. Use special anti-rotation washers to stop new taps with smaller lugs from turning in old tap holes.

TIPS TO SAVE TROUBLE

- to undo stubborn back-nuts, add extra leverage to the crowsfoot by hooking a wrench handle into its other end
- if this fails, squirt penetrating oil around the back-nuts. Leave for a while and try again
- in really stubborn cases, remove the basin completely, and turn it upside down on the floor so you have more room to work
- grip the tap body with an adjustable spanner to stop it turning as you use the crowsfoot; otherwise the tap lugs could crack the basin

REMOVING OLD TAPS

1 *It's best to change taps by removing the basin completely. Loosen the two tap connectors carefully with an adjustable spanner.*

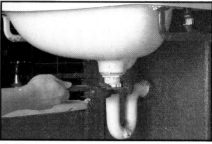

2 *Disconnect the waste trap connector using an adjustable wrench. Take care not to damage the trap, particularly if it is lead or copper.*

3 *Undo any screws holding the basin to its brackets on the wall, and lift it clear of the brackets before lowering it carefully to the floor.*

4 *Check the condition of the back-nuts, which may be badly corroded. It's a good idea to apply penetrating oil and leave this to work for a while.*

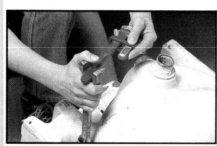

5 *Use the crowsfoot (with extra leverage if necessary) to undo the back-nut. If more force is needed, grip the tap itself with a wrench to stop it turning.*

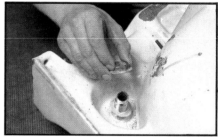

6 *Remove the back-nut and any washers beneath it and the basin. Old washers like these should always be replaced with new washers.*

inaccessible — back-nut secures the tap to the basin. The nuts of the swivel tap connectors joining the pipes to the taps are usually easily undone with a wrench or spanner of the appropriate size. The back-nuts can be extremely difficult — even for professional plumbers!

There are special wrenches and basin or 'crows foot' spanners that may help, but they won't perform miracles and ceramic basins can be very easily damaged by heavy handedness. The best course of action is to disconnect the swivel tap connectors and to disconnect the trap from the waste outlet. These are secured by nuts and are easily

undone. Then lift the basin off its brackets or hanger and place it upside down on the floor. Apply some penetrating oil to the tap tails and, after allowing a few minutes for it to soak in, tackle the nuts with your wrench or crowsfoot · spanner. You'll find they are much more accessible. Hold the tap while you do this to stop it swivelling and damaging the basin.

Fitting the new taps

When fitting the new taps or mixer, unscrew the back-nuts, press some plumber's putty round the tail directly below the tap body or fit a plastic washer onto the top tail.

FITTING NEW TAPS

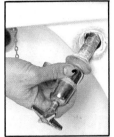
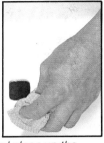

1 *Remove the tap and clean up the basin surround, chipping away scale and any old putty remaining from when the tap was originally installed.*

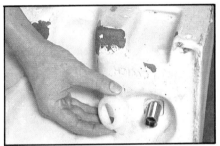

3 *Twist the tap so that it's at the correct angle to the basin and is firmly bedded on the putty. Then push a top-hat washer onto the tail.*

5 *Tighten up the back-nut until the tap assembly is completely firm, using the crowsfoot or an adjustable spanner. Repeat the process for the other tap.*

7 *When all is secure, remove any surplus putty from around the base of the taps, wiping it over with a finger to leave a smooth, neat finish.*

2 *Now take one of the new taps and fit a washer or plumber's putty around the top of the tail before pushing it into the hole in the basin.*

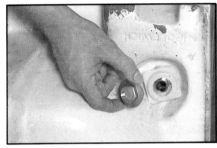

4 *With the top-hat washer firmly in place, take the new back-nut and screw it up the tail of the tap by hand.*

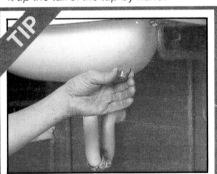

6 *Reconnect all the pipework. Use tap-tail adaptors if the new taps have shorter tails than the old ones.*

8 *Turn the water back on. Check that the flow from the taps is regular and that the waste trap is not leaking. If it is, tighten up its connectors slightly.*

Push the tails through the holes in the basin. Slip flat plastic washers over the tails where they protrude from beneath the basin, screw on the back-nuts and tighten them up. Make sure that the taps or mixer are secure, but don't overtighten them. To make tightening easier, (and undoing, if ever necessary) use top-hat washers.

All that remains to be done is to connect the swivel tap connectors to the tails of the new taps or mixer. You will see that a tap connector consists of a lining – with a flange – that is inserted into the tap tail and is then secured by the coupling nut. This nut is provided with a washer to ensure a watertight connection. When renewing taps you may well need to renew this small washer.

It is possible that when you come to connect the water supply pipes to the taps you will get an unpleasant surprise. The tails of modern taps are slightly shorter than those of older ones and the tap connectors may not reach. If the water supply pipes are of lead or of copper it is quite likely that they will have enough 'give' to enable you to make the connection but, if not, there are extension pieces specially made to bridge the gap.

Bib taps

If you're replacing existing bib taps with those of a more modern design, it's a relatively simple matter of disconnecting and unscrewing the old ones and fitting the new taps in their place. However, it's quite possible that you'll want to remove the bib taps altogether and fit a new sink with some pillar taps. This will involve a little more plumbing work. To start with, turn off the water supply and remove the taps and old sink. If the pipework comes up from the floor, you'll need to uncover the run in the wall to below where the new sink will go. You should then be able to ease the pipes away from the wall and cut off the exposed sections. This will allow you to join short lengths of new pipe, bent slightly if necessary, to link the pipe ends and the tap tails. Alternatively, if the pipes come down the wall you'll have to extend the run to below the level of the new sink and use elbow fittings to link the pipe to the tap tails. In either case it's a good idea to fit the taps to the new sink first and to make up the pipework runs slightly overlong, so that when the new sink is offered up to the wall you can measure up accurately and avoid the risk of cutting off too much pipe. Rather than having to make difficult bends you can use lengths of corrugated copper pipe. One end of the pipe is plain so that it can be fitted to the 15mm supply pipes with either a soldered capillary or compression fitting; the other end has a swivel tap connector.

JOINTS FOR COPPER PIPE

Joining copper pipe is one of the basic plumbing skills. Compression and capillary joints are easy to make and once you've mastered the techniques, you'll be prepared for a whole range of plumbing projects.

C onnecting pipes effectively is the basis of all good plumbing as most leaks result from poorly constructed joints. For virtually all domestic plumbing purposes you will only have to use compression or capillary joints. Compression joints are easy to use but expensive, while capillary joints are cheap but need some care in fitting.

If you are making a join into an existing pipe system remember to make sure the water supply has been turned off at the relevant stop-valve either on that section or below the cold water storage cistern, and the pipe has been completely drained.

Preparing the pipes
Before joining pipes together, check that the ends are circular and have not been distorted. If they have been dented, cut back to an undamaged section of the pipe using a hacksaw with a sharp blade or a wheel tube cutter (see pages 185-187).

The ends should also be square and a simple way of checking this is shown overleaf (see *Ready Reference*). Use a file to make any correction and remove ragged burrs of metal. If you're using a capillary joint clean up the sides of the pipe with abrasive paper or steel wool.

Compression joints (friction joints)
A compression joint, as its name implies, is made by compressing two brass or copper rings (known as olives or thimbles) round the ends of the pipes to be joined, so forming a watertight seal. There are two main types of compression joint – the non-manipulative fitting and the manipulative fitting.

Although not the cheapest means of joining a pipe, a non-manipulative joint is the easiest to use and requires only the minimum of tools. It comprises a central body made of brass or gunmetal with a cap-nut at each end which, when rotated, squeezes the olive tightly between the pipe end and the casing. This is the most commonly used type of compression joint suitable for most internal domestic plumbing purposes.

A manipulative joint is now rarely used in indoor domestic water systems. Because it

cannot be pulled apart it is sometimes used for underground pipework, but capillary joints will do equally well in these situations.

The joint usually comprises a male and a female union nut. These are slipped over the pipe ends which are then flared ('manipulated') using a special steel tool called a *drift*. Jointing compound is smeared on the inside of the flares and a copper cone is inserted between them. The nuts are then screwed together to complete the seal.

How a compression joint works
The olive (thimble) is the key part of a non-manipulative compression joint. When the cap-nut is rotated clockwise the olive is forced between the casing and the pipe and is considerably deformed in the process.

A watertight seal is dependent upon the pipe ends having been well prepared so they butt up exactly to the pipe stop in the casing. This forms a primary seal and ensures that the pipe is parallel to the movement of the rotating cap-nut. An even pressure is then

applied to the olive so that it does not buckle under the strain of tightening.

What size of pipework and fittings?
Pipework is now sold in metric dimensions, but plumbing in your home may be in imperial sizes. The metric sizes are not exactly the same as their imperial equivalents – check the table (*Ready Reference*, right) which shows the different ways pipe can be bought.

These differences can cause problems. With capillary joints you have to use adaptors when converting pipe from one system to another. Adaptors are also needed for some compression joints although the 12mm, 15mm, 28mm and 54mm sizes are compatible with their imperial equivalents. This means if you already have imperial compression joints you can connect in new metric pipework, without replacing the joints.

Adaptors are made with different combinations of metric and imperial outlets to fit most requirements. A supplier will advise on what replacements to use.

HOW OLIVES MAKE A WATERTIGHT SEAL

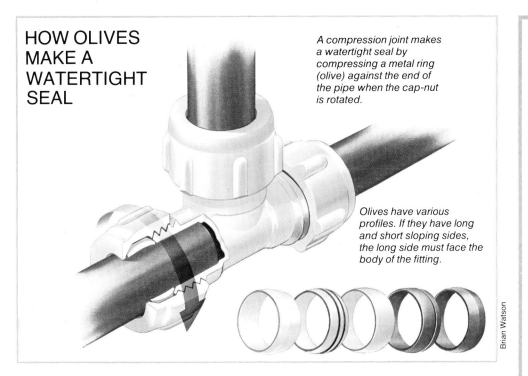

A compression joint makes a watertight seal by compressing a metal ring (olive) against the end of the pipe when the cap-nut is rotated.

Olives have various profiles. If they have long and short sloping sides, the long side must face the body of the fitting.

Brian Watson

Capillary joints

A capillary joint is simply a copper sleeve with socket outlets into which the pipe ends are soldered. It is neater and smaller than a compression joint and forms a robust connection that will not readily pull apart.

Because it is considerably cheaper than a compression joint it is frequently used when a number of joints have to be made and is particularly useful in awkward positions where it is impossible to use wrenches.

Some people are put off using capillary fittings because of the need to use a blow-torch. But modern gas-canister torches have put paid to the fears associated with

paraffin lamps and are not dangerous.

How a capillary joint works

If two pipes to be joined together were just soldered end to end the join would be very weak because the contact area between solder and copper would be small. A capillary fitting makes a secure join because the sleeve increases this contact area and also acts as a brace to strengthen the connection.

Molten solder is sucked into the space between the pipe and fitting by capillary action, and combines with a thin layer of copper at the contact surface thus bonding the pipe to the fitting. To help the solder to

What happens when solder melts

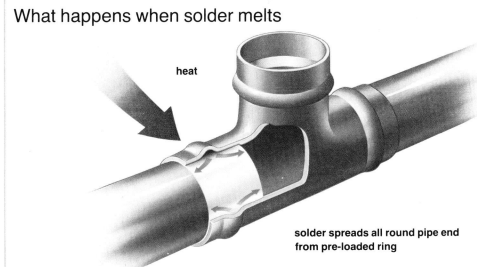

heat

solder spreads all round pipe end from pre-loaded ring

Brian Watson

MAKING A COMPRESSION JOINT

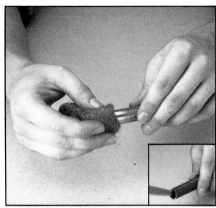

1 Check that the end of the pipe is square using a file to make any correction and to remove burr. Clean pipe end and olive with steel wool.

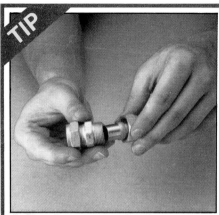

2 The olive goes on after the cap-nut. If it has both long and short sloping sides, make sure the long side faces the main body of the compression fitting.

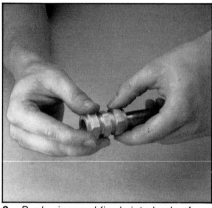

3 Push pipe end firmly into body of fitting so that it rests squarely against pipe stop. Screw up cap-nut tightly with your fingers.

4 Make pencil mark on cap-nut and another aligning on body of fitting to act as guide when tightening cap-nut with wrench.

5 Use one wrench to secure body of fitting and the other to rotate the cap-nut clockwise. About 1 1/2 turns is sufficient to give a watertight seal.

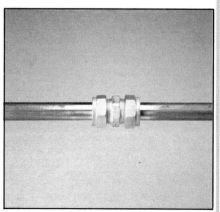

6 Repeat operation to join other pipe to fitting. If water seeps through when supply is turned on, tighten cap-nut further by half a turn.

'take' the copper needs to be clean and shining. Therefore flux is applied to prevent oxides forming which would impair the solder-copper bond.

Types of capillary joint

The most common type of capillary joint has a ring of solder pre-loaded into the sleeve. It is known as an integral ring or 'Yorkshire' fitting – the name of a leading brand.

The 'end feed' type of capillary joint is virtually the same as an integral ring fitting, but you have to add the solder in a separate operation. The sleeve is slightly larger than the pipe and liquid solder is drawn into the space between by capillary action.

Flux and solder

Essential in the soldering operation, flux is a chemical paste or liquid which cleans the metal surfaces and then protects them from the oxides produced when the blow-torch heats the copper so a good metal-solder bond is formed. Mild non-corrosive flux is easy to use as it can be smeared onto the pipe and fitting with a clean brush or even a finger. Although it is best to remove any residue this will not corrode the metal. There is an acid-corrosive flux which dissolves oxides quickly, but this is mostly used with stainless steel. The corrosive residue must be scrubbed off with soapy water.

Solder is an alloy (mixture) of tin and lead and is bought as a reel of wire. Its advantage in making capillary joints is that it melts at relatively low temperatures and quickly hardens when the heat source (blow-torch) is removed.

Blow-torches

A blow-torch is an essential piece of equipment when making capillary joints. It is easy, clean and safe to use providing you handle it with care. Most modern torches operate off a gas canister which can be unscrewed and inexpensively replaced (larger cans are relatively cheaper than small). Sometimes a range of nozzles can be fitted to give different types of flames, but the standard nozzle is perfectly acceptable for capillary joint work.

Using a blow-torch

When using a blow-torch it's most convenient to work at a bench, but you'll find most jointing work has to be carried out where the pipes are to run. Pipework is usually concealed so this may mean working in an awkward place, such as a roof space, or stretching under floorboards. However, always make sure you are in a comfortable position and there's no danger of you dropping a lighted blow-torch.

Jem Grischotti

MAKING A CAPILLARY FITTING

1 Make sure the pipe end is square, then clean it and the inner rim of the fitting with steel wool or abrasive paper until shining.

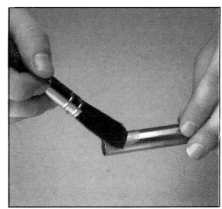

2 Flux can be in liquid or paste form. Use a brush, rather than your finger, to smear it over the end of the pipe and the inner rim of the fitting.

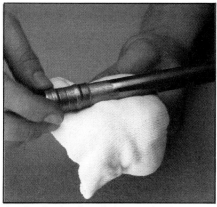

3 Push pipe into fitting so that it rests against pipe stop, twisting a little to help spread the flux. Remove excess flux with a cloth.

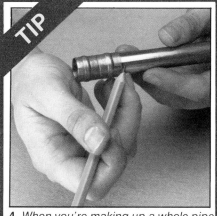

TIP

4 When you're making up a whole pipe run, it helps to make corresponding pencil marks on pipe ends and fittings as a guide for correct lining up.

5 Make other side of joint in same way, then apply blow-torch. Seal is complete when bright ring of solder is visible at ends of fitting.

6 For an end feed fitting, heat the pipe, then hold the solder to mouth of joint. A bright ring all the way round signifies a seal.

Jem Grischotti

Ready Reference

WHICH TOOLS?

For cutting pipe:
● hire a **wheel tube cutter** (which ensures perfectly square pipe ends)

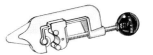

or use a **hack saw**
● use a **metal file** for removing ragged burrs of metal and for squaring ends of pipe that have been cut with a hacksaw. A half-round 'second-cut' type is ideal.

For compression joints:
● use two adjustable **spanners** or **pipe wrenches** (one to hold the fitting, the other to tighten the cap-nut)

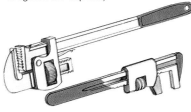

● **steel wool** to clean the surface of pipes before assembling a joint.

For capillary joints:
● a **blow-torch** to melt the solder
● **steel-wool** for cleaning pipe surfaces
● **flux** to ensure a good bond between the solder and copper
● **solder** because even if you're using integral ring fittings (which already have solder in them) you may need a bit extra
● **glass fibre** or **asbestos mat** (or a ceramic tile) to deflect the torch flame from nearby surfaces.

TIP: CUTTING PIPE SQUARELY

For a perfect fit, pipe ends must be cut square. If you're using a hacksaw, hold a strip of paper round the pipe so its edges align and saw parallel to the paper edge. Use the same trick if you have to file an inaccurately-cut end.

TIP: PROTECT NEARBY JOINTS

With capillary fittings, the heat you apply could melt the solder in nearby fittings. To help prevent this, wrap them in wet cloths.

When working near to joists and floor-boards. glass. paintwork and other pipework with capillary joints it is important to shield these areas with glass fibre matting or a piece of asbestos.

Applying the heat
When making a capillary joint gradually build up the temperature of the copper by playing the flame up and down and round the pipe and then to the fitting. When the metal is hot enough the solder will melt and you can then take away the flame. The joint is complete when a bright ring of solder appears all round the mouth of the fitting. Stand the torch on a firm level surface and turn it off as soon as you have finished. Where two or more capillary joints are to be made with one fitting, for example the three ends of a tee, they should all be made at the same time. If this is not possible wrap a damp rag round any joints already made.

Repairing a compression joint
If a compression joint is leaking and tighten-ing of the cap-nut doesn't produce a watertight seal you'll have to disconnect the fitting and look inside – after turning off the water supply. If a cap-nut is impossible to move. run a few drops of penetrating oil onto the thread. If that doesn't do the trick. you'll have to cut it out and replace the fitting and some piping.

Once you have unscrewed one of the cap-nuts there will be enough flexibility in the pipe run to pull the pipe from the casing. Usually the olive will be compressed against the pipe. First check that it is the right way round (see page180) and if it isn't replace it with a new one making sure that it is correctly set.

Sometimes the olive is impossible to remove and needs to be cut off with a hacksaw – make the cut diagonally. Reas-semble the joint following the procedure on page 182 and repeat the operation for the other end of the pipe. Turn on the water supply to check that the repair is watertight.

Repairing a capillary joint
Poor initial soldering is usually the reason why a capillary fitting leaks. You can try and rectify this by 'sweating' in some more solder but if this doesn't work you'll have to remake the joint.

Play the flame of the blow-torch over the fitting and pipe until the solder begins to run from the joint. At this stage you can pull the pipe ends out of the sockets with gloved hands. You can now reuse the fitting as an end feed joint or replace it with a new integral ring capillary connection.

If you reuse the fitting clean the interior surface and the pipe ends with abrasive paper or steel wool and smear them with flux. Then follow the procedure for making an end feed capillary joint.

REPAIRING A COMPRESSION JOINT

1 Unscrew cap-nut using wrenches. There's enough flexibility in pipe run to pull pipe from casing. Check that olive fits, and isn't damaged.

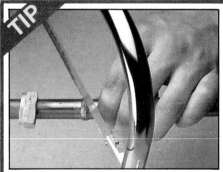

2 A damaged olive must be removed. Use a hacksaw and to make it easier make the cut on the diagonal – but take care not to cut into the pipe itself.

3 Prepare end of pipe with steel wool or abrasive paper. Slip on new olive and finger tighten cap-nut. Rotate cap-nut 1 1/2 turns using wrenches.

REPAIRING A CAPILLARY JOINT

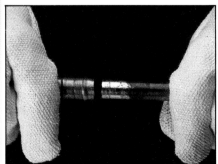

1 Drain pipe and wrap a damp cloth round nearby joints. Play flame on fitting and pull pipe from rim using gloved hands.

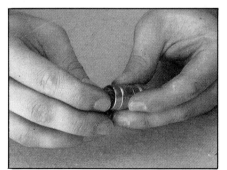

2 If you remake both sides of joint use a new fitting. A spent integral ring fitting, thoroughly cleaned, can be used as an end feed joint.

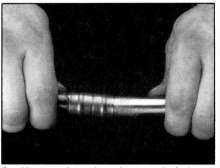

3 Use steel wool to clean end of pipe and inside of fitting. Brush with flux and push pipe into socket. Apply blow-torch to melt solder.

Jem Grischotti

CUTTING & BENDING COPPER PIPE

One of the advantages of domestic copper pipe is that it's easy to cut and bend. Few tools are required and even if you've only a few bends to make in a pipe run, it makes sense to know how it's done. Making accurate bends may need some practice, but it's cheaper than buying specially-shaped fittings.

In all plumbing water has to be carried from a source to a fixture and often then to some type of exit where it can disperse as waste. Basic to all of this is that water must run smoothly with nothing causing resistance to the flow — an important factor when the pressure is low.

Generally the best plumbing practice is to make pipe runs as straight and direct as possible. But sometimes bends are unavoidable (like, for example, when pipe has to go around a room or to turn down into an area below) and if available fittings are neither right for the angle nor attractive to look at, then you'll have to bend the pipe to suit.

Copper piping, because it is both light and resistant to corrosion, is a popular choice for home plumbing work. It can be joined with either capillary or compression fittings (see the techniques on pages 180-184) and when bends are needed you can create the angles in several ways.

The first essential is to accurately work out the pipe lengths you require. Once you've made the measurement double check it — it's quite easy to forget to allow for the pipe that will fit into the socket ends of the joints. You can make the actual marks on the pipe with pencil as this is clearly visible on copper and is a good guide when you come to cutting.

Cutting pipe accurately

For smaller pipe sizes, a sharp-bladed hacksaw is the best tool to use to make the cut. You'll need to hold the pipe firmly, but if you use a vice be careful not to over-tighten the jaws and crush the bore of the pipe (see *Ready Reference*, page 187).

It's important to cut the pipe square so that it butts up exactly to the pipe stop in the joint. This will ensure the pipe is seated squarely in the fitting which is essential for making a watertight seal. It will also help to make that seal. It's surprising how near to square you can get the end just cutting by eye. But the best way to make a really accurate cut is to use a saw guide. This can be made very easily by placing a small rectangle of paper round the pipe with one long edge against the cut mark. By bringing the two short edges of the paper together and aligning them you effectively make a template that's square to the pipe. All you then have to do is hold the paper in place and keep the saw blade against it as you cut. Any burr that's left on the cut edges can be removed with a file.

If you intend to carry out a lot of plumbing, or are working mainly in the larger pipe sizes, it may be worthwhile buying (or hiring) a wheel tube cutter. Of course using one of these is never absolutely essential, but it does save time if you've more than, say, half a dozen cuts to make. And once you have one you'll use it for even the smallest jobs. It's quick to use and will ensure a square cut without trouble every time. You simply place the pipe in the cutter and tighten the control knob to hold it in place. The cutter is then rotated round the pipe and as it revolves it cuts cleanly into the copper. This circular action automatically removes burr from the outside of the pipe, but burr on the inside can be taken away with the reamer (a scraping edge) which is usually incorporated in the tool.

Bending copper pipe

If a lot of changes of direction are necessary in a pipe run it's cheaper and quicker to bend the pipe rather than use fittings. This also makes the neatest finish particularly if the pipework is going to be exposed. Under a pedestal wash-basin, for example, the hot and cold supply pipes rise parallel to each other in the pedestal before bending outwards and upwards to connect to the two tap tails.

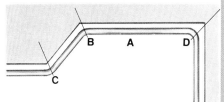

Using fittings in this situation would be more costly as well as possibly being unsightly, while the cheaper alternative, making bends, means the pipework is less conspicuous. The pipe can also be bent to the exact angle required so this method of changing direction is not limited by the angles of the fittings. And with fewer fittings in a pipe system there are fewer places where leaks can occur.

The smaller sizes of copper pipe, those most commonly used in domestic plumbing (15mm, 22mm and 28mm), can be bent quite easily by hand. The technique of annealing — heating the pipe to red heat in the vicinity of the bend to reduce its temper (strength) and so make bending easier — is unnecessary when working in these pipe sizes. But you will need to support the pipe wall, either internally or externally, as the bend is made. If you don't you'll flatten the profile of the pipe. Using it in this condition would reduce the flow of water at the outlet point.

For small jobs a bending spring is the ideal tool, supporting the pipe internally. It is a long hardened steel coil which you push into the pipe to the point where the bend will be made. It's best used for bends near the end of the pipe, since the spring can be easily pulled out after the bend is made. However, it can be used further down the pipe if it is attached to a length of stout wire (which helps to push it into place, and is vital for retrieving it afterwards).

Bending techniques
You actually bend the pipe over your knee, overbending slightly and bringing back to the required angle. The spring will now be fixed tightly in the pipe and you won't be able simply to pull it out. However, its removal is quite easy. All you have to do is to insert a bar — a screwdriver will do — through the ring at the end of the spring and twist it. This reduces the spring's diameter and will enable you to withdraw it. It's a good idea to grease the spring before you insert it as this will make pulling it out that much easier (also see *Ready Reference* page 187).

Slight wrinkles may be found on the inside of the bend, but these can be tapped out by gentle hammering. It's wise not to attempt this before taking out the spring. If you do you'll never be able to remove it.

Bending springs are suitable for 15mm and 22mm diameter pipe. But although it is possible to bend 28mm pipe as well, it's advisable to use a bending machine instead. This is also preferable if you have a lot of bends to make. And if you don't want to go to the expense of buying one, you can probably hire a machine from a tool hire shop.

A bending machine consists of a semi-circular former that supports the pipe externally during the bending operation and a roller that forces the pipe round the curve when the levers of the machine are brought together. The degree of bend depends on how far you move the handles.

Flexible pipe
This is a kind of corrugated copper pipe which can be bent easily by hand without any tools. You can buy it with two plain ends for connection to compression joints or with one end plain and one with a swivel tap connector for connection to a tap or ball-valve.

As it's the most expensive way of making a bend, it's not cost effective to use it when you have to make a number of changes of direction in a pipe run. It's not particularly attractive to look at so it is best used in places where it won't be seen. As such it's most commonly used for connecting the water supply pipes to the bath taps in the very confined space at the head of the bath. And it can make the job of fitting kitchen sink taps easier, particularly when the base unit has a back which restricts access to the supply pipes.

CUTTING COPPER PIPE

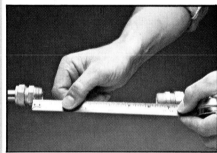
1 Make an accurate measurement of the proposed pipe run. Don't forget to allow extra for the pipe that will fit inside the joints.

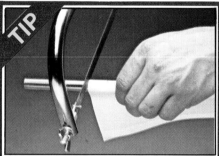
2 Use a simple paper template to help you cut pipe squarely. Wrap the paper round the pipe and align the edges.

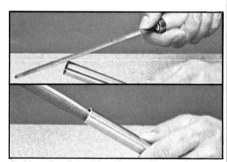
3 Use the flat side of your file to clean any burr from the outside of the pipe. The curved side of the file can be used to clean the inside.

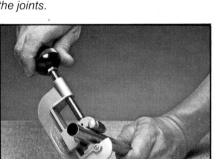
4 When using a wheel tube cutter, position the cutting mark on the pipe against the edge of the cutting wheel, then tighten the control knob.

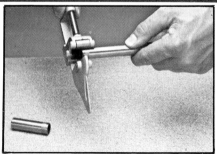
5 Once the pipe is clamped in place, rotate the cutter so it makes an even cut. The rollers on the tool will keep the blade square to the pipe.

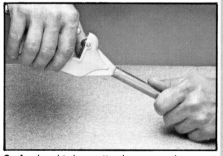
6 A wheel tube cutter leaves a clean cut on the outside of the pipe, but any burr on the inside can be removed with the reamer (an attachment to the tool).

BENDING COPPER PIPE

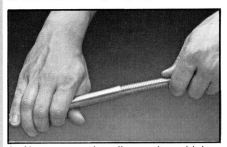

1 *Always use a bending spring which is compatible in size with the pipe. Smear it with petroleum jelly.*

2 *Overbend the pipe slightly, and then bend it back to the required angle.*

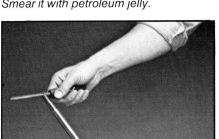

3 *Put a screwdriver through the ring at the end of the spring. Twist it, then pull the spring out.*

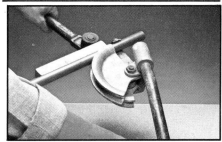

4 *To use a bending machine, open the levers and position the pipe as shown, then slide the straight former on top.*

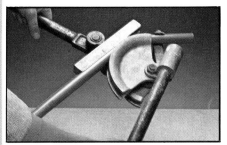

5 *Raise the levers so the wheel runs along the straight edge and the pipe is forced round the circular former.*

6 *Bend the pipe to the required angle, then remove by opening the levers, and taking out the straight former.*

FLEXIBLE COPPER PIPE

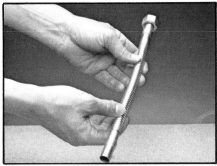

1 *Although relatively expensive, flexible pipe is ideal for making awkward bends in the pipe run to connect to taps.*

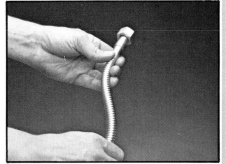

2 *It's easy to hand bend the pipe to the required shape, but don't continually flex it or the thin wall will split.*

Jem Grischotti

Ready Reference

PIPE LENGTHS

Draw a rough sketch plan of the complete pipe run, then work out:

● how many 2 metre lengths you'll need
● where to join them in on the straight (not at a bend)
● how many fittings you'll need to connect the pipes to each other.

TIP: CUTTING PIPE

Copper pipe can be crushed in the jaws of a vice so use a bench hook when cutting with a hacksaw. Pin a scrap of wood beside it to hold the pipe snugly.

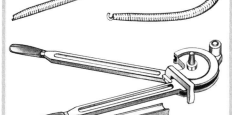

BENDING AIDS

For 15mm and 22mm pipe use a *bending spring* to match the pipe size. It's a flexible coil of hardened steel about 600mm (2ft) long.

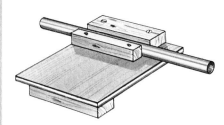

For 28mm pipe hire a *pipe bending machine* which supports the outside of the pipe wall as it bends.

TIP: REMOVING BENDING SPRINGS

For bends over 600mm (2ft) from the pipe end use a wire coathanger with a hooked end to turn and withdraw the spring.

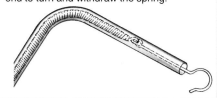

187

CONNECTING NEW PIPES TO OLD

Improvements or additions to a domestic plumbing system inevitably involve joining new pipework into old. How you do this depends largely on whether the existing pipework is made of lead, iron or more modern materials – copper, polythene or even unplasticised PVC.

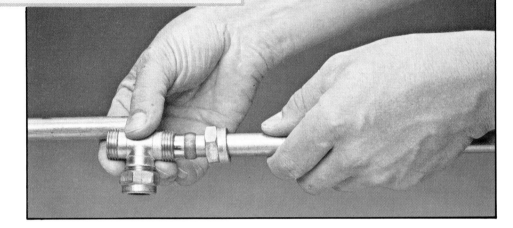

The principle of joining into existing pipework is quite straightforward. You decide where you will need your new water supply – at a bedroom basin or an outside tap, for example – and then pick a convenient point on the plumbing system to connect up your 'branch line'. At this point you have to cut out a small section of the old pipe and insert a tee junction into which the branch pipe will be fitted. That's all there is to it: laying the branch pipe will simply involve routine cutting, bending and joining of new pipe, and final connection to the new tap or appliance at the other end.

Before you can begin the job, however, you have to do some reconnaissance work to identify what sort of existing pipework you have. You might be tempted to relate the plumbing to the age of the house, thinking that an old house will have an old system with lead or iron pipework. But this isn't a reliable guide. Many old properties have been modernised and so may actually have a more up-to-date system than a house built relatively recently.

Until the 1950s the only types of pipe used in domestic plumbing were lead and iron, but then these were superseded by thin-walled copper piping. Today there are other alternatives too: stainless steel is sometimes used as an alternative to copper, and polythene and UPVC (unplasticised polyvinyl chloride) pipes can be installed for cold water supplies only.

Check the table (see *Ready Reference*, right) for the type of pipe you can use. While copper is the most common one for new work, it must *never* be joined to galvanised iron because of the severe risk of electrolytic corrosion of the iron if the galvanising is not in perfect condition.

First things first

Before cutting into a pipe run you'll first have to turn off the water supply to the pipe and then drain it by opening any taps or drain cocks connected to it. But this need not be too inconvenient if you make up the complete branch line before you turn the

water off so you are without water only while you make the final branch connection.

Connecting into copper pipe

When taking a branch from a copper pipe it's probably easier to use a compression tee fitting rather than a capillary fitting. A compression fitting can be made even if there is some water in the pipe run – capillary joints need the pipe to be dry – and you won't have to worry about using a blow-torch and possibly damaging other capillary joints nearby (if they are heated up, their solder will soften and the joint will leak).

It's quite easy to work out how much pipe to cut out of the main run in order to insert a tee junction (of either compression or capillary fittings). Push a pencil or stick into the tee until it butts up against the pipe stop. Mark this length with your thumbs, then place the stick on top of the fitting so you can mark the outside to give a guide line. Next you have to cut the pipe at the place where the branch has to be made and prepare one of the cut ends (see the pictures on page 190). Now connect to the pipe the end of the tee that doesn't have the guide line marked on the casing and rest the tee back against the pipe. You will now be able to see where the pipe stop comes to and you can then mark the pipe to give you the second cutting point. Remove the section of pipe with a hacksaw and prepare the pipe end.

With a compression fitting put on the other cap-nut and olive. If you gently push the pipe

and tee sideways to the pipe run this will give you more room to position the body before you allow the pipe end to spring into place. When this is done the cap-nut can be pushed up to the fitting and can be tightened with your fingers. Both sides of the tee can then be tightened using your wrenches to give the cap-nuts about one-and-a-quarter turns.

Remember that you must use a second wrench to grip the body of the fitting so it stays still as the cap-nut is tightened. If it should turn, other parts of the joint which have already been assembled will be loosened or forced out of position, and leaks will result. The connection into the main pipe run is now complete and you can connect up the branch pipe.

If you are using a capillary tee fitting there are a number of points to bear in mind. It's easiest to use one with integral rings of solder (this saves the bother of using solder wire) and after the pipe ends and the inside rims have been prepared and smeared with flux the fitting can be 'sprung' into place. The branch pipe should also be inserted at this stage so all the joints can be made at the same time.

When using the blow-torch, it is important to protect the surrounding area from the effects of the flame with a piece of glass fibre matting, asbestos or the back of a ceramic tile. It's also worthwhile wrapping damp cloths round any nearby capillary joints to protect them from accidental over-heating and thus 'sweating'.

IDENTIFYING YOUR PIPEWORK

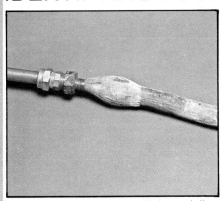

1 Lead pipes are grey and give a dull thud when knocked. You can nick the surface with a knife. Look for smooth bends and neat even swellings – these are 'wiped' soldered joints. Repairs are often made using copper pipe.

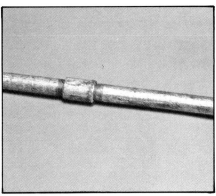

2 Iron pipes have a grey galvanised or black finish and give a clanging sound when knocked. A knife will only scrape along the surface. Look for the large threaded joints which appear as a collar on the pipe or at a bend.

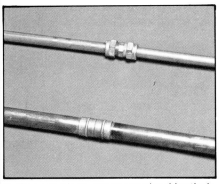

3 Copper pipes are recognised by their familiar copper colour. Changes of direction are often made by bends in the pipe itself or by using angled fittings. The joints will be either the compression or capillary type.

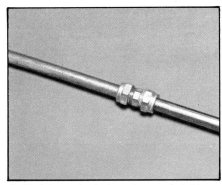

4 Stainless steel pipes have a bright silvery surface. They come in the same sizes as copper and can be joined in the same way. Bends are only found in sizes up to 15mm. These pipes are not commonly used in the home.

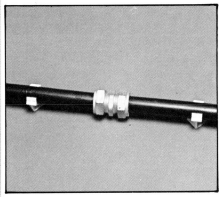

5 Polythene pipes are usually black and are soft enough to be slightly compressed between the fingers. Joints are made with metal compression fittings which require special gunmetal olives and liners.

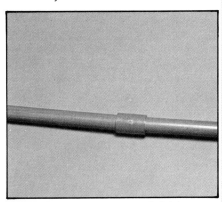

6 UPVC pipes are grey and rigid. Connections and changes in direction are made by angled joints which fit like slim collars over the ends of the pipes. These are fixed in place using solvent weld cement.

Ready Reference

WHAT JOINS TO WHAT?
Use this table as a guide to choosing new pipework – the first material mentioned is the best or most usual choice.

Existing pipe	New pipework
copper	copper, stainless steel, polythene
lead	
iron	iron, stainless steel, polythene
stainless steel	stainless steel, copper, polythene
polythene	polythene, copper, stainless steel
UPVC	copper, stainless steel, polythene

CONNECTING OLD TO NEW
Fitting metric to imperial pipework can be complicated by the slight differences in pipe diameters. The problem connections are:

copper to copper (compression fittings)
● some metric fittings can be used directly with imperial-sized pipes (eg, 15mm fittings with 1/2in pipe and 28mm fittings with 1in pipe)
● with other sizes you need to buy special adaptors or larger olives to replace those inside the fittings, so to connect a 15mm branch into existing 3/4in pipe you'll need a tee 22 x 22 x 15mm with special olives for the 22mm ends of the tee.

copper to copper (capillary fittings)
● metric capillary fittings with integral solder rings are not compatible with imperial pipes, but straight adaptors are available to connect the two sizes of pipe
● use these to join in short lengths of metric pipe, the other ends of which are connected to opposite ends of the metric tee
● with end-feed type fittings, extra solder can be added to make a good joint with imperial-sized pipe.

copper to stainless steel – as for copper to copper connections, but usually compression fittings only.

stainless steel to copper – as above for copper to stainless steel.

stainless steel to stainless steel – as for copper to copper.

Connecting into lead pipe

Inserting a tee junction into lead pipe involves joining the run of the tee into two 'wiped' soldered joints. Join short lengths of new copper pipe into opposite ends of a compression tee. Measure the length of this assembly, and cut out 25mm (1in) less of lead pipe. Join the assembly in with wiped soldered joints – a job that takes a lot of practice, and one you may prefer to leave to a professional plumber until you have acquired the skill. You then connect the branch pipe to the third leg of the tee.

Connecting into iron

Existing iron pipework will be at least 25 years old, and likely to be showing signs of corrosion. Extending such a system is not advisable – you would have difficulty connecting into it, and any extension would have to be in stainless steel. The best course is to replace the piping completely with new copper piping.

Connecting into polythene pipe

If you have to fit a branch into a polythene pipe it's not a difficult job, especially if you use the same material. Polythene pipes are joined by compression fittings similar to those used for copper. Polythene hasn't yet been metricated in the UK and each nominal pipe size has a larger outside diameter than its copper equivalent. So you'll have to use either special gunmetal fittings for polythene pipe (still made to imperial sizes) or else an ordinary metric brass fitting a size larger than the pipe – 22mm for 1/2in polythene.

You also need to slip a special metal liner inside the end of the pipe before assembling each joint to prevent the pipe from collapsing as the cap-nuts are tightened. In addition, polythene rings are used instead of metal olives in brass fittings. Apart from these points, however, inserting a tee in a length of polythene pipework follows the same sequence as inserting one into copper.

Connecting into UPVC pipe

As with polythene it's an easy job to cut in a solvent weld tee – a simple collar fitting over the ends of the pipe and the branch. After you've cut the pipe run with a hacksaw you have to roughen the outsides of the cut ends and the insides of the tee sockets with abrasive paper and then clean the surfaces with a spirit cleaner and degreaser. Solvent weld cement is smeared on the pipe ends and the insides of the sockets, and the pipe ends are then 'sprung' into the sockets.

You have to work quickly as the solvent begins the welding action as soon as the pipes meet. Wipe surplus cement off immediately, and hold the joint securely for 15 seconds. After this you can fit your branch pipe to the outlet of the tee.

CUTTING INTO METRIC COPPER PIPE

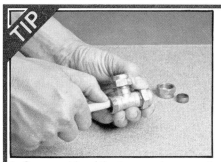

1 On one side of the tee, push a pencil or piece of dowelling along the inside until it butts against the pipe stop. Mark this length with your thumb.

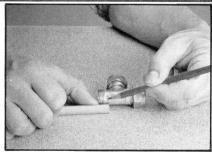

2 Now hold the marked length of dowel against the outside of the fitting so you can see exactly where the pipe stops. Mark this position on the fitting.

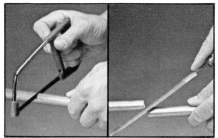

3 Having turned off the water and drained the supply pipe, cut it at the place where you want the branch to join in. Clean one of the ends with steel wool.

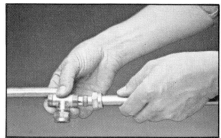

4 Now slip a cap-nut and then an olive over the cleaned pipe end and connect up the unmarked end of the tee fitting to the pipe.

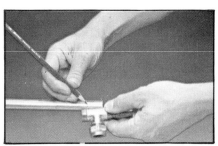

5 Allow the tee to rest alongside the pipe run. The mark on the front of the fitting is your guide to where the pipe has to be cut again.

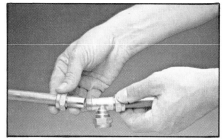

6 Cut the pipe at this mark, thus taking out a small section. Clean the end and slip a cap-nut and olive into place. Spring the pipe end into the tee.

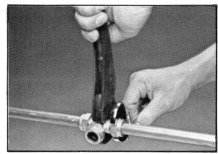

7 Support the fitting with a wrench while tightening the cap-nuts on both ends of the tee with an adjustable spanner or wrench.

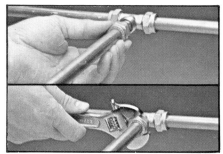

8 Insert the cleaned end of the branch pipe into the tee and tighten the cap-nut 1 1/4 turns with a wrench, holding the fitting to stop it from twisting.

JOINING METRIC TO IMPERIAL PIPE

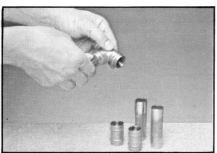

1 Cut two short lengths of metric pipe and prepare the pipe ends, the metric/imperial adaptors and also the tee junction.

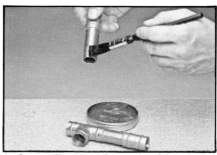

2 Smear flux over the ends of the pipe, inside the rims of the adaptors and each opening on the tee. Then assemble the fitting.

3 With the water turned off and the pipe drained, cut it where you want to make the connection. Prepare one of the ends with steel wool.

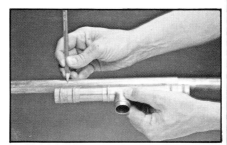

4 Hold the fitting so the pipe stop of one adaptor rests against the cut. Now you can mark the other pipe stop position on the pipe run.

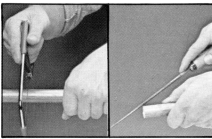

5 Cut out the section of pipe and prepare the newly-cut end. Don't forget to apply the flux, smearing it on the outside of both pipe ends.

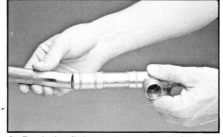

6 Push the fitting onto one end of the supply run, then gently spring the other end into place so that the tee junction is correctly positioned.

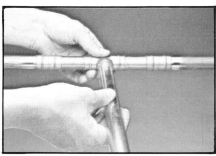

7 Prepare the end of the branch pipe and push it into the tee. Make sure that all the pipe ends are butting up fully against the pipe stops.

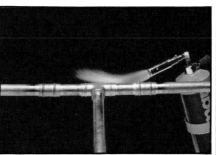

8 Make all the joints at the same time. Rings of solder round the mouths of the fittings indicate that sound, watertight connections have been made.

Ready Reference

CONVENIENT CUTTING

Try to join into existing pipework at a point where you have room to manoeuvre. If space is very tight
● use a junior hacksaw instead of a full-sized one, or
● use a sawing wire for cutting pipes in corners

THE RIGHT TEE

Your branch line may be the same diameter as the main pipe, or smaller (it should never be larger). Tees are described as having all ends equal (eg, 15 x 15 x 15mm), or as having the branch reduced (eg, 22 x 22 x 15mm).

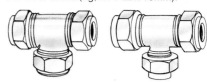

SUPPORTING THE PIPEWORK

All pipework needs supporting at intervals along its length with pipe clips (usually plastic or metal). Fit them at
● 1.2m (4ft) intervals on horizontal pipe runs
● 1.5m (5ft) intervals on vertical pipe runs.

TO SAVE TIME AND TROUBLE

● hold the body of a compression fitting securely with one wrench or spanner while doing up the cap-nut with another
● wrap nearby capillary fittings in damp cloths when soldering in new ones
● make up the entire branch line before cutting in the branch tee
● have cloths handy for mopping up when cutting into existing pipework
● if you're using compression fittings on a vertical pipe run, stop the lower cap-nut and olive from slipping down the pipe by clipping a clothes peg or bulldog clip to it
● keep a replacement cartridge for your blow-torch in your tool kit so you don't run out of gas in the middle of a job.

JOINING INTO PLASTIC PIPES

1 Polythene pipe is joined by a compression fitting with a larger olive than usual (right hand) and pipe liners to support the pipe walls.

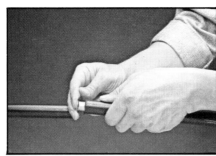

2 Turn off the water supply and then cut the pipe. Use a file to remove any rough edges and then insert a liner into one end of the pipe.

3 Undo the compression fittings and slip a cap-nut over the pipe end containing the liner; then slip on the olive.

4 Mark the pipe stop on the outside of the tee, join the tee to the prepared end, then mark across the pipe stop to show where the pipe is to be cut.

5 Cut out the section of pipe and connect the other end of the tee. Hold the fitting securely while you tighten the cap-nuts 1 1/4 turns.

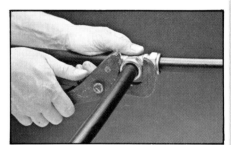

6 Insert the branch pipe into the tee fitting and again use a wrench or adjustable spanner to give the cap-nuts 1 1/4 turns.

7 With UPVC pipe, mark the pipe stops on the outside of the tee. Use these as a gauge to cut out a small section of pipe with a hacksaw.

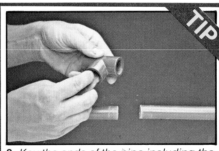

8 Key the ends of the pipe including the branch and the inside of the tee with abrasive paper. This is essential when using solvent-weld cement.

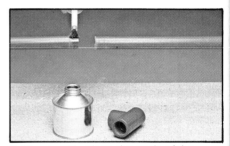

9 Thoroughly clean the ends of the pipes with a degreaser, which you apply with a brush, and leave until completely dry.

10 Once you've done this, spread solvent weld cement on the contact surfaces. Take care not to inhale the fumes as you work.

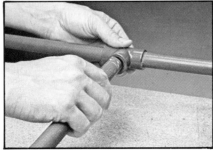

11 Make all the connections at the same time, and check to ensure that all the pipes are pushed right into the tee. Hold for 30 seconds.

12 As soon as you've made all the connections, use a cloth to remove any surplus cement from the pipes. Water shouldn't be turned on for 24 hours.

JOINING PLASTIC PIPING

Most waste pipes installed today are made of plastic, which is cheap, lightweight and easy to work with. A little practice and careful measuring will enable you to replace all parts of your system.

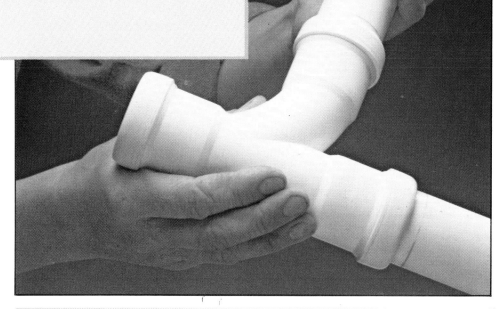

Waste systems draining baths, basins and sinks used to be made of lead, heavy galvanised steel with screwed joints, or copper. Soil pipes from WCs were traditionally cast iron, as was all the outside pipework for both waste and soil disposal. Nowadays waste and soil pipes are made of one or other of a variety of plastic materials, which may be used for repairs, extension work or complete replacement of an existing system.

These plastic pipes are lightweight and easily cut, handled and joined. They are made of materials usually known by the initials of their chemical names – UPVC (unplasticised polyvinyl chloride), MPVC (modified polyvinyl chloride), ABS (acrylonitrile butadiene styrene) and PP (polypropylene). CPVC (chlorinated polyvinyl chloride) is usually used for hot and cold water supply pipes. Pipes and fittings are available in white, grey or a copper colour, depending on type and manufacture.

All these materials are satisfactory for domestic waste systems and – with one exception – can all be joined in the same way: either by push-fit (ring-seal) jointing or by solvent welding.

The exception is PP pipe. This was first developed because of its good resistance to very hot water and chemical wastes, and was therefore extensively used in industry. Nowadays, however, it is frequently used in the home for waste or rainwater drainage. The big difference between PP and other plastic pipes used in waste drainage is that it cannot be solvent-welded. All joints must be push-fit. In most situations this is no great disadvantage but it does make it important to be able to distinguish PP from other plastics. It has a slightly greasy feel and, when cut with a fine toothed saw, leaves fine strands of fibrous material round the cut edges.

Sizes

When buying plastic pipe and components it is wise to stick to one brand only. Pipes and fittings from different makers, though of the same size, are not necessarily interchangeable. Most suppliers stock the systems of only one manufacturer, although the same

PREPARING THE PIPE ENDS

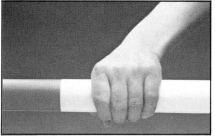

1 *To make sure that you cut the pipe squarely, hold a sheet of paper around it so that the edges meet and overlap each other. This is your cutting line.*

2 *Hold the pipe firmly and cut it with a hacksaw, using gentle strokes. You may find it easier to use a junior hacksaw, which gives a finer cut.*

3 *When you've cut the pipe, use a piece of fine glass paper to clean off the burr left by sawing.*

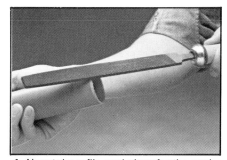

4 *Now take a file and chamfer the end of the pipe all round the edge to a 45° angle. Try to keep the chamfer even.*

Ready Reference

THE TOOLS YOU'LL NEED
● hacksaw – a junior or larger – for cutting the lengths of pipe as you need them
● piece of paper – to help cut the pipe truly square
● tape measure
● file – for chamfering the pipe ends
● fine glasspaper – to abrade pipes and sockets for solvent-welding, and for cleaning up the ends of pipes where you have cut them
● pencil – for marking the cutting points and socket depths to find the working area of the pipe.

VITAL ACCESSORIES
● solvent cement – for solvent-welding
● cleaning fluid – for cleaning the pipe ends and socket fittings when making solvent-weld joints
● petroleum jelly – for lubrication when inserting the pipe into the socket in push-fit joint assemblies
● tissues or rag for cleaning off excess solvent or petroleum jelly.

TYPES OF PIPE
Unplasticised PVC (UPVC) is used for all waste pipe applications.
Modified PVC (MPVC) has rubber or some other plasticiser added to make it more resistant to shock.
Chlorinated PVC (CPVC or MUPVC) is used where very hot water discharge occurs, such as washing machine out-flows.
Polypropylene (PP) is an alternative to PVC and can withstand hot water – but it expands a lot and is only suitable on short runs.
Acrylonitrile butadiene styrene (ABS) is stronger than UPVC and is used for waste connection mouldings.

SAFETY TIPS
● don't smoke when you are solvent-weld jointing – solvent cement and solvent cement cleaner become poisonous when combined with cigarette smoke
● don't inhale the fumes of solvent-weld cement or cleaning fluid – so avoid working in confined spaces
● don't get solvent-weld cement on any part of the pipe you're not joining as this can later lead to cracking and weaknesses, especially inside sockets where the solvent cement can easily trickle down
● hold all solvent-weld joints for 15 seconds after joining and then leave them undisturbed for at least 5 minutes – if hot water is going to flow through the pipe don't use it for 24 hours.

SOLVENT-WELD JOINTING

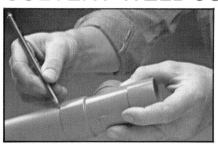

1 *Push the end of the pipe into the socket of the fitting as far as it will go. Mark the pipe at this point with a pencil as a guide to the length within the joint.*

2 *Take the pipe out of the fitting and, with a file, roughen the whole of the end surface that will be inside the fitting up to the pencil mark.*

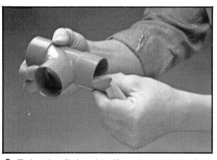

3 *Take the fitting itself and roughen the inside of the socket with fine glass paper. This will provide a key for the solvent cement.*

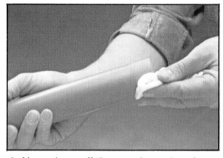

4 *Now clean off the roughened surface of the pipe and socket with spirit as recommended by the manufacturer to remove all dust and debris.*

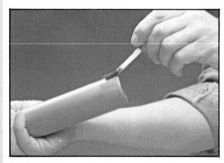

5 *Apply the solvent cement to the roughened end of the pipe, making sure that the whole roughened area is covered. Try and keep it off your fingers.*

6 *Also apply solvent cement to the socket of the fitting. Try to use brush strokes along the line of the pipe.*

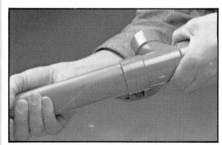

7 *Gently push the pipe fully home into the socket. Some manufacturers suggest a slight twisting action in doing this but check their instructions first.*

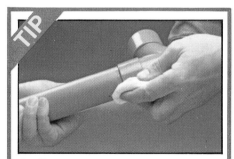

8 *Remove any excess solvent at the edge of the socket with a clean cloth, hold the joint in position for 15 seconds.*

PUSH-FIT JOINTING

1 *Cut the pipe squarely as in solvent-weld jointing and remove the burr, then take the fitting and clean the socket out with the recommended cleaner.*

2 *Check that the rubber seal is properly seated in the socket. You may find seals are supplied separately and you will have to insert them.*

3 *Now chamfer the end of the pipe to an angle of 45°, and smooth off the chamfer carefully with fine glass paper so that no rough edges remain.*

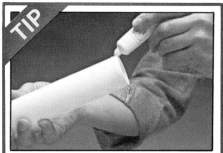

4 *Lubricate the end of the pipe with petroleum jelly over a length of about 5mm (3/16in).*

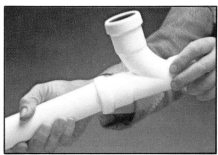

5 *Push the pipe into the socket gently but firmly. Then push it fully home and check that all is square, otherwise you may damage the sealing ring.*

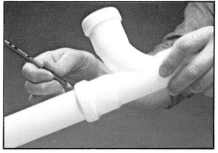

6 *Now make a pencil mark on the pipe at the edge of the socket – you can easily rub it off later if you want to – to act as a guide in setting the expansion gap.*

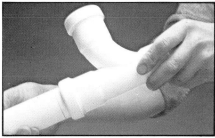

7 *Gently pull the pipe out from the fitting so that your pencil mark is about 10mm (3/8in) away from the fitting to allow for expansion when hot water is flowing.*

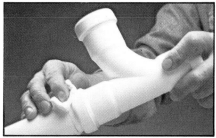

8 *The joint is now complete. Wipe off any excess petroleum jelly. Don't lose the expansion allowance when joining the other side of the fitting.*

manufacturer may make both PP and either PVC or ABS systems.

It is worth asking the supplier if there is an instruction leaflet supplied by the maker. There are slight variations in the methods of using each particular make of pipe and fitting. The manufacturer's instructions, if available, should be followed to the letter.

Buying new pipe
Existing waste pipe is likely to be imperial in size – 1½in internal diameter for a sink or bath and 1¼in internal diameter for a wash basin.

Metric sized plastic pipes are normally described – like thin-walled copper tubes – by their external diameter, though at least one well-known manufacturer adds to the confusion by using the internal diameter. Both internal and external diameters may vary slightly – usually by less than one millimetre between makes. This is yet another reason for sticking to one make of pipe for any single project.

The outside diameter of a plastic tube that is the equivalent of a 1¼in imperial sized metal tube is likely to be 36mm and the inside diameter 32mm. The outside diameter of the equivalent of a 1½in pipe is likely to be 43mm and the inside diameter 39mm. If in doubt, it is usually sufficient to ask the supplier for waste pipe fittings for a basin waste or – as the case may be – a bath or sink waste. Plain-ended plastic pipe is usually supplied in 3m (10ft) lengths, though a supplier will probably cut you off a shorter piece.

Joining solvent-weld types
Solvent-weld fittings are neater and less obtrusive than push-fit ones and they offer the facility of pre-fabrication before installation. However, making them does demand a little more skill and care and – unlike push-fit joints – they cannot accommodate the expansion (thermal movement) that takes place as hot wastes run through the pipe. A 4m length of PVC pipe will expand by about 13mm (just over ½in) when its temperature is raised above 20°C (70°F). For this reason, where a straight length of waste pipe exceeds 1.8m (6ft) in length, expansion couplings must be introduced at 1.8m intervals if other joints are to be solvent-welded. This rarely occurs in domestic design, however, and use of push-fit or solvent-weld is a matter of personal preference.

Although the instructions given by the different manufacturers vary slightly, the steps to making solvent-weld joints follow very similar lines. Of course, the first rule is to measure up all your pipe lengths carefully. Remember to allow for the end of the pipe overlapping the joint. When you've worked out pipe lengths cutting can start.

Ready Reference

TYPES OF FITTINGS
A number of fittings are available in both solvent-weld and push-fit systems – here are just a few of them. Check the complete range before you plan a new system – special bends and branches may exist that will make the job much easier.

Solvent-weld 92½° bend

Push-fit 157½° bend

Expansion coupling solvent-weld/push-fit

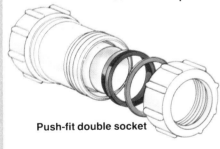

Push-fit double socket

Solvent-weld adaptor

JOINING SOIL PIPES

These are joined in the same way as plastic waste pipes but are much bigger – about 100mm (4in) in diameter – so they take longer to fit. They also have some different fittings, such as a soil branch for use where the outlet pipe joins the stack, and access fittings with bolted removable plates for inspection. There are also special

connectors to link to the WC pan, via a special gasket, and to link to the underground drainage system which is traditionally made of vitrified clay.

The accurate moulding of the fittings and the ease of assembly means that you can confidently tackle complete replacement of a soil system.

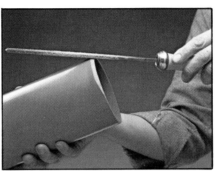

1 *Soil pipes are joined in the same way as their narrower waste counterparts, but as they're bigger take special care with cutting and chamfering.*

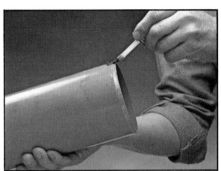

2 *You have got a lot more area to cover with the solvent cement so you must work speedily – but don't neglect accurate application.*

3 *The soil branch pipe has a swept entry into the main stack fitting. This is one of the most important joints in the system, so make sure you get it right.*

4 *When you finally push the pipe into the fitting socket make quite sure that it goes right home against the pipe stop inside the fitting.*

Cut the pipe clean and square with a hacksaw or other fine-toothed saw. A useful tip to ensure a square cut is to fold a piece of newspaper over the pipe and join the edges beneath it. The paper will then act as a template.

Remove all internal and external 'burr' or roughness at the end of the pipe, then use a file to chamfer the outside of the pipe end to about 45°. Not all manufacturers recommend this, but it does provide an extra key for the solvent.

Insert the pipe end into the fitting and mark the depth of insertion with a pencil. Using medium grade abrasive paper, or a light file,

lightly roughen the end of the pipe, as far as the pencil mark, and also roughen the interior of the socket. Thoroughly clean the roughened surfaces of the socket and the pipe end using a clean rag moistened with a spirit cleaner recommended by the manufacturer of the fittings.

Select the correct solvent cement (PVC pipes need a different solvent cement from ABS ones; once again, buy all the materials needed at the same time from the same supplier). Read the label on the tin and stir only if instructed.

Using a clean paintbrush apply the solvent cement to the pipe end and to the inside of the fittings, brushing in the direction of the pipe. It is usually necessary to apply two coats to ABS pipes and fittings. The second coat should be brushed on quickly before the first has dried.

Push the pipe fully home into the fitting (some, but not all, manufacturers suggest that this should be done with a slight twisting action). Remove excess solvent cement and hold the assembled joint securely in position for about 30 seconds. If hot water will be flowing through the pipe, don't use it for 24 hours to give time for the joint to set completely.

Joining ring-seal types

Preparation for ring-seal or push-fit jointing is similar to that for solvent welding. The pipe end must be cut absolutely squarely and all the burr removed. You should draw a line round the cut end of the pipe 10mm from its end and chamfer back to this line with a rasp or shaping tool, then clean the recess within the push-fit connector's socket and check that the sealing ring is evenly seated. One manufacturer supplies sealing rings separately, and they should be inserted at this point. The pipe end should now be lubricated with a small amount of petroleum jelly and pushed firmly into the socket past the joint ring. Push it fully home and mark the insertion depth on the pipe with a pencil. Then withdraw it by 10mm (which is the allowance made for expansion). The expansion joint that is inserted into long straight lengths of solvent-welded waste pipe consists of a coupling with a solvent-weld joint at one end and a push-fit joint at the other.

As with solvent-weld jointing, individual manufacturers may give varying instructions. Some, for instance, advise the use of their own silicone lubricating jelly. Where the manufacturer supplies instructions it is best to follow these exactly.

Fittings

PVC pipe can be bent by the application of gentle heat from a blow-torch, but this technique needs practice and it is best to rely on purpose-made fittings. Sockets are used for joining straight lengths of pipe, tees for right-angled branches, and both 90° and 45° elbows are usually available. If you need to reduce the diameters from one pipe to another you can use reducing sockets. These are really sockets within sockets which can be welded together, one taking the smaller diameter pipe and the other the larger. Soil outlet pipes from WCs are joined in the same way; they are merely bigger – usually 100mm (4in) – in diameter. Sockets work in the same way, but the branch-junction with the main soil stack must be of a specially 'swept' design.

HOW PLASTIC FITTINGS WORK

Solvent-weld joints

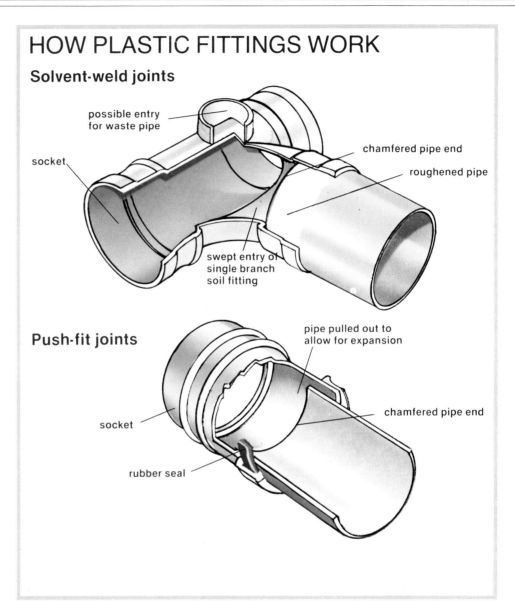

possible entry for waste pipe

socket

chamfered pipe end

roughened pipe

swept entry of single branch soil fitting

Push-fit joints

pipe pulled out to allow for expansion

chamfered pipe end

socket

rubber seal

SPECIAL FITTINGS

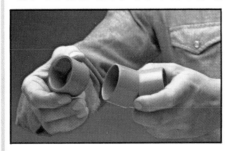

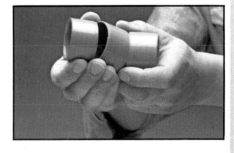

Special fittings are available when pipe fitting is not straightforward. This is a reducing adaptor for push-fit fittings where you need to join a

32mm pipe to a 40mm pipe. You join the relevant pipe to the mating part of the adaptor and then join the two adaptor parts together.

USING PLASTIC PIPE AND FITTINGS

Plastic pipe and fittings can now be used for hot water supplies and central heating. They are easy to work with and allow the DIY plumber to tackle a wide range of jobs.

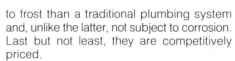

Over the last twenty years plastic has become the most popular plumbing material for above and below ground drainage, for rainwater collection and disposal, and for subsoil drainage. In the form of black polythene tubing it has also become a material widely used for water transportation on camping sites and farms. In the home, however, it has not proved popular. Although this lack of interest can partly be attributed to the conservatism of plumbers and householders, the main reason has been that up until now the plastic pipes that have been available have been suitable for cold water supplies only. This has meant that plumbers, who have had no choice but to use copper or some other metal for the hot water or central heating system, have almost always tended to use the same material when dealing with the cold water system. Householders have doubted the ability of plastic pipework to do a good, life-long job, and have also tended to resist its use on grounds of taste: quite simply, in places where pipework is exposed to view the combination of plastic and copper (or stainless steel or iron) is not one that is very pleasing to the eye.

Now, however, all this has changed. Recently the National Water Council (NWC) gave its approval to two proprietary systems of plastic plumbing, one made out of polybutylene and the other of chlorinated polyvinyl chloride (CPVC), both of which can now be used for cold *and* hot water supply as well as for wet central heating systems. These two rival plumbing systems should hold a special appeal for the DIY enthusiast and – now that they have gained the NWC's approval – there is nothing to prevent them gaining widespread acceptance.

The advantages of plastic pipework

The most obvious advantage is the lightness of the pipework, which makes for ease of handling, but the most important benefit is the ease with which plastic can be cut and joined. This means that the level of skill you require to undertake a particular plumbing task is greatly reduced, as is the amount of time you require to carry it out. Both systems are also strong and durable, more resistant

to frost than a traditional plumbing system and, unlike the latter, not subject to corrosion. Last but not least, they are competitively priced.

Plastic pipes are less vulnerable to frost because plastic is a poor conductor of heat compared to metal (which means that, unlike metal, it provides a certain amount of insulation), and because it has greater elasticity. This means that plastic pipes are not only less likely to freeze than metal ones, but also that in the event of their doing so they are much less likely to burst. The greater degree of insulation that plastic provides also brings other benefits: it results in less heat being lost from pipe runs between radiators (or between the hot water cylinder and the hot taps), as well as meaning that less insulation is necessary for pipework that needs to be protected against the cold.

Plastic pipes aren't subject to corrosion for the simple reason that plastic isn't attacked by the water supply. Electrolytic corrosion, which results in the build up of hydrogen gas and black iron oxide sludge (magnetite) and can ultimately lead to leaky radiators and early pump failure, is therefore far less of a problem when a central heating system is fitted with plastic pipes.

This also means that plastic is a safer material to use for your drinking water supply pipes than metal, the use of which can, under some circumstances, present a health risk.

One final point to be borne in mind before you replace metal pipes with plastic ones is that plastic is a non-conductor of electricity. This means that all-plastic plumbing systems cannot be used to earth a domestic electricity supply (see *Ready Reference*).

You can obtain both polybutylene and CPVC tubing in the 15mm (½in), 22mm (¾in) and 28mm (1in) diameters commonly used in domestic hot and cold water supply and in small-bore central heating. However, in other respects – particularly as regards the flexibility of the two different types of tubing and methods of cutting and jointing – the two systems differ. So, before you undertake a plumbing task using plastic pipes and fittings, you'd do well to consider which system best suits your particular application.

Polybutylene tubing

Polybutylene tubing is brown in colour and naturally flexible; in this respect it differs from CPVC tubing, which is rigid. As well as being available in 3m (10ft) lengths in all three diameters, it is also obtainable as a 100m (390ft) coil in the 15mm (½in) size, and as a 50m (195ft) coil in the 22mm (¾in) size. This flexibility, and the long lengths in which the tubing is available, is particularly useful as it cuts down the time you need to spend on installation, and reduces the number of fittings necessary (which means less cost). You can thread polybutylene pipes under floors and between joists with minimal disturbance, their flexibility also allowing you to take them through apertures and round obstacles that would otherwise present serious difficulties. You can bend the tubing cold to easy bends with a minimum radius of eight times the pipe diameter; 15mm (½in) tube can therefore be bent to a minimum radius of 120mm (4¾in) and 22mm (¾in) to a minimum radius of 176mm (7in). You must, however, provide a clip on either side of the bend to secure it. The flexibility of polybutylene tubing means that

POLYBUTYLENE PIPE AND FITTINGS

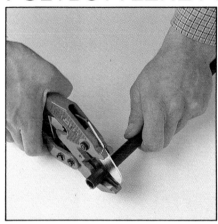

1 *The best way to cut polybutylene pipe is with the manufacturer's shears. These are easy to use and ensure that you get a square-cut pipe end every time.*

2 *Alternatively, you can cut polybutylene pipe with a hacksaw or a sharp knife. If you use this method don't forget to clean off any burr or swarf with a file.*

3 *Before jointing the pipe, insert a stainless steel support sleeve into the pipe end. This prevents the tube end getting crushed within the fitting.*

4 *Polybutylene pipe can be used with ordinary compression fittings. The joint is made in exactly the same way as one made using ordinary copper pipe.*

5 *Within a polybutylene fitting a grab ring holds the pipe in place, while an 'O' ring ensures a watertight seal. The two are separated by a spacer washer.*

6 *The witness lines on the body of the fitting indicate the length of pipe hidden within it when the joint is assembled. Remember to allow for this.*

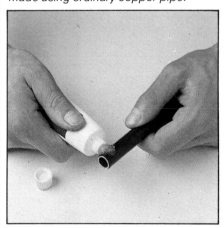

7 *Before inserting polybutylene pipe into a polybutylene fitting, apply a special lubricant to both the pipe end and the interior of the socket.*

8 *Make the joint without unscrewing or even loosening the cap-nuts. Simply thrust the pipe end into the socket until it meets the pipe stop inside.*

9 *The pipe can be withdrawn only if you unscrew the cap-nut. To re-use the joint, crush and discard the grab ring, and then replace it with a new one.*

CPVC PIPE AND FITTINGS

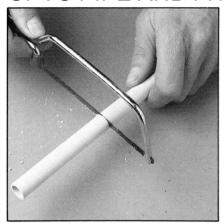

1 You can cut CPVC pipe with either a fine-toothed saw or an ordinary pipe cutter. If using a saw, make sure that you hold it at right-angles to the pipe.

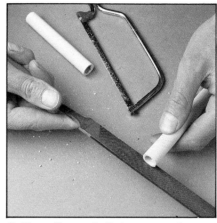

2 Use a file or a knife to remove the swarf from the pipe end. Check that the pipe fits snugly in the socket, and that the fitting is free from imperfections.

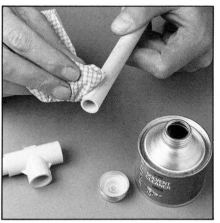

3 Before making a joint with CPVC the surfaces to be solvent-welded must first be cleaned. Use the manufacturer's special solvent cleaner for this purpose.

4 Immediately afterwards, apply the solvent weld cement, brushing this liberally on the tube end and only sparingly in the interior of the fitting socket.

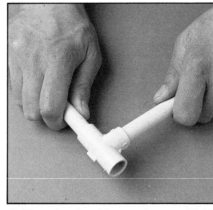

5 The solvent-weld cement goes off fairly rapidly, so you must make the joint as soon as you've applied it. Push the pipe home with a slight twisting motion.

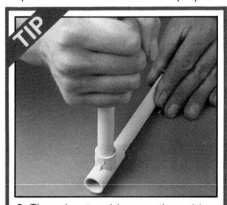

6 The solvent-weld cement's rapid setting time also means you must make adjustment for alignment immediately. Do not remove surplus cement.

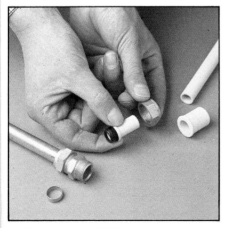

7 You can join CPVC pipe to copper using a compression fitting and a two-part adaptor. Discard the olive as the first part of the adaptor is self-sealing.

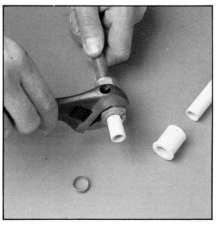

8 Tighten up the compression fitting in the usual way. Use a second spanner to hold the body of the fitting before giving the coupling nut a final turn.

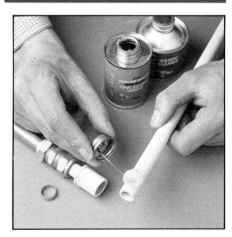

9 Having solvent-welded the two parts of the adaptor together, complete the fitting by solvent-welding the CPVC pipe to the second part of the adaptor.

you will have to give continuous support to any visible horizontal pipe runs in order to eliminate the possibility of unsightly sagging (see *Ready Reference*).

You can cut polybutylene tube with a sharp knife or a hacksaw. However, for speed of operation and to ensure an absolutely square cut pipe end every time, the manufacturers recommend that you use their specially designed pipe shears. It would certainly be worthwhile investing in a pair of these shears before embarking on a major project that involved the marking of a large number of joints.

You can join polybutylene tubing by using either non-manipulative (Type 'A') compression joints (as used with copper), or else the manufacturer's own patent push-fit connectors. One of the advantages of being able to use Type 'A' compression joints with tubing is that it enables you to replace a length of copper pipe with polybutylene tubing using the existing compression tee or coupling.

When using polybutylene tubing with this type of joint the procedure you follow is identical to that which you adopt with copper pipe (see the techniques on pages 180-184). But in order to prevent the collapse of the tube end when the cap-nut is tightened, you must insert a purpose-made stainless steel support sleeve into the tube end. And if you use jointing compound to complete a threaded fitting connected to polybutylene pipe, make sure none comes into contact with the polybutylene.

The patent polybutylene joints and fittings are available in the usual range of straight couplings, tees, elbows, reducing fittings and tap and tank connectors, and in appearance they resemble their brass compression counterparts. But there is one important difference – you don't have to loosen or unscrew the cap-nuts to make a joint. To make a connection you simply have to push the prepared pipe end into the fitting (see step-by-step photographs). Polybutylene fittings have one further advantage in that they allow you to rotate a pipe that has been inserted into one of them, even when it is filled with water. This means, for example, that a polybutylene stop-valve can rest neatly against a wall until you need to use it. You then pull the handle away from the wall so you can open and close it easily.

CPVC tubing
CPVC tubing differs from the polybutylene type in two basic ways. First, it is rigid rather than flexible, which means that it is only available in relatively short lengths of 2m (6ft 6in) or 3m (9ft 9in). Secondly, it is joined by a process known as solvent welding, a slightly more involved procedure than making a push-fit or compression connection (see

step-by-step photographs). Superficially, CPVC tubing can be distinguished from polybutylene by its off-white colour. An hour after the last joint has been made you can flush through the system and fill it with cold water; before filling with hot water you need to wait at least four hours.

CPVC pipe does expand when hot water passes through it, but this won't cause a problem in most domestic systems unless one of the pipe runs exceeds 10m (33ft), which is unlikely. In this case you will have to create an expansion loop using four 90° elbows and three 150mm (6in) lengths of pipe.

The manufacturers of CPVC tubing provide an exceptionally wide range of fittings to meet every eventuality. There are 90° and 45° elbows, equal and unequal tees, reducing pieces, tap and ball-valve connectors, stop-valves and gate-valves, and provision for connection to existing copper or screwed iron fittings. The connectors for copper tubing have a solvent-weld socket at one end and a conventional Type 'A' compression joint at the other. Those for iron fittings have a solvent-weld fitting at one end and either a male or female threaded joint at the other. If you are connecting a fitting to an existing iron socket, make sure that you render the screwed connection watertight by binding plastic PTFE tape round the male thread before screwing home.

What system to use
Neither system is 'better' than the other, and each has its merits and its drawbacks. The polybutylene tubing is flexible and available in extremely long lengths which reduce the number of joints you will have to use, as well as enabling you to get through or round obstacles that might prove difficult were you using the CPVC system. On the other hand the push-fit polybutylene joints are bulkier and more obtrusive than those used with the CPVC system.

Bearing in mind this, and the fact that the rigid CPVC pipes will be less prone to sagging than the flexible polybutylene tubing, the CPVC system is probably the more acceptable one in situations where plumbing is exposed to view. The more complex construction of the polybutylene joints – the cause of their bulkiness – also makes them relatively expensive: which means that the smaller number necessary for carrying out a given plumbing task won't always cost you less than the greater number necessary with CPVC. However, polybutylene joints, unlike CPVC ones, can be used more than once.

Lastly, in case your decision to opt for one system or the other is influenced by the colour of the material out of which it is made (dark brown for polybutylene and off-white for CPVC), you can paint both systems with ordinary household paints.

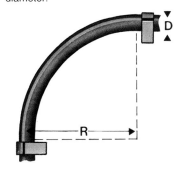

PLUMBING IN KITCHEN APPLIANCES

Washing machines and dishwashers can be a great boon in the house. They are best plumbed into a water supply and the waste outlet, otherwise you'll find they don't save as much on time and effort.

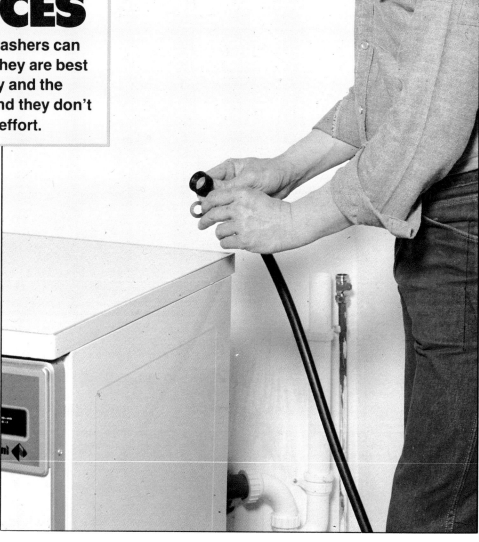

These days you'll probably opt for an automatic washing machine that fills and empties itself according to a pre-set programme, and so can be left unattended. There is a choice between top loaders and front loaders, although the latter are by far the more common. Obviously top loaders can't fit under a work surface, but drum-type top loaders tend to be narrower and this may suit your particular space requirements.

Dishwashers are almost always automatic, except for some small, cheaper sink-top models. They, too, are available as top or front loaders, though again front loaders are by far the more popular. They are also easier to load and unload, as with top loaders it's easy for crockery and cutlery to slip to the bottom of the machines.

Washing machines have become almost a necessity in busy family homes, especially where there are young children. Dishwashers are far less common, but sales are developing rapidly as more and more people wake up to their advantages. It's a simple matter to stack a dishwasher with dirty crockery direct from the meal table and then turn it on before going to bed at night. Again, for a family the labour saving is considerable.

Some washing machines don't have to be plumbed in. The inlets can be attached to the kitchen taps when the sink isn't being used, and the outlet can be hooked over the edge of the sink. The same goes for dishwashers, which usually require only a cold water feed. But to keep things really neat and tidy as well as more practical, it is best to create permanent connections for both the water supply and the waste outlet. In most kitchens this should be a fairly easy task, provided you have room for the machines in the first place.

As far as the capacities of washing machines and dishwashers go, you don't really have much choice. Washing machines have a capacity of about 4-5kg (9-11lb) and dishwashers will function quite happily provided you stack them up within the obvious tray limitations. It's important to follow the manufacturers' instructions for day-to-day maintenance. Many washing machines need their outlet filter cleaned regularly, as do dishwashers. They may also need regular doses of salts, not to mention rinse aids.

Water supply

There are a number of ways in which you can arrange the water supply. One of them is sure to suit your plumbing system or the layout of your kitchen or utility room. A washing machine may need a hot and cold supply; dishwashers and some cheaper washing machines need only a cold supply.

Let's first consider the conventional means of plumbing in – the means that a professional plumber would almost certainly adopt if you called him in to do the job for you. It is likely to be most satisfactory where the machine is to be positioned in the immediate vicinity of the kitchen sink and the 15mm (½in) hot and cold supply pipes to the sink taps are readily accessible and in close proximity to each other.

The technique is to cut into these two pipes at a convenient level, after cutting off the water supply and draining the pipes, and to insert into them 15mm compression tees. From the outlets of the tees lengths of 15mm (½in) copper tube are run to terminate, against the wall, in a position immediately adjacent to the machine. Onto the ends of these lengths of pipe are fitted purpose-made stop-cocks. These are usually provided with back-plates that can be screwed to the wall after it has been drilled and plugged. The outlets of the stop-cocks are designed for connection to the machine's inlet hose or hoses.

As an alternative, which is best used where the hot and cold water pipes in the kitchen are in close proximity to the position of the machine, you can use a special patent valve. This is a 'tee' with a valve outlet designed for direct connection to the washing machine hose. There are compression joints at each end of the tee and the valve is particularly

PLUMBING IN A WASHING MACHINE

Plumbing in a washing machine shouldn't present too many problems. Normally it's sited next to an existing sink, so you'll know that the water supply pipes and drainage facilities are close at hand.

Most machines are run off separate 15mm (½in) hot and cold supplies (1 & 2) taken from tees (3) inserted in the pipe runs to the sink. You should also insert some form of stop-valve (4) into the pipes so the machine can be isolated for repairs. You'll have to use female/male connections (5) to join the copper pipes to the machine's rubber inlet hoses (6).

When the water has been used, it's fed into a rubber drain hose (7) which should be loosely inserted into the top of the stand-pipe (8). This in turn connects to a 75mm (3in) trap and from here the waste water is taken in 38mm (1½in) pipe to discharge in the gully outside below the grille.

Dealing with single-stack drainage

From the trap at the bottom of the stand-pipe (11) the waste water is conducted to the main drainage stack (12) where the pipe is connected via a fitting known as a strap boss(13).

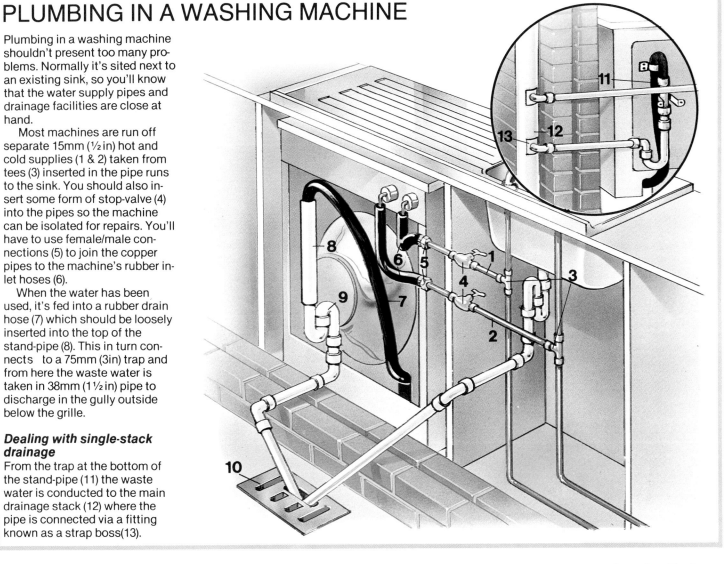

easily fitted because there is no tube-stop in one of these joints. This cuts out the difficult business of 'springing' the cut ends of the pipe into the tee.

Then there are valves which can be connected without cutting a section out of the water supply pipes. With one such valve the pipe is drained and is then drilled with a 8mm (⁵⁄₁₆in) bit. A back-plate is then fitted to the wall behind it and a front-plate, with a short projecting pipe and a rubber seal that fits into the hole in the pipe, is clamped to it. The washing machine valve then screws into this front-plate.

Yet another valve is self-tapping and screws its own hole in the water pipe. This, so the makers claim, can be done without cutting off the water supply and draining the pipe.

A valve which depends upon drilling the water supply pipe will not permit the same flow of water as one in which the pipe is cut and a tee inserted. It must be said, though,

that this seems to make very little difference in practice, but obviously in the former case the tightening of the connection must be more than sufficient for it to work properly.

Putting in drainage

The simplest method is undoubtedly to hook the machine's outlet hose over the rim of the kitchen or utility room sink when required. However, this method isn't always convenient and is certainly untidy. An alternative is to provide an open-ended stand-pipe fixed to the kitchen wall into which the outlet hose of the machine can be permanently hooked. The open end of the stand-pipe should be at least 600mm (24in) above floor level and should have an internal diameter of at least 35mm (1⅜in). A deep seal (75mm or 3in) trap should be provided at its base and a branch waste pipe taken from its outlet to an exterior gully, if on the ground floor, or to the main soil and waste stack of a single stack

system if on an upper floor. As with all connections to a single soil and waste stack this should be done only under the supervision of the district or borough council's Building Control Officer. Manufacturers of plastic drainage systems include suitable drainage stand-pipes and accessories in their range of equipment (the trap and pipe being sold as one unit).

It is sometimes possible to deal with washing machine or dishwasher drainage by taking the waste pipe to connect directly to the trap of the kitchen sink and this course of action may be suggested at DIY centres and by builders' merchants staff. But it must be stressed that this is not recommended by the manufacturers of washing machines, who consider that it involves a considerable risk of back-siphonage. This could lead to waste water from the sink siphoning back into the machine. In the case of a washing machine this could mean considerable problems.

PLUMBING IN A DISHWASHER

1 Start by working out how to run the waste outlet. This will often mean making a hole in the wall using a club hammer and cold chisel.

2 Measure up the run on the inside, then cut a suitable length of 38mm (1½in) PVC plastic waste pipe and push it through the hole you have made.

3 Make up the outside pipe run dry, to ensure it all fits, then solvent weld it. It's useful to put in an inspection elbow in case of blockages.

6 Carry on assembling the run on the inside using standard waste pipe fittings. Try to keep the run close to the wall for a neat appearance.

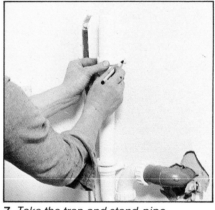

7 Take the trap and stand-pipe, which you can buy as a standard fitting or make up yourself, and mark the bracket positions on the wall.

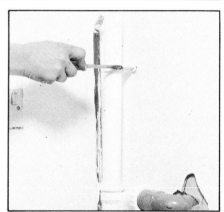

8 Drill and plug the wall, and fix the stand-pipe in position. Make sure that it is fully supported and vertical and the trap is screwed tight.

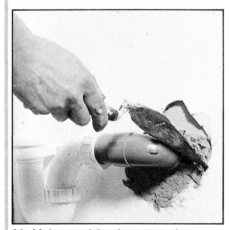

11 Make good the damage to the wall both on the inside and out; the plastic pipe will be held firmly in place by the mortar and plaster.

12 You can now move the machine into position and connect it up. The inlet hose has a female screwed connector, which must have a washer in it.

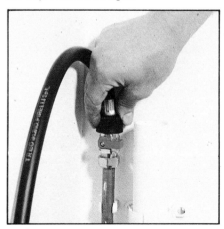

13 With the washer in place, screw up the connector to the tap on the inlet pipe; it's enough to hand-tighten this connection.

4 If the run terminates in a gully drain, then make sure that you fit the pipe so that the end is situated below the level of the water.

5 When you have completed the outside waste run, replace the grid. Cut away as much of it as necessary to fit round the pipe, using a hacksaw.

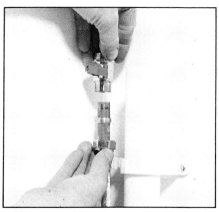

9 Run the cold water supply using 15mm (¹/₂in) pipe via a tee cut into the domestic cold supply, and attach a running tap to the end.

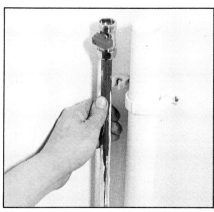

10 Secure the supply pipe to the wall using pipe brackets, then go back and make sure that all your connections are sound.

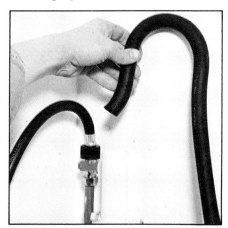

14 Take the outlet hose from the machine and place it in the top of the stand-pipe. You should not attempt to make the connection airtight.

15 Move the machine exactly into position and check that it is level; if not, adjust the feet. Then turn on the water and test the machine.

Ready Reference

INSTALLATION CHECKLIST

When installing a washing machine or dishwasher, remember that:
● it's usual to take the water supply from the domestic cold water system; if you want to use the mains you may need a pressure reducer, so check with the manufacturer's literature
● if the machine takes a hot and cold supply you will have to ensure that there is sufficient pressure in the hot supply and that this is the same as that from the cold
● to operate at maximum efficiency, the machine should stand on a level surface and this should be firm; washing machines in particular are extremely heavy when full of water.

BATHROOM REGULATIONS

If you want to put your washing machine in the bathroom then there are electrical rules that must be obeyed:
● it must be permanently wired in
● you must not be able to touch the controls when you're in the bath or shower.

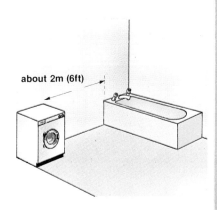

about 2m (6ft)

TIP: CHECK DIMENSIONS

If the machine is going to be put between existing units or under a work surface you'll have to measure up carefully before you buy. Make sure there is enough space behind for the plumbing work.

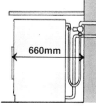

660mm

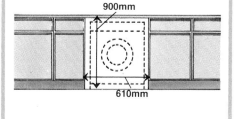

900mm

610mm

INSTALLING A SHOWER

Showers have become a part of the modern home, whether fitted over the bath or in a separate cubicle. They save time, space and energy and are quite easy to install once the design is right.

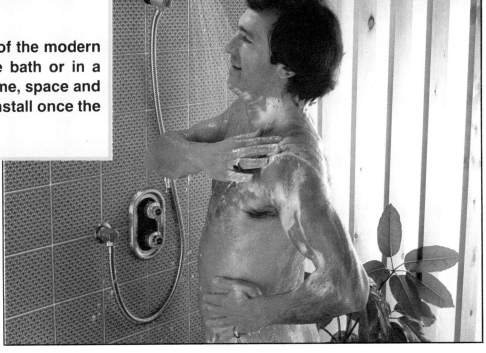

shower from Mira

It is possible for four or five members of a family to have showers at the same time – and with the same amount of hot water – that would be needed for just one of them to have a bath. Showers, if properly installed, are safer for use by the elderly and the very young than a sit-down bath and need less cleaning. They are also more hygienic to use than a bath, as the bather isn't sitting in his own soapy and dirty water, and can rinse thoroughly in fresh water.

Where a shower is provided in its own cubicle, as distinct from over a bath, it takes up very little extra space. One can be provided in any space which is at least 900mm (36in) square, and can be put in a variety of locations such as a bedroom, on a landing, in a lobby or even in the cupboard under the stairs.

Yet shower installation can all too often prove to be a disappointment. Poorly designed systems may provide only a trickle of water at the sprinkler, or may run icy cold until the cold tap is almost turned off, and will then run scalding hot.

So, although it is possible to provide a shower in virtually any household, it is important that you match the shower equipment and your existing hot and cold water systems. If you have a cylinder storage hot water system, which is by far the commonest kind of hot water supply to be found in British homes, a conventional shower connected to the household's hot and cold water supplies is likely to be the most satisfactory and the easiest to install. But the hot and cold water systems must comply with certain quite definite design requirements if the shower is to operate safely and satisfactorily.

Pressure

The most important requirement is that the hot and cold supply pipes to the shower must be under equal water pressure. With a cylinder storage hot water system, whether direct or indirect, hot water pressure comes from the main cold water storage cistern supplying the cylinder with water. The cold water supply to the shower must therefore also come from this cistern (or perhaps

from a separate cistern at the same level); it must not be taken direct from the cold water main. It is, in fact, illegal to mix, in any plumbing appliance, water which comes direct from the main and water coming from a storage cistern.

However, quite apart from the important question of legality, it is impossible to mix streams of water satisfactorily under such differing pressures. The shower will inevitably run either very hot or very cold, depending on which stream is the high-pressure one.

The cold water storage cistern must also be high enough above the shower sprinkler to provide a satisfactory operating pressure. Best results will be obtained if the base of the cold water storage cistern is 1.5m (5ft) or more above the sprinkler. However, provided that pipe runs are short and have only slight changes of direction, a reasonable shower can be obtained when the vertical distance between the base of the cistern and the shower sprinkler is as little as 1m (39in). The level of the hot water storage tank in relation to the shower doesn't matter in the least. It can be above, below or at the same level as the shower. It is the level of the cold water storage cistern that matters.

There is yet another design requirement for conventional shower installation which sometimes applies. This is that the cold water supply to the shower should be a separate 15mm branch direct from the cold water storage cistern, not as a branch from the main bathroom distribution pipe. This is a safety precaution. If the cold supply were

taken as a branch from a main distribution pipe, then flushing a lavatory cistern would reduce the pressure on the cold side of the shower causing it to run dangerously hot. For the same reason it is best for the hot supply to be taken direct from the vent pipe immediately above the hot water storage cylinder and not as a branch from another distribution pipe, though this is rather less important. A reduction in the hot water pressure would result in the shower running cold. This would be highly unpleasant, although not dangerous.

Mixers

Showers must have some kind of mixing valve to mix the streams of hot and cold water and thus to produce a shower at the required temperature. The two handles of the bath taps provide the very simplest mixing valve, and push-on shower attachments can be cheaply obtained. Opening the bath taps then mixes the two streams of water and diverts them upwards to a wall-hung shower rose. These very simple attachments work quite satisfactorily – provided that the design requirements already referred to are met. However, it isn't always easy to adjust the tap handles to provide water at exactly the temperature required.

A bath/shower mixer provides a slightly more sophisticated alternative operating on the same principle. With one of these, the tap handles are adjusted until water is flowing through the mixer spout into the bath at the required temperature. The water is then

206

CHOOSING THE RIGHT SHOWER TYPE

The type of shower you can install depends on the sort of water supply you have in your home. This chart will help you make the right selection.

Hot and cold water stored → **Is there 1m (3ft) between cistern base and shower rose?**

Cold taps from mains hot water stored → **Can new cold water cistern be installed?**

No water storage → **Consider instantaneous water heater shower**

- Is there 1m (3ft) between cistern base and shower rose? ← YES — Can new cold water cistern be installed? — NO → Consider instantaneous water heater shower
- Is there 1m (3ft)... → NO → **Can cistern be raised or a pump be fitted?**
- Can cistern be raised or a pump be fitted? — NO → Consider instantaneous water heater shower
- Is there 1m... → YES → **Consider mixer-type shower**
- Can cistern be raised or a pump be fitted? → YES → Consider mixer-type shower

Consider instantaneous water heater shower → **How is domestic hot water heated?**

How is domestic hot water heated? → **Instantaneous gas water heater** / **Non-storage electric water heater**

Consider mixer-type shower → **Will children or the old use the shower?**

Will children or the old use the shower? → YES → **Use thermostatic mixer-type shower**
Will children or the old use the shower? → NO → **Use manual or thermostatic mixer-type shower**

Instantaneous gas water heater → **Mixer-type shower can be used with some gas water heaters**

Non-storage electric water heater → **Is there a gas supply in the house?**
Is there a gas supply in the house? → YES → Mixer-type shower can be used with some gas water heaters
Is there a gas supply in the house? → NO → **Install instantaneous electric shower**

Mixer-type shower can be used with some gas water heaters → **If heater suitable, use mixer-type shower**

Non-storage electric water heater → Install instantaneous electric shower

Ready Reference

WHY HAVE A SHOWER?
Showers have many advantages over baths:
- they are hygienic as you don't sit in dirty, soapy water and you get continually rinsed
- they are pleasant to use. Standing under jets of water can be immensely stimulating, especially first thing in the morning
- they use a lot less water per 'wash' than a bath, which saves energy and is also an advantage where water softeners are in use
- economy of hot water usage means that at peak traffic times there is more water to go round
- showers take less time, they don't have to be 'run', and users can't lay back and bask, monopolizing the bathroom
- easy temperature adjustment of a shower gives greater comfort for the user and lessens the risk of catching cold in a cold bathroom.

SHOWER LOCATION

You don't have to install a shower over a bath or even in the bathroom. A bedroom is one alternative site, but landings and utility rooms are another possibility. Provided a supply of water is available, the pressure head satisfactory, and the disposal of waste water possible, a shower can provide a compact and very useful house improvement in many parts of the home.

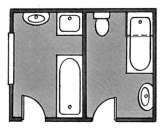

In a bathroom a shower will usually go over a bath, which is the easiest and most popular position. In a larger bathroom a cubicle is a good idea.

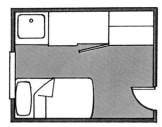

In a bedroom a shower can be easily fitted at the end of built-in wardrobes.

---

diverted up to the head by turning a valve.

Then there are manual shower mixers. These are standard equipment in independent shower cubicles and may also be used over a bath. With a manual mixer the hot and cold streams of water are mixed in a single valve. Temperature, and sometimes flow control, is obtained by turning large knurled control knobs.

Finally, there are thermostatic shower mixing valves. These may resemble manual mixers in appearance but are designed to accommodate small pressure fluctuations in either the hot or cold water supplies to the shower. They are thus very useful safety devices. But thermostatic valves cannot, even if it were legal, compensate for the very great difference of pressure between mains supply and a supply from a cold water storage cistern. Nor can they add pressure to either the hot or cold supply. If pressure falls on one side of the valve the thermostatic device will reduce flow on the other side to match it.

Thermostatic valves are more expensive but they eliminate the need to take an independent cold water supply pipe from the storage cistern to the shower and can possibly reduce the total cost of installation.

Where a shower is provided over an existing bath, steps must be taken to protect the bathroom floor from splashed water. A plastic shower curtain provides the cheapest means of doing this but a folding, glass shower screen has a much more attractive appearance and is more effective.

Electric showers
You can run your shower independently of the existing domestic hot water system by fitting an instantaneously heated electric one. There are a number of these on the market nowadays. They need only to be connected to the rising main and to a suitable source of electricity to provide an 'instant shower'. You are recommended to have these installed professionally.

Installing a bath/shower mixer
To install a shower above a bath, first disconnect the water supply, and drain the cistern (see the techniques on pages 107-108). Remove the bath panel, if there is one, and disconnect the tap tails from the supply pipes. Then unscrew and remove the tap back-nuts and take the taps off.

You can now fix the new mixer in place (see the techniques on pages 177-179). Finally decide on the position for the shower spray bracket and fix it in place.

HOW TO ADAPT YOUR SYSTEM

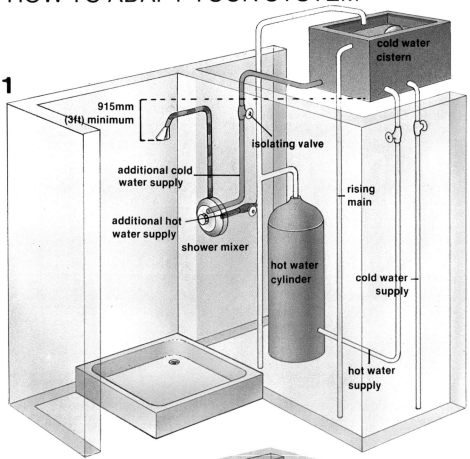

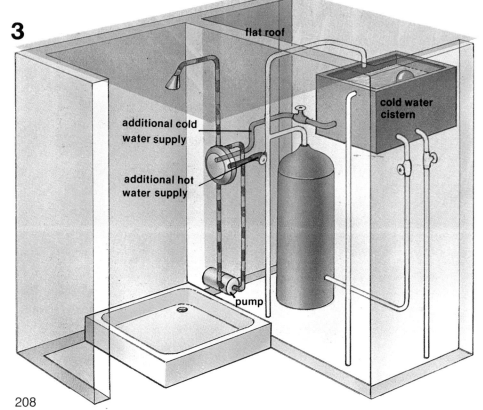

1 : Just add pipework

◁ The most common domestic plumbing system has a cold water cistern in the loft which feeds a hot water tank. In this case you must check that the vertical distance from the bottom of the cold cistern to the shower outlet head is at least 915mm (3ft). To install a shower you must take a 15mm cold water supply direct from the cistern to the cold inlet of the mixer, and a 15mm hot water supply from the vent and draw-off pipe, which emerges from the hot water tank, to the hot water inlet of the mixer.

2 : Raise the cistern

▷ In many older houses the cold water cistern may be in the airing cupboard immediately above the hot water tank, or in another position but still beneath ceiling height. This will usually mean that there is insufficient pressure for a mixer-type shower on the same floor. To get round this problem the cistern can be raised into the loft by extending the pipework upwards. Moving an old galvanised cistern will be rather arduous so this is a good opportunity to replace it with a modern plastic one, (see a future issue).

3 : Install a pump

◁ In some homes which have flat roofs it is impossible to raise the cistern indoors to provide a sufficient pressure head for a shower on the same floor. While you could consider putting the cistern on top of the roof this would involve providing extensive insulation and is an unsatisfactory solution. Pump-assisted mixer showers are available which will artificially increase the pressure head when the shower is turned on and these are fairly simple to install. As they are electrically operated they should be situated outside the bathroom area.

4 : Add a new cistern

▷ Many modern houses have combination hot and cold water storage units which are supplied and installed as one unit. They have a disadvantage in that cold water capacity is about one-third of the hot water cylinder and would provide an insufficient supply for a shower. This problem can be overcome by installing a pump and a supplementary cold water storage cistern. To ensure similar hot and cold pressures at the shower the supplementary cistern must be at a comparable level with the combination unit's cold water storage .

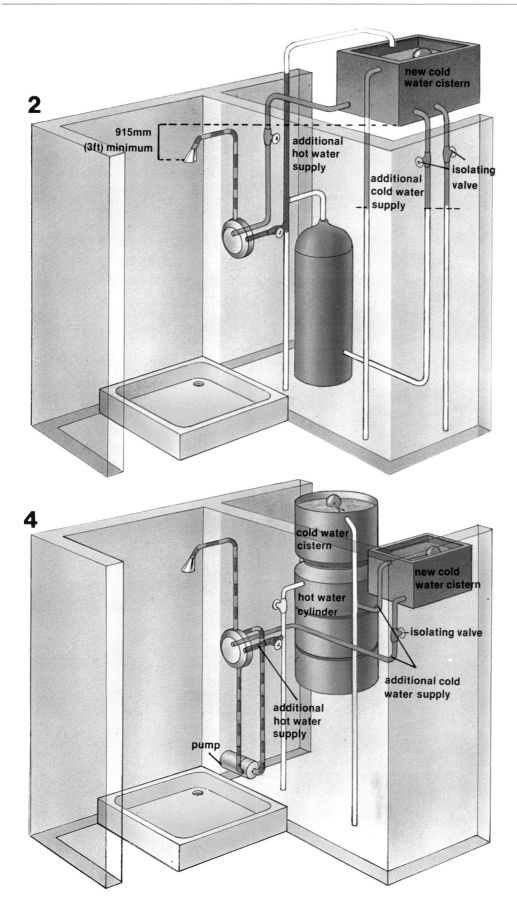

2

915mm
(3ft) minimum

new cold
water cistern

additional
hot water
supply

additional
cold water
supply

isolating
valve

4

cold water
cistern

new cold
water cistern

hot water
cylinder

isolating valve

additional cold
water supply

additional
hot water
supply

pump

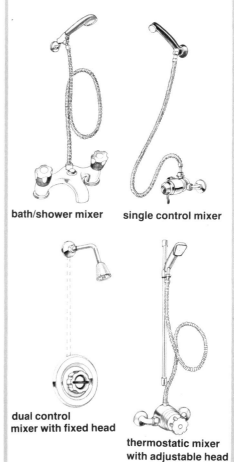

Ready Reference

TYPES OF SHOWER

There are two basic types of shower:
● those attached to a mixer on a bath
● those independent of the bath, discharging over their own bases, in their own cubicles.

Bath showers may be attached to a mixer head on which you have to adjust both taps, or they may simply fit over the tap outlets. The shower head in either case is detachable and may be mounted at whatever height you require.

Independent showers have fixed position heads or are adjustable. They may have a single control mixer, or a dual control which means that you can adjust the flow as well as the temperature. Thermostatic mixing valves are also available which can cope with small pressure fluctuations in the hot and cold water supply. These only reduce pressure on one side of the valve if that on the other side falls; they cannot increase the pressure unless they have already decreased it.

bath/shower mixer   single control mixer

dual control
mixer with fixed head

thermostatic mixer
with adjustable head

CONNECTING SHOWER FITTINGS

Before you get to grips with installing a new shower cubicle, you ought to select the type of control fitting you're going to use. Your choice may affect the way you organise the plumbing.

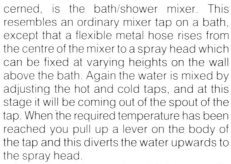

Once you've decided where you're going to site your shower – over a bath or in a separate cubicle – you'll have to determine what type of fitting you're going to use to run it. In order for the shower to work effectively, you need to be able to control the rate of flow of water and also, more importantly, it's temperature. There's nothing worse than standing under a stuttering supply of water that's hot one minute and cold the next. So it's the job of the shower fitting to provide this control fast and effectively.

Some fittings work by having individual taps to control the hot and cold water supplies, while the more sophisticated types have a simple valve or a mixer. How they are connected up to the water supply depends primarily on their design. For example, instantaneous showers (not recommended for DIY fitting) need only to be connected to the mains cold water supply, as they heat all the hot water required just before it comes out of the shower rose. A hot water supply is therefore unnecessary. But for all other showers, the temperature of the water is controlled by mixing together separate supplies of hot and cold water which may also be at different pressures.

The simplest fittings

Before proper showers over a bath and separate shower cubicles became popular, it was quite common to find a rather makeshift device being used to supply a spray of water. This consisted of a length of rubber hose with a rose attached at one end and two connectors fitted at the other which slipped over the hot and cold taps on the bath. By adjusting these taps you could regulate the flow and temperature of the water. In fact the principle of this very basic mixing valve was used in early shower cubicles. Gate valves on the hot and cold distribution pipes were used to control the flow, and the two supplies were mixed at a 'tee' in the pipework before being fed in a single pipe to an overhead shower rose.

Mixer taps

An improvement on this very simple arrangement, as far as showers over baths are concerned, is the bath/shower mixer. This resembles an ordinary mixer tap on a bath, except that a flexible metal hose rises from the centre of the mixer to a spray head which can be fixed at varying heights on the wall above the bath. Again the water is mixed by adjusting the hot and cold taps, and at this stage it will be coming out of the spout of the tap. When the required temperature has been reached you pull up a lever on the body of the tap and this diverts the water upwards to the spray head.

Nowadays, showers in cubicles normally have what's known as a manual mixing valve. This has two inlets, one for the hot and another for the cold supply; but the temperature is regulated by turning just one mixer knob. The flow may also be adjusted by turning another knob which is set round the outside of the temperature control. In this way you can control the water more quickly and positively than you could do if you had to adjust two separate taps (which tends to be a bit of a juggling act).

Shower mixers are constantly being improved so that they are more convenient and safer to use. With one modern manual mixing valve, for example, the temperature of the water is controlled by turning a knurled knob, not unlike the handle of a tap. And the flow and on/off control is worked by pushing in or pulling out this knob. You can therefore control the flow and temperature of the water

in one movement. Another advantage of this kind of control is that the shower can be stopped instantly if the pressure on the cold side falls (as a result of a toilet being flushed or cold water being drawn off elsewhere in the house, for example). If this happened the shower would suddenly run very hot, but by flicking the control knob downwards the flow ceases. It's not so serious if the pressure falls on the hot side, because the shower would just run cold. But again, to prevent discomfort the flow can be stopped quickly by flicking the control knob.

However, prevention is better than cure and there are ways of organising the plumbing so that this problem can't arise. To alleviate the danger it's best to run the 15mm (½in) cold water supply pipe to the shower direct from the cold water storage cistern and not as a branch from the 22mm (¾in) distribution pipe to the bathroom. This will supply a continuous volume of cold water provided the cistern is working properly.

Thermostatic valves

Of course it may mean too much of an upheaval to lay in a new pipe run, but instead you could install a special thermostatic mixing valve. This enables you to pre-set the temperature of the shower water and this will remain constant despite fluctuations of pressure in the hot and cold supplies. And apart from this, thermostatic mixers provide

INSTALLING A FIXED ROSE

1 To mount the wall fixing, thread one end of the double-ended screw supplied into the hole in the base of the casting.

2 With the flange in place, screw the fitting into the shower wall using a pre-drilled fixing hole. The inlet hole must point downwards.

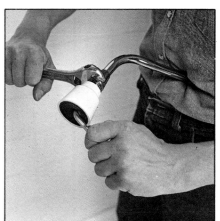

3 Screw the outlet rose onto the outlet pipe by removing the rose and inserting an Allen key into the recess you will find inside.

4 Attach the outlet fitting to the wall fixing, by tightening the fixing nut on the rose so it crushes the olive. But don't chip the chrome.

5 Make sure that the outlet rose swivels firmly but freely on its ball bearing, and that it emerges at right angles to the wall.

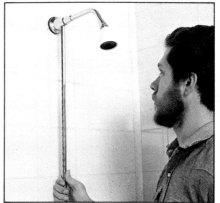

6 Screw the supply pipe in to the outlet supply until it is tight against the washer, and check that it is truly vertical.

7 Attach the supply pipe to the thermostatic control unit and mark the position of the supply pipe holes on the shower wall.

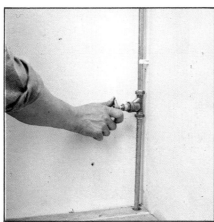

8 Turn off the water supplies via stop-valves, if fitted, and tee off the supply pipes to feed the hot and cold inlets of the shower mixer.

9 Drill holes in the shower wall so that the supply pipes can be fed through from behind and connected up to the shower mixer.

INSTALLING AN ADJUSTABLE ROSE

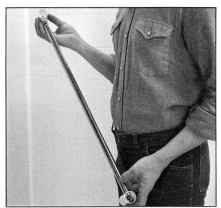

1 Fit the two wall fixing brackets to the end of the runner, and align them both so that they are pointing in the same direction.

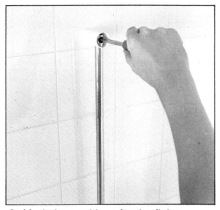

2 Mark the positions for the fixing screws on the shower wall, drill the holes and then proceed to screw on the uppermost bracket.

3 Slide on the movable rose support and fix the lower bracket to the wall. Cover the screw entry holes with plastic caps.

4 Take the one-piece shower head and rose and screw on the flexible hose, making sure that the fibre washer is correctly placed.

5 Hold the wall supply point fixing in place and mark the wall for drilling. Drill the hole, making sure you don't damage the tiled surround.

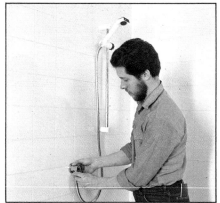

6 Insert the fixing and screw it up tight. Then take your chosen mixer, drill its fixing holes and plumb in the supply pipes.

just that extra margin of safety and assurance against discomfort.

Before buying a thermostatic mixing valve, it's important that you recognise its limitations as well as its advantages. These valves can deal with relatively minor fluctuations in pressure that can result from water being drawn off from one or other of the supply pipes. They can't accommodate the great differences in pressure between a hot water supply under pressure from a storage cylinder and a cold supply taken direct from the main (in any case, you should never arrange your shower plumbing in this way). Some thermostatic valves even require a greater working 'hydraulic head' (the vertical distance between the cold water cistern and the shower rose) than the 1m (3ft) minimum that is usual for manual mixers. So it's a good idea to check on these points and on the 'head' available before you buy one of them.

Shower pumps

An inadequate 'head' is, of course, one of the commonest reasons why a shower won't work properly. Although the minimum distance between the base of the cold water cistern and the shower rose must be 1m (3ft), for best results this distance ought to be 1.5m (5ft) or more.

However, all is not lost if you can't get this head because you can install a shower pump. They're expensive but they can make the difference between a stimulating shower and a miserable, low-pressure trickle, which isn't much good to anyone.

Different types of pump are controlled in different ways. Some have manual switches which are controlled by a pull-cord. In this case the pump is only switched on after the water has begun to flow, and is turned off before it has been stopped. Other pumps are operated automatically when the water is

turned on at the shower by the movement of water in the pipes.

You can install a simple pump between the mixer and the shower rose outlet, but you may find it difficult to conceal. On the other hand, automatic pumps must be connected into the water supply before it reaches the mixer, so it's easier to choose a convenient site where the pump can be hidden from view or disguised.

Shower pumps need quite a lot of plumbing in, and if you're not careful about planning you may end up with a lot of exposed pipework. It's also worth remembering that when you wire up the electricity supply you have to connect the pump to a fused connection unit with a double-pole switch. And if the pump is situated inside the bathroom it must be protected from steam and water (except in the case of units specially designed to be inside the shower cubicle).

THREE TYPES OF SHOWER

There are several types of shower mixer available on the market. They fall into two types – those which simply mix the hot and cold flows, and those which make an effort to provide the mixed flows at a constant, pre-set, temperature. All of them are usually finished in chrome and the controls are made of a strong plastic which will resist most knocks and blows.

Surface-mounted mixer
Left: This is a surface-mounted mixer control with separate supply pipes emerging through the wall to supply the control which provides power over flow and temperature.

Built-in mixer
Right: This built-in control is supplies from behind the shower wall so that the supply pipes are hidden. These fittings are also available in a gold finish.

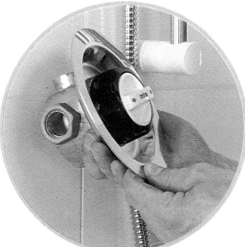

Thermostatic mixer
Left: This thermostatic mixer is also supplied from behind and provides two separate controls – one for pre-setting the temperature, and one for adjusting the flow of the water once the user is inside the shower.

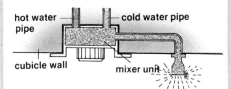
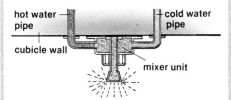
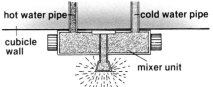
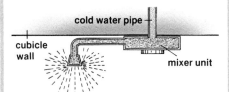

REPLACING A WASHBASIN

Replacing a washbasin is fairly straightforward. It's a job you'll have to undertake if the basin is cracked – but you may also want to change the basin if you're redesigning your bathroom and adding some up-to-date fittings.

Apart from replacing a cracked basin, which you should do immediately, the most common time to install a new basin is when you're improving a bathroom or decorating a separate WC. The chances are that the basin you'll be removing will be one of the older ceramic types, wall-hung, a pedestal model or built into a vanity unit.

The main advantage of a wall-hung basin is that it doesn't take up any floor space and because of this it is very useful in a small bathroom, WC or cloakroom. You can also set the basin at a comfortable height, unlike a pedestal basin whose height is fixed by the height of the pedestal. However, it's usual to fit a wall-hung basin with the rim 800mm (32in) above the floor.

Vanity units are now increasing in popularity. In fact they're the descendents of the Edwardian wash-stand, with its marble top, bowl and large water jug. The unit is simply a storage cupboard with a ceramic, enamelled pressed steel or plastic basin set flush in the top. The advantage of vanity units is that you have a counter surface round the basin on which to stand toiletries. There is rarely, if ever, sufficient room for these items behind or above conventional wall-hung or pedestal basins. Usually the top has some form of plastic covering or can be tiled for easy cleaning.

Fittings for basins

It's a good idea to choose the taps and waste fittings at the same time you select the basin, so everything matches. You could perhaps re-use the taps from the old basin, but it's doubtful if these will be in keeping with the design of the new appliance. As an alternative to shrouded head or pillar taps, you could fit a mixer, provided the holes at the back of the basin are suitably spaced to take the tap tails. But remember that because of the design of most basin mixers, you shouldn't use them if the cold water supply is directly from the mains.

Ceramic basins normally have a built-in overflow channel which in most appliances connects into the main outlet above the trap. So if you accidentally let the basin overfill you reduce the risk of water spillage.

PUTTING IN A NEW BASIN

You should have little trouble installing a new washbasin in the same place as the old one. It's also a good opportunity to check the pipe runs. If they're made of lead it's a good idea to replace them.

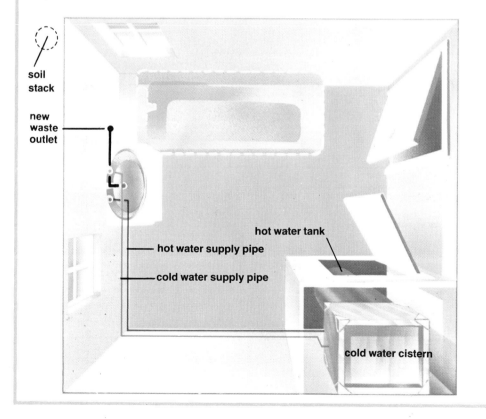

soil stack

new waste outlet

hot water tank

hot water supply pipe

cold water supply pipe

cold water cistern

Vanity unit basins are usually sold complete with a waste and overflow unit which resembles that of a modern stainless steel sink. A flexible tube connects the overflow outlet of the basin with a sleeve or 'banjo' unit which fits tightly round a slotted waste fitting.

With both types of basin the flange of the waste outlet has to be bedded into the hole provided for it in the basin on a layer of plumber's putty. The thread of the screwed waste must also be smeared with jointing compound to ensure a watertight seal where the 'banjo' connects to it.

Traps

The outlet of the waste must, of course, connect to a trap and branch waste pipe. At one time it was the practice to use 'shallow seal' traps with a 50mm (2in) depth of seal for two-pipe drainage systems, and 'deep seal' traps with a 75mm (3in) depth of seal for single stack systems. Today, however, deep seal traps are always fitted.

Of course, the modern bottle trap is one of the most common types used. It's neater looking and requires less space than a traditional U-trap. Where it's concealed behind a pedestal or in a vanity unit you can use one made of plastic, but there are chromium-plated and brass types if you have a wall-hung basin where trap and waste will be clearly visible. The one drawback with bottle traps is that they discharge water more slowly than a U-trap. You can now also buy traps with telescopic inlets that make it much easier to provide a push-fit connection to an existing copper or plastic branch waste pipe.

Connecting up the water supply

It's unlikely that you'll be able to take out the old basin and install a new one without making some modification to the pipework. It's almost certain that the tap holes will be in a different position. To complicate matters further, taps are now made with shorter tails so you'll probably have to extend the supply pipes by a short length.

If you're installing new supply pipes, how you run them will depend on the type of basin you're putting in. With a wall-hung basin or the pedestal type, the hot and cold pipes are usually run neatly together up the back wall and then bent round to the tap tails. But as a vanity unit will conceal the plumbing there's no need to run the pipes together.

You might find it difficult to bend the required angles, so an easy way round the problem is to use flexible corrugated copper pipe which you can bend by hand to the shape you need. You can buy the pipe with a swivel tap connector at one end and a plain connector, on which you can use capillary or

ASSEMBLING A VANITY UNIT

1 Cut a hole in the vanity unit with the help of the template provided or, if the hole is precut, check the measurement against that of the sink.

2 Prop the basin up while you install the mixer unit. Start with the outlet spout which is fixed with a brass nut and packing washers.

3 Now take the water inlet assembly and check that the hot and cold spur pipes are the right length so that the tap sub-assemblies are correctly positioned.

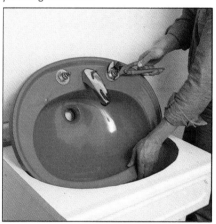

4 Fix the assembly in position with the brass nuts supplied by the manufacturer. Make sure that all the washers are included otherwise the fitting won't be secure.

5 Now complete the tap heads by first sliding on the flange which covers up the securing nut; next put on the headwork and tighten the retaining nut.

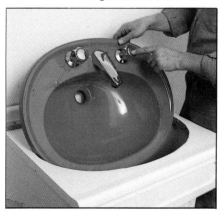

6 Finish off the tap assembly by fitting the coloured markers into place (red for hot is usually on the left), and gently pressing home the chrome cap.

Ready Reference

BASIN SIZES

On basins, the dimension from side to side is specified as the length, and that from back to front as the width.

Most standard sized basins are between 550 and 700mm (22 and 28in) long, and 450 to 500mm (18 to 20in) wide.

BASIN COMPONENTS

tap

waste outlet

bracket for wall fixing

tap-washer

back-nut

waste back washer

connecting nut

waste back-nut

supply pipe

trap

THE SPACE YOU'LL NEED

2200mm

1000mm

400mm   700mm

Think about the space around your basin particularly if you are installing a new one. You not only need elbow room when you are bending over it, such as when you are washing your hair, but also room in front to stand back – especially if you put a mirror above it. Here are the recommended dimensions for the area around your basin.

PLUMBING IN A VANITY UNIT

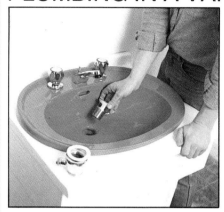

7 Now insert the waste outlet. Make sure the rubber flange is fitted properly and seats comfortably into the basin surround.

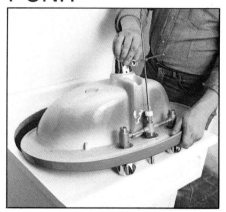

8 Turn the basin over; secure the outlet and the pop-up waste control rods. These may need shortening depending on clearance inside the vanity unit.

9 Before you put the basin into its final position put a strip of mastic around the opening in the vanity unit to ensure a watertight seal.

10 Press the basin gently into position and fix it to the underside of the top of the vanity unit. Attach the waste plug to its keeper.

11 Now fix the inlet pipes to the two mixer connections and screw on the waste trap. Take the doors off the vanity unit to make access easier.

12 Turn the water back on and check for leaks. Check the pop-up waste system works, then put the doors of the vanity unit back on.

When fitting the taps all you have to do is to remove the back-nuts and slip flat plastic washers over the tails (if they aren't there already). The taps can then be positioned in the holes in the basin. When this has been done more plastic washers (or top hat washers) have to be slipped over the tails before the back-nuts are replaced. It's important not to overtighten these as it's quite easy to damage a ceramic basin.

. Because some vanity unit basins are made of a thinner material, you may find that the shanks of the taps fitted into them will protrude below the under-surface of the basin. The result is that when the back-nut is fully tightened, it still isn't tight against the underside of the basin. To get round the problem you have to fit a top hat washer over the shank so the back-nut can be screwed up against it.

Mixers usually have one large washer or gasket between the base of the mixer and the top of the basin and you fix them in exactly the same way.

When you've fitted the taps you can then fit the waste. With a ceramic basin you'll have to use a slotted waste to enable water from the overlfow to escape into the drainage pipe. Getting this in place means first removing the back-nut so you can slip it through the outlet hole in the basin – which itself should be coated with a generous layer of plumber's putty. It's essential to make sure that the slot in the waste fitting coincides with the outlet of the basin's built-in overflow. You'll then have to smear jointing compound on the protruding screw thread of the tail, slip on a plastic washer and replace and tighten the back-nut. As you do this the waste flange will probably try to turn on its seating, but you can prevent this by holding the grid with pliers as you tighten the back-nut.

Finally, any excess putty that is squeezed out as the flange is tightened against the basin should be wiped away.

A vanity unit will probably be supplied with a combined waste and overflow unit. This is a flexible hose that has to be fitted (unlike a ceramic basin, where it's an integral part of the appliance). The slotted waste is bedded in in exactly the same way as a waste on a ceramic basin. You then have to fit one end of the overflow to the basin outlet and slip the 'banjo' outlet on the other end over the tail of the waste to cover the slot. It's held in position by a washer and back-nut.

Fitting the basin
Once the taps and waste have been fixed in position on the new basin, you should be ready to remove the old basin and fit the new one in its place. First you need to cut off the water supply to the basin, either by turning off the main stop-valve (or any gate valve on

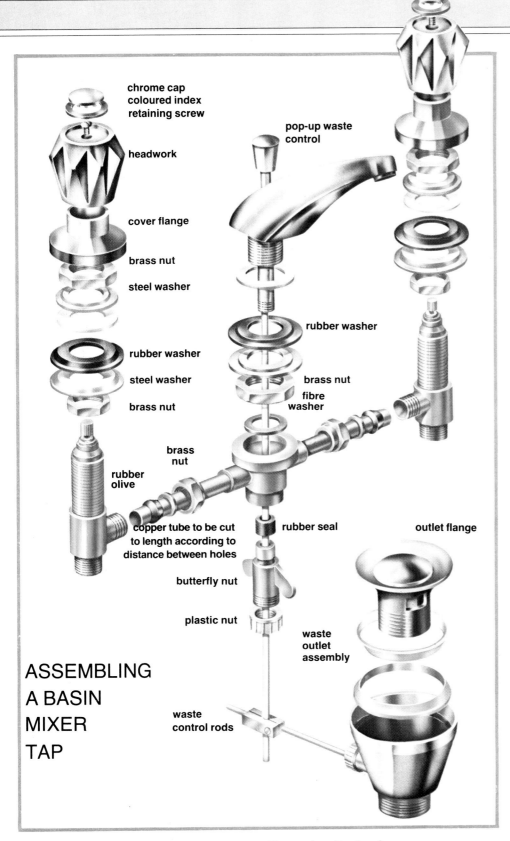

chrome cap
coloured index
retaining screw

headwork

cover flange

brass nut

steel washer

rubber washer

steel washer

brass nut

brass nut

rubber olive

copper tube to be cut to length according to distance between holes

pop-up waste control

rubber washer

brass nut
fibre washer

brass nut

rubber seal

butterfly nut

plastic nut

waste control rods

outlet flange

waste outlet assembly

ASSEMBLING A BASIN MIXER TAP

compression fittings at the other. If you're using ordinary copper pipe, the easiest way to start is by bending the pipe to the correct angle first, and then cutting the pipe to the right length at each end afterwards. See techniques on pages 185-187.

Preparing the basin
Before you fix the basin in position, you'll need to fit the taps (or mixer) and the waste. It's much easier to do this at this stage than later when the basin is against the wall because you will have more room to manoeuvre in.

Ready Reference

TYPES OF BASIN

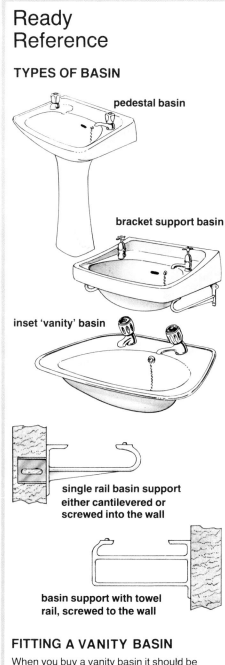

pedestal basin

bracket support basin

inset 'vanity' basin

single rail basin support either cantilevered or screwed into the wall

basin support with towel rail, screwed to the wall

FITTING A VANITY BASIN

When you buy a vanity basin it should be supplied with a template to guide you in cutting your work surface or vanity unit. This should also include fitting instructions, and necessary fixing screws and mastic strip. It may look like this.

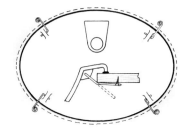

the distribution pipes) or by tying up the ball-valve supplying the main cold water storage cistern. Then open the taps and leave them until the water ceases to flow. If the existing basin is a pedestal model you'll have to remove the pedestal which may be screwed to the floor. Take off the nut that connects the basin trap to the threaded waste outlet and unscrew the nuts that connect the water supply pipes to the tails of the taps. These will either be swivel tap connectors or cap and lining joints. You'll need to be able to lift the basin clear and then remove the brackets or hangers on which it rests.

You'll probably need some help when installing the new basin as it's much easier to mark the fixing holes if someone else is holding the basin against the wall. With a pedestal basin, the pedestal will determine the level of the basin. The same applies with a vanity unit. But if the basin is set on hangers or brackets, you can adjust the height for convenience.

Once the fixing holes have been drilled and plugged, the basin can be screwed into position and you can deal with the plumbing. Before you make the connections to the water supply pipes you may have to cut or lengthen them to meet the tap tails. If you need to lengthen them you'll find it easier to use corrugated copper pipe. The actual connection between pipe and tail is made with a swivel tap connector – a form of compression fitting.

Finally you have to connect the trap. You may be able to re-use the old one, but it's more likely you'll want to fit a new one. And if its position doesn't coincide with the old one, you can use a bottle trap with an adjustable telescopic inlet.

FITTING A PEDESTAL BASIN

1 Stand the basin on the pedestal to check the height of the water supply pipe runs and the outlet. Measure the height of the wall fixing points.

2 When you're making up the pipe run to connect to the tap tails, plan it so the pipes are neatly concealed within the body of the pedestal.

3 Line up the piped waste outlet and fix the trap to the basin outlet. A telescopic trap may be useful here to adjust for a varying level.

4 Move the whole unit into its final position, screw the basin to the wall, connect the waste trap to the outlet, and connect up the supply pipes.

CHAPTER 8

Wiring

TRACING ELECTRICAL FAULTS

When the lights go out or an electrical appliance won't work, the reason is often obvious. But when it isn't, it helps to know how to locate the fault and put it right.

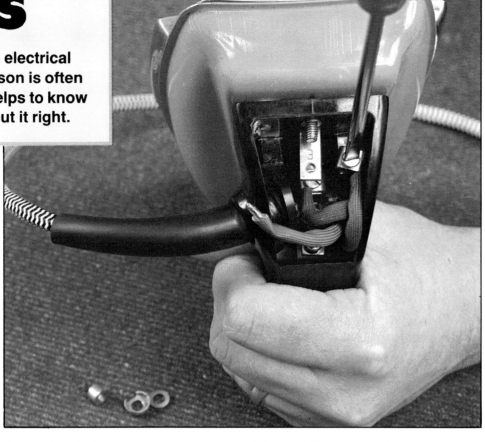

Most people's immediate reaction to something going wrong with their elecricity supply is to head for the meter cupboard, muttering darkly about another blown fuse. Fuses do blow occasionally for no immediately obvious reason, but usually there is a problem that needs to be pin-pointed and put right before the power can be restored. It's no use mending a blown fuse, only to find that when the power is restored the fuse blows again because the fault is still present.

Tracing everyday electrical faults is not particularly difficult. You simply have to be methodical in checking the various possible causes, and eliminating options until you find the culprit. More serious faults on the house's fixed wiring system can be more difficult to track down, but again some careful investigation can often locate the source of the trouble, even if professional help has to be called in to put it right.

Safety first
Before you start investigating any electrical faults, remember the cardinal rule and switch off the power at the main switch. When fuses blow, it is all too easy to forget that other parts of the system may still be live and therefore dangerous, and even if you know precisely how your house has been wired up it is foolish to take risks. If the fault appears to be on an electrical appliance, the same rules apply: always switch off the appliance *and* pull out the plug before attempting to investigate. Don't rely on the switch to isolate it; the fault may be in the switch itself.

It's also important to be prepared for things to go wrong with your electrics; even new systems can develop faults, and in fact a modern installation using circuit breakers will detect faults more readily than one with rewireable or cartridge fuses, so giving more regular cause for investigation. Make sure that you keep a small emergency electrical tool kit in an accessible place where it won't get raided for other jobs; it should include one or two screwdrivers, a pair of pliers, a handyman's knife, spare fuses and fuse wire, and above all a *working* torch. There is nothing more annoying when the lights go out than finding the torch does not work.

Check the obvious
When something electrical fails to operate, always check the obvious first – replace the bulb when a light doesn't work, or glance outside to see if everyone in the street has been blacked out by a power cut before panicking that all your fuses have blown. Having satisfied yourself that you may have a genuine fault, start a methodical check of all the possibilities.

A fault can occur in a number of places. It may be on an appliance, within the flex or plug linking it to the mains, on the main circuitry itself or at the fuseboard. Let's start at the appliance end of things. If something went bang as you switched the appliance on, unplug it immediately; the fault is probably on the appliance itself. If it simply stopped working, try plugging it in at another socket; if it goes, there's a fault on the circuit feeding the original socket. If it doesn't go, either the second socket is on the same faulty circuit as the first one (which we'll come to later) or there may be a fault in the link between the appliance and the socket – loose connections where the cores are connected to either the plug or the appliance itself, damaged flex (both these problems are caused by abuse of the flex in use), or a blown fuse in the plug if one is fitted.

Plug and flex connections
The next step is to check the flex connections within the plug and the appliance. The connections at plug terminals are particularly prone to damage if the plug's cord grip or flex anchorage is not doing its job; a tug on the flex can then break the cores, cutting the power and possibly causing a short circuit. If the connections are weak or damaged, disconnect them, cut back the sheathing and insulation and remake the connections. Make sure that the flex is correctly anchored within the body of the plug before replacing the cover.

If the plug contains a fuse, test that it has not blown by using a continuity tester, or by holding it across the open end of a switched-on metal-cased torch – see *Ready Reference*. Replace a blown fuse with a new one of the correct current rating; 3A for appliances rated at 720W or below, 13A for higher-rated appliances (and all colour televisions).

Next, check the flex connections within the appliance itself. Always unplug an appliance before opening it up to gain access to the terminal block, and then remake any doubtful-looking connections by cutting off the end of the flex and stripping back the outer and inner insulation carefully to expose fresh conductor strands. If the flex itself is worn or

REWIRING A PLUG

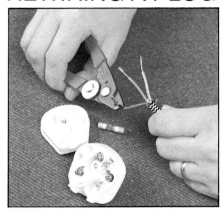

1 *Strip the outer sheathing carefully, cut each core 12mm (¹/₂in) longer than is necessary to reach its correct terminal and then remove 12mm of core sheathing.*

2 *Twist the strands of each core neatly and form a loop that will fit round the terminal screw. Connect the cores as shown here and screw down the studs.*

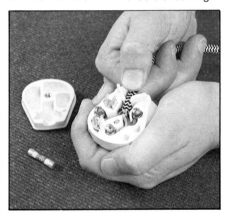

3 *Check that the core insulation reaches right to each terminal, and that there are no loose strands visible. Then fit the flex securely in the cord grip.*

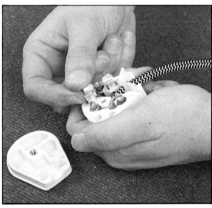

4 *Lastly, in a fused plug press in a cartridge fuse of the correct rating for the appliance concerned, and screw the plug top firmly on.*

damaged, take this opportunity to fit new flex of the correct type and current rating – see *Ready Reference*, step-by-step photographs and pages 224-225 for details. Make sure you re-use any grommets, heat-resistant sleeving, special captive washers and the like that were fitted to the appliance.

Lastly, check the flex continuity; it is possible that damage to the flex itself has broken one of the cores within the outer sheathing. Again use a continuity tester for this, holding the two probes against opposite ends of each core in turn, or use your metal-cased torch again, touching one core to the case and the other to the battery. Replace the flex if *any* core fails the test; the appliance may still work if the earth core is damaged, but the earthing will be lost and the appliance could become live and dangerous to anyone using it in the event of another fault developing in the future.

Lighting problems

Similar problems to these can also occur on lighting circuits, where the pendant flex linking ceiling roses to lampholders can become disconnected or faulty through accidental damage or old age. If replacing the bulb doesn't work, switch off the power at the mains and examine the condition of the flex. Look especially for bad or broken connections at the ceiling rose and within the lampholder. Replace the flex if the core insulation has become brittle, and fit a new lampholder if the plastic is discoloured (both these problems are caused by heat from the light bulb). If the lampshade ring will not turn you will have to cut this with a hacksaw.

Mending blown fuses

A circuit fuse will blow for two main reasons, overloading and short circuits – see *Ready Reference*. Too many appliances connected

Ready Reference

COMMON FAULTS

Many electrical breakdowns in the home are caused by only a few common faults. These include:
● overloading of circuits, causing the circuit fuse to blow or the MCB to trip
● short circuits, where the current by-passes its proper route because of failed insulation or contact between cable or flex cores; the resulting high current flow creates heat and blows the plug fuse (if fitted) and circuit fuse
● earthing faults, where insulation breaks down and allows the metal body of an appliance to become live, causing a shock to the user if the appliance is not properly earthed and blowing a fuse or causing the ELCB to trip otherwise
● poor connections causing overheating that can lead to a fire and to short circuits and earthing faults.

TIP: TESTING FUSES

You can test suspect cartridge fuses (both circuit and plug types) by holding them across the open end of a switched-on metal-cased torch, with one end on the casing and the other on the battery. A sound fuse will light the torch.

CHOOSE THE RIGHT FLEX

When fitting new flex to an appliance, it's important to choose the correct type and current rating. The table below will help:

Size (mm²)	Rating amps	watts	Use
0.5	3	720	Light fittings
0.75	6	1440	Small appliances
1.0	10	2400	Larger appliances
1.5	15	3600	
2.5	20	4800	

If you are buying flex for pendant lights, remember that the maximum weight of fitting that each size of twin flex can support is
● 2kg (4¹/₂lb) for 0.5mm² flex
● 3kg (6¹/₂lb) for 0.75mm² flex
● 5kg (11lb) for larger sizes.

Select circular **three-core PVC-insulated flex** for most appliances, **unkinkable** or **braided flex** for irons, kettles and the like, **two-core flex** for non-metallic lamps and light fittings or for double-insulated appliances, and **heat-resisting flex** for powerful pendant lights and for heater connections.

to a circuit will demand too much current, and this will melt the fuse. Similarly, a short circuit – where, for example, bare live and neutral flex cores touch – causes a current surge that blows the fuse.

If overloading caused the fuse to blow, the remedy is simple: disconnect all the equipment on the circuit, mend the fuse and avoid using too many high-wattage appliances at the same time in future. If a short circuit was to blame, you will have to hunt for the cause and rectify it before mending the fuse – see photographs on the next page.

When a circuit fuse blows, turn off the main switch and remove fuseholders until you find the one that has blown. Then clean out the remains of the old fuse wire, and fit a new piece of the correct rating for the circuit – 5A for lighting circuits, 15A for circuits to immersion heaters and the like, and 30A for ring circuits. Cut the wire over-long, thread it loosely across or through the ceramic holder and connect it carefully to the terminals. Trim the ends off neatly, replace the fuseholder in the consumer unit and turn on the power again. If the fuse blows again, and you have already checked for possible causes on appliances, flexes and lighting pendants, suspect a circuit fault – see below.

If you have cartridge fuses, all you have to do is find which cartridge has blown by removing the fuseholder and testing the cartridge with a continuity tester or metal-cased torch. A blown cartridge fuse should be replaced by a new one of the same current rating. Again, if the new fuse blows immediately, suspect a circuit fault.

If you have miniature circuit breakers (MCBs) you will not be able to switch the MCB on again if the fault that tripped it off is still present. Otherwise, simply reset it by switching it to ON or pressing in the centre button.

Earth leakage circuit breakers (ELCBs)
If your installation has an ELCB, it will trip off if an earthing fault occurs – for example, if a live wire or connection comes into contact with earthed metal. Like an MCB, it cannot be switched on again until the fault is rectified – a useful safety point. However, it will not trip off in the event of a short circuit between live and neutral, or when overloading occurs.

The high-sensitivity current-operated ELCB, in addition to detecting earth faults, also protects against the danger of electric shocks by tripping off if it detects current flowing to earth through the human body. It can do this quickly enough to prevent the shock from causing death.

Tracing circuit faults
If you have checked appliances, flexes, plug connections and pendant lights, and a fault is still present, it is likely to be in the fixed

REPLACING FLEX

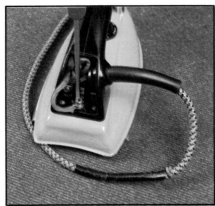

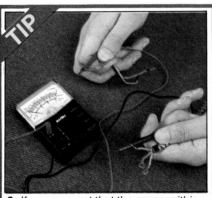

1 *To replace damaged flex, remove the appropriate cover plate or panel from the appliance. Make a note of which core goes where before undoing it.*

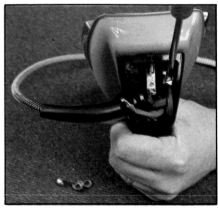

2 *Loosen the cord grip within the appliance and withdraw the old flex. Here heat-resisting sleeving has been fitted; save this for re-use.*

3 *If you suspect that the cores within apparently undamaged flex are broken, test each core in turn with a continuity tester.*

4 *Connect in the new flex by reversing the disconnection sequence, re-using grommets, sleeving and washers. Make sure each connection is secure.*

wiring. Here, it is possible to track down one or two faults, but you may in the end have to call in a professional electrician.

The likeliest causes of circuit faults are damage to cables (perhaps caused by drilling holes in walls or by nailing down floorboards where cables run), ageing of cables (leading to insulation breakdown, and overheating) and faults at wiring accessories (light switches, socket outlets and so on). Let's look at the last one first, simply because such items are at least easily accessible.

If the cable cores are not properly stripped and connected within the accessory, short circuits or earth faults can develop. To check a suspect accessory such as a socket outlet, isolate the circuit, unscrew the faceplate and examine the terminal connections and the insulation. Ensure that each core is firmly held in its correct terminal, and that each core has insulation right up to the terminal,

so that it cannot touch another core or any bare metal. There is usually enough slack on the mains cable to allow you to trim over-long cores back slightly. Check that the earth core is sleeved in green/yellow PVC, and try not to double over the cable as you ease the faceplate back into position; over-full boxes can lead to short circuits and damage to cable and core insulation ... and more trouble. You can carry out similar checks at light switches and ceiling roses. Any damaged accessories you find should be replaced immediately with new ones.

Damage to cables is relatively easy to cure provided that you can find where the damage is. If you drilled or nailed through a cable, you will of course be able to pin-point it immediately. Cable beneath floorboards can be repaired simply by isolating the circuit, cutting the cable completely at the point of damage and using a three-terminal junction

REPAIRING A CIRCUIT FUSE

1 *Switch off the mains and locate the blown fuse. Then remove the remains of the old fuse wire and clean off any charring that has occurred.*

2 *Feed in a length of fuse wire of the correct rating and wind each end round the terminal before tightening up the screw. Don't pull the wire taut.*

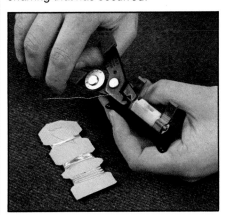

3 *Trim off the unwanted ends of fuse wire neatly with wire strippers, then replace the fuse carrier in the fuse box and restore the power.*

4 *Test a suspect cartridge fuse with a continuity tester or torch (see* Ready Reference) *and replace it by pressing in a new fuse of the correct rating.*

box to link the cut ends. Cable buried in plaster must be cut out and a new length of cable inserted between adjacent accessories to replace the damaged length. Where this would involve a long length of cable (on a run to a remote socket, for example) it is acceptable to use junction boxes in nearby floor or ceiling voids to connect in the new length of cable. You will then have to make good the cutting-out.

Tracking down a break in the cable elsewhere in the installation is a difficult job best left to a qualified electrician. If, however, you find that your house is wired in rubber-sheathed cable and faults are beginning to occur, don't waste time and effort trying to track them down; you need a rewire. Unless you know what you are doing, this is certainly a job for the electrician.

If you are unable to trace an electrical fault after checking all the points already de-

scribed, call in a professional electrician who will be able to use specialist test equipment to locate the fault. Do *not* attempt to bypass a fault with a makeshift wiring arrangement, and NEVER use any conducting foreign body such as a nail to restore power to a circuit whose fuse keeps blowing. Such tricks can kill.

Regular maintenance
You will find that a little common-sense maintenance work will help to prevent a lot of minor electrical faults from occurring at all. For example, it's well worth spending a couple of hours every so often checking the condition of the flex on portable appliances (especially those heavily used, such as kettles, irons, hair driers and the like) and the connections within plugs. Also, make a point of replacing immediately any electrical accessory that is in any way damaged.

Ready Reference

CHECKLIST FOR ACTION
When something goes wrong with your electrics, use this checklist to identify or eliminate the commonest potential causes of trouble.

Fault 1
Pendant light doesn't work
Action
● replace bulb
● check lighting circuit fuse/MCB
● check flex connections at lampholder and ceiling rose
● check flex continuity.

Fault 2
Electrical appliance doesn't work
Action
● try appliance at another socket
● check plug fuse (if fitted)
● check plug connections
● check connections at appliance's own terminal block
● check flex continuity
● check power circuit fuse/MCB
● isolate appliance if fuses blow again.

Fault 3
Whole circuit is dead
Action
● switch off all lights/disconnect all appliances on circuit
● replace circuit fuse or reset MCB
● switch on lights/plug in appliances one by one and note which blows fuse again
● isolate offending light/appliance, and see Faults 1 and 2 (above)
● check wiring accessories on circuit for causes of short circuits
● replace damaged cable if pierced by nail or drill
● call qualified electrician for help.

Fault 4
Whole system is dead
Action
● check for local power cut
● reset ELCB if fitted to system (and see Faults 1, 2 and 3 if ELCB cannot be reset)
● call electricity board (main service fuse may have blown).

Fault 5
Electric shock received
Action
● try to turn off the power
● grab victim's clothing and pull away from power source, but DO NOT TOUCH WITH BARE HANDS
● keep victim warm
● if victim is conscious, keep warm and call a doctor; don't give brandy or food
● if breathing or heartbeat has stopped, CALL AN AMBULANCE and give artificial respiration or cardiac massage.

CABLE & FLEX

Two types of wiring are used in the domestic electrical circuits. Fixed cables are normally concealed, and carry electrical current to switches, ceiling lights, and socket outlets. Flexible cords (flexes) connect portable appliances and light fittings to the fixed wiring.

Fixed wiring

This consists mostly of PVC-sheathed cable containing three copper conductors (cores). The core insulated in red PVC is the 'live' and the one in black the 'neutral' though in lighting circuits in the cable to the switch both the black and red are live. (The black core is required to have a piece of red sleeving on it to indicate this, although this is often omitted by incompetent electricians. Cables having two red conductors are made for contract work, but rarely stocked and sold retail). The third core is the earth and this is uninsulated, but when exposed after the sheathing is removed ready for wiring up it must be sleeved in green/yellow striped PVC before being connected to the earth terminal. In some wiring circuits PVC-sheathed cables having one core only are used, for example, where a live core is looped out of a switch or a neutral core is looped out of a light, to supply an additional light or lights. Three-core and earth cable is used for two-way switching. The conductors are insulated in red, blue and yellow; the colour coding is for purposes of identification only.

Cables

PVC-sheathed and insulated, two-core and earth

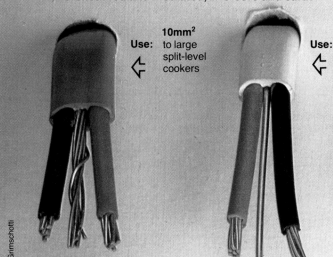

Use: 10mm² to large split-level cookers

Use: 6mm² circuits to cookers over 12kW

Use: 4mm² circuits for small cookers, instantaneous water heater (up to 7kW), 30A radial circuit

Use: 2.5mm² ring main, power circuit (eg, 20A radial circuit), immersion heater, instantaneous water heater (up to 5kW)

Jem Grimschotti

Flexible cords

Flexible cords are made in various sizes and current ratings and the types you'll most often come across are: *parallel twin unsheathed, circular PVC-sheathed, circular braided, unkinkable* and *heat-resisting*. Each conductor is made up of a number of strands of copper and it is this which gives the cord its flexibility.

The insulation used round the conductors now conforms to an international colour coding standard – brown denotes the live wire, blue the neutral, and green/yellow the earth, when it is part of the flex. Transparent or white insulation is used for a flex that carries a low current and where it doesn't matter which wire is connected to the live and neutral terminals of an appliance. It is used mainly for table lamps that need no earth.

Parallel twin unsheathed

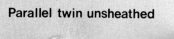

Circular PVC sheathed two-core, and two-core and earth

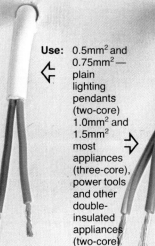

Use: 0.5mm² and 0.75mm² — plain lighting pendants (two-core) 1.0mm² and 1.5mm² most appliances (three-core), power tools and other double-insulated appliances (two-core)

Circular braided (rubber insulated)

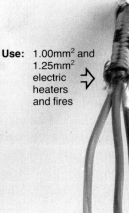

Use: 1.00mm² and 1.25mm² electric heaters and fires

Cables for fixed wiring

Most domestic wiring is now supplied in metric sizes which refer to the cross-sectional area of one of the conductors, whether it is composed of one or several strands of wire. Most common sizes of cable are 1.0mm² and 1.5mm² used for lighting, and 2.5mm² used for power circuits.

Cable with grey sheathing is intended to be concealed in walls or under floors; white sheathing is meant for surface mounting.

PVC-sheathed and insulated, three-core and earth

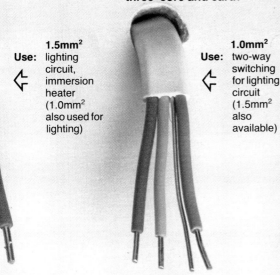

1.5mm²
Use: lighting circuit, immersion heater (1.0mm² also used for lighting)

1.0mm²
Use: two-way switching for lighting circuit (1.5mm² also available)

Unkinkable

Use: 1.25mm² and 1.5mm² electric irons, percolators and kettles

Heat-resisting

Use: 0.5mm² and 0.75mm² lighting pendants with 100W-200W bulbs 1.25mm² and 1.5mm² immersion heater

Safety with electricity
● never work on a circuit with current on. Turn off at mains and isolate circuit by removing relevant fuse. Keep this with you until you restore supply
● never touch plugs and sockets with wet hands
● remove plugs from socket when working on appliance
● always use the correct fuse wire when mending a fuse

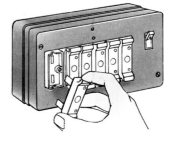

The importance of earthing
Earthing is an essential safety feature of all wiring systems. To complete a circuit, electricity either flows down the neutral conductor of the supply cable or it flows to earth. That is why you get a shock if you touch a live wire. The idea of earthing is to connect all metal fittings and appliances in the house with a good conductor – the 'earth wire' in cables and flexes. If a fault occurs that makes this metal live, the presence of the earth wire prevents the voltage from rising much above earth voltage. At the same time, the fault greatly increases the current being drawn to the metal via the supply conductor, and this current surge is detected by the circuit fuse, which

'blows' and cuts off the current flow.
The earth conductor links socket outlets and appliances (via their plugs) and is connected to a main earthing terminal at the house fuse box or consumer unit. This is usually connected to the outer metal sheath of the underground supply cable.

All metal pipework in the house is also earthed by being connected to the earth terminal – this is called 'cross bonding'.

Old wiring
Some old installations may still be using lead-sheathed or tough rubber-sheathed (TRS) wiring, with the conducting wires insulated in vulcanized rubber, or vulcanized rubber insulated, taped and braided

wire. These insulating materials deteriorate with age (about 25-30 years) so the wiring can become dangerous. Therefore it really does need to be replaced with modern PVC-sheathed and insulated cable.

The right connection
The plug is the vital link between any electrical appliance and the mains and must be connected up correctly if it is to do its job properly. With flex in the new colour codes, connect the BRown core to the Bottom Right terminal, the BLue core to the Bottom Left one and the green-and-yellow core (if present) to the top terminal. With cores in old colour codes, Red goes to the bottom Right terminal, BLack to Bottom Left and green to top.

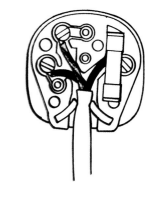

Old colour codes
Before the introduction of new international colour codes, flex used red insulation to denote the live conductor, black for the neutral and green for the earth.

Warning: Electricity is dangerous.
In some countries, including Australia, West Germany and the USA, regulations stipulate that all home electrical work must be carried out by a qualified electrician.

CEILING LIGHTS AND SWITCHES

Most ceiling lights are positioned centrally in a room to give general lighting. But by adding another light, or changing the position of an existing fitting, you can highlight particular areas and enhance the decoration.

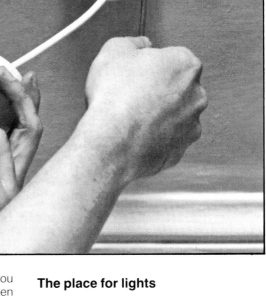

Keith Morris

Putting in a new pendant ceiling light and switch, or changing the position of an existing one, usually presents few problems – even if you have little or no experience of electrical work.

A pendant is the most common ceiling light and consists of a lampholder wired to a length of flexible cord which hangs from a ceiling rose. Another type can be plugged into the ceiling rose – in this case the flexible cord has to have a special fitting which slots into a batten holder.

Know your system

Installing a new ceiling light requires making a simple connection into a nearby lighting circuit either by inserting a junction box or at an existing loop-in rose and then running a cable to a switch. In order to connect into the circuit you'll first need to know how the lights in your house are wired and which lights belong to which circuit. Then you'll be able to work out whether you can actually add another light to the circuit that is nearest to the new light's position.

There are two principal methods of wiring a lighting circuit. In the loop-in method the cable runs from ceiling rose to ceiling rose, stopping at the last one on the circuit, and the switches are wired into the roses. With the junction box system the cable runs to a number of junction boxes each serving a switch and a light. You may well find that both methods have been used in the same circuit to simplify and reduce the cable runs.

It's possible to connect into a nearby rose provided it's a loop-in type. You can check this simply by turning off the power and unscrewing the rose cover. A loop-in rose will have more than one red insulated wire going into the central terminal bank of the three in-line terminal banks. However, it can be quite fiddly to fit another cable, given that the terminal banks are very small, so you might find it easier to insert a junction box in the main circuit. And if there isn't a loop-in rose you'll have to use this method anyway.

Earthing for lighting circuits

Modern lighting circuits are protected by an earth. But if you've got a fairly old system (it's

likely to be based on junction boxes), you might find that it doesn't have one. So when you're extending such a circuit, you're now required to protect the new wiring, light fitting and switch by installing an earth. Consequently, you have to use two-core and earth cable for the extension, which will most probably connect into the existing circuit at a junction box. You then have to run a 1.5mm² earth cable from this point to the main earthing point.

Circuit additions

Usually there's a lighting circuit for each floor of a house and in a single storey dwelling there are likely to be two or more. But it's easy to identify the individual circuits simply by switching on all the lights, turning off the power and taking out a 5A fuse from the consumer unit or switching off an MCB. When you restore the power you'll know that the lights that remain off all belong to the same circuit.

Generally speaking, a lighting circuit serves six to eight fixed lighting points. In fact it can serve up to 12 lampholders provided the total wattage of the bulbs on the circuit doesn't exceed 1,200 watts. This means that unless other lights have previously been added – wall lights for example – there shouldn't be a problem of connecting in another light.

Remember, when adding up the bulb wattages, a bulb of less than 100 watts counts as 100 watts and not its face value.

The place for lights

Apart from bathrooms, where special regulations apply, you can position lights and switches in any place you like inside the house. But bear in mind they are there to fulfil a function, so switches, for example, should be conveniently located – by a door is often the most satisfactory position. Usually they are set on the wall 1.4 metres (4ft 6in) above floor level. But they can be higher or lower to suit your needs.

You mustn't install pendant lights, especially plain pendants with exposed flexible cords, in a bathroom. This is for your safety. Flexes can become frayed, and if, say, you tried to change a bulb while standing in the bath and touched an exposed conductor you could electrocute yourself. Consequently, all light fittings here must be of the close-mounted type and preferably totally enclosed to keep off condensation. If instead you use an open batten lampholder it must be fitted with a protective shield or skirt which makes it impossible for anyone changing the bulb to touch the metal clamp.

A wall-mounted switch must also be out of reach of a person using the bath or shower. In modern small bathrooms, however, this is often impossible. The alternative is to place the switch just outside the room by the door, or to fit a special ceiling switch operated by an insulating cord which doesn't have to be out of reach of the bath or the shower.

PREPARING THE CABLE RUN

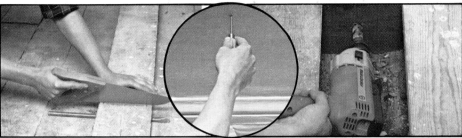

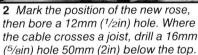

1 *Raise the floorboard above the proposed location of the new light and any others necessary for laying the power supply and switch cables.*

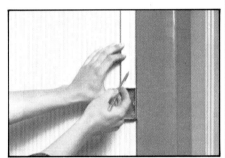

2 *Mark the position of the new rose, then bore a 12mm (¹/₂in) hole. Where the cable crosses a joist, drill a 16mm (⁵/₈in) hole 50mm (2in) below the top.*

3 *If the new rose can't be screwed to a joist, drill a 12mm (¹/₂in) hole in a wooden batten to coincide with the hole in the ceiling and fix the batten in position.*

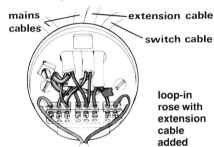

4 *If flush-fitting the switch and chasing in the cable, use a mounting box and a length of conduit to mark their positions on the wall.*

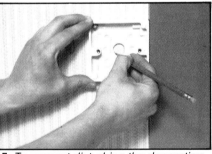

5 *To prevent disturbing the decoration in one room, you can bring the switch cable down the other side of the wall and surface-mount the switch.*

6 *Use a small bolster chisel and club hammer to channel out a groove in the wall to take the switch cable and to chop out the recess for the switch.*

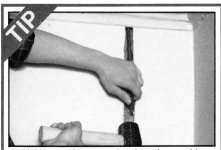

7 *With cornices, make the channel in the wall first, then drive a long cold chisel gently up the back.*

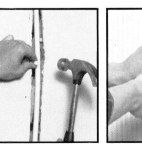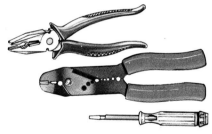

8 *Fix the conduit in place with old nails, although you can also use clout nails. Drill and plug the fixing holes for the box and screw it into place.*

Mounting box: MK

Keith Morris

Ready Reference

LIGHTING BASICS

● Extensions to lighting circuits are usually wired in 1.00mm² two-core and earth PVC-sheathed and insulated cable.
● You can extend from an existing rose only if it is of the loop-in variety with three banks of terminals; such roses can accommodate up to four cables. If you have older roses, extensions must be made via a junction box.

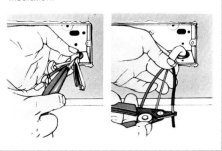

mains cables — extension cable

switch cable

loop-in rose with extension cable added

TOOLS FOR THE JOB

Electrician's pliers have cutting edges on the jaws and insulated handles.
Wire strippers can be adjusted to the diameter of the insulation to be stripped.
Handyman's knife – ideal for cutting back the sheathing of the cable.
Screwdrivers – a small one is best for the terminal fixing screws and a medium sized one for the fixing screws on the rose and switch.

HOW TO STRIP CABLE

● Use handyman's knife to cut sheathing between neutral and earth cores.
● Use wire strippers to remove core insulation.

LAYING THE CABLE

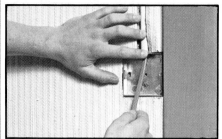

1 *Run the cable from where it joins the existing circuit to the new rose and lay in the switch cable. Allow 200mm (8in) for connections.*

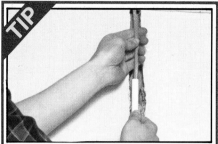

2 *With the switch cable, you might find it easier to pull down the required length and then slide on the conduit before fixing it in place.*

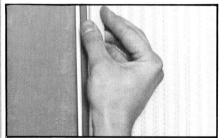

3 *It's not a good idea to leave cable exposed on a wall. When surface-mounting, the cable should be laid in PVC trunking with a clip-on cover.*

4 *If the cable is brought down on the other side of the wall to the switch, you'll need to drill a hole through so the cable enters the back of the box.*

FIXING THE SWITCH

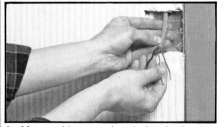

1 *After making good, strip back about 100mm (4in) of sheathing; take off 15mm (⅝in) of insulation and bend over the exposed wire; sleeve the earth wire.*

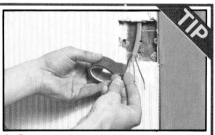

2 *Because the switch is wired into the 'live' of the circuit, the black wire is live and not neutral; mark it as such with red PVC tape.*

3 *Connect the earth wire to the earth terminal of the metal box and the two conductors to the terminals on the back of the faceplate.*

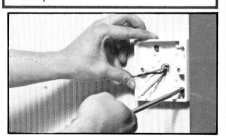

4 *Make sure a surface-mounted box is square before connecting the switch. With a flush fitting squareness can be adjusted when attaching the faceplate.*

Putting in switches

There is a great variety of switches available, but all perform the same function of breaking or completing an electrical circuit so you can turn the light off or on. Modern switches are of the rocker type; a one-gang switch has a single switch on the faceplate; a two-gang switch has two switches on the same faceplate, and so on. Dimmer switches are slightly different in that you can vary the power flowing to the bulb (so reducing or increasing its brightness) by rotating a control knob.

With a new light, you can either connect it into an existing switch position (fitting a two-gang switch in place of a one-gang one, for example) or a new switch. Depending on how you connect into the existing circuit, you'll have to run the switch cable above the ceiling from a rose or a junction box down the wall to where you are going to locate it. If you want to conceal the cable on the down drop you'll have to cut a shallow channel – which will damage the existing decoration. Or, you can surface-mount it in trunking.

Making the connection

Once you've decided where you want to put the light fitting and switch, you then have to decide where it's best to make the connection into the existing circuit.

Wiring runs may require some detective work to find out what each cable is doing – you don't want to connect into a switch cable by mistake. This may mean climbing into the roof space or raising a few floorboards. You'll need to do this anyway to run in the new cables to the required positions. As cable is expensive, it's best to plan your runs to use as little as possible. But when you measure along the proposed route, don't forget to allow about 200mm extra at the switch, rose and junction box for stripping back the conductors and joining in.

Changing the position of a ceiling light is even easier than adding a new one. If after you've turned off the power you undo the existing rose you'll see immediately the type of lighting circuit you are dealing with.

If there is only a black, a red and an earth wire going into it on the fixed wiring side then you have a junction box system. All you have to do is to disconnect the wires from the rose and reconnect them to the respective terminals of a new three-terminal junction box that you'll have to put in directly above the old fitting. You can then lead off another cable from this junction box to the repositioned ceiling rose. The switch remains unaffected.

If the rose is a loop-in type, you have to carry out a similar modification, but this time the switch wires have to be incorporated in the new junction box, which must be a four-terminal type.

FITTING THE NEW ROSE AND LAMPHOLDER

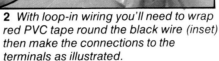

Ceiling rose: MK

1 *Fix the new rose to the ceiling. Strip back 75mm (3in) of sheathing and 8mm (¹⁄₃in) of insulation from the conductors, and sleeve the earth wires.*

2 *With loop-in wiring you'll need to wrap red PVC tape round the black wire (inset) then make the connections to the terminals as illustrated.*

3 *With junction box wiring, the earth is connected to the earth terminal, the black conductor goes to the neutral bank and the red to the SW terminal.*

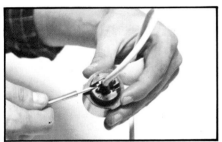

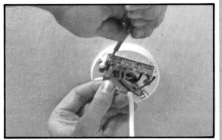

Lampholder: MK

Keith Morris

4 *Strip back the sheathing and insulation of one end of the flex and connect the blue and brown conductors to the two terminals of the lampholder.*

5 *Screw on the cap and then slip the rose cover over the flex. Cut the flex to length and prepare the free end for connecting to the rose.*

6 *At the rose, connect the blue conductor to the terminal on the neutral side and the red to the SW side. Hook the wires over the cord grips.*

CONNECTING INTO THE CIRCUIT

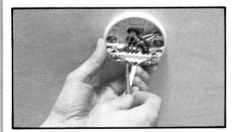
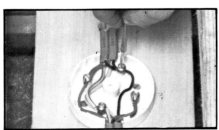

1 *When connecting into a loop-in rose, undo the fixing screws and pull the fitting a little way from the ceiling. But keep all the wires in place.*

2 *Tap out a knockout, then draw down through it about 200mm (8in) of the cable that leads to the new ceiling rose, or else feed the cable up from below.*

3 *Prepare the cable by stripping back about 75mm (3in) of sheathing and 10mm (³⁄₈in) of insulation from the conductors. Sleeve the earth wire.*

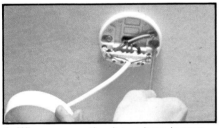
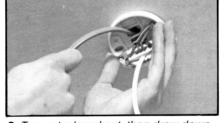

Keith Morris

Junction box: MK

4 *Connect the earth to the earth terminal, the black to the neutral terminals and the red to the central in-line terminals.*

5 *When connecting in at a junction box, use a four-terminal type mounted on a batten. Connect the wires to the terminals as shown.*

6 *When taking out an old loop-in rose, disconnect the switch and feed cables and connect up the two feed cables as shown in a three-terminal junction box.*

ADDING A POWER POINT

Electrical equipment is now used more and more in the home. You should never overload an existing socket, but fit an extra one instead.

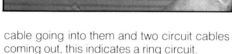

Keith Morris

There's nothing really difficult about installing a new power point. It's easier than putting in a new light as you don't have to worry about a switch cable.

Ever since the early 1950s, the power supply to the sockets has almost always been wired as a ring circuit, where the cable starts and ends at the consumer unit. Houses re-wired since then will almost certainly have had this system installed. This means that once you've decided where you want the new outlet point – by a shelf in the living room for a hi-fi system, or over a worktop in the kitchen, for example – all you then have to do is to run a 'branch' or 'spur' to it from a convenient point on a nearby ring circuit.

The connection could be made at any socket on the ring (unless it already has a spur coming from it), or by using a three-terminal junction box inserted into the cable run. Each spur can have either two singles or one double socket fitted to it, or else a fused connection unit. But new regulations will come into force from the beginning of 1983 and then you'll only be able to install one single or one double socket on the spur.

Checking your circuits
Although it's very likely that your house has ring circuits for the power supply, it's important to make sure. A ring circuit serves a number of 13A power outlets, and the sockets themselves take the familiar three-pin plugs with flat pins. But having this type of socket doesn't necessarily mean you've got a ring circuit – a new radial circuit may have been installed with these fittings, or an old radial circuit may simply have been modernised with new socket outlets. If in doubt, get an electrician to check the circuit.

First you've got to check whether you've got a modern consumer unit or separate fuse boxes for each of the circuits. Having a consumer unit is a fair indication that you've got ring circuit wiring, and if two cables are connected to each individual 30A fuseway in the unit this will confirm it. Normally each floor of the house will have a separate ring circuit, protected by a 30A fuse or MCB.

If you have separate fuse boxes, look for the ones with 30A fuses. If they have one supply

cable going into them and two circuit cables coming out, this indicates a ring circuit.

It's easy to identify the sockets on any particular circuit simply by plugging in electrical appliances, such as table lamps, turning off the power and then removing a 30A fuse from the fuse box or consumer unit, or switching off a 30A MCB. When you restore the supply, the equipment that remains off will indicate which sockets are on the circuit.

Dealing with radial circuits
Where a house hasn't got ring circuits, then the power sockets will be supplied by some form of radial circuit. Because there are different types of radial circuit, each governed by separate regulations controlling the number and location of sockets on the circuit, the size of cable to be used and the size of fuse protecting it, it's not possible to connect a spur to a nearby radial circuit. In all probability you'll have to install a new circuit starting at a new, separate fuse box or else at a spare fuseway in a consumer unit.

If you've still got unfused 15A, 5A and 2A round-pin plugs, then this is a sure sign of very old radial circuits, which were installed more than 30 years ago. Rather than extending the system you should seriously consider taking these circuits out and replacing them with ring circuits, as the wiring will almost certainly be nearing the end of its life. You'll then be able to position the new sockets exactly where you want them. If you're in any doubt about the

circuitry in your house you should contact your local electricity authority or a qualified electrician before carrying out any work.

Adding a spur to a ring
Once you've established you're dealing with a ring circuit and what sockets are on it, you'll need to find out if any spurs have already been added. You can't have more spurs than there are socket outlets on the ring itself. But unless the circuit has been heavily modified, it's unlikely that this situation will arise. You'll also need to know where any spurs are located – you don't want to overload an existing branch by mistake.

You can distinguish the sockets on the ring from those on a spur by a combination of inspecting the back of the sockets and tracing some cable runs (see *Ready Reference*). But remember to turn off the power first.

When you've got this information, you can work out whether it's feasible to add to the ring circuit. And you'll have a good idea where the cable runs.

Installing the socket
It's best to install the socket and lay in the cable before making the final join into the ring, since by doing this you reduce the amount of time that the power to the circuit is off.

You can either set the socket flush with the wall or mount it on the surface. The latter is the less messy method, but the fitting stands proud of the wall and so is more conspicuous.

FLUSH FITTING IN A BRICK WALL

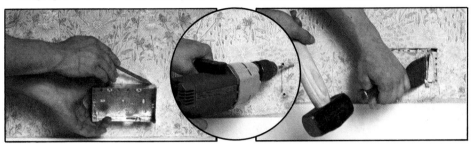

1 *Decide where you want to position the socket, then pencil round the mounting box as a guide for where to chop out the wall.*

2 *Drill slightly within the pencil lines to the depth of the mounting box, then work along the lines with a bolster chisel before chopping out the recess.*

3 *Channel a cable run down the back of the skirting using a long, thin cold chisel. Alternatively, use a long masonry bit and an electric drill.*

4 *Thread the cable up from under the floor, through some PVC conduiting behind the skirting and into the mounting box.*

5 *Push the box into position, then use a bradawl to mark where the fixing holes are to go in the recess. Remove the box and drill and plug the holes.*

6 *Set the box back into place and screw it tightly into the recess. Check that it is level, and then make good if necessary with plaster or filler.*

Flush-fixing a socket on a plasterboard wall is a little more involved.

If you choose to surface-mount the socket, all you have to do is to fix a PVC or metal box directly to the wall after you've removed the knockout (and, if metal, use a grommet) where you want the cable to enter. The socket can then be screwed directly to this.

Laying in the cable

Because cable is expensive, it's best to plan the spur so that it uses as little cable as possible. When you channel cable into a wall you'll need to chase out a shallow run, fix the

cable in position with clips, then plaster over it. But the best method of all is to run the cable in oval PVC conduiting. It won't give any more protection against an electric drill, but it'll prevent any possible reaction between the plaster making good and the cable sheathing. Always channel horizontally or vertically, and never diagonally, so it's easier to trace the wiring run when you've completed decorating. You can then avoid the cable when fixing something to the wall.

Normally the cable will drop down to below floor level to connect into the circuit. Rather than remove the skirting to get the cable down

Keith Morris

FLUSH FITTING IN A PLASTERBOARD WALL

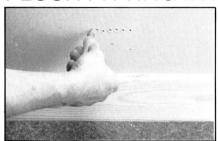

1 Knock along the cavity wall to locate a stud near where you want the socket. Pierce the wall with a bradawl to locate the centre of the upright.

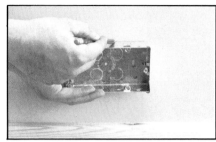

2 Position the box centrally over the stud and pencil round it. Be as accurate as you can because eventually the box should fit neatly in the opening.

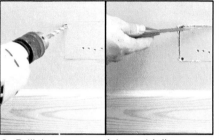

3 Drill the corners of the guidelines. Push a pad saw (or keyhole saw) into one of them and cut along the lines. The plasterboard will come out in one piece.

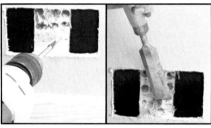

4 Once you've exposed the stud, you'll need to remove some of the wood so the box can be fully recessed. You can do this with a drill and chisel.

5 Use a long drill bit to drill down through the baseplate of the stud partition. Try and keep the drill as upright as possible.

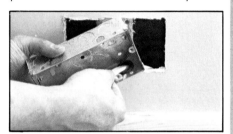

6 Lay the cable from the point where it joins the main circuit and thread it up through the hole in the baseplate and into the box.

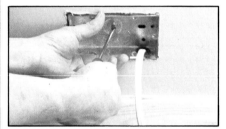

7 Set the box in the recess and fix it in place by screwing to the stud. The cable end can now be prepared and connected to the socket terminals.

8 Where there is no stud to fix to, fit special lugs to the box sides. These press against the plasterboard's inner face when the faceplate is attached.

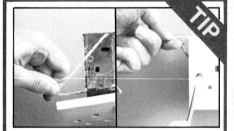

9 Before manoeuvring the box into the recess, thread some string through the front so you can hold it in position.

Jem Grischotti

CONNECTING THE NEW SOCKET

1 Strip back the sheathing of the cable by running a sharp knife down the side of the uninsulated earth. Avoid damaging the other cores.

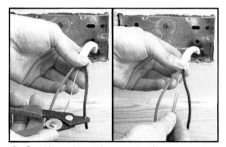

2 Set the wire strippers to the correct gauge and remove about 9mm (3/8in) of insulation from the cores. Sleeve the earth core in green/yellow PVC.

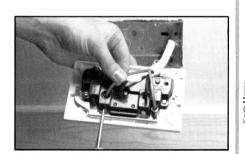

3 Connect the three cores to the relevant terminals of the socket, making sure no exposed core is showing. Then screw the socket into position.

Keith Morris

the back you can use a long steel cold chisel to chip out a groove. You'll then have to drill down through the end of the floorboard with a wood bit. Alternatively, you can use a long masonry bit with an electric drill to complete the task.

But if the floor is solid, the ring is usually in the ceiling void above, in which case the branch will drop down from the ceiling. And this will involve a considerable amount of channelling out if you want to install the new socket near floor level.

Stud partition walls also present a few problems. If the socket is near the floor, you should be able to get a long drill bit through the hole you cut for the socket to drill through the baseplate and floorboard. You can then thread the cable through. But if the socket is to be placed higher up the wall, noggings and sound insulation material may prevent the cable being drawn through the cavity. In this case you will probably have to surface-mount the cable.

In fact, surface-mounting is the easiest method of running the cable. All you do is fix special plastic conduit to the wall and lay the cable inside before clipping on the lid. But many people regard this as an ugly solution.

When laying cable under ground floor floorboards you should clip it to the sides of the joists about 50mm (2in) below the surface so that it doesn't droop on the ground. Cable in the ceiling void can rest on the surface.

When you have to cross joists, you'll need to drill 16mm (5/8in) holes about 50mm (2in) below the level of the floorboards. The cable is threaded through them and so is well clear of any floorboard fixing nails.

Connecting into the circuit

If you use a junction box, you'll need one with three terminals inside. You have to connect the live conductors (those with red insulation) of the circuit cable and the spur to one terminal, the neutral conductors (black insulation) to another, and the earth wires to the third. Sleeve the earth wires in green/yellow PVC first.

You might decide that it's easier to connect into the back of an existing socket rather than use a junction box, although this will probably mean some extra channelling on the wall. Space is limited at the back of a socket so it may be difficult to fit the conductors to the relevant terminals. However, this method is ideal if the new socket that you're fitting on one wall is back-to-back with an existing fitting. By carefully drilling through the wall a length of cable can be linked from the old socket into the new.

CONNECTING INTO THE CIRCUIT

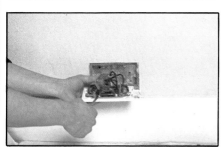

1 *Unscrew a nearby socket to check that it's on the ring – normally there'll be two red, two black and two earth wires. Sometimes the earths are in one sleeve.*

2 *Usually it's easier to push the new cable up into the mounting box from below the floor, although you might prefer to take it the other way.*

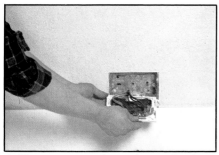

3 *Prepare the cores and sleeve the earth of the new cable, then connect them into the appropriate terminals on the back of the socket.*

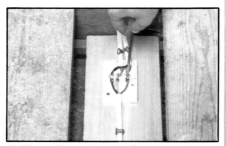

4 *If installing a junction box use a three-terminal type. Connect the red conductors to one terminal, the blacks to another and the earths to a third.*

Ready Reference

SOCKET MOUNTINGS

Metal boxes are recessed into the wall and provide a fixing for the socket itself. Knockouts are provided in the back, sides and ends to allow the cable to enter the box. Rubber grommets are fitted round the hole so the cable doesn't chafe against the metal edges.

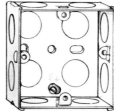

Elongated screw slots allow box to be levelled when fixed to wall.

Adjustable lugs enable final adjustments to level of faceplate on wall.

Boxes are usually 35mm deep, but with single-brick walls boxes 25mm deep should be used, along with accessories having deeper-than-usual faceplates.

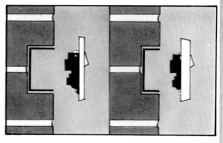

Lugs can be fitted to a metal box so that it can be fitted into stud partition walls.

Surface-mounted boxes (usually white plastic) are 35mm deep, and are simply screwed to the wall surface where required.

TIP: FIT SAFETY PLATES

Safety plates can be fitted to sockets to prevent young children playing with them.

PROBLEMS

● **Crumbly plaster** There's little that can be done other than cutting back to sound area. Position box and socket as required then make good surrounding area.

● **Poor bricks** Because of soft bricks you can quite easily chop out too big a recess for the box. Pack the recess with dabs of mortar or plaster.

● **Cavity Walls** To prevent breaking through into the cavity only chop out a recess big enough to take a shallow box, about 25mm (1in).

RUNNING CABLE

The hardest part of the average electrical job is running the cables: it takes up a lot of time and a lot of effort. But there are certain techniques used by experts which can make it much easier.

Before you get involved in the details of how to install the wiring, there's one simple question you must answer. Does it matter if the cable runs show? This is because there are only two approaches to the job of running cable. Either you fix the cable to the surface of the wall, or you conceal it. The first option is far quicker and easier but doesn't look particularly attractive; it's good enough for use in, say, an understairs cupboard. For a neater finish, using this method, you can smarten up the cable runs by boxing them in with some trunking. Many people, however, prefer to conceal the wiring completely by taking it under the floor, over the ceiling, or in walls.

TYPICAL CABLE RUNS

More and more electrical equipment is now being used in the home. And the chances are that sooner or later you will want to install a new power point, wall or ceiling light, or another switch. In which case you will have to get power to your new accessory. To do that will involve running cable from an existing circuit or installing a completely new one. Running cable to a new appliance can be the hardest part of any job and, as the illustration on the right shows, you will be involved in trailing cable across the roof space or ceiling void, channelling it down walls and threading it behind partitions as well as taking it under floorboards. But it's much easier than it seems. There are a number of tricks of the trade that will make any electrical job simpler and less time consuming. For example, once you can 'fish' cable, the daunting task of running it under a floor is simple.

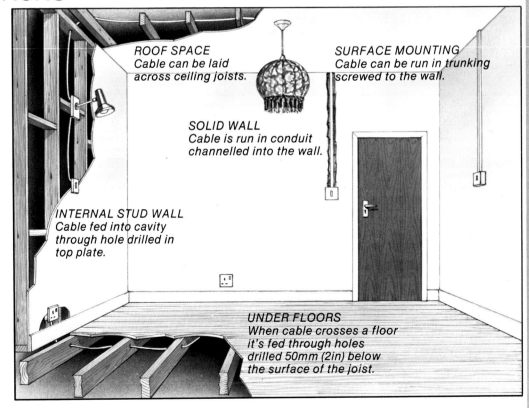

ROOF SPACE
Cable can be laid across ceiling joists.

SURFACE MOUNTING
Cable can be run in trunking screwed to the wall.

SOLID WALL
Cable is run in conduit channelled into the wall.

INTERNAL STUD WALL
Cable fed into cavity through hole drilled in top plate.

UNDER FLOORS
When cable crosses a floor it's fed through holes drilled 50mm (2in) below the surface of the joist.

SURFACE MOUNTING CABLE

1 *To run cable in trunking, cut the trunking to length and fix the channel half to the wall with screws and wall plugs at 450mm (18in) centres.*

2 *Run the cable and press it firmly into the channel as far as it will go, carefully smoothing it out to avoid kinks and twists.*

3 *Next, snap the trunking's capping piece over the channelling, tapping it firmly along its length with your hand to lock it into place.*

4 *If the cable is to be on show, merely secure it every 225mm (9in) with cable clips. Fit them over the cable and drive home the fixing pins.*

Planning the route

Having made your decision you must now work out a suitable route for the cable to follow.

If it is to be surface-mounted – with or without trunking – run the cable around window and door frames, just above skirting boards and picture rails, down the corners of the room, or along the angle between wall and ceiling. This not only helps conceal the cable's presence, but also protects it against accidental damage. This last point is most important, and is the reason why you must never run cable over a floor.

With concealed wiring, the position is more complicated. When running cable under a floor or above a ceiling, you must allow for the direction in which the joists run – normally at right angles to the floorboards – and use an indirect route, taking it parallel to the joists and/or at right angles to them.

When running cable within a wall, the cable should *always* run vertically or horizontally from whatever it supplies, *never* diagonally.

Surface-mounting techniques

If you are leaving the cable on show, all you need do is cut it to length, and fix it to the surface with a cable clip about every 225mm (9in), making sure it is free from kinks and twists. With modern cable clips, simply fit the groove in the plastic block over the cable and drive home the small pin provided.

Surface mounting cable within trunking involves a bit more work. Having obtained the right size of PVC trunking, build up the run a section at a time, cutting the trunking to length with a hacksaw. Once each piece is cut, separate it into its two parts – the

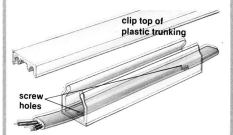
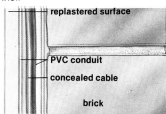

channelling and capping – and fix the channel to the wall with screws and wall plugs at roughly 450mm (18in) intervals (you may have to drill screw clearance holes in the channelling yourself).

Continue in this way until the run is complete. Turn corners by using proprietary fittings or by angling the ends of two pieces of trunking to form a neatly mitred joint, then run the cable. Press this firmly into the channel, and finish off by snapping the capping pieces firmly into place.

Concealing cables in walls

There are two ways to conceal cable in a wall. With a solid wall, chop a channel (called a 'chase') out of the plaster using a club hammer and bolster chisel, carefully continuing this behind any skirting boards, picture rails, and coverings. You could now run the cable in this chase and plaster over it. However, to give the cable some protection, it is better to fit a length of PVC conduit into the chase and run the cable through this before replastering.

To continue the run either above the ceiling or through the floor before you position the conduit, use a long drill bit so you can drill through the floor behind the skirting board. If a joist blocks the hole, angle the drill sufficiently to avoid it.

With a hollow internal partition wall, the job is rather easier, because you can run the cable within the cavity.

First drill a hole in the wall where the cable is to emerge, making sure you go right through into the cavity. Your next step is to gain access to the timber 'plate' at the very top of the wall, either by going up into the loft, or by lifting floorboards in the room above. Drill a 19mm (¾in) hole through the plate, at a point vertically above the first hole, or as near vertically above it as possible.

All that remains is to tie the cable you wish to run to a length of stout 'draw' wire – single-core earth cable is often used – and then to tie the free end of this wire to a length of string. To the free end of the string, tie a small weight, and drop the weight through the hole at the top of the wall. Then all you do is make a hook in a piece of stout wire, insert it in the cavity, catch hold of the string and pull it (and in turn the draw wire and cable) through the hole in the room below.

What are the snags? There are two. You may find that, at some point between the two holes, the cavity is blocked by a horizontal timber called a noggin. If this happens, try to reach the noggin from above with a long auger bit (you should be able to hire one) and drill through it. Failing that, chisel through the wall surface, cut a notch in the side of the noggin, pass the cable through the notch, and then make good.

The second snag is that you may not be

CHASING OUT SOLID WALLS

1 *Mark out the cable run using a length of conduit, and chop a channel ('chase') in the wall to receive it, using a club hammer and a bolster chisel.*

2 *Continue the chase behind any coving, skirting board, or picture rail by chipping out the plaster there with a long, narrow cold chisel.*

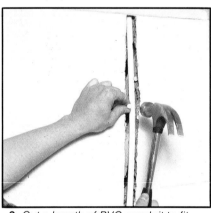

3 *Cut a length of PVC conduit to fit, and lay it in the chase, securing it temporarily with clout nails driven into the wall's mortar joints.*

4 *Pull the cable through the conduit, then make good the wall by filling in over the conduit with plaster or cellulose filler.*

able to reach the top plate to drill it. In which case, either give up the ideas of having concealed wiring, or try a variation on the second method used to run cable into the cavity from below the floor.

Here, it is sometimes possible to lift a couple of floorboards and drill up through the plate forming the bottom of the wall. Failing that you have to take a very long drill bit, drill through the wall into the cavity, then continue drilling through into the timber plate. You can now use the weighted string trick to feed the cable in through the hole in the wall, and out under the floor.

Running cable beneath a floor

The technique for running cable beneath a suspended timber floor depends on whether the floor is on an upper storey and so has a ceiling underneath, or is on a ground floor with empty space below. If it's a ground floor, it may be possible to crawl underneath and secure the cable to the sides of the joists with cable clips, or to pass it through 19mm (¾in) diameter holes drilled in the joists at least 50mm (2in) below their top edge. This prevents anyone nailing into the floor and hitting the cable.

If you cannot crawl underneath, then the cable can be left loose in the void. But how do you run it without lifting the entire floor? The answer is you use another trick, called 'fishing'.

For this, you need a piece of stiff but reasonably flexible galvanised wire, say 14 standard wire gauge (swg), rather longer than the intended cable run, and a piece of thicker, more rigid wire, about 1m in length. Each piece should have one end bent to form a hook.

Lift a floorboard at each end of the

COPING WITH STUD WALLS

1 Drill a hole in the wall where the cable is to emerge, then bore a second hole in the wooden plate forming the top of the wall.

2 Tie a weight to a length of string and lower this through the hole in the wall plate. Tie the free end of the string to a stout 'draw' wire.

3 If the weight gets blocked on its way to the hole in the wall, use a long auger bit to drill through the noggin obstructing it.

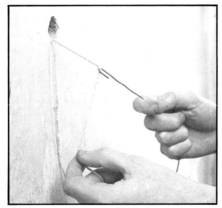

4 Fish out the weighted string through the hole in the wall, using a piece of wire bent to form a hook. Now, pull through the draw wire.

5 Tie the draw wire to the cable you wish to run, then return to the hole in the wall's top plate, and use the string to pull up the draw wire.

6 Then use the draw wire to pull the length of cable through. Remember, do this smoothly and don't use force if there's an obstruction.

Ready Reference

TRICKS OF THE TRADE

Hollow internal partition wall

Drill a hole in the top or bottom plate, then drill another in the wall where the cable is to emerge. Drop a weighted piece of string through one of the holes and hook it out through the other. Use this to pull through a stout draw wire which is attached to the cable.

● if the weighted piece of string gets obstructed by a noggin or its way to the hole in the wall, use a long auger bit to drill through the noggin.

● don't pull the cable through with the weighted string – the string tends to snap

● never run cable down the cavity of an external wall– treat these as solid walls.

Under floors

Use a technique known as fishing:
● lift the floorboards at either end of the run
● thread stiff wire beneath the floor through one hole and hook it out of the other with another piece of wire
● use the longer piece of wire to pull the cable through.

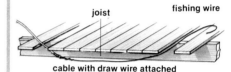

joist　　**fishing wire**

cable with draw wire attached

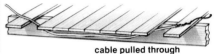

cable pulled through

● if there's a gap beneath a ground floor you can 'fish' the cable diagonally across the room under the joist

● if the gap under the joists is large enough you can crawl in the space clipping the cable to the joists

● where the cable crosses the joists at right angles, run it through holes drilled 50mm (2in) below their top edges.

Over ceilings

If you can get above the ceiling into a loft, you can clip the cables to the joists. Otherwise you'll have to 'fish' the cable across (see above).

If you can't get above the ceiling and fishing doesn't work you'll have to surface-mount the cable.

INDEX